CW01369088

The Story of Rufino

The Story of Rufino

Slavery, Freedom, and Islam in the Black Atlantic

JOÃO JOSÉ REIS, FLÁVIO DOS SANTOS GOMES
and
MARCUS J. M. DE CARVALHO

TRANSLATED BY H. SABRINA GLEDHILL

OXFORD
UNIVERSITY PRESS

OXFORD
UNIVERSITY PRESS

Oxford University Press is a department of the University of Oxford. It furthers
the University's objective of excellence in research, scholarship, and education
by publishing worldwide. Oxford is a registered trade mark of Oxford University
Press in the UK and certain other countries.

Published in the United States of America by Oxford University Press
198 Madison Avenue, New York, NY 10016, United States of America.

This book is a translation of
O alufá Rufino: Tráfico, escravidão e liberdade no Atlântico Negro (c. 1822– c. 1853) © 2010 João José Reis,
Flávio dos Santos Gomes, and Marcus J. M. de Carvalho. São Paolo: Companhia das Letras, 2010.

© English translation © Oxford University Press 2020

All rights reserved. No part of this publication may be reproduced, stored in
a retrieval system, or transmitted, in any form or by any means, without the
prior permission in writing of Oxford University Press, or as expressly permitted
by law, by license, or under terms agreed with the appropriate reproduction
rights organization. Inquiries concerning reproduction outside the scope of the
above should be sent to the Rights Department, Oxford University Press, at the
address above.

You must not circulate this work in any other form
and you must impose this same condition on any acquirer.

CIP data is on file at the Library of Congress
ISBN 978-0-19-022436-3

1 3 5 7 9 8 6 4 2

Printed by Integrated Books International, United States of America

The translation of this work was published with the financial support of the
National Library Foundation | Ministry of Citizenship.
Obra publicada com o apoio da Fundação Biblioteca Nacional | Ministério da Cidadania.

MINISTÉRIO DA CIDADANIA
Fundação BIBLIOTECA NACIONAL

MINISTÉRIO DA
CIDADANIA

PÁTRIA AMADA
BRASIL
GOVERNO FEDERAL

CONTENTS

Preface vii

PART I

1. Rufino's Africa 3
2. Enslaved in Bahia 9
3. Enslaved in Porto Alegre 20
4. Farroupilha and Freedom 34
5. Freedman in Rio de Janeiro 40
6. Rio de Janeiro, a City in Fear 51

PART II

7. Rufino Joins the Slave Trade 63
8. Luanda, Slave-Trading Capital of Angola 75
9. Readying the *Ermelinda* 82
10. Rufino's Employers 96
11. Passengers, Shippers, and Cargo 109
12. The *Ermelinda* Goes to Sea 118
13. The Equipment Act 126

14. Sierra Leone 138

15. Among Akus and African Muslims 153

16. The Trial of the *Ermelinda* 162

17. Dirty Tricks 174

18. Back to Sea 180

PART III

19. Counting the Costs 189

20. Rufino's Recife 196

21. A Man of Faith and Sorcery 206

22. Tense Times in Rufino's Recife 217

23. A Free Man 222

24. The Malês of Recife and a Doctrinal Dispute 229

   Epilogue 241

Acknowledgments 245
Notes 247
Sources and Works Cited 283
Name Index 299
Subject Index 303

PREFACE

The written history of Africans in Brazil during slavery times is largely based on police records. The central character of this book is no exception. On September 2, 1853, Rufino José Maria was arrested in his home on 78, Rua da Senzala Velha (Old Slave Quarter Street), in the parish of São Frei Pedro Gonçalves in Recife, the capital of the northeastern province (now state) of Pernambuco. He was a freedman of the Nagô ethnic nation, as the Yoruba-speaking Africans, who currently inhabit southwestern Nigeria and the eastern part of the neighboring Republic of Benin, were called in Brazil. The Nagôs became known throughout Brazil for organizing a number of rebellions in the province (now state) of Bahia in the first half of the nineteenth century. In Salvador, the capital of Bahia, Nagô Muslims known as Malês–from the Yoruba *imàle*–led the famous slave revolt of January 1835 and probably participated in prior uprisings and conspiracies as well, there having been at least thirty of them between 1807 and 1835. Rufino was also Muslim and as such, bore the name Abuncare (possibly derived from Abdul Karim), which he brought from his homeland.

Rufino's arrest in 1853 took place amid a tense atmosphere of rumors, accusations, and repression related to a slave conspiracy involving several plantations on the outskirts of Recife. Many African homes were searched, and on two occasions, so were the streets and taverns in the city center. However, the only suspicious items the police discovered in Rufino's home were a large number of Arabic manuscripts—the same type of materials seized from the African rebels in Bahia nearly twenty years earlier. In 1835, the so-called Malê writings became notorious throughout Brazil thanks to newspaper reports, since they were portrayed as being the most intriguing and mysterious and therefore dangerous aspect of the rebellion. However, the story Rufino told the police was far from being a rebel's tale. It was primarily that of an urbane, peace-loving Muslim, albeit a devout one with a rich life experience replete with adventures and misadventures on the Atlantic trade routes.

There are two complementary reports on Rufino's life, both based on his police interrogation. One of them is the official transcript of his interrogation, drafted by a police clerk, which contains the signatures of three witnesses to the investigation. Rufino himself signed the document as well, in Arabic. Unfortunately, we have only been able to find a copy that does not contain his signature.[1]

The other report is a long article written by a witness to the interrogation published a few weeks later in the *Jornal do Commercio*, a newspaper based in Rio de Janeiro, the largest city and capital of Brazil, the seat of the imperial court. The unsigned article ends with the observation, "Private letter." It describes the circumstances in which the writer obtained the information, as he seems to have had free access to the back rooms of police power in Recife: "Out of curiosity, I went to see the black man who had to be interrogated, and finding some singular things in his responses, primarily when he said that being a priest in this land is *a trade*, I am enclosing some notes about that Muslim priest, which can be read as a curiosity. I owe these notes to the pen of another curious soul who was there with me." That other "curious soul" could also have been one of the witnesses.

Therefore, there is an explicit partnership in the production of the document that basically recounts Rufino's life, sometimes repeating the official statement taken down by the police clerk and sometimes adding new information. The report published in the *Jornal do Commercio* was written by someone with an anticlerical mindset who was inclined toward religious tolerance. He defended Rufino's right to practice his religion legally and freely, which nevertheless meant limiting it to household worship—as was the case with Rufino—according to the constitution then in force in the country. It is a basically favorable report about the African freedman that recommended his immediate release.[2]

These two documents not only provide a wealth of information about Rufino but also set out a trail of clues that enabled us to follow his footsteps from the time he left Africa until his arrest nearly thirty years later. Unfortunately, the presence of this particular African was not documented in all the places (or archives) we scoured as we followed his trail. As is generally the case with biographies of people of Rufino's social rank, direct information about him frequently evaded us. We often got very close to him, to the point of seeing his shadow in a corner of the archives, but we came across other characters who, in their eagerness to stand out, seemed to want to steal the spotlight from the African. Many of them were men of wealth and power: slave owners, slave traders, bosses, officials, and journalists. This book also tells their stories, particularly of individuals involved in the transatlantic slave trade during the period when it was already illegal. Thus, we have managed to gain an understanding of Rufino's circumstances and experiences through the people who crossed his path. We have also been able to reconstruct the turbulent world in which he lived and traveled and which he helped create in several corners of the Atlantic.

This is not a typical book about African slavery in Brazil. It involves that dimension, among others, but in these pages the reader will primarily find a narrative of Atlantic history. Rufino's life takes us on a journey that begins in Òyó, the African kingdom where he was born; goes on to Salvador, where he first arrived in Brazil as a slave; then to Porto Alegre, in the southernmost part of the country, where he was taken by his young master, sold, and later purchased his manumission. As a freedman he moved to Rio de Janeiro, the port where he shipped out as a sailor on a slaver bound for Luanda, the main entrepôt of the Angolan slave trade, ending up in Sierra Leone, the British colony he would visit on two occasions, and finally settling down in Recife, the capital of Pernambuco province, where he chose to live and work as a diviner, healer, and Muslim teacher. Aside from these locales, Rufino also spent time aboard slave ships on the Atlantic. Therefore, this book is largely a history of the slave trade, its economy, organization, and business strategies; its trading posts, ships, the various figures involved; its atrocities and the campaign to suppress it when the African freedman was engaged in the infamous commerce in human flesh. Thus, this is more than one man's biography; it is a social history of the slave trade and slavery in the Atlantic basin guided by the experiences of Rufino José Maria, also known by his Muslim name, Abuncare.[3]

The Story of Rufino

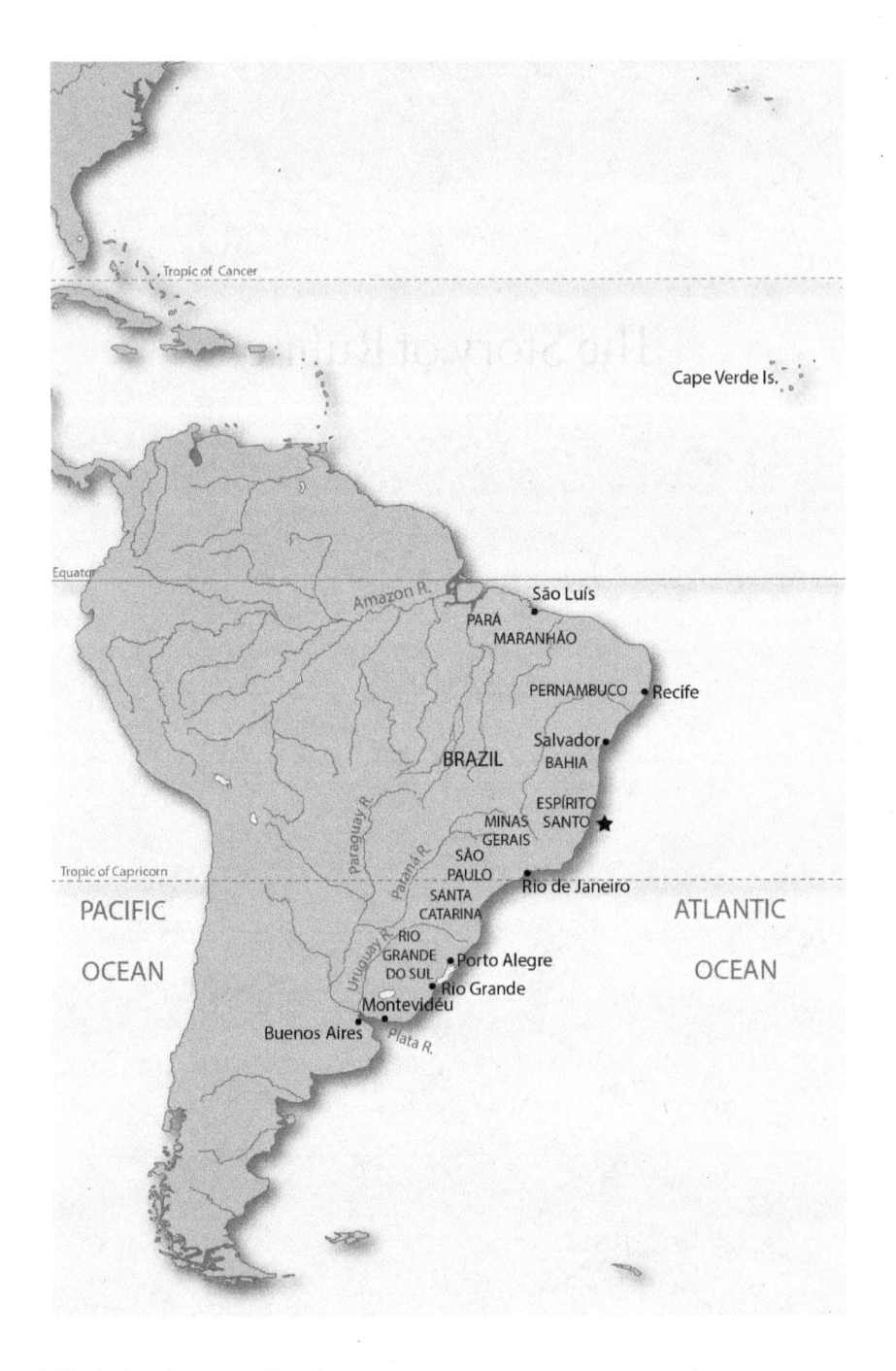

Mid-nineteenth-century Brazil

PART I

We constantly have one foot on a volcano.
Jornal do Commercio, September 25, 1853

1

Rufino's Africa

Rufino told his interrogators that he was "a son of the kingdom of Ọ̀yọ́"— probably the capital, Ọ̀yọ́ Ile—where he was born in the early nineteenth century. Ọ̀yọ́ stood out at that time as one of the most powerful states in the interior of the Bight of Benin region. It controlled most of the Yoruba-speaking realms for a considerable time in the eighteenth and early nineteenth centuries. It also subjugated the kingdoms of Dahomey to the west, Borgu to the north, and Nupe to the northeast, which became its vassal states. Ọ̀yọ́ dominated major slave trade routes leading from the interior to ports in the bights of Benin and Biafra. Ọ̀yọ́ financed a good part of its military might—particularly its cavalry, which was unrivaled in Yorubaland—through active participation in the trade in human beings.

By the beginning of the nineteenth century, Ọ̀yọ́ was facing a few challenges to its hegemony in the region. Dahomey and Nupe were struggling to free themselves from its grip, and, more important, the kingdom was rocked by internal strife. In about 1796, a warrior named Afonja, the *are-ona-kakanfo* (commander in chief of Ọ̀yọ́'s provincial army, the most powerful of its military leaders), rebelled against the recently installed *Alafin* (or *aláàfin*, king of Ọ̀yọ́). He claimed that he had earned that title through merit and had a hereditary right to it. Afonja was not only an important military chief but also the political leader (*baálè*) of the city of Ilorin, located in the southeast of Ọ̀yọ́ Ile.

From his base in Ilorin, Afonja resisted the authority of successive Ọ̀yọ́ kings for two decades. Then, in 1817, he decided to make a decisive gambit by inciting a major slave rebellion in Ọ̀yọ́. That powerful kingdom not only engaged in the slave trade but was a major consumer of forced labor—that is, it was a slave-trading state that governed a slavocracy. Most slaves in Ọ̀yọ́ originated from areas north of the kingdom, and most of them were Hausa Muslims. The Hausa-speaking peoples occupied a vast territory in the northern region of what is now Nigeria. That is where a Muslim state known as the Sokoto Caliphate was formed in about 1809 under the leadership of the Fulani, a major ethnic group also present in that region, who were devoted followers of Islam and responsible for a jihad that began in 1804.

Led by Uthman Dan Fodio—a charismatic preacher, scholar, author of erudite religious works and militant leaflets, and poet—the jihad marked a radical change in the history of the Hausas and neighboring peoples. Initially, the targets of the holy war were mainly Hausa chiefs accused of oppressing good Muslims, which included enslaving them, and tolerating a style of Islam that was syncretized with the local "pagan" religion. However, many followers of that traditional faith fought alongside the jihad warriors to rid themselves of frequently tyrannical political leaders. The enslaved Hausas in Ọ̀yọ́ were chiefly the victims of this political-religious conflict that revolutionized the region, a movement focused mainly on Islamic reform, pitting orthodox Muslims against others accused of being "relaxed." The conflict developed into a war of expansion throughout Hausa territory and beyond its borders, including the Yoruba-speaking region where Rufino lived. The 1817 Hausa slave rebellion in Ọ̀yọ́ marked the beginning of wide-scale Muslim penetration among the Yoruba.

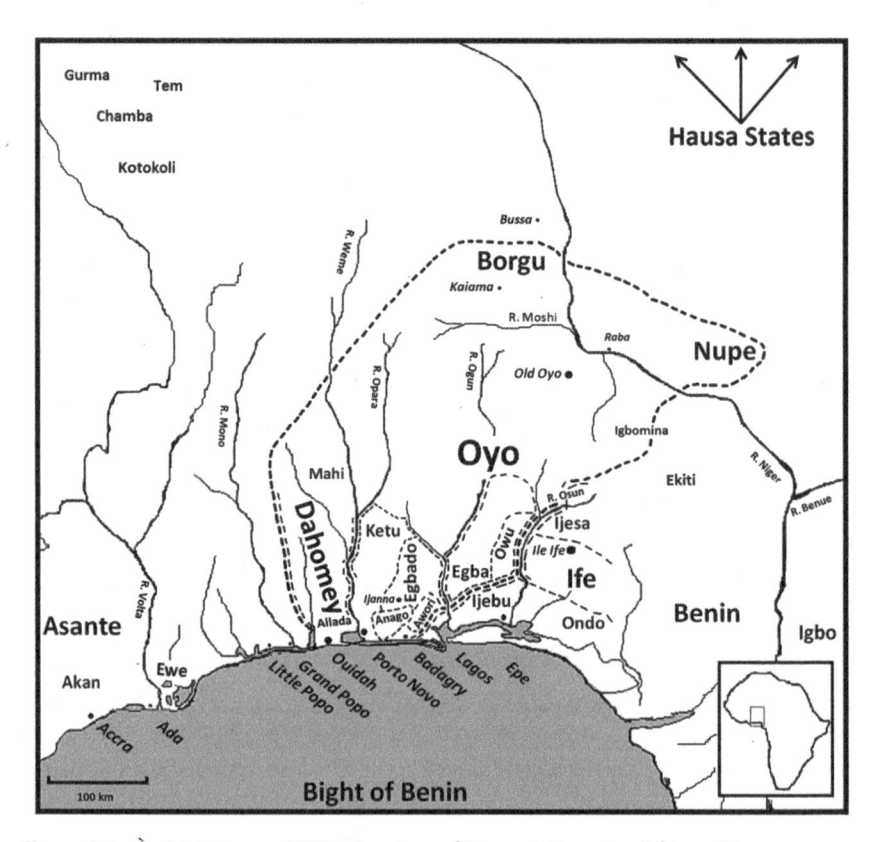

Figure 1.1 Ọ̀yọ́ territory, c. 1780. Courtesy of Henry B. Lovejoy, African Diaspora Maps Ltd.

Enslaved Hausas worked in several sectors of Ọ̀yọ́'s economy, but they were primarily livestock herders. Their veterinary skills made them essential for tending the horses that the powerful kingdom used for military purposes, and many were soldiers serving the Ọ̀yọ́ army. Thus, the Yorubas' Hausa slaves played an important role in the region's political economy, and their rebellion had a disastrous and decisive impact on Ọ̀yọ́. They were encouraged to leave their masters en masse by a Muslim preacher known among the Yorubas as Alimi. He was a free man of Fulani origin, steeped in the ideology of jihad, whom the Alafin had allowed to preach in his realm without realizing that he was preparing his own downfall. However, when the uprising took place in 1817, Alimi was living in Ilorin and issued his appeal to the Hausa slaves in response to Afonja's suggestions. The alliance between Afonja and the Hausa Muslims helped accelerate the decline of the ancient and powerful Ọ̀yọ́ empire. A series of civil wars followed in the wake of the 1817 slave uprising, with disastrous consequences over the course of the next two decades and beyond. The victims of these conflicts crowded the slave ports and the holds of ships that relentlessly crossed the Atlantic, bound for Brazil.[1]

Therefore, Rufino grew up during a turbulent time in his native land and within a family that he declared to be Muslim. Yoruba Muslims called themselves *imàle*, an expression that gave rise to the term *Malê* used for Yorubas in Brazil. Rufino stated that he began learning Arabic, the language of Islam, in Ọ̀yọ́, and that his own father was an *alufá* (or *àlùfáà*), "a sort of priest and schoolteacher, who not only taught religious precepts but had other functions," according to the accurate definition in the unsigned article published in *Jornal do Commercio*.[2] However, the names he gave for his parents were Yoruba, not Islamic. His father's name was Ocochê (or Ocoshé, Okọṣe), which could have different meanings, such as "wayward child" or "carrier and guardian of the oshe," the oṣe being the double-headed axe that is the paramount symbol of the Òrìṣà (or Orisha) Ṣàngó (or Shango). This was the most important divinity in Ọ̀yọ́'s pantheon, closely linked to its royal lineages—for Ṣàngó is said to have been one of the first alafins—whose worship was also widespread among the common folk. If Ocochê had that meaning, then Rufino's father may have been a devotee and perhaps even a priest of Ṣàngó, and not an *alufá* at all. But it is also possible that Rufino's paternal family may have been belated converts to Islam. As for his mother's name, Bixoumi (Bishoumi), there are at least three possibilities: it could mean "she is with Èṣù (or Eshu)," the well-known Yoruba messenger divinity and lord of the crossroads; or "born to guard and protect me," or even "born in the water."[3]

Rufino may have preferred to give the police his parents' traditional names, since it was customary among Muslims in his homeland to retain their ethnic names even when they also had Islamic ones. In Bahia in 1835, for example, many of the Muslims arrested after the rebellion were known by their Yoruba names: Ajayi, Alade, Aliyu, Dada, Licutan, Ojo, and others.[4] Unless he did so in his signature, which we have yet to find, Rufino himself did not identify himself by his Muslim name, Abuncare, during his interrogation eighteen years later. We only know it because of an article published in the Rio de Janeiro newspaper *Correio Mercantil*, whose author met the African while he was in prison and wrote: "[he is] called Rufino here, and Abuncare in his homeland."[5]

In the early decades of the nineteenth century there was a considerable, albeit minority, Muslim community in Ọ̀yọ́. It was made up of free and enslaved immigrants from the north (chiefly Hausas) as well as the native Ìmàle. We know that there had been a Yoruba Muslim community in Ọ̀yọ́ since at least the late seventeenth century, and they had coexisted peacefully with Orisa devotees, including the kingdom's rulers. According to oral history sources, the Alafin himself was responsible for confirming the local Ìmàle leaders. Muslims with a greater or lesser command of written Arabic, both Yorubas and foreigners, made a living from producing and selling amulets containing passages of the Qur'ān and other religious texts, which were considered to embody extraordinary protective powers. Even the Ọ̀yọ́ kings and generals prized these talismans and carried them about in war and peacetime.

However, after the 1817 uprising, relations became tense between the Muslim minority and the majority of Orisha worshipers in Ọ̀yọ́. Rallied by Solagberu, a prosperous Yoruba merchant, the Ìmàle decided to leave Ọ̀yọ́ in large numbers and join the rebels in Ilorin to escape the Alafin's persecution. He, in turn, was spurred by his priests to view Muslims in general—even his fellow Yorubas—as real or potential political adversaries.

The forces gathered in Ilorin came to be formed, on one side, by Muslims of Yoruba, Hausa, and Fulani origin, and, on the other, Orisa people, who were the majority in that locale too. Ilorin was so closely identified with its leader that it was known as the city of Afonja. Despite the growing Muslim influence among his hosts, Afonja never converted to Islam and kept well-tended shrines for pagan gods at home, probably giving precedence to Ṣango. This must have displeased the Muslims profoundly, particularly his ally Alimi, who hoped to see the powerful warlord embrace Islam. Such a disparate alliance could not have been entirely harmonious. Conflicts between Muslims and followers of the local religion were a common occurrence in Ilorin. According to historian Robin Law, in about 1823–1824, Fulani and Hausa Muslims rose up against Afonja and killed him. After that coup, Ilorin was governed by foreign devotees of Allah who nevertheless somewhat respected their local Orisa-worshiping allies, reserving a secondary place for them on the governing council of what was now the Emirate of Ilorin.

The Yoruba Muslims, who did not take sides in that recent conflict, became a subordinate group in their own country within the coalition that founded the

Figure 1.2 Chained slaves on their way to the coast for sale. From Sarah Tucker, *Abeokuta; or, sunrise within the tropics: an outline of the origin and progress of the Yoruba mission* (London: James Nisbet and Co., 1853).

Emirate of Ilorin, a state with loose ties to the Sokoto Caliphate. The first emir of Ilorin is believed to have been Abdul Salami, Alimi's son. A member of the Fulani ethnic group, Salami founded the dynasty that still holds power in Ilorin (and whose legitimacy Afonja's descendants still contest). Soon, the new Fulani- and Hausa-controlled government would use tremendous violence to subjugate the native Muslims led by Ṣolagberu, who were showing growing opposition to foreign rule.[6]

Although they were Muslims, Rufino's family did not fall victim to the Alafin of Òyó. According to Rufino's statement, "Having been a prisoner of war of the *Hausa*, I was transported to Bahia."[7] Therefore, he was captured by fellow

Figure 1.3 African captives being embarked on a slave ship. "The Celebrated Piratical Slaver *L'Antonio* with others of the black craft lying in the Bonny River." National Maritime Museum, London.

Muslims from a different ethnic group and sold as a slave, which must have occurred in the early 1820s. Rufino's story suggests that Muslims of different ethnic backgrounds fought on opposite sides in these conflicts. The Hausas who captured and sold him were probably former slaves who had rebelled against Ọ̀yọ́ and were now allies of Afonja. The date Rufino gave for his arrival in Bahia is close to the one that Robin Law suggests for the coup against Afonja (ca. 1823–1824), but Rufino seems to have been captured shortly before that. Taken from the region of Ọ̀yọ́ Ilẹ, the capital of the kingdom, or a nearby community, to the Atlantic coast in a journey with few stops for rest, he must have walked for about a month—probably tied to other prisoners—and most likely sailed for Bahia from Lagos, the most active slave port in the Bight of Benin at that time.[8]

2

Enslaved in Bahia

The estimated date of Rufino's capture is based on his statement that he arrived in the city of Salvador at the age of seventeen, "in the time of Madeira's war."[1] He was referring to Brigadier Ignácio Luís Madeira de Mello, who commanded the Portuguese garrison in Bahia during the struggle for Brazil's independence in 1822 and 1823. Appointed by the government in Lisbon to replace a Brazilian as military commander of the province of Bahia, Madeira de Mello's new post was contested by Bahian military and civil elites alike. That situation swiftly developed into rejection by the populace as well, followed by the skirmishes and open conflicts that went down in history as the War for Independence in Bahia. While the brigadier led the Portuguese during the occupation of Salvador, the Brazilians concentrated their forces in the Recôncavo, the region of sugar plantations and tobacco farms where most of Bahia's enslaved population resided. Led by the slave owners of the Recôncavo and aided by troops sent from Rio de Janeiro by the recently enthroned Emperor Pedro I, the Brazilian party eventually won a conflict characterized by a series of small battles and large numbers of fighters—about 15,000 on the Brazilian side alone. The Portuguese were driven out of Bahia in early July 1823.[2]

Madeira led the Portuguese troops based in Salvador from February 15, 1822 to July 2, 1823. Rufino arrived there at some point during that period, which lasted exactly one year, four months, and seventeen days, during which time the Portuguese general was the master of the city. Since Rufino would have been a newly arrived slave, or a *boçal* (an African with a poor command of Portuguese language and local mores) during that period, he must have learned about the tense political-military situation from fellow Yoruba speakers already living in Salvador. He may have witnessed the activities of the poor black and mixed-race people who stayed in the city under Madeira and who, on some occasions, contested Portugal's military occupation with jeers and stone throwing. However, it is also possible that Rufino's master had left Salvador by then, taking his slave with him to the safety of the plantation zone. Most of the city's residents, particularly the elite, generally sought refuge behind Brazilian lines in the Recôncavo. There, black freedpersons

The Story of Rufino. João José Reis, Flávio dos Santos Gomes, and Marcus J. M. de Carvalho, Translated by H. Sabrina Gledhill, Oxford University Press (2020) © Oxford University Press.
DOI: 10.1093/oso/9780190224363.001.0001

and slaves—most of them without their masters' permission—enlisted in the fight against Madeira in hopes of being rewarded with social recognition and manumission later on. Ironically, the African left a war-torn land, Ọyọ, only to arrive in the middle of the Luso-Brazilian conflict in Salvador.[3]

In Bahia, Rufino was purchased by an apothecary, João Gomes da Silva, a *pardo* (light-skinned mulatto) man who had practiced that profession since at least the beginning of the century.[4] In 1806, for example, he issued a receipt for 4,560 réis (the price of seven hens) for medicine he prepared for Captain Vicente Ferreira de Andrade. The concoction does not seem to have worked, because the captain died, but not before making his friend the apothecary the third executor of his will, a responsibility that would only befall him if the first two appointees turned down the post. By the time he was Rufino's master, about fifteen years later, João Gomes was not just any apothecary. In early September 1816, he was selected as the exclusive supplier of medicine to the hospital and orphanage of the Santa Casa de Misericórdia da Bahia, which meant that he supplied the most important philanthropic institution and the largest consumer of medicinal drugs in the captaincy. The terms of his appointment obliged him to ensure that "all the remedies supplied are composed of the best ingredients and manufactured with the utmost perfection." Furthermore, like his predecessor, he would have to supply all medicines given to patients in the months of February and June of each year free of charge.[5]

Made during a period when there were no more than one hundred inpatients at the hospital, the contract with the Santa Casa became a liability for the apothecary when that number exceeded two hundred in 1825. At the beginning of that year, Rufino's master complained that he had accumulated a loss of three million six hundred thousand réis—a small fortune that would have been enough to buy a little over ten slaves—and asked that the annual donation of medicine be reduced from two months to just one.[6] He wrote that his situation reflected "such calamitous times" in the city, perhaps a reference to the recent Revolt of the Periquitos, a mutiny of predominantly black and mixed-race soldiers that began with the murder of the general commander of the army in Bahia. It was a combination of two movements—protests against corporal punishment in the barracks and sympathy for the radical liberalism of civilian agitators—but it did not lack an element of racial tension. During the soldiers' turbulent yet generally peaceful occupation of the city between October and December 1824, retail goods were in short supply and prices soared. However, despite the apothecary's dramatic (and self-serving) assessment, it was hardly a calamity. João Gomes's decisive argument for gaining the sympathies of the Santa Casa's directors may have been the additional claim that since 1797 he had been a member of the powerful confraternity whose members included the elite of Bahian society. Some, however, may have been men of merely middling circumstances like

Figure 2.1 View of Salvador, Bahia, and its port in 1826. Painting by G. Scharf, 1826. Museu de Arte de Bahia.

him, who was, moreover, of mixed race and therefore placed in the category of a "lesser brother," a subordinate position reserved for those who did not belong to the ranks of white plantation owners, merchants, and high officials who ran the brotherhood. The board of directors eventually granted the brother apothecary's request.[7]

João Gomes stayed on as the Santa Casa's apothecary until he was "let go" in August 1829. The previous year, during several meetings, the directors discussed the institution's debts to Gomes and his possible replacement as a supplier of drugs to the hospital and orphanage for reasons that are unclear—perhaps because he was overcharging. In August, the treasurer informed the board that the debt for medicine supplied in the previous seventeen months totaled four million and a half réis—enough to purchase nearly twenty slaves. It would be paid off in monthly installments of four hundred thousand five hundred réis. On that occasion, there was no mention of a "donation," but of medicine supplied at a 40 percent discount. They even discussed firing him, but the board voted to keep him on until, a year later, the Santa Casa opened a call for tenders for a new apothecary, and João Gomes did not submit a bid. He tried to regain his former position several times over the course of the 1830s, and his last request

Figure 2.2 The Santa Casa de Misericórdia da Bahia, on the ground floor of which, to the right of its church, Rufino´s master kept his pharmacy. Watercolor by Diógenes Rebouças. From Diógenes Rebouças and Godofredo Filho, *Salvador da Bahia de Todos os Santos no Século XIX* (Salvador: Odebrecht, 1985).

was dated 1836, the year prior to his death. However, the Santa Casa decided that he should bid for the job on the same footing as the other candidates, which he apparently refused to do.[8]

In addition to his contract with the Santa Casa, João Gomes was also the apothecary for the Medical-Surgical College of Bahia, where he lectured in pharmacology until 1821, around the time when Rufino arrived in Salvador.[9] In addition to these two jobs, the apothecary presumably sold his drugs to other clients and may even have shipped them to other provinces. When they visited Oieiras, in Piauí province, in 1819, German botanist Johann B. Spix and biologist Karl von Martius observed that all the medicine sold there was imported from Bahia and Maranhão.[10]

The apothecary's trade provided Rufino's master enough income to purchase the African and other slaves. Eight years before becoming the Santa Casa's apothecary, he was already a slave owner. In 1808, the records show that one of his former slaves, Rita Maria da Conceição, from the Angola nation, died and was interred in the burial vault of the Jesus, Mary, Joseph confraternity in the Carmelite convent in Santíssimo Sacramento da Rua do Passo parish, where the apothecary lived at the time. In 1815, another of his slaves, Elena, from the Hausa nation, died of phthisis, as tuberculosis was then called. She was buried in a white shroud in Passo parish church. The following year, he buried a two-year-old boy named Ciríaco, a *crioulo* (a black person born in Brazil), the son of another slave named Elena—this time a member of the Jeje (Gbe-speakers) nation—who died of "paralysis." Slaves died and slaves were born in the apothecary's household. In 1831, when he was living in Sé parish in a house rented from the Santa Casa, he took to the baptismal font Venancia, a four-month-old *crioula*, probably born of the same mother as Ciríaco. The following year, he had Clementina's son Anselmo baptized at the age of four months. He was described as *pardo*. The same day, the apothecary had an adult slave woman, Florinda, a Nagô, baptized as well. Three years later, on March 9, 1834, three more of João Gomes' slaves were taken to the baptismal font: Elena, the daughter of Vicência, seven months old; João, Florinda's son, one year old; and Felicidade, a black woman of the Nagô nation. So far that makes twelve people the apothecary owned, including Rufino. We have not found any baptismal records for Rufino or for any other of the apothecary's male slaves. It should be noted that João Gomes did not usually buy men. He generally purchased African women, who probably worked as slaves for hire as well as doing housework. They also bore children, thereby adding to their mixed-race master's possessions. Rufino was therefore an exception in the strategy this master used to form his contingent of slaves. Elena, Clementina, and perhaps Florinda, among others, may have lived alongside the African under João Gomes's roof, a townhouse on Rua Direita da Sé, conveniently located across the street from the Santa Casa charity hospital.[11]

According to Rufino, the apothecary trained him as a cook, contrary to Johann Baptist von Spix and Karl Friedrich von Martius's opinion that masters preferred to employ slaves from Congo and Angola in domestic service "due to their greater docility and fluency of speech."[12] Illusions of docility aside, the German travelers, who went on a scientific expedition to Brazil between 1817 and 1820, were unwittingly alluding to the fact that those Africans had already become familiar with the Portuguese language spoken in Brazil while they lived in Portugal's possessions in those regions. It should be noted that, from among his slaves, João Gomes chose to train an African from the Nagô nation as a cook. That job was not unusual among male slaves in Brazilian cities. When he visited Bahia in 1817, the French traveler L. F. Tollenare had his food prepared by a male slave, as he noted in his journal: "I lead a solitary life, only accompanied by a black man who serves me as a cook."[13] The foreigner was merely adapting to a widespread custom in Brazil. In Rio de Janeiro, nearly all enslaved men advertised in the newspapers as domestics in the mid-nineteenth century were cooks.[14] In Salvador, eleven of the twenty-nine slaves in a sample of postmortem inventories carried out in that city between 1800 and 1820 were listed as cooks. When rural

Figure 2.3 Receptacles such as these were used to store medicine at the Santa Casa pharmacy. Museu da Santa Casa de Misericórdia da Bahia.

towns and cities are added to the sample, the proportion of male cooks drops slightly: twenty-one men to forty women. Naturally, many of the women listed under the category of "domestic service" also worked in the kitchen, but men—albeit few—were also listed as domestics. However, saying that a slave (male or female) was a cook emphasized a specialization among domestic labor. At the same time, the kitchen where the slave worked may have been somewhere other than his master's house—in a hotel, hospital, barracks, prison, or ship—in short, anywhere where he or she could be hired or rented out. The occupations of three of the slaves found in the abovementioned sample are described as "sailor and cook."[15] Therefore Rufino's occupation was no exception in the world of male slaves in Brazil.

There is evidence that slaves worked as apothecaries in eighteenth-century Brazil, including Bahia. That situation probably continued in the following century. Rufino may have worked as a house slave, but his activities were not limited to that. His skills as a cook may have been useful in concocting drugs for his master's apothecary shop, and he may have helped work with herbs, roots, and chemicals. There were also medicines of animal and mineral origin. In this case, he may have become a *prático de botica* (lay apothecary) or *moço do boticário* (apothecary's boy). An apothecary's lab was very much like a kitchen, full of pots, pans, bowls, mugs, cups, goblets, amphorae, colanders, jugs, funnels, knives, and mortars, where a range of culinary methods was used to produce powders, electuaries, ointments, plasters, ointments, tablets, infusions, oils, syrups, elixirs, decoctions, apozems, and other solutions. It may also have produced food for the patients—such as "medicinal" chicken, using lean meat—when the apothecary and his assistants worked just like ordinary cooks. In addition to "cooking" medicine (and chicken), Rufino's master may have taught him to use them, because at that time apothecaries often did the work of physicians, in the role of apothecary–medicine man. Amid their pots, pans, and infusions, these professionals had a *soupçon* of sorcery. In 1818, Spix and Martius saw a large quantity of "English specifics and miraculous remedies" in Salvador's pharmacies. The travelers must have entered João Gomes's apothecary shop three or four years before Rufino landed in Bahia, because they visited the Santa Casa hospital, where his establishment was on the ground floor, facing the street, right below that institution's administrative offices.[16]

An apothecary shop was not just a place for mixing medicinal formulas, and prescribing and selling drugs. Since colonial times, it had also been a venue where men gathered "at certain times of the afternoon or evening to discuss politics or religion, converse about a variety of topics, or simply to shoot the breeze," according to medical historian Lycurgo Santos Filho. It was also a place for "passionate" games of cards and dice, according to Spix and Martius's report on what they saw in Bahia. Both João Gomes's shop and home were located at addresses where large numbers of people came and went—in government offices, the city council, the governor's palace, numerous churches, shops, and homes. In addition to medicine—and possibly other things—the apothecary sold the Santa Casa's lottery tickets to help finance its charitable work. In 1827, João Gomes handed over 160,000 réis to that institution for the 4,000 tickets he had sold for a lottery that would benefit the charity hospital, the main consumer of his drugs. The first prize was 8 million réis—enough to purchase about twenty-five slaves.[17]

Aside from his contacts with the Santa Casa, João Gomes's extensive social network and prestige—which were typical of an apothecary—led to his being chosen to act as the executor of wills made by people of all walks of life, ranging from Captain Vicente Ferreira to the African freedwoman Efigênia do Sacramento. As her executor, Gomes wrote, signed, and delivered the manumission letter of the Mina slave, Matilde—with whom the apothecary must have frequently discussed the matter. Efigênia had freed Matilde in her will for the price of 40,000 réis, payable in three years—terms that the future African freedwoman fulfilled. João Gomes also signed several documents related to real estate transactions and manumission letters as a proxy and witness. The apothecary shop must have been responsible for most of the relationships established and the trustworthy reputation that João Gomes had built up in Salvador. If Rufino worked at his master's shop, he would have had the opportunity to interact with all sorts of people, which may have helped him learn more about the world of white people in which he now lived as the slave of a *pardo*, mixed-race master.[18]

Rufino may have taken advantage of his master's social contacts, particularly the poorer customers. The apothecary's relations with that portion of the city's population were clear in his performance at the baptismal font and probably reflected the color of his skin. His many godchildren included Aprigio, a *pardo* child baptized in April 1828, the illegitimate child of Francisca da Pureza Pereira. The following month, he stood as godfather for Leopoldina, the illegitimate daughter of Florinda Izidora da Conceição. In 1829, he did so for a freed *crioula* girl, Maria, age six months, the legitimate daughter of Domingos and Izabel, a married slave couple whose master, Captain José Teixeira de Oliveira, must have been a friend of the apothecary. The child may have been freed at the font as a sign of her master's affection for her and/or in recognition of the good service rendered by the baby's parents. The apothecary was also the best man at weddings, such as that of two Jeje freedpersons, Felipe Ignácio, 45, a merchant, and Caetana de Menezes, 40, in 1807. The Africans were his neighbors in Passo parish, and in addition to João Gomes, they invited Lieutenant Antonio Gonçalves Marins to witness their union.[19]

João Gomes da Silva was married to Maria Rosa de Jesus, who was *parda* like him. She died on February 2, 1837, at the age of 64 of an "internal disease" and was buried in a black shroud in Misericórdia church. The apothecary passed away eight months later—also of an internal malady (possibly a broken heart). He was 68 years old. His death certificate states that he was white. Was he whitened by age or social climbing? He was buried in a white shroud in Ajuda chapel, a few steps from Misericórdia. Gomes, and his wife had at least six children: Maria Roza, Anna Roza, João Junior, Bernardino, Manoel, and Francisco. Maria Roza died of malaria at the age of 19 in 1812. Her father gave her a lavish funeral: fourteen priests accompanied the unmarried young woman's body to Passo parish church, where she was buried in the habit of Our Lady of the Conception. Three years later, his eighteen-year-old daughter Anna died of tuberculosis, a few days after the Hausa slave Elena died of the same contagious disease. Anna also had a splendid funeral, accompanied by twelve clerics and the parish priest. The apothecary's sons João Junior, Bernardino, and Manoel joined the Santa Casa confraternity on the same day—July 16, 1828. The first two may have been ill, possibly the victims of some kind of epidemic, because they died a few weeks later. They may have joined the institution to enjoy a good death with the pomp lavished on its members. Rufino witnessed this intense family drama year after year.[20]

Rufino spent the 1820s in Salvador, where most of the slaves were African. At the time, the city had a population of roughly 55,000 to 60,000 inhabitants, about 42 percent of whom were slaves. Sixty-three percent of those slaves were born in

Africa. Rufino found thousands of Nagôs in Bahia and must have witnessed the arrival of thousands more. The 1820s, especially the second half of the decade, saw the height of the century's slave trade to Bahia. Bahian slave traders, who controlled the flow of ships coming from the Bight of Benin—mainly the ports of Ouidah, Porto Novo, Badagry, and Lagos— intensified their operations in the years following 1826 because they feared that the treaty signed that year between Brazil and Britain would end the transatlantic trade in human beings within four years. The exacerbation of the civil war in Ọ̀yọ́ and its ramifications in the south of Yoruba territory helped intensify that pillage by producing slaves in mass quantities. Historian David Eltis estimates that 291,400 Yoruba speakers departed for Bahia in the first half of the nineteenth century. Most were enslaved illegally, because since 1817 the transatlantic slave trade had been banned north of the equator following a treaty between Portugal and Britain signed two years earlier. Like thousands of fellow Nagôs, Rufino himself was a "contraband slave"—and therefore free in the eyes of the law. In the mid-1830s, his nation represented about 30 percent of the enslaved Africans in Salvador, and most came from the Ọ̀yọ́ region and its neighboring dependencies, including Ilorin. Rufino must have come across people from his portion of Yorubaland, some of whom he may have known on the other side of the Atlantic. Now, all of them were enslaved in Bahia.[21]

Urban slaves mainly worked as domestics—just as Rufino appears to have done—or they worked outdoors or as slaves for hire. The latter mainly worked as porters, carrying heavy loads, and as litter bearers, street vendors, and artisans. They negotiated payment of a weekly fee with their masters and could keep anything left over for themselves. These agreements were not legally binding, but masters followed a custom that gave many slaves a chance to save up enough money to buy their freedom. Rufino may have worked as a slave for hire—as a cook or in another occupation, possibly selling cooked food in the streets. That was a common activity for slaves—especially women—in large cities like Salvador, Rio de Janeiro, and Recife, and even smaller ones like Porto Alegre. As was common in the urban slave environment, it is possible that Rufino engaged in more than one occupation, both indoors and outdoors.[22]

While Rufino lived in Bahia, his fellow Nagôs staged several rebellions, all of them in the sugar-growing region of the Recôncavo and the outskirts of Salvador, except for one that erupted in the city center. Most of the slave uprisings took place in the 1820s—sixteen all told—due, for the most part, to the intensification of the slave trade during that period. The rebels were generally recent arrivals from Africa, or *boçais* (sing. *boçal*), though their leaders were *ladinos*— that is, slaves and even freedpersons who had been there much longer and were already accustomed to the local culture and language.

Figure 2.4 Sedan chair porter, a typical occupation of urban slaves in Salvador and other large cities in Brazil. Detail of "Hospice de N. S. Piedade à Bahia." From Johann Moritz Rugendas, *Malerische Reise in Brasilien* (Paris: Engelmann & Cie., 1835).

We have detailed information about at least three rebellions staged during the war for independence, one on Itaparica Island in May, another in the village of São Mateus in September, and the third on the outskirts of Salvador, in an area called Pirajá, in December. They all took place in 1822. That is the year when Rufino most likely arrived in Bahia. The December uprising was actually an attack by slaves on the Brazilian forces, incited by the Portuguese. It resulted in the summary execution of at least fifty of the rebels captured. Other revolts occurred in 1826 and 1827. And there were several in 1828. The 1826 uprising involved slaves who had taken refuge in the Urubu *quilombo* (maroon community) in a rural area outside Salvador. That incident demonstrated the primacy of the Nagôs, both in the prisoners' statements and the presence in that *quilombo* of an African cult house that apparently belonged to that ethnic group. And in April 1830, there was a rebellion in the city itself, where warehouses full of newly arrived Africans were attacked on Ladeira do Taboão near Pelourinho, in Sé parish—the same district where Rufino's master had his apothecary shop.[23]

We do not know whether Rufino was one of the rebels, what he thought about the uprisings, or if he quietly supported those revolts. There is no direct evidence of Muslim participation in any of them. Muslims like Rufino would only appear clearly on the front lines during the 1835 rebellion. Before then they seemed to be gathering their forces, recruiting followers, and converting other Nagôs to Islam, perhaps originally without even considering the possibility of staging a radical mass slave uprising. It is likely that, as Abuncare, he belonged to a Malê group and, as such, attended or even conducted prayer sessions and Qur'ānic writing exercises, ritual suppers, and celebrations of the Muslim calendar, all of which were common practice among the Malês in the late 1820s and the 1830s in Bahia. Therefore, he must have gathered and prayed to Allah with fellow Muslims who later organized the armed uprising. As a result, he might perhaps have been part of the group of Malê insurgents when the revolt broke out on January 25, 1835, in Salvador, not far from his master's house, had it not been for the fact that, by then, he no longer lived in Bahia. Otherwise he might just have adhered to a kind of non-militant Islam, not only in Brazil but since his days in Ọ̀yọ́ country.

Rufino only spent eight years in Salvador, although the police scribe in Pernambuco incorrectly wrote "eighteen years"—information that conflicts with other passages of the interrogation conducted in 1853. The Malê told his interrogators that he had left Salvador (where he arrived "in the time of Madeira's war") "before [Emperor] Pedro went to Lisbon." He remembered the major milestones in his life in distinctly Yoruba fashion by associating them with equally important political events that he seems to have observed attentively.[24] Regarding the time when he left the province of Bahia, Rufino referred to the period immediately following Pedro I's abdication as Emperor of Brazil (he returned to Portugal in April 1831), a time of intense political turbulence in the country marked by growing opposition to the sectors associated with Portuguese interests, along with demonstrations in the streets and agitation in the press by liberal radicals and republicans.[25]

3

Enslaved in Porto Alegre

Rufino told his interrogators that he traveled south to the province of São Pedro do Rio Grande do Sul in the company of his "young master"—his master's son, army cadet Francisco Gomes. It is very likely that Gomes had been deployed to serve on the imperial border where, for at least three years, Emperor Pedro I had been waging a fruitless war with Uruguay that continued until that country won its independence in 1828. Intensified military recruitment for that war was one reason for the emperor's low popularity and the pressure that forced him to abdicate the throne.

At some point between 1830 and March 1831, Francisco Gomes arrived in Rio Grande do Sul along with Rufino, who may have accompanied him as a valet to save part of the annuity of 130,000 réis that families paid the army for the food and comfort of their cadet sons.[1] The slave's life there must have been even more unstable than the one he had experienced thus far. In Salvador, he had had just one master; in Rio Grande do Sul, he would have three, including Francisco Gomes. We do not know anything about the period he spent there with his young master, except that, for some reason, Gomes decided to sell him.

Since the first decades of the nineteenth century, several provinces—including Rio Grande do Sul—had become major buyers of slaves from the north. The region gained a reputation for harsh slavery because that was where masters sold their rebellious slaves. At the time, Nicolao Dreys, a French merchant who lived in Porto Alegre from 1817 to 1827, wrote that "when a black man from other provinces of Brazil showed any sort of vicious disposition, Rio Grande was the destination that was inflicted on them as punishment," adding that slaves were offered for sale in Rio de Janeiro's newspapers as long as they were sent to that southern province. Dreys himself did not agree that slavery there was as harsh as masters from other provinces believed it to be. In any event, seigniorial punishment alone does not explain the booming southward trade in slaves, especially from Rio de Janeiro. For the most part, it was simply due to market demands in Rio Grande do Sul.[2]

The Story of Rufino. João José Reis, Flávio dos Santos Gomes, and Marcus J. M. de Carvalho, Translated by H. Sabrina Gledhill, Oxford University Press (2020) © Oxford University Press.
DOI: 10.1093/oso/9780190224363.001.0001

Traders often accompanied slaves to sell them in person. On August 7, 1835, for example, Manuel Avelindo da Costa, a Portuguese, arrived in Porto Alegre from Bahia aboard the brig *Travassos* with ten of his own slaves. The following month, the sumac *Novo Acordo* brought from Bahia Antonio, Sofia, Maria, José, and Irena, all of them African-born, and a creole woman named Rita, accompanied by another Portuguese, Antonio José Duarte, and a Brazilian, Antonio José Moreira. Apparently, Rufino's master had not gone to Rio Grande do Sul with the intention of selling him, but like these others, that is precisely what he did.[3]

Rufino was purchased by José Pereira Jardim, a merchant based in Porto Alegre, and served him as a slave for at least two years. When Jardim went bankrupt and fled to Montevideo to escape his creditors, the African was auctioned off along with the merchant's other assets. We have not been able to find the records of that transaction, but Rufino said he was "sold at public auction and bought by judge Peçanha." The full name of Rufino's new owner was José Maria de Salles Gameiro de Mendonça Peçanha, and he apparently put his slave to work as a house servant.

Under José Maria Peçanha, the Muslim slave would be cooking for a powerful man who became Chief of Police of Rio Grande do Sul in May 1833. Peçanha was born in Rio de Janeiro, the son of José Feliciano da Rocha Gameiro and Ana Preciosa de Mendonça Peçanha e Mascarenhas. Among other posts, his father had been a criminal magistrate in Rio de Janeiro when Tiradentes, the famous leader in an anti-Portuguese conspiracy in Minas Gerais in 1789, was executed three years later. In Portugal, among other posts, Gameiro was a member of His

Figure 3.1 Porto Alegre and surroundings in mid-nineteenth century. From Herman Rudolf Wendroth, *O Rio Grande do Sul em 1852: aquarelas* (Porto Alegre: Governo do Rio Grande do Sul, 1983).

Royal Highness's Supreme Court, as well as an appellate court judge, a magistrate for the Royal Tobacco Contract, and General Superintendent of Police in the northern city of Oporto (Porto), where he lived in mid-1808, which means that he was there when it was regained from French control.[4]

Rufino's master followed in his father's footsteps in many ways. After obtaining a law degree from Coimbra University in 1818, he pursued a brilliant legal career, reaching the post of minister of the Supreme Court. The province where he held the highest post in the police force was not unfamiliar to him. At the beginning of his career, between the late 1810s and mid-1820s, Peçanha was a visiting magistrate and tutelary judge in Porto Alegre. He took a medical leave of absence in April 1819, which he spent in Rio de Janeiro, returning the following year. Shortly thereafter, he would be active as visiting magistrate in the towns of Rio Pardo and São João da Cachoeira, as well as holding the post of probate judge, a position that gave him privileged information about local estates. He married the daughter of a potentate from Rio Pardo and had become an appellate court judge in Porto Alegre by August 1823, when, soon after Brazil's independence from Portugal, he was accused of judicial malfeasance for allegedly persecuting the political enemies of the president of the provisional, local post-independence governing junta, Marshal João de Deus Mena Barreto, the future Viscount of São Gabriel, his father-in-law. One of his accusers at the time would call Rufino's future master a despot, "servile to his totalitarian father-in-law and his private interests," and therefore an "odious minister."[5]

In 1824, Peçanha experienced another career advancement when he became an appellate court judge in Bahia. Appointed for a term that ended in 1829, he assumed the post but apparently never took the bench.[6] There are indications that he never left Rio Grande do Sul during that period. There are reports of three of his adult slave women being in Porto Alegre when he should have been in Bahia: Maria, an African, Leonarda, a creole, and Felippa, another African. The first two appear in death certificates for babies: Maria's son Francisco was three months old when he died of dysentery, in May 1824; Leonarda lost two sons: Firmino, who died of impetigo at the age of three months in June 1826, and Agostinho, who was five months old when he died of smallpox in January 1828. There is also a record of the birth in early October 1830 of Madalena, the daughter of Felippa, a "black woman from the Coast [of Africa]," who was also Peçanha's slave. The godfather was a *pardo* slave, Frederico, and his godmother was a slave named Madalena. Rufino must have lived under Peçanha's roof along with all of these enslaved women and their surviving children—and perhaps even cooked for them.[7]

The hallmarks of Peçanha's activities as police chief were dedication to duty and political prudence. He sent daily reports to the president of the province, informing him of all the events related to law enforcement in the city. They were based on reports he received from the justices of the peace regarding crimes and other offenses committed, arrests, and the departure of long-standing residents and arrival of new ones in their respective districts. Periodically, Peçanha would visit the city jail. Among other things, he heard the prisoners' complaints, which he reported to his superior, the president of Rio Grande do Sul province.

Peçanha also had a modest political career in Rio Grande do Sul. In 1833 and 1834, he presided over the General Provincial Council, an agency that advised the president of the province on administration-related matters. The following year, he was elected to the recently installed Provincial Assembly, the institution that succeeded that Council. In order to take his seat as an assemblyman, Peçanha requested a leave of absence from his post as chief of police, but he soon returned to it.[8]

While working in the kitchen as a cook and probably in the streets of Porto Alegre as a hired-out slave, Rufino followed these and other moves in his master's life in politics and the police force because, after sending off sometimes tense reports from his office, Peçanha would return home to eat an invigorating meal prepared by his slave. Rufino spent nearly four years in Porto Alegre, most of the time under Peçanha's control.

During that period, Rio Grande do Sul's economy was based on the production of *charque*, or beef jerky, which was exported to other parts of the country and mainly consumed by the poor and enslaved population. Working in groups averaging sixty to one hundred men, slaves represented the majority of the workforce at the *charqueadas* that produced *charque*. When they were well run, Nicolao Dreys—who believed slavery in that province to be pleasant—compared them with "a penitentiary establishment."[9] Over the course of the nineteenth century, thousands of slaves arrived in Rio Grande do Sul, either from overseas or re-exported from other provinces—mainly Rio de Janeiro and Bahia, which was a distant second—to work in this central industry and other secondary sectors of its economy. In 1802, the number of slaves traded annually reached nearly 1,000 and was as high as 1,466 in 1817. The number of slaves in the region in 1802 totaled 12,970. It soared to 20,611 in 1819, representing 31 percent of the population. Estimates are that, by 1840, there were 40,000 souls in Rio Grande do Sul's enslaved population. In 1846, Porto Alegre had 12,355 inhabitants, roughly 17 percent of whom were slaves.[10]

In the first half of the 1830s, when Rufino lived in Porto Alegre, the city was growing rapidly. French traveler Arséne Isabelle, who visited the provincial capital in 1834, heard from local informants that a house was built every day. In the streets, Isabelle observed that enslaved blacks were veritable "industrious men, workers" who spent their lives ensuring "the subsistence and all the pleasures of life of their indolent masters." In the port, he noted that blacks unloaded the heavy cargo and carried it to its destinations. When he walked through the city, the Frenchman felt like a fish out of water because he could not see any whites, just black people working "among he-goats and she-goats, of which the streets are full." The traveler's and Rufino's paths might have crossed one day. In addition to men, Isabelle also saw many black women during his walks in Porto Alegre. At the time, black women of the Mina nation enjoyed a good reputation for the quality of the sweets they sold in the city streets. In fact, they had already caught the attention of other foreign travelers in the previous decade, such as Saint-Hilaire, who wrote in 1820: "as in Rio de Janeiro, the hawkers are black women; some squat next to their wares to sell them; others have stalls arranged in a disorderly fashion."[11]

Urban slavery in Porto Alegre took on sharper contours in the 1830s, driven by the growing number of slaves for hire, greengrocers, porters and litter bearers, artisans, and house slaves who circulated in the streets and served in their masters' homes. Every day, the newspapers advertised the sale of slaves with a range of skills. A "good-looking" twenty-four-year-old mulatto man, who was heathy and "free of vice," was said to be a good coachman, cook, and cobbler. Another ad asked if anyone had a carpenter for sale. Most of the slaves sold or rented out were men and women with the skills required to work in domestic service. "For rent, a slave woman who can wash, starch, sew and cook," reads one such notice. An African woman from the Borno nation was advertised as being a good washerwoman and cook, "and also suitable for all kinds of work." Her twelve-year-old creole daughter was also up for sale as an apprentice domestic, but whoever bought the mother did not buy the daughter, who was still being advertised on her own later on. In the same shops that sold slaves, merchants also displayed all kinds of goods, including a variety of books and musical instruments.[12]

The daily reports the justices of the peace sent to the chief of police and Rufino's master clearly show slavery taking shape in the city, often with the help of outsiders. The justice of the central district of Porto Alegre informed Chief Peçanha on March 28, 1833, that the new president of the province, José Mariani, 34, a bachelor from Bahia, had taken up residence there along with his two slaves, José and Atanásio. José Mendes, his wife, two children, and three slaves moved to the same district from Rosário parish in April 1834. Most of the seigneurial families of Porto Alegre owned between one and three slaves, but there were also masters with much larger slaveholdings, often employing most of them as slaves for hire.[13] Joaquim Olavo de Jesus, for example, was married with two daughters. A rancher from Rio Pardo, he moved to the capital in April 1835, taking with him eleven slaves, "including males and females," who were supposed to work in a variety of occupations as domestics and hired-out slaves. The jeweler Tito Livo da Costa, 28, had come from further away, Rio de Janeiro, the previous year, in the company of Maria Maciel, 32, possibly his wife, and the slaves Silvestre, from the Rebolo nation: Joaquim, a Benguela; Paulina, a Mozambique; Feliciana, a creole; and Carolina, a mulatto. It is unlikely that all these slaves were going to be put to work as domestics. Some may have helped out in their master's jewelry shop while others worked in the streets. Among the five slaves of the Portuguese João José Santana, 30, married and the father of a four-month-old daughter, some may also have worked outside their master's home. In addition to his family and slaves, his household also included a woman with two children aged eighteen and twelve. These records of changes of address suggest that Porto Alegre was expanding and becoming a dynamic urban center where business and work opportunities were growing and driving the increase of slavery.[14]

As in other slave cities, enslaved blacks found many ways to challenge seigneurial control in Porto Alegre. Dealing with escapes, for example, was part of the daily routine of masters and police authorities. Eleven slaves on a list of seventeen who were jailed in the city in October 1833 were described as having an "absent Master." Alongside advertisements for the purchase, sale, or rental of slaves, the newspapers repeatedly published announcements about fugitives. One day, two slaves fled "at dawn" from the town of Triunfo, presumably heading for Porto Alegre. Another day, Antonio, a slave of the Cabinda nation, vanished, taking an army uniform that he must have worn to disguise himself as a soldier. Another escapee was a "little mulatto" (*mulatinho*) called Amaro, just eight years old, thin, with large eyes and a soft voice.

Runaways often formed maroon communities called *quilombos*. In late October 1835, one such settlement was raided in the Miraguaia district. The attackers met with resistance, and one *quilombo* member was wounded and arrested while another was killed. The dead man's head was cut off and sent to Peçanha in Porto Alegre as proof that the mission was accomplished, as well as being a kind of trophy that proclaimed the barbaric nature of slavery in Rio Grande do Sul. Among those arrested for escaping and more serious offenses, the majority were African-born slaves. In an accounting of prisoners in late February 1834, twelve of the fifteen slaves in the city jail were born in Africa. Some had already received a range of sentences, including death or life in the galleys for homicide. Months later, black prisoners tried to escape through the roof, taking advantage of "the dark night," according to the jailer in his report to Rufino's master.[15]

Escaping was a nonviolent way of contesting the conditions of slavery, but slaves were also known to attack their masters, and some even killed them. In June 1835, Peçanha wrote to the president of the province to warn him that he had prosecuted a slave from Viamão—then a parish of Porto Alegre—"for the murder perpetrated against his own master."[16]

Due to the growth of the enslaved population, the need to control it became part of the order of the day. In February 1834, Peçanha sent instructions regarding police patrols to the president of the province for his approval. They banned "gatherings of slaves on any occasion or in any place, nor may they carry sticks or other instruments that might do harm, even if they are not forbidden weapons." Further on, the new rules ordered that gatherings of slaves in taverns and bars should be avoided. These instructions also reinforced existing municipal ordinances that punished the owners of taverns, bars, and bodegas who allowed slaves to hang around their establishments, "never consenting to their gambling, conversing, eating, playing [instruments] or dancing." The penalty was a 2,000 réis fine for the first infraction and 4,000 réis thereafter. Another ordinance established that slaves found outside after the city council's bell sounded the curfew without a pass from their master or the person responsible for them would be taken home to determine whether they were authorized to be out after hours. If not, they were jailed overnight. There were more lenient rules against gatherings of free people "without a just purpose" and even for violating the curfew.[17]

However, many slaves were not intimidated by police control. In late November 1833, a block inspector from Rosário parish arrested twenty-five blacks for being found "in an illicit gathering" in the home of one of them, Antonio Castelhano, whose surname must have come from a Spanish-speaking country in the river Plate region. Eight of them were freedpersons, eleven were male slaves, and six were female slaves. Antonio had to sign a declaration of good behavior and move out of that district. The rules of residence of the time forbade slaves from living outside their masters' homes, a custom and prohibition that were common to most cities in Brazil. In an official letter dated August 1835, Peçanha wrote that he was about to take action against two slaves who had rented homes in the city center. In addition to challenging state control of what happened behind closed doors, slaves and freedpersons took their insubordination to the streets. The black freedwoman Brízida, for example, confronted the police patrol "with some hardly decent words," most likely because she was involved in some sort of behavior that was considered improper. She was arrested for insolence, of course, as was a black slave charged with "insulting with words" a police patrol that attempted to stop him from engaging in some sort of "disorderly" conduct.[18]

When Rufino lived in Porto Alegre, Arséne Isabelle described a harsh form of slavery replete with punishments, mainly lashings, regularly administered by masters and mistresses for the slightest transgression. Salt and pepper were rubbed in the resulting wounds. This is how the French traveler described the city's pillory:

> Every day, from seven to eight in the morning, you can watch a bloody drama in Porto Alegre. If you go to the shore, next to the arsenal, in

front of a church, before the instrument of torture of a divine lawgiver, you will see a pillar raised on a stone pedestal and against it ... a shapeless lump, something certainly belonging to the animal kingdom.... It is a black man!... A black man sentenced to two hundred, five hundred, a thousand or six thousand lashes! Keep going, leave this scene of desolation: the wretch is nothing but a group of mutilated members, difficult to recognize under the bloody pieces of his flagellated skin.

Isabelle was a republican and abolitionist, a man who thought "the aristocracy of skin [color] will go the way of all aristocracies!"[19] Therefore, one might assume that he was exaggerating what he saw in a monarchical and slavocratic Brazil. We have not found any contemporary documents that match what Isabelle wrote about how masters treated their slaves—whippings followed by pepper and salt rubbed in the wounds—but we did find confirmation of his description of the pillory in Rio Grande do Sul's capital, which in fact stood in front of the church of Nossa Senhora das Dores—Our Lady of Sorrows (but literally Our Lady of Pain)—symbolizing the convergence between seigneurial and divine justice. The men Isabelle saw whipped during his time in Porto Alegre could have included the African Gabriel, the slave of Francisco da Costa, sentenced to 2,000 lashes for murder. Gabriel was admitted to hospital in early February 1834 to be treated for his wounds. Another might have been the Africans Manoel, the slave of Francisco de Souza, and Luiz, owned by the "late Bilhano," who were both sentenced to 6,000 lashes for murder and were hospitalized in mid-February of the same year. Even women were not spared, although they received fewer lashes. The slave Catarina, also owned by Bilhano, was supposed to receive 4,000 lashes. Luiz and Catarina were apparently being punished for their master's murder.

Slaves received lighter sentences for lesser crimes. In April of the following year, one of the many to be punished was Manoel, a black man owned by Maria Lucinda de Mattos, sentenced to one hundred lashes "for carrying a pointed knife," a forbidden weapon. His mistress demanded that the sentence be carried out immediately so she could have her slave back at work sooner rather than later. In the case of João, another black man arrested for fighting with two other blacks, his master asked Peçanha to punish him with fifty lashes. The chief of police immediately obliged and sent the slave home. From his exalted post, Rufino's master presided over this veritable massacre of enslaved folk in Rio Grande do Sul.[20]

Rufino's Porto Alegre included some people from his homeland, both enslaved and freed, with whom he certainly crossed paths. There is not yet a great deal of data about the slave trade to Rio Grande do Sul in the 1830s, when Rufino arrived in that southern province, but in the 1820s, of the 872 imported from other provinces, 86 percent came from Rio de Janeiro and 11.5 percent from Bahia. That migration included a growing number of slaves from the Mina nation, although they were numerically fewer than Africans from Angola, Congo, and Mozambique. Mina slaves came from the area the Portuguese called Costa da Mina (Mina Coast) in West Africa, namely the litoral of the Bight of Benin, also known as the Slave Coast. Mina was a generic name that included Nagôs, Jejes, and Hausas, which were not always accurate ethnonyms either. They were also strongly present in the *charqueadas* of Pelotas. Between 1780 and 1831, African-born Minas represented 13.2 percent of the enslaved workforce employed the meat industry. In a sampling of Africans hauled into court in Rio Grande do Sul between 1818 and 1833, 25 percent were Minas, followed by 18 percent Benguelas, 12 percent Congos, and 10.5 percent Angolas. The remainder were also of West Central African origin, including 7 percent Cabindas. Later on, the number of West Africans increased. Among the 114 escaped Africans sent to jail in Rio Grande between December 1856 and July 1859, 43 percent were Minas, and that figure surpasses 45 percent if those specifically identified as Hausas and Nagôs are included.[21]

Although more systematic research remains to be done, recently obtained data shows that, over the course of the nineteenth century, the Minas forged considerable ethnic communities in the region, especially in the cities of Pelotas, Rio Grande, and Porto Alegre. This can be seen in manumission records. Among the Africans freed in Pelotas between 1832 and 1849, Minas in general, together with those specifically listed as Nagôs, represented 41.5 percent. In the city of Rio Grande, the percentage of manumissions obtained by West African slaves (listed as Minas, Nagôs, Hausas, Jejes, etc.) soared from 15.8 in the 1810–1830 period to 56.7 percent in 1831–1850, whereas their presence in the enslaved population only rose from 11.2 to 22 percent, respectively. In Porto Alegre, the number of manumissions obtained between 1748 and 1888 benefited 932 West African slaves, 1,099 from West Central Africa (Angolas, Congos, etc.), and sixty-eight from East Africa (mostly Mozambicans). Considering that West African slaves were in the minority, the conclusion is that they did very well in the race for freedom. More accurate records exist for the period between 1800 and 1835 in the capital of Rio Grande do Sul and its outskirts: West Africans represented 21 percent of slaves but 34 percent of those who obtained manumission. Those from Central West Africa represented 71 percent of the enslaved and just 66 percent of freedpersons. The specific data for the second half of the nineteenth century (1858–1887) confirm this: Nagôs—Rufino's nation—made up 60 percent of freed Africans, followed by Minas in general, who represented 36.2 percent.[22]

These last figures suggest that when Rufino lived in Porto Alegre, Nagôs had become a major presence, since many of the slaves freed in the 1850s onward would have arrived there in the 1830s, just like Rufino. However, they particularly began arriving there after the 1835 Muslim revolt in Bahia. The term *nagô* only began to appear in the records of the port city of Rio Grande after that date.[23] Therefore, Rufino must have witnessed the arrival of many fellow Nagôs who, like him, had once lived in Bahia, some of whom he had probably met there.

The Minas who lived in Rio Grande do Sul, particularly in Porto Alegre, included slaves and freedpersons who were Muslims like Rufino. Evidence of this includes the fact that in October 1838, the police discovered a "black Mina club" in the capital and confiscated Muslim papers from its members. When Francisco Alvares Machado became president of the province in 1841, he found those papers and carried out an inconclusive investigation to determine the meaning of the "hieroglyphics" written on them. In a letter to the minister of justice, Machado explained that the justice of the peace of the city's first district had received an anonymous tip about "a house that served as a school for blacks, where they learned to read and write." It was the headquarters of the Mina club. More than two years had passed, but the president still feared a rebellion similar to the one staged by Nagô Muslims, or Malês, in Bahia. Suspecting that those writings were subversive, he sent them to Rio de Janeiro for translation. Since he already had a separatist uprising to deal with—the Farroupilha revolt—he took pains to avoid an even worse problem: a slave rebellion in Rio Grande do Sul that could exploit divisions among the whites.

The same concerns assailed the president of the province in 1838. He tried to find a translator among the Africans in Porto Alegre, and when that failed, he sent some of the documents seized—two books and other manuscripts—to Rio Grande. There, on November 6, the city magistrate and interim police chief, Manoel Joaquim de Souza Medeiros, interrogated a Hausa freedman named José, 79, who said that he had arrived there as a slave in 1796. He declared that in his homeland he had been the son of a "priest," someone who "exercised the duties of his religion." He was most likely a *malomi* or *malam*, in short, a Muslim cleric and teacher. José understood the writing shown to him but claimed that he could not translate it into the white man's language. However, he attempted to ease the mind of the judge in charge of the investigation by explaining that it did not contain plans for a revolt but prayers from his homeland that were each used to achieve specific aims. In the words the scribe wrote down, "they were prayers that are used on various occasions as well as when they were about to die." José added that he did not understand what was written on sheets of paper that were shown to him.

The judge used the following investigative method to determine the sincerity of José's statement: he gave him a blank sheet of paper and told him to write "in his language" the words dictated to him, starting with the name of God. He wrote Allah twice in the short form the Hausas frequently used instead of the Arabic "long" form to write the name of God. He correctly wrote down the "name of his homeland" as Hausa. He also wrote his own name, José (written as something like Jojer or Jujer), and his original name, which he said was Muhammad, but the police scribe understood to be Muamba, which meant fraud or mischief. His father's name, Fu or Fau, and the like, is unclear, and his mother's was Hafsat. According to a specialist we consulted regarding these translations, the Hausa form of the name of God shows that these words were written in Ajami, the Hausa language written in Arabic script. The calligraphy is sometimes poor, probably due to the trembling hands of an elderly individual, compounded perhaps by the stress of interrogation.[24]

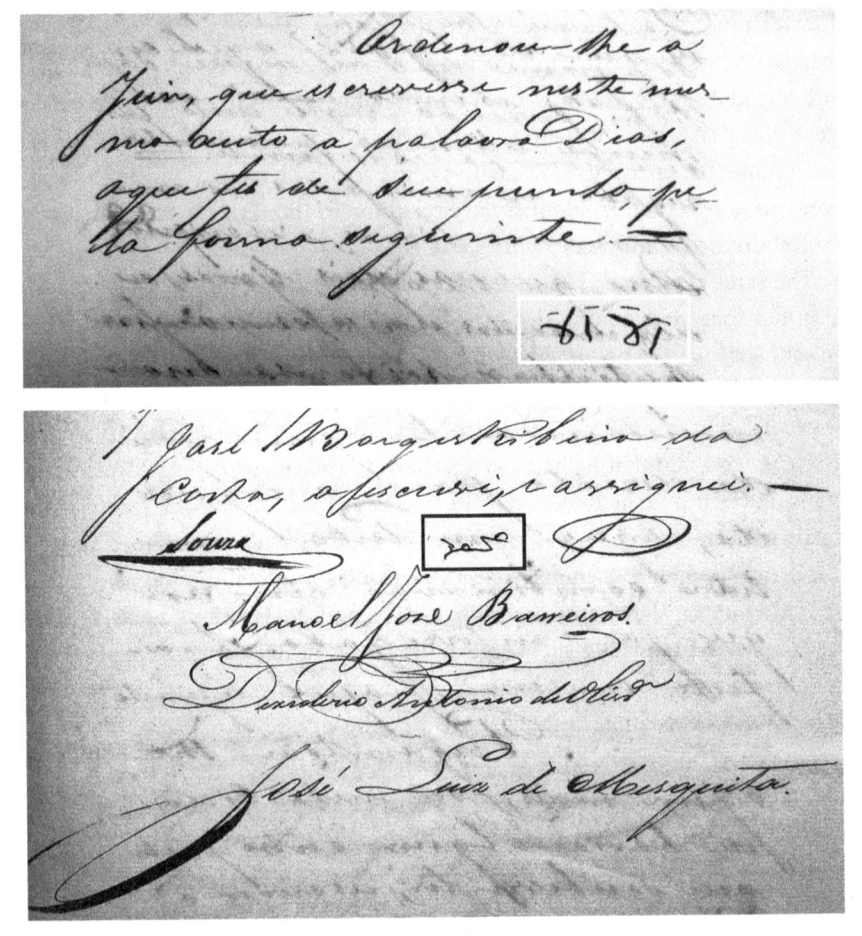

Figures 3.2a and 3.2b Muhammad writes "God" and signs his name in 1838. Arquivo Nacional, Rio de Janeiro.

Once this was done, the chief of police ordered José to write the same words underneath each question, as written down by the scribe. He then asked the scribe to compare the two, attesting that the words had been written "from right to left," and concluded that the aged Hausa had given consistent answers on both sheets of paper. Once he had finished his statement and it had been read out, the African—in a gesture that signified that he had not fully abandoned his personal and religious identity—signed his black Muslim name, Muhammad, "according to the style and with the characters of his homeland" in the words of the scribe. Beside his signature are the initials of the police chief, followed by the signatures of the witnesses present. They included Muhammad's former master and legal representative, Manoel José Barreiros, who at the beginning of the interrogation was incorrectly identified as the freedman's "*senhor*" (master). Barreiros had accompanied his former slave, who lived in his household, to the meeting with the police, and before the judge he officially vouched for the African´s good behavior over the years. This shows the value of a *patrono* (patron), a term used at the time to describe the status of a former master in the life of a slave he had freed. Since he enjoyed that protection, the police let Muhammad go. However, he would soon find himself under arrest for being a Muslim.[25]

Among the surviving documents found in a Muslim "school" in Porto Alegre, probably from the same investigation conducted in 1838, there is a manuscript of prayers elegantly bound in leather that was donated in 1855 to the Brazilian Historical and Geographic Institute (Portuguese acronym, IHGB) by Henrique de Beaupaire-Rohan. A lexicographer and politician during the imperial period, he must have received it from an official from Rio Grande do Sul in 1840 when he visited Porto Alegre as the military engineer assigned to fortify the city against the Farroupilha rebels. Passages from the Qur'ān are transcribed in the book, among other devotional writings, including excerpts from a seventeenth-century poem celebrating Muhammad, a popular text throughout the Islamic world. One passage from the *Qaṣīdat al-Burda* speaks of love:

> How can you deny love after the testimony borne against you by [such] irrefutable witnesses as your tears and exhaustion?
> Love has ingrained two lines [in your face] with sorrow and disease.
> Yes! The ghost of my beloved visited me in the night and left me sleepless
> Love mingles pleasures with pain.[26]

The story of this investigation and documents like this attest to the presence of literate Muslims in Porto Alegre who got together to teach, pray, memorize, recite, and copy verses of the Qur'ān and other Islamic texts, as well as devotional and love poetry. Rufino probably came into contact with these people and

Figures 3.3a and 3.3b Book manuscript confiscated at a Muslim "club" in Porto Alegre, containing passages of the poem *Qaṣīdat al-Burda*. Instituto Histórico e Geográfico Brasileiro, Rio de Janeiro.

may have even been a member of this or some other Muslim fraternity where he would certainly have been known as Abuncare and may even have read or handled the devotional book housed in the IHGB. But by October 1838, when "a black Mina club" was raided and those writings confiscated, Rufino had already left the capital of Rio Grande do Sul.

4

Farroupilha and Freedom

Confirming the Nagôs' success in gaining their freedom, Rufino would obtain his in the last months of 1835. Ironically this took place not long after the Revolt of the Malês in Bahia, who sought to win collective freedom by force. Rufino said he paid Police Chief José Maria Peçanha 600,000 réis for his manumission, the average price of a slave in Rio Grande do Sul. However, the freedom document registered in book 10 of the First Notary's Office of Porto Alegre does not mention the amount paid, nor does it stipulate that it was granted free of charge. It also lacks a conditional clause setting restrictions on the freedom granted, which was a common practice. The document simply identifies Rufino as belonging to the Nagô nation and states that, from that date forward, he enjoyed "full liberty" and could "take care of his work and industry and own his own property when acquired as the free person he has now become." His letter of manumission shows two dates: November 20, the day Peçanha wrote it, and December 17, when it was registered at the notary's office.[1] But what did his freedom cost? Had the slave reached an informal agreement with the judge? Did Peçanha have some reason to omit the amount received in the official document? Or was Rufino not telling the truth when he said he had paid for his freedom?

We believe Rufino, because he had no apparent reason to lie. It may be significant that the judge wrote that he was not granting a manumission letter but an *alvará* (charter or patent) of freedom to Rufino, a legal term that was unusual for a document of that nature. An *alvará*—derived from the Arabic *al-baraa*, "letter, bank note, receipt"—is a document issued by a judicial authority like the judge, "in favor of someone, certifying, authorizing or determining acts and rights."[2] It is possible that Peçanha had proceeded this way out of judicial habit, but he may have intended to safeguard the freedman's recently acquired rights even more effectively, particularly in a province experiencing turbulent times. As a result, Rufino's freedom paper was especially powerful in legal terms compared to manumissions granted privately by ordinary masters. Peçanha had expressed himself as judge and master when writing that document. Because it was an

The Story of Rufino. João José Reis, Flávio dos Santos Gomes, and Marcus J. M. de Carvalho, Translated by H. Sabrina Gledhill, Oxford University Press (2020) © Oxford University Press.
DOI: 10.1093/oso/9780190224363.001.0001

authoritative legal act, it may not have been opportune to stipulate the specific amount paid for that transaction, or even that any financial transaction was involved. That would explain its silence regarding the price Rufino claimed to have paid the judge for his freedom.

In 1835, the year Rufino became a freedman, the same Porto Alegre notary's office registered just four manumissions of West Africans—two Mina women, a Nagô woman, and Rufino. This confirms the general rule for Brazil, which was also true for Porto Alegre, that women outstripped men in the race for freedom. Two of the African women received their manumissions free of charge, and another received her freedom in exchange for the bondage of another African woman: Feliciana, of the Mina nation, the slave of Manoel Tavary da Silva, gave him a Cabinda slave named Joaquina to serve him in her place. Manumission through substitution was a common expedient in this sort of transaction throughout the country.[3]

We do not know what Rufino's life was like as Peçanha's slave, but if he managed to save up enough money to pay for his manumission, he must have worked as a hired-out slave, which was not unusual in Porto Alegre. It is also likely that he used his knowledge, however slight, of Arabic to write and sell amulets, an activity that paid as well as a full day's work in Bahia and likely in Porto Alegre, too. Based on the earnings of slaves for hire from 1830 to 1860, historian Valéria Zanetti observes that the slaves could keep for themselves as much as a third of what they made from working outside their masters' homes.[4] Therefore, out of their monthly earnings of, say, 17,920 réis, slaves were entitled to about 5,920 réis, enough to buy a bushel of cassava meal in 1842 or 37 bottles of Brazilian brandy in 1836, based on prices then charged in Porto Alegre. (In Rio in 1833, it would have been enough for two pairs of pants, two shirts, a blanket, and a pair of shoes, with 400 réis to spare.)[5] Hired-out slaves would have to use some of that money to buy food and pay rent, if they lived outside their masters' homes. If the same calculation can be used for Rufino, he would have had to save up money for over eight years of work in the streets of Porto Alegre without spending anything on himself to purchase his freedom for the amount he claimed to have paid—600,000 réis. But he only spent half that time as a slave in Porto Alegre. Perhaps Rufino had already saved up part of the money for his manumission during his time under slavery in Bahia.

However he obtained the funds required to buy his freedom, Rufino seems to have found in the police chief a master who was open to negotiation, a master who, despite his role in law enforcement—being responsible, among other things, for the sometimes harsh control of the city's slaves—may have tolerated his slave's religion and even been favorably impressed by his familiarity with the world of literacy. At the same time, Rufino must have used his intelligence, diligence, and discipline to be—or at least appear to be—a good and loyal slave.

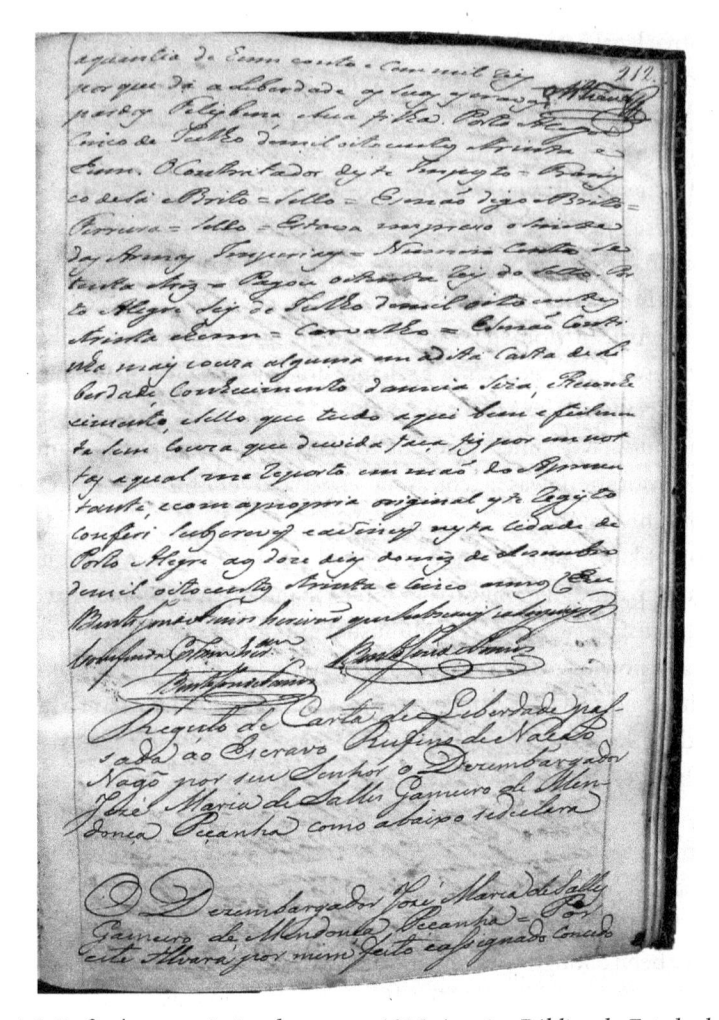

Figure 4.1 Rufino's manumission document, 1835. Arquivo Público do Estado do Rio Grande do Sul.

The fact that he had his master's permission to build up assets, the unconditional terms of the letter of manumission, and the circumstance of it being written as a charter are all factors that point in that direction. The freedman's loyalty to and the equivalent reciprocity from his former master was also expressed in the name he adopted: Rufino José Maria, former slave of José Maria Peçanha. The African probably would not have taken the name of a tyrannical master.

Two months before Rufino's manumission, on September 20, 1835, the liberal, federalist, and republican Farroupilha Revolt began with the invasion of Porto Alegre by the rebels, who held the town for almost a year. According to an eyewitness, Daniel Hillebrandt, a German doctor, during the occupation local authorities were threatened by scores of "Indians" (probably racially mixed folks) and Blacks.[6] The tensions that led that movement to erupt had already been seething openly since the previous year. Rufino was living with a master who was under pressure. The disturbances Peçanha reported to the president of the province that year included the first conflicts between liberals and conservatives that would soon lead to regional revolt. In October 1834, the first demonstrations were held to celebrate approval of a constitutional amendment, an achievement for the liberals that would give the provinces more autonomy, partly because it created provincial legislative assemblies after more than a decade of liberal pressure following Brazil's independence from Portugal. The streets of Porto Alegre would see violent clashes for a few days when the president of the province, Antonio Rodrigues Braga, was away from the capital. Police chief Peçanha wrote several vexed letters begging him to return, because he felt that he could not keep the situation under control. In one of those missives, written on October 21, he declared that he had "exhausted the legal means at my disposal . . . to restore public confidence." At the time, the Viscount de Castro, a hard-core conservative who was angered by the public unrest, took aim from his house at the crowd that was hailing the reforms and chanting "death to the Caramurus," as the partisans of the return of Pedro I to power were called (after the newspaper *O Caramuru*, the mouthpiece of this political group). After firing a few shots at the demonstrators, de Castro fled on horseback. A reading of Peçanha's reports during that crisis gives the impression that he was a rootless individual, a man of the law without a political calling—at least that he lacked the easy access to local potentates who could have helped him put out the fire. In any event, he may merely have been a truly cautious soul.[7]

One of the longest of Brazil's many regional uprisings of that period, the Farroupilha Revolt (1835–1845) mobilized ranchers and beef jerky producers against the centralizing policies of the Imperial Court in Rio de Janeiro. The rebels demanded protection against tough external competition with their products from neighboring countries, namely Uruguay and Argentina, and further privileges included in the constitutional amendment passed the previous year granting more autonomy for their province. It was a "white men's" revolt but, in the course of the struggle, it also came to include the free poor and slaves whom the rebels freed for the specific purposes of waging war against the "legalist" forces siding with the Rio government. In many cases, the white rebels reneged on that promise of freedom. We do, however, know that over fifty slaves joined in the first Farroupilha attack on Porto Alegre. Furthermore, the rebels were accused of starting or spreading rumors of slave uprisings. On their part, the legalists also promised slaves their manumission: any that deserted from the Farroupilhas' ranks would be freed and sent outside the province.[8]

Municipal judge Vicente Ferreira Gomes replaced Peçanha as the head of the police force, which was under Farroupilha control in early December 1835, and decided to take a hard line with the slaves. It may be that due to the soaring revolutionary passions in the province, slaves became unruly without necessarily joining the movement. In fact, the movement itself turned against them, at least in Porto Alegre. Judge Ferreira Gomes argued that Peçanha's slave control policies were of "little profit" because punishment was only called for slaves found breaking the 9p.m. curfew "without due authorization" to spend a night in jail. Because of that, he said, bond people were out of control and had even armed themselves with daggers and perpetrated abuses. The police chief asked the recently installed Farroupilha president to allow him to introduce the punishment of fifty lashes for slaves found in the streets after curfew without permission, "a measure that is not only fair but will have the infallible result of [preventing] so many crimes from being committed." The president partially approved his idea. The new guideline became an edict that established that the penalty for breaking the curfew should be twenty-five lashes for the first offense and fifty for repeat offenders.[9] Rufino did not remain in Farroupilha-controlled Porto Alegre to witness the stricter control of slaves, nor did he take sides in the conflict. That is what he stated in his 1853 deposition in Recife. It is possible that he obtained his manumission sooner than planned due to the uprising, or his master may finally have agreed to the slave's long-standing freedom project for the same reason. Peçanha may have decided that it would be good business to sell Rufino his freedom, given the tense climate in São Pedro do Rio Grande do Sul province. He would prevent his slave from trying to desert to the rebel ranks or take advantage of the political and military turmoil and simply abscond. Peçanha himself seemed to have been getting ready to leave Porto Alegre. When he wrote Rufino's letter of manumission in November, he was no longer chief of police. Claiming to be "in very poor health," he had resigned on September 30, 1835. However, he still served for about ten days under the government headed by Marciano Pereira Ribeiro, the fourth vice president of the province, who replaced the legalist president Antonio Rodrigues Braga, whom the Farroupilhas had run out of Porto Alegre along with the other vice presidents. Braga set up a parallel government in Rio Grande do Sul's Atlantic port, the city of Rio Grande.

Nevertheless, Peçanha did not leave Porto Alegre immediately, and there are indications that he initially joined the rebel regime. At least until early December 1835, he attended meetings of the rebel Farroupilha Provincial Assembly as an assemblyman. On November 28, 1835, for example, he was present when Vice President Marciano reported the province's successes to the assemblymen, praising the movement effusively and criticizing his predecessor's administration. And until early December, Peçanha was appointed as a member of the Assembly's committees, such as Public Education and the Statistics, Civil, and Judiciary Division. His absence was only reported in the records of that lawmaking body on the fourth day of that month, "with informed cause." He may

Figure 4.2 The city of Rio Grande's busy port in the mid-nineteenth century. From Herman Rudolf Wendroth, *O Rio Grande do Sul em 1852: aquarelas* (Porto Alegre: Governo do Rio Grande do Sul, 1983).

have secretly left Porto Alegre to meet with the deposed government in Rio Grande. Accordingly, a few days later, on December 12, we find legalist president Antonio Braga's signature on an official dispatch—"I [hereby] grant the permission requested"—in response to an unknown request from Peçanha. He may have once again asked for medical leave to go to Rio de Janeiro. Politically fickle, five years later Peçanha would be mentioned in a letter from merchant Ladislau Brandão to Domingos José Almeida, war minister of the Farroupilha government, in a context suggesting that Rufino's former master was not only present in Rio Grande do Sul during the revolutionary period but also on friendly terms with then-rebel president Bento Gonçalves da Silva, the celebrated leader of the southern revolt. By then, however, Peçanha would already be serving as a member of the Supreme Court in Rio de Janeiro, to which he was appointed in late 1838.[10]

5

Freedman in Rio de Janeiro

Rufino declared that he left Rio Grande do Sul and went to Rio de Janeiro "when the Farrapos war was beginning," according to the report on his arrest published in *Jornal do Commercio* in 1853. Both that article and the transcription of his statement to the police give the impression that he set off for Rio soon after his manumission was registered in mid-December 1835.

However, there is another possibility. Due to suspicions of a Muslim conspiracy in Porto Alegre in 1838, the authorities sent confiscated documents to the city of Rio Grande, where a Hausa freedman named José in Brazil interpreted them. This transpired toward the end of November of the same year. A month later, the interim police chief who interrogated José, Manoel Joaquim de Souza Medeiros, ordered the deportation of two African freedmen to Rio de Janeiro aboard the patache *Beleza do Sul.* Their names: José and Rufino. These men were suspected of "promoting a conspiracy of people of color," and, before being expelled from the province, they were forced to sign a "statement of responsibility" promising never to return to Rio Grande do Sul. To put this measure in perspective, the legalist government was then deporting from the province all the black people they arrested or who turned themselves in, whether slaves or freedpersons, who took part in the Farroupilha Revolt. Taking advantage of these circumstances, the president of the province had Rufino and José sent to the chief of police of Rio de Janeiro, the notorious Euzébio de Queiroz, who, seeing that they were Africans and therefore foreigners, recommended to the Minister of Justice that both of them be deported—"I believe it will be convenient to toss them out of the Empire," he wrote, as if he were dealing with rubbish. "Out of the Empire" meant sending them back to Africa.[1]

We suspect that José was Muhammad, the man who interpreted the Arabic documents mentioned in chapter 3, and Rufino, which was not a common name, may well have been our main character. This is what could have happened: instead of traveling directly from Porto Alegre to Rio de Janeiro between December 1835 and January 1836, Rufino may have gone to Rio Grande (where the official anti-Farroupilha government was based), possibly in the company of his former

The Story of Rufino. João José Reis, Flávio dos Santos Gomes, and Marcus J. M. de Carvalho, Translated by H. Sabrina Gledhill, Oxford University Press (2020) © Oxford University Press.
DOI: 10.1093/oso/9780190224363.001.0001

master, Judge José Maria Peçanha. After that, he may have stayed on and got involved with the local Muslim community until the Porto Alegre police raided that Islamic school, and confiscated papers were sent to Rio Grande for translation in late 1838. Although the Hausa freedman José (or Muhammad) explained that the documents did not contain any subversive writings and was allowed to go home after cooperating with the police, the local authorities remained on the alert. They even recommended that the justices of the peace ban and investigate all gatherings of blacks within their jurisdictions. Between the time José gave his statement and the date he was deported, the police discovered a link between José and Rufino—who, in the name of Allah, would have overcome past feuds between Hausas and Nagôs in Africa—belying José's claim that he did not know any other blacks who could read those documents. But he likely knew Rufino José Maria.

According to this version of Rufino's travels, he would then have arrived in Rio de Janeiro between late 1838 and early 1839, and not three years earlier as he stated in Recife in 1853, when he had good reason to omit the real reason for his leaving Rio Grande do Sul. Having just been arrested in Recife on suspicion of conspiracy, he could not reveal that he had been suspected of the same crime fifteen years earlier. If this narrative is correct, we would just need to discover how

Figure 5.1 View of the city of Rio de Janeiro, 1820s. Drawing by Augustus Earle, engraving by Edward Finden. From Maria Graham [Lady Maria Callcott], *Journal of a voyage to Brazil and residence there, during part of the years 1821, 1822, 1823* (London: Longman, Hurst, Rees, Orme, Brown, and Green, 1824).

he managed to avoid the deportation recommended by Euzébio de Queiroz. One possibility is that Peçanha, who had just taken his seat on the Supreme Court of Rio de Janeiro (in November 1838), interceded on behalf of his former slave. Another, more plausible alternative is that instead of leaving the ship that was supposed to drop him off in some African port, as was common practice in those cases, Rufino had joined the slave trade aboard that same vessel.

Unfortunately, we cannot confirm this version of events because we do not yet know if the Rufino who was expelled from the province of Rio Grande was in fact our Rufino, nor can we be sure that the José who accompanied him was the same one also named Muhammad who was interrogated in 1838. The coincidence of names, however, makes this version a strong possibility.

In any event, the Rufino who was interrogated in 1853 did end up in Rio de Janeiro, either between 1835 and 1836 or 1838 and 1839, and found an extraordinary African Tower of Babel there. The most populous city in the empire, Rio had also become the largest African city in the Americas in the first half of the nineteenth century. Estimates vary, but all of them indicate that Africans were disembarking in that city on a massive scale. Mauricio Goulart suggests that 570,000 Africans arrived there between 1801 and 1830, and Mary Karasch

Figure 5.2 A slave market in Rio de Janeiro, 1820s. Drawing by Augustus Earle, engraving by Edward Finden. From Maria Graham [Lady Maria Callcott], *Journal of a voyage to Brazil and residence there, during part of the years 1821, 1822, 1823* (London: Longman, Hurst, Rees, Orme, Brown, and Green, 1824).

has posited that at least 900,000 to 950,000 Africans were imported to Rio in the first half of the nineteenth century. More recent estimates indicate that during the period between 1811 and 1830 alone, approximately 610,000 Africans landed in Rio, from where most went on to work on coffee and sugar plantations in the interior. Many, however, remained in the city.[2] In 1821, there were over 40,000 slaves in Rio's urban parishes alone, and in the 1830s that number would surpass 50 percent of the population. Nearly 80 percent of the slave contingent was African. In 1849, by a conservative estimate, Africans made up 66.5 percent of the nearly 79,000 slaves in the largest slaveholding city in the western world.[3]

It may have been an African Tower of Babel, but different from the ethnic makeup of Salvador, another major African metropolis in the Brazilian Empire. In Rio, the predominant groups were West Central Africans (originating mainly from what is now Angola) and East Africans (from what is now Mozambique). They were mainly Bantu speakers, who rubbed shoulders with a much smaller number of West Africans, locally known as Minas. Tens of thousands of Africans formed nations that were often created along the routes of the Atlantic slave trade and under slavery—Angolas, Cabindas, Benguelas, Congolese, Rebolos, Cassanges, Songos, Monjolos, Ganguelas, Moanges, Cabundás, Mofumbes, Macuas, Inhambanes, Quilimanes, Mozambiques—and the list goes on. In most cases, Rufino would have been familiar with these groups, because he had come across them in Bahia and Porto Alegre, but never in such large numbers.

In Rio de Janeiro, the Nagô Rufino would have joined the ranks of the Mina nation. They were Africans from Cape Verde, Gabon, São Tomé and Calabar, Hausas, Jejes, and Nagôs. According to historian Manolo Florentino, the Minas reached no more than 3 percent of Africans whom the slave trade deposited in Rio between 1790 and 1830.[4] Mary Karasch has found that the number of Minas ranged from 1.5 to nearly 7 percent in the first half of the nineteenth century. That figure is very different from Africans from the Congo-Angola area (nearly 80 percent) and from Mozambique (18 percent).[5] In a sample of two hundred inventories studied by Luis Carlos Soares covering the period between 1810 and 1849, Minas totaled just 3.7 percent.[6] The results of our own study of 997 inventories were similar, at 4 percent. Some data suggest that many of the Minas who landed in Rio were sent to the interior of that province or re-exported to other parts of Brazil. For example, in a sample we gathered of 36,647 adult Africans—most of them recent arrivals—baptized in the main urban parishes (Candelária, Santíssimo Sacramento, São José, Santana, and Santa Rita), Minas represented 13 percent between 1801 and 1830.

In short, although the sources vary, all of them indicate that Minas formed a small to very modest part of the African population of Rio de Janeiro. Rufino therefore belonged to a small minority during the time he spent in Rio, which appears to have been brief. Nevertheless, Minas were over-represented among

BENGUELA **ANGOLA**

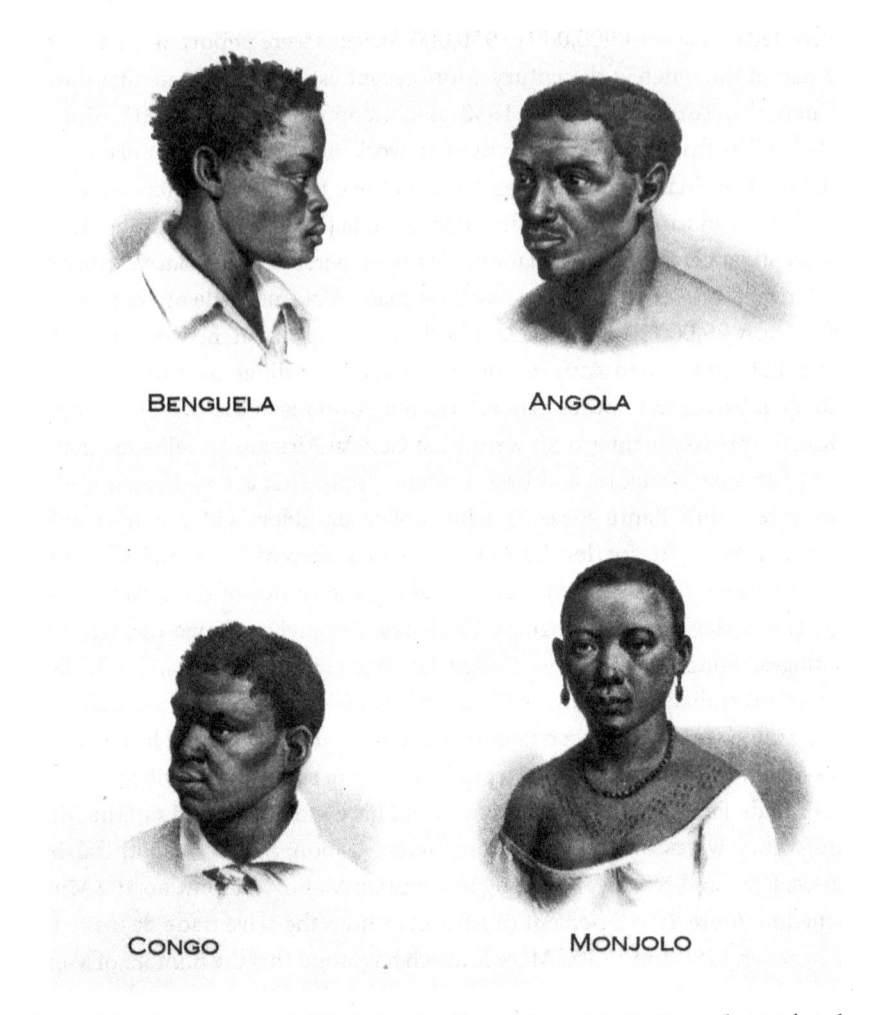

CONGO **MONJOLO**

Figure 5.3 African nations in Rio de Janeiro. From Johann Moritz Rugendas, *Malerische Reise in Brasilien* (Paris: Engelmann & Cie., 1835).

Africans arrested for some sort of crime in that city. They made up 5.7 percent of the 3,435 escaped African slaves captured between 1810 and 1830.[7] Historian Leila Algranti has found an even larger number: of a total of 2,492 Africans arrested by the Rio police between 1810 and 1821, 8.8 percent were Minas, and Thomas Holloway states that Minas represented 15.7 percent of the Africans arrested in Rio de Janeiro in 1850, which may reflect an increase in their presence in the city during that period.[8]

However, the larger proportion of Minas in the prison population also resulted from their frequent encounters with the police in the streets. Although they were the minority in the entire contingent of Africans, the Minas controlled an important part of the job market in the streets of Rio. Between 1851 and

1870, Africans in general were strongly represented in that sector, at 83.9 percent. Minas made up 32.7 percent of them. They primarily worked as porters, carrying heavy loads through the city, but they were also artisans. African street vendors were mainly women, who sold a range of products like cloth wrappers, black soap, straw mats, and other items imported from Africa, in addition to a variety of foodstuffs, both raw and cooked.[9] Female Mina vendors lent a touch of elegance to the streets of Rio, parading in their African wrappers and head-ties, adorned with clusters of amulets called *balangandās,* and elaborate hairstyles.[10] Charles Expilly, a French visitor, enthusiastically wrote that the Mina women were "superb creatures."[11] However, there is some exaggeration about the predominance of Mina women—as well as their monopoly on charm—in that sector of the urban market, because of all the African slave women who worked as street vendors between 1825 and 1850, just 26 percent were Minas, the rest being either Creoles or Bantu-speaking Africans. At any rate, the proportion of Minas was significant for a group that represented a small minority among black women in Rio de Janeiro. There were many Nagô women among the Mina grocers, although they made up just 5.5 percent of all Minas in the city. Women from Rufino's nation represented 36 percent of that gender, ethnic, and occupational group.[12]

Just as in Porto Alegre, so in Rio de Janeiro the Minas' prosperity reflected their success in purchasing freedom. According to Manolo Florentino, although they made up just 9 to 15 percent of the city's slave population—much larger percentages than those found by most authors—they represented 45 percent of the paid manumissions registered between 1840 and 1859.[13] Sheila Faria has found that in the first half of the nineteenth century, 52 percent of Mina men and 62 percent of women from that nation paid for their freedom. This indicates that they had privileged access to the market that enabled them to make and save up enough money to invest in their manumission.[14]

When Rufino arrived in Rio de Janeiro as an African freedman, there was a considerable population of freedpersons in the city. In 1849, it reached over 10,000 souls in the urban parishes alone.[15] The growing number of Mina freedpersons must already have been noticeable in the 1830s. It unsettled the Rio police because they knew that many freedmen and women had played an active role in the Muslim Revolt in Bahia in 1835. In Rio, the effort to break up "gatherings" of slaves was concentrated in neighborhoods where African freedpersons lived. There was talk of "African clubs," supposedly venues for subversive meetings but in most cases nothing more than the homes of freedpersons where urban slaves lived as their tenants.[16]

The problem of "public safety" became a growing concern in the increasingly dense population of the city. Between 1810 and 1821, practitioners of Capoeira and escaped slaves made up nearly one quarter of arrests in Rio de

Figures 5.4a and 5.4b Black porters and street vendor in Rio de Janeiro. From Henry Chamberlain, *Vistas e costumes da cidade e arredores do Rio de Janeiro em 1819–1820* (Rio de Janeiro: Livraria Kosmos Editora/São Paulo: Erich Eichner & Cia. Ltda., 1943) and Daniel P. Kidder and J. C. Fletcher, *Brazil and the Brazilians: Historical and Descriptive Sketches* (Philadelphia: Childs and Petterson; Boston: Phillips, Sampson & Co., 1857).

Janeiro. That situation deteriorated during the following decade, evidenced by the number of fugitive slave notices published in the *Jornal do Commercio* and *Diário do Rio de Janeiro*. Nearly 90 percent of fugitives were African, including recently arrived youths. Each of these newspapers published over one hundred notices per month. In short, running away was a daily headache for the masters, many of whom were small proprietors with between one and three slaves, including domestics and hired-out hands whose earnings provided their owners' livelihood.[17]

While escaped slaves, Capoeira groups, and hired-out slaves were roaming about in the streets, there was turbulence in the upper political strata. In late 1835, Diogo Antonio Feijó became regent after holding the post of Minister of Justice during the period of three-man regencies that followed Pedro I's abdication in 1831. One of the main feats of Feijó's administration, in a context of increasingly diverse armed conflicts in several parts of the empire, was the creation of the National Guard, which strengthened local landowners and the central government both politically and militarily.[18]

Clashes did not just take place in palaces, ministries, and parliament, but spread to the churches, taverns, bars, workshops, newspaper offices, streets, and squares. There was an "explosion of the public voice," according to historian Marco Morel. Newspapers proliferated, many of which were just political rags run by people who aspired to careers in public life. Parliamentary debates, international news, and commonplace episodes of urban life became ammunition for an intense shoot-out in the press.[19] In 1835, the newspaper *Pão D'Assucar* stood as one of the main forums for political disputes. In February, for example, it published an editorial stating that the news about the slave rebellion in Bahia was serving as a pretext for attacks on liberals.[20] Police repression in those days was allegedly used to harass the government's political adversaries, because "mere indications give rise to arrests, which can be occasioned by the testimony of two individuals: this gives rise to terrible vengeance."[21]

More than any other city in the empire, Rio de Janeiro lived under the "reign of opinion" because the press, but also the tavern, had become an informal instrument for political action against the government. Newspapers representing diverse groups and ideologies argued among themselves over projects for nation building and foresaw the consequences of political activities in Brazil and the world.[22] In 1835 and 1836, fear of slave insurrections provided an excuse for debating the Regency's directives on subjects like banning the transatlantic slave trade, replacing slaves with European settlers, and creating Brazilian colonies in Africa for freed and free Africans, the former being ex-slaves, the latter captives confiscated as contraband after the prohibition of the Brazilian slave trade in 1831. Despite this ban, the trade in slaves from Africa thrived, going on full force and blatantly. Major and minor officials at the local, provincial, and national levels, police and judicial authorities, legislators, provincial presidents, and ministers of the empire—everywhere someone was somehow complicit in the illegal slave trade. This was especially true after 1837, when the conservatives came to power. They were openly in favor of the trade, and they even tried to reactivate it with proposals to reform and even revoke the law that had banned it.[23]

According to British Foreign Office estimates, nearly 40,000 Africans were smuggled into Brazil in 1836 and 1837. Their main destination was Rio de Janeiro. In the last six weeks of 1836 alone, fourteen ships disembarked about 6,150 Africans in the vicinity of the city.[24] Given that thousands of slaves were brought to Brazil illegally, the number confiscated by the authorities proved to be insignificant—just 900 between 1834 and 1836.[25] Meanwhile, some newspapers reported clandestine arrivals, and the police claimed to be combating the human traffickers. On February 2, 1836, an African was arrested on suspicion of being a runaway, but the captain of the guard discovered that he was a recently arrived African who could only communicate with the help of a seasoned "fellow countryman" familiar with the local customs and language. The police then found that the arrested man belonged to the Benguela nation and, according to him, "had come from his land aboard a big ship with many others."[26]

If Rufino was not deported in 1839, as we suspect, but instead spent some time in Rio as a freedman, news of the intense activity of local slavers must have reached him. But why did he decide to work in the slave trade? We have seen that Africans of the Mina nation in that city were well represented among hired-out slaves and small merchants. Fifteen percent of the 464 Minas with specialized occupations who appear in inventories conducted between 1801 and 1835 worked as hired-out slaves, whereas 8.4 percent were cooks and just 2 percent sailors. Rufino may have decided that in the second half of the 1830s, the deck of a ship would be more lucrative, and safer, than dry land. Working in Rio must have been difficult for two reasons. First, there was a major exodus of slaves and freedpersons from Bahia to the imperial capital after the Revolt of the Malês, possibly saturating the job market in which Minas typically worked; and second, potential employers of African freedpersons were wary, particularly of those with Rufino's profession, due to the fear that Minas like him inspired in those days—because cooks could easily poison their white bosses' families. Difficulty finding a job may explain the advertisement that a cook published in *Diário do Rio de Janeiro* in January 1835, offering his services to "anyone who needs a foreign black man who speaks Italian, French and Portuguese."[27] He was not Rufino. In this case, it was someone who spoke three European languages and may have been European himself, because he described himself as a "foreign black" and not an "African."

In the Atlantic city of Rio de Janeiro, there was no lack of success stories of Africans who became sailors and traveled—sometimes fled—to other parts of the world, including Africa. In the 1830s, notices abounded in the newspapers of fugitive slaves who worked in the maritime industry. They boarded a ship and disappeared from their masters' sight forever. In one case, the African Manoel—"very resourceful, speaks good Portuguese, as well as English, a passable cook"—sailed to Lisbon and Pernambuco before vanishing. In another, Carlos, from the Mina-Santé nation (therefore an Ashanti) was a middleman in the poultry business, a fishmonger, and a sailor who passed himself off as a freedman and fled, probably under the protection of St. Iphigenia, of whose confraternity he was a member. Then there was "the black from the Mina nation by name of Frederico, generally known by the nickname Tapá" (therefore probably from the Nupe ethnic group, called by the Yoruba term *tapá* in Brazil), a sailor and cook who often traveled to West Africa and the province of São Pedro do Rio Grande do Sul. He, too, escaped overseas.[28]

Creole and African sailors, whether enslaved or freed, frequently sailed across the Atlantic in many directions. In 1836 and 1837, the Brazilian consulate in London claimed expenses for clothing, housing, hospitalization, health care, and passage for sailors working aboard British ships who declared themselves "Brazilian subjects." In July 1836, the expenses reported were for housing, food, clothes, shoes, and money for two freed sailors. One of them was José João, 20, who was born in Bahia and "arrived in London having come from Rio de Janeiro as a cook aboard the British ship *Ranger of Jersey*." The other was a Creole named Silvestre, 36, also from Bahia, who "arrived in London, traveling as a cook aboard the British ship *Odessa*."[29] They both worked in the legitimate maritime industry in the service of the British on the Brazil–Europe route. Rufino would find employment in the more dangerous adventure of the illegal trade in African slaves, which the British Navy was vigilantly engaged in suppressing.

Rufino must have realized that he could find protection and a good life—as well as good money—by enlisting as a worker in the slave trade. It was also an easy occupation, in many cases exempt from customs protocols for sailors. At the time Rufino said he arrived in Rio, the chief of police, Euzébio de Queiroz, complained of "abuses" by ships' captains when preparing the rosters of their vessels because "many people who want to exit without passports, particularly ships sailing for Africa, travel with a large number of sailors, chandlers and barbers."[30] Rufino was a cook, but we do not know if he traveled without a passport. He may have. And once again, he may even have sailed as a deportee.

We do not know when Rufino arrived in Rio de Janeiro from Porto Alegre, under what circumstances, or how long he stayed there. In his 1853 account, he also failed to explain why he decided to leave Rio. But his time in the capital of the empire was crucial, because there he probably decided—or was somehow forced to decide—to sail to Africa aboard a slave ship. What Rufino saw and perceived in Rio de Janeiro, whether in the streets or a prison cell, may have influenced him to take the paths that would affect the rest of his life. This necessitates a closer look at the city he found after leaving Porto Alegre, particularly what awaited an African visitor—specifically, a member of the Mina nation.

6

Rio de Janeiro, a City in Fear

Whether he arrived in early 1836 or early 1839, Rufino landed in Rio de Janeiro at a politically charged time for the Africans who lived there. For him, as a Muslim, the situation would have been even more critical. The repercussions of the Muslim revolt in Bahia reverberated in the Brazilian capital for several years. As a preventive measure, the imperial government introduced strict regulations controlling the lives and movements of the Africans there, particularly the Minas. They included the Nagôs, the African nation mainly responsible for the Bahian rebellion and Rufino's own ethnic group. Several waves of witch hunts took place in Rio in the months and years that followed the January 1835 revolt.[1]

In December 1835, close to Rufino's possible arrival in Rio, rumors circulated of a planned insurrection. According to the chief of police, "in different districts, some blacks have said that around Christmas they will rise up and wreak havoc." Farther away from the capital, in the town of Itaboraí, there were reports of "a gathering of fifty or more blacks to commit the crime of insurrection."[2] In the first days of January 1836, Rio's police chief also received reports of "two hubs of insurrection" in the parishes of São João de Meriti and Santo Antonio de Jacutinga, closer to the imperial court.[3]

In the city center, Mina Africans from São José parish became the main target of suspicion. One of them was arrested while carrying a note hidden in his cap that allegedly contained instructions about a rebellion planned for Christmas 1835.[4] As in Salvador, there were fears of uprisings in Rio involving slaves from nearby rural parishes. The justice minister advised the chief of police that, according to private letters from Maricá and Itaboraí, "some blacks affirm that there was an agreement between them and those from the City [of Rio], and that one Andrade, a *pardo* freedman, who has a grocery store on Rosário Street, is one of the agents of the plan that will be put into effect." It was reported that they had already "enlisted over three thousand blacks" to join the insurrection.[5] The situation was somewhat unusual, because the report indicated an alliance between blacks and mulattos, or *pardos*, with the latter in the leadership for that matter, which was a rare mix in such rebellions.

The Story of Rufino. João José Reis, Flávio dos Santos Gomes, and Marcus J. M. de Carvalho, Translated by H. Sabrina Gledhill, Oxford University Press (2020) © Oxford University Press.
DOI: 10.1093/oso/9780190224363.001.0001

Over the course of 1835 and 1836, "terrifying" news of "a slave insurrection" spread throughout Rio de Janeiro province, and rumors came up here and there of "symptoms of slave insurrection" according to the vexed president of the province.[6] Given the fears of a black rebellion, repression and intolerance reared their heads, set off for the outlying parishes, and spread into the countryside. The far-off town of Campos, for example, urgently requested extra ammunition in the form of "two thousand packaged cartridges" from the War Ministry for the local police force. This was due to reports that the Malês of Salvador had developed an astonishing plan for staging a rebellion in conjunction with slaves from that township in Rio de Janeiro province. The municipal judge stated that, having arrested "some blacks who were wearing a kind of ribbon, I learned that they had received orders from Bahia to rebel here too, and that ribbon was the signal for the day of the insurrection."[7] The ribbon was probably attached to their clothes, hats, or more likely caps, which were a common item of apparel among Africans. The ribbon might also have been some kind of amulet used to protect the rebels' bodies.

Previously, in March 1835, the government sent troops to Praia Grande parish, on the other side of Guanabara Bay, to suppress "some kind of attempted insurrection."[8] Complaints and preventive measures led to indiscriminate persecution. A special meeting of the City Council of Santo Antônio de Sá in the Guanabara Bay area decided that, although no signs of the planned rebellion had been found, patrols should be posted in several parts of town, just in case. The justice of the peace of Magé recommended raiding the slave quarters, whipping their occupants, and detaining freed Africans to get "the best effects for somehow instilling terror into the scoundrels" in response to the "slaves' spirit of insubordination," which was believed to have spread there after the events in Bahia.[9]

Amid the fears fueled by rumors and reports, followed by investigations and sometimes blind repression, it was hard to distinguish between facts and delusions. In May 1835, a black man from the Mina nation named Manoel José Henriques was arrested in the Candelária district and charged with "raising the tricolor flag on a pole and using insulting expressions."[10] When in doubt, the net even fell on Catholic devotees. In Piaraí, banners saying "Long Live the Holy Cross" were seized from slaves, although it was later discovered that they belonged to a festival crowning a black king, a common feature in black brotherhoods all over Brazil, especially the most popular ones, honoring Our Lady of the Rosary.[11] But in Areias, fifty blacks were arrested in a single sweep during festivities where streamers and other items were confiscated. Things got even worse in São João do Príncipe, where over one hundred slaves were arrested and charged with conspiracy. One truly amazing arrest involved three Africans who were enjoying a card game in Resende.[12] Regarding that episode, the confused justice of the peace from neighboring Areias parish declared that the charges were "presented under such and so varied circumstances that to date we have not been able to reach a sound judgment in this regard."[13] And they probably never would. The highest authorities of the province soon realized that uncontrolled panic reigned in those parts. The president of Rio warned the minister of justice that rumors of "plans" for slave insurrections were "tinged with the color of fear."[14]

But the government itself had helped stoke fear. As soon as he heard of the Bahia rebellion, the justice minister recommended that Rio's police take "indispensable" measures to ensure "the peace of mind of the capital's residents," thereby avoiding a "reproduction of the scenes in Bahia." The Provincial Assembly of Rio de Janeiro also sent a motion to the empire's chief authorities regarding the presence of black "secret societies" in the city.[15]

Africans, particularly the Minas, were the main target of surveillance and repression. In March 1835, a bulletin from Regent Feijó to Police Chief Euzébio de Queiroz ordered that, "to ease the minds of the residents of this capital," the justices of the peace should undertake "the most scrupulous examination of black Minas who may reside in their respective districts, to see if others are meeting in their dwellings in such a way as to cause suspicion."[16] The authorities' strategy was to conduct police raids at dawn on the homes of African freedpersons, particularly those known for their weird religious practices.[17] In March 1835, there were reports of "a black man" living on Valongo Street, "close to the Theater, to whom many others pay the greatest reverence, and go there to initiate themselves in religious principles."[18] Unfortunately, those principles were not described in detail. They could have been Islamic, but they could just as well have been Candomblé rituals. There was danger everywhere and to suit all tastes. In October 1836, an anonymous columnist for the *Jornal do Commercio* newspaper expressed fear of a Malê rebellion in Rio and concluded, "We always have one foot on a volcano."[19]

From then on, all African freedpersons living in the imperial capital were closely watched from several fronts. In mid-March 1835, the imperial government ordered the city's justices of the peace to "organize a complete map of the men of color in your respective districts," which should include their names, nations, addresses, living conditions, and professions. Not even black Catholic confraternities escaped this vigilance. They were watched day and night. Thenceforth, the confraternities were obliged to inform the authorities about "the dates and times of meetings and if there was evidence that they had any seditious tendencies or political ends that could be dangerous to society." A model bureaucrat, the justice of the peace of Sacramento fired off reports about two major confraternities based in his parish—Santo Elesbão and Santa Efigênia, and São Domingos. The first had been controlled by Minas in Rio since the eighteenth

Figure 6.1 African festive gatherings such as this in the 1820s became a target of police control in the 1830s. "Negro fandango scene, Campo St. Anna nr. Rio", 1820–1824. Watercolor by Augustus Earle. The National Library of Australia, Canberra.

century.[20] However, the justice of the peace eased the government's fears by writing that, having "conducted the necessary investigations of their meetings," he had found that the confraternities "only dealt with subjects regarding Divine Worship and their own welfare."[21] The authorities anxiously awaited information from the justices of the peace of the outlying parishes of Engenho Velho and Lagoa "regarding the conduct of the black Minas and freedmen."[22]

The city's revelries were also impacted by the police crackdown. Historian Martha Abreu describes the 1830s, particularly the period immediately after 1835, as a "difficult situation" for Rio's folk festivals, including those which expressed Catholic devotions such as the feast of the Holy Spirit, held annually in Campo de Santana, a large plaza that was the main meeting place for Rio's residents. Stalls could no longer be set up in advance, and they had to be taken down immediately after the three-day festival to prevent crowds from gathering. The stall owners were obliged to sign a document undertaking responsibility for any disturbances on their premises. Permits for folk dances held during religious street festivals were rescinded in 1837. But the heaviest prohibition fell on festive expressions primarily involving black people, generally to the beat of drums.[23]

Africans' movements in the city were monitored more carefully, and that included changes of address. In December 1835, for example, Inspector Sebastião José Ferreira notified the justice of the peace of the second district of Santana that "a black freedman, a caulker" had moved to "reside on this block on the

7th day of this month, in the house no. 288, bringing with him three black freedwomen and a slave woman"; and "on the 10th of this month, the Mina black man Eugênio Joaquim José Maurício and his wife left house no. 276, which they had rented."[24]

The close watch kept on the homes of slaves and freedpersons in 1835 and 1836 can also be seen in Rio's police reports.[25] The port was also subject to close vigilance. On March 9, 1836, Antonio João de Carvalho, a black man from Luanda, Angola, was detained by the authorities when he tried to land in Rio de Janeiro. They used the law of November 7, 1831 against him, since in addition to banning the slave trade, article no. 7 also prohibited freed Africans from entering Brazilian ports. Antonio João argued that he was not "a freedman but free, and since he was freeborn, the Law referred to status and not color," and that he was arriving in Brazil with a mission that was above suspicion: being ordained a priest.[26] We do not know if the government allowed the Angolan to follow his religious vocation in Brazil.

The anti-African sentiment in Rio continued until the end of the 1830s. A series of municipal ordinances and the vigilant eyes of the police restricted religious festivals, games of billiards, and dances enjoyed by the black population. The preferred target was still the Mina nation, whose numbers were growing in the city's demographics. In 1837, Chief of Police Euzébio de Queiroz came up with a solution that was already being practiced systematically in Bahia: "The right measure to take with dangerous black Minas in all parts and whose numbers here are growing due to migration from Bahia is to make them leave for their own country, not waiting for a time when they cause fear and suspicion."[27] He was implementing that policy in 1838 when he recommended the deportation of the two African freedmen sent to Rio de Janeiro from Rio Grande, one of whom may have been Rufino José Maria.

Whether willingly or forced, Africans came and went from the port of Rio under the watchful gaze of the authorities. In 1835, slave traders tried to get around the restrictions on the traffic in Africans from the north to supply the labor market in the capital and the interior, where coffee plantations were beginning to thrive. The law of April 13, 1835 required a clean criminal record for "certain slaves coming from Bahia."[28] Ships arriving from that port were often banned from disembarking Africans without the proper paperwork, and sometimes their human cargo was returned to Salvador on "suspicion that they were criminals from the African sedition." In March, Euzébio de Queiroz himself issued express orders to the port authorities: "do not allow anyone to land, even with a passport, without presenting a police record." The following month, certainly to avoid depriving the provincial economy of much-needed labor, the police chief explained that that requirement should "be understood to be limited to those who brought here for sale and who could have been involved in the insurrection of January 24 and 25, [meaning] adult African men, mainly Minas, and never extending to children, women, creoles and *pardos*."[29] The government had drawn a clear line around the area from which it expected danger—from *men* born in Africa. In May, African slaves arriving in Salvador aboard the brig *Triunfo* were barred from landing because they looked suspicious. The vessel was only authorized to unload its human cargo when proof arrived from Bahia that the African men aboard had not played any role in the "African sedition."[30] In another case, in June 1836, a black man named Antônio Nagô, had been imprisoned aboard the *Pedro 2º* for seventeen months. He had come from Bahia aboard the smack *São Domingos* without a "proper passport."[31] Antônio Nagô was probably a freedman—one of many—who was fleeing a Bahia that had become the scene of intolerance and persecution of Africans and their ways.

It was the immigration of freedmen like Antônio and not slaves sold from the northern province that most concerned Euzébio de Queiroz. In May 1835, for example, Rio's chief of police had located two African freedmen suspected of involvement in the Muslim rebellion in Bahia and had them summarily deported to Africa.[32] If Rufino arrived in Rio in early 1836, he might have seen the Portuguese brig *Funchalense* anchored there. It had come from Bahia, and its captain claimed that he was docking for repairs. The ship was considered dangerous because it carried forty-six "black freedmen of the Mina nation." Although he presented a document signed by Bahia's police chief guaranteeing that all of the black men on board had clean records, they were treated with suspicion and closely watched. They were not allowed to land, and agents of the police vigilantly observed their transfer to another ship. Those Africans were probably freedmen fleeing persecution in Bahia and returning to Africa, with a stop in Rio de Janeiro.[33] In those days, a large number of African freedmen and women made the voyage back to Africa in small or large groups. Two hundred and thirty-four embarked in the month of February alone.[34] The *Jornal do Commercio* reported on February 6, 1836: "The English ship *Parampine* is about to embark in the coming days to Onim [Lagos], on the Mina Coast, taking aboard over one hundred and fifteen black Mina freemen who not only chartered said vessel but also loaded it on their own account with a large quantity of spirits, textiles and other goods."[35] They might have been escaping, but the Minas had not lost their business acumen.

Although newspapers occasionally claimed that these repressive measures aimed to intimidate the political opposition, the climate of apprehension that had overtaken the imperial capital reverberated in their pages, thus fueling collective fear. For example, an article published in June 1835 asked that measures be taken against a "menacing prospect" of slave insurrections in Rio. Any complaint about slave unrest that arrived through letters to the editors occupied the news for days. A *Pão d'Assucar* writer asked in November 1835 that "we do not overlook any news of that nature, no matter how unlikely it may seem." Regarding an item republished from Salvador's *Correio Mercantil,* the Rio newspaper assessed: "if we give ourselves up to the hazards of the future, if we do not take immediate steps against the Africans who live among us, horrific scenes will arise in this wretched Brazil, and who knows how far it could go."[36]

The Bahian revolt had reignited the debate on definitively abolishing the slave trade, in keeping with the unenforced law of 1831. Now, the argument often brought into play was that staunch enemies of public order were being introduced to Brazil. The *Aurora Fluminense* wrote that "the imagination quails at the consequences of the imprudent and cruel African trade."[37] Along with the debate on banning the slave trade, the idea of creating a Brazilian colony in Africa—like Britain's Sierra Leone—began to gain traction to provide a destination for free Africans who had been confiscated as contraband, and freedpersons whom the government might consider undesirable. In short, the end of the importation of enslaved Africans would be supplemented by the expulsion of those who were not. It was a plan—and a very popular one under those circumstances—to de-Africanize Brazil.[38]

"Arabic writings," like those brought from Salvador to be interpreted by Mina Africans in Rio de Janeiro, those reported in the press, or found by the police-fed rumors of slave insurrections in the empire's capital. The suspicions they aroused in Rio de Janeiro were similar to those held by the authorities of Rio Grande do Sul two years earlier (as we have seen in chapter 3).

By order of the minister of justice, several "writings" found among the African Malês were sent from Salvador to be translated in Rio in early February 1835—therefore, soon after the uprising. This was based on the supposition that those involved in the rebellion would not reveal anything about their contents, often for fear of retaliation from rebels still at bay. Police Chief Euzébio de Queiroz wrote to the minister of justice regarding the results of his investigations. In addition to what might be revealed about the events that transpired in Salvador—very little—it is interesting to see what they learned about the black Muslims in Rio itself. The police chief obtained "a translation made by a black man from a language that is foreign to him into one that is even more foreign." According to Queiroz, his informant revealed that "Nagôs cannot read or write, but they customarily send some young men to be educated in a neighboring nation of men of lighter complexion who wear long beards on their chins; therefore the writings are not in the Nagô language but in that other language, which only more educated Nagôs understand."[39] We can interpret this information to mean that the Nagôs were often sent to Hausa country, north of Yoruba territory, to study Arabic and be schooled in Islam with lighter-skinned Fulani teachers. This information did not greatly exacerbate the authorities' concerns, although it revealed once again that the Malês—who were also present in Rio—were not unsophisticated in terms of intellectual preparation in the world of the written word, although less so than their Hausa and Fulani neighbors.

The subject of writing would come up again in Rio's police records on other occasions. In the latter days of 1835, for example, the justice of the peace of Santana parish ordered the investigation of a house on Rua Larga de São Joaquim, which was apparently the venue of "meetings of black Minas, called a school of reading and writing" like the ones found in Bahia in 1835 and in Porto Alegre in 1838. It was clearly a Qur'ānic school, a madrasa. The lessons were held daily, in the afternoons, and must have involved prayers in the direction of Mecca, passing through Africa. On that occasion, the Rio police reported that they had confiscated from the slaves a book with "African characters." The justice of the peace of São José parish sent the manuscript to the chief of police because he suspected that it contained "pernicious doctrines that could compromise [the safety of] families and disturb the peace, as the dire examples that have occurred in some provinces and principally Bahia attest."[40] The astute police chief sent the justice of the peace some guidelines to follow during the investigation:

> 1st that he must call in two or more people who appear knowledgeable, have them decipher those characters separately and observe if the decipherments match or differ on essential points.
>
> 2nd that he must have the Africans included in this business watched carefully and assiduously, as well as any other who may cause suspicion, to determine the houses and places they frequent both day and night, and the people they converse with and deal with, which is essentially necessary for the questioning and research that must be conducted.[41]

We do not know any more details about the investigation, but, as in other cases, they probably involved religious writings and not manifestos or plans for political rebellion.

The Muslim papers were still tormenting the authorities toward the end of the decade. In 1839, in Rio de Janeiro, "to facilitate the understanding of some manuscripts of black Minas," the police asked the Public Library to lend it a "dictionary that exists there from Arabic to Latin in 4 volumes" for the use of a Frenchman, José Poix, recruited to translate those documents.[42] This occurred shortly after information reached Rio of a conspiracy of "men of color" in Rio Grande do Sul, accompanied by two prisoners, one of whom may have been Rufino José Maria.

There were many Muslims among the Africans in Rio de Janeiro, and their numbers grew as migrating freedpersons and exported slaves arrived in Rio from Bahia after the 1835 rebellion. According to Mary Karasch, several foreign visitors observed "a significant contingent of Muslim slaves in the city" from that year forward on different occasions. As in Salvador, Porto Alegre, and Rio Grande, Africans in Rio included slaves and freedpersons who could read and write Arabic. They were frequently the targets of police investigations until at least the middle of the century, long after the period when the Malês terrified Brazil from north to south. The penchant of these devotees of Allah for devotional readings and writings generated a considerable trade in copies of the Qur'ān, which were purchased in the city's bookshops. The written word, however, was not just studied to understand the messages of Allah and his Prophet. For example, protective amulets were one of the main uses of Qur'ānic texts and other writings, in addition to Cabalistic numbers and symbols drawn on pieces of paper that were carefully folded and enclosed in small leather or cloth pouches. These and other "magic" charms worn by followers of Islam were observed by a traveler—and a qualified Muslim, an Imam—three decades later. In the mid-1860s, he criticized as unorthodox the poor knowledge of doctrine and lax customs of the Muslims in Rio de Janeiro, a large number of whom, he had learned, had come from Bahia after the 1835 uprising.[43]

In Rio de Janeiro, Rufino encountered an extremely tense situation for a Muslim Nagô. If he did not get involved in the transatlantic slave trade immediately, he must have been in contact with other Muslims, as he had probably been in Porto Alegre, possibly in Rio Grande, and before that, in Bahia. There is no doubt that he came across former companions who migrated to Rio on their own account or were sold from Bahia, and that they told him about what was going on in the city where he had first disembarked in Brazil and spent nearly a decade. He would therefore have heard first-hand reports from eyewitnesses, possibly rebels who managed to escape, about the uprising that had shaken Brazil's main Malê city to its core. And in Rio, Rufino found a city that feared that its vast African population might want to emulate the Bahian rebels—a city that was constantly seeing the specter of holy war in the slightest African religious expression. The whites' fear that an African volcano would erupt was equivalent to the Africans' fears at the disproportionate reaction to every rumor of slave rebellion. Rufino must have decided that it would not be a good idea to live there as a freedman.

PART II

Today... the black hold, deep,
Foul, close, filthy,
Stalked by the plague...
And sleep always broken
By the hauling of a corpse,
And the splash of a body in the sea...
Castro Alves, "Slave Ship" (1870)

7

Rufino Joins the Slave Trade

Rufino found a job in the transatlantic slave trade at a time when, despite being illegal, it was a thriving, growing, and promising business, even for minor players like the African freedman. Between 1831 and 1835, and 1836 and 1840, Brazil's slave imports grew by over 150 percent, from 93,700 to 240,600.[1] The decision to make a living at sea may not have been entirely unusual for someone who had seen and sailed on ships most of his life, including slave ships like the one in whose hold he had crossed the Atlantic in chains. Even a minor port like Porto Alegre, where he had lived for at least five years, was by no means idle. Monsieur Isabelle reported that he had always seen "some fifty ships, both domestic and foreign" there.[2] There would have been more transatlantic vessels in the city of Rio Grande, and that may have been where the recently freed Rufino set sail for Rio de Janeiro, the busiest port in Brazil.

Rufino entered the slave trade through the back door by signing on as a cook aboard a slave ship, although the exact date when he did so is unknown. He had practiced that occupation while enslaved. Cooks were key crewmembers on any ship at the time, although their occupation was not considered a specialized trade and was therefore viewed as inferior to those of other seafarers, such as coopers, blacksmiths, carpenters, navigators, pilots, and even common sailors. In Brazil and other parts of the Atlantic, the ship's galley was usually manned by blacks. Luiz Geraldo Silva shows indications of this in announcements regarding escaped slaves who had worked as ship's cooks. The presence of black cooks was underscored by historians W. Jeffrey Bolster regarding American ships in general, and Emma Christopher and Marcus Rediker with regard to those which specifically engaged in the British slave trade before it was banned in 1807. Bolster explains the ambiguous position of ship's cooks. They prepared meals for the captain's mess and the crew, and in the case of slavers, they also fed the captives in the hold. They were supposed to report sailors for stealing small amounts of food. If they failed to do so, the captain would punish them harshly for poor management of the ship's stores. For both black and white crewmen, the punishment was often whipping. At the same time, the cook could favor some of

The Story of Rufino. João José Reis, Flávio dos Santos Gomes, and Marcus J. M. de Carvalho, Translated by H. Sabrina Gledhill, Oxford University Press (2020) © Oxford University Press.
DOI: 10.1093/oso/9780190224363.001.0001

the crewmembers by giving them more and better food than others. Therefore, they enjoyed bargaining power among their shipmates, who generally ate little and poorly.[3]

However, maritime historian Marcus Rediker considers the position of cook aboard a slave ship to be of little importance compared to those of the other crewmembers. Although he was part of the maritime working class, Rediker argues, the cook worked separately from the rest of the crew for hours on end, handling pots, kettles, and stove in the cramped space that was his exclusive territory aboard the ship. He did not play a direct role in the collective process of organizing the voyage per se, making him somewhat isolated from the other crewmen.[4]

However, this does not seem to be so, especially in the case of a slave ship. Although a cook might not have been directly involved in the procedures that enabled the vessel to sail from one port to another, he played an essential part in the sustenance of the people who participated in it fully, as he fed them on a daily basis. For slavers, what really mattered was the survival of the people being transported in the hold. Any lapse on the cook's part could result in lost profits. If he let spoiled ingredients get into the captives' rations, it could lead to fatal dysentery. One of the main causes of death aboard slave ships was diarrhea, a condition historically linked to ingesting bad food and water. Another serious problem during long voyages was scurvy—known as "Luanda disease." According to modern science, it is caused by a lack of vitamin C, but based on experience seafarers have long known that it was due to a lack of fresh food, particularly citrus fruits, which had been used to combat it since colonial times. Scurvy "caused swelling all over the body, including the gums, loosening teeth and making it hard to ingest food."[5] Although the disease mainly resulted from the slaves' poor nutrition before embarking, conditions aboard the vessel could hasten or delay the onset of its symptoms. The cook played a decisive role in the effort to prevent this and other ailments, and therefore to avoid financial losses for their employers.

It was vital to feed the slaves enough to keep them alive, despite their being weakened by hunger and thirst and depressed by the absolute horror of their position. Food for the captives had to be cooked every day, and properly. They ate rice, yams, and ground grains, preferably corn meal, a staple that could be replaced with manioc flour, which was cheaper on the Brazilian slave routes. Sometimes—twice a week, according to one slave's statement—some dried meat added animal protein to their rations.[6] The humidity and scorching tropical heat did not help keep food fresh. If the flour or rice went off, the results could be disastrous. The cook aboard a slave ship, in short, was one of the main crewmembers responsible for keeping slaves alive within acceptable profit margins– perhaps even more so than the ship's surgeon, if one was available at all.[7] It should be added that Rufino had spent nearly eight years as the slave of an apothecary from whom he may have learned something about preparing and administering medicine. Therefore, it is possible that, in addition to cooking, he also worked as the ship's apothecary. Furthermore, as a Muslim, he could make protective amulets for his co-workers (and the ship itself) in that perilous maritime trade.

Rufino's first job was aboard a small ship, the schooner *Paula*. This type of vessel was one of the most widely used in transatlantic slave transportation at the time, second only to the speedy brigs, a large number of which were built in the United States.[8] Schooners were ships with shallow drafts and two or three masts. They generally weighed 144 tons and carried a crew of eighteen men, although larger ships could carry up to twenty-two. In theory, they could transport up to 360 slaves, but they often carried more.[9]

The conditions in which slaves were transported across the Atlantic are a tale of pure horror. Slave traders packed their ships with as many captives as possible, aware that although it would increase the mortality rate, it would also mean a greater profit. The ban on the slave trade made conditions in the hold even worse because traders no longer had to meet the standards of customs officials and other authorities regarding the permitted number of slaves and conditions for transporting human cargo. The number of days on board also increased, according to Eltis and Richardson, "because captives were held longer on the coast [of Africa] to avoid anti-slave-trade patrols and were often disembarked under hazardous conditions away from port facilities." As a result, between 1776–1830 (legal trade)[10] and 1831–1851 (illegal trade), the average voyage length to Pernambuco, for instance, increased from 26.7 to 35.4 days, and slave mortality more than doubled, from 7.1 percent to 15.5 percent in the same period.[11] Depending on the number of days it took to cross the ocean, ships could run out of food and water, and if there were too many mouths to feed, some were fed to the sharks, those "invariable outriders of all slave ships crossing the Atlantic" in the words of novelist Herman Melville.[12] A former slave trader, a physician born in the United States and naturalized Brazilian citizen, testified to members of the British Parliament in the late 1840s that slaves were "put like books upon a shelf," lying on their sides: "there is plenty of room for them to lie flat, but not enough for them to elevate." Just breathing was a harrowing exercise in mere survival. The heat, humidity, lack of air, and chronic shortage of water were exacerbated by the stench of excrement that grew stronger every day. According to the statement made two days later by a slave who underwent that experience, the captives "were so closely packed together that there was no room to get anything at all in between them." He said that "many died in consequence of the excessive heat and of the want of water," a point the man emphasized more than once: "many, from absolute suffocation, from the want of drink, died."[13]

Lack of drinking water, along with diarrhea and vomiting, led to dehydration, which was, in the end, the most lethal factor in the Middle Passage. It generally caused a swift and concomitant drop in sodium and potassium levels in the body, resulting in cramps, apathy, vomiting, and a spike in blood pressure. "This process," write Kipple and Huggins, "affects the brain cells in such a way that the victims are not aware of thirst and their need for water, and they enter a dreamlike state which ends in sudden death when potassium loss finally produces heart failure."[14]

> **Conditions Aboard a Slave Ship Captured in 1829, According to Reverend Robert Walsh**
>
> When we mounted her decks we found [the ship to be] full of slaves. She was called the Feloz [Veloz], commanded by Captain José Barbosa, bound to Bahia.... She had taken in, on the coast of Africa, 336 males and 226 females, making in all 562, and had been out seventeen days, during which she had thrown overboard 55 [dead]. The slaves were all enclosed under grated hatchways between decks. The space was so low that they sat between each other's legs and [were] stowed so close together that there was no possibility of their lying down or at all changing their position by night or day. As they belonged to and were shipped on account of different individuals, they were all branded like sheep with the owner's marks of different forms. These were impressed under their breasts or on their arms, and, as the mate informed me with perfect indifference "burnt with the red-hot iron." Over the hatchway stood a ferocious-looking fellow with a scourge of many twisted thongs in his hand, who was the slave driver of the ship, and whenever he heard the slightest noise below, he shook it over them and seemed eager to exercise it....
>
> But the circumstance which struck us most forcibly was how it was possible for such a number of human beings to exist, packed up and wedged together as tight as they could cram, in low cells three feet high, the greater part of which, except that immediately under the grated hatchways, was shut out from light or air, and this when the thermometer, exposed to the open sky, was standing in the shade, on our deck, at 89°. The space between decks was divided into two compartments 3 feet 3 inches high.... into the first were crammed the women and girls, into the second the men and boys: 226 fellow creatures were thus thrust into one space 288 feet square and 336 into another space 800 feet square.... We also found manacles and

fetters of different kinds, but it appears that they had all been taken off before we boarded.

The heat of these horrid places was so great and the odor so offensive that it was quite impossible to enter them, even had there been room.... The officers insisted that the poor suffering creatures should be admitted on deck to get air and water.... It is impossible to conceive the effect of this eruption—517 fellow creatures of all ages and sexes, some children, some adults, some old men and women, all in a state of total nudity, scrambling out together to taste the luxury of a little fresh air and water. They came swarming up like bees from the aperture of a hive till the whole deck was crowded to suffocation front stem to stern, so that it was impossible to imagine where they could all have come from or how they could have been stowed away. On looking into the places where they had been crammed, there were found some children next the sides of the ship, in the places most remote from light and air; they were lying nearly in a torpid state after the rest had turned out. The little creatures seemed indifferent as to life or death, and when they were carried on deck, many of them could not stand.

After enjoying for a short time the unusual luxury of air, some water was brought; it was then that the extent of their sufferings was exposed in a fearful manner. They all rushed like maniacs towards it. No entreaties or threats or blows could restrain them; they shrieked and struggled and fought with one another for a drop of this precious liquid...

It was not surprising that they should have endured much sickness and loss of life in their short passage.... Indeed, many of the survivors were seen lying about the decks in the last stage of emaciation and in a state of filth and misery not to be looked at....[15]

Rufino had survived this excruciating experience and would see others go through it from a more privileged position aboard the *Paula*. We have not found any record of a schooner with that name, but we have found that name twice, associated with another class of ship, a barque, in 1827, and twice for a galley in 1829. This may have been the same ship on which Rufino sailed roughly six to ten years later. His memory may have failed him with regard to the type of vessel, but it is also possible that the same ship changed the number, shape, and size of its masts and sails, and when that happened, a schooner became a galley, which then became a barque, and so on. All three times the *Paula* is mentioned, its owner is listed as Joaquim José da Rocha, a famous slave trader who sailed the route between the coast of Angola and Rio de Janeiro, the same route Rufino says he covered aboard the ship of the same name.

The first records for the *Paula* date back to the time when the slave trade was still legal on the route it plied. In 1827, under the command of Captain José Antonio de Souza Cardoso, the *Paula* carried 466 slaves from the southern Angolan port of Benguela to Rio de Janeiro. Forty of those Africans died during the crossing. In late June 1828, the *Paula* set off on another voyage that ended in mid-January 1829. Under Captain Antônio Teodoro dos Santos, it was transporting 550 slaves, of whom 524 reached Rio de Janeiro alive. On a third voyage, whose start date is unknown, but which ended in Rio de Janeiro on November 24, 1829, the same captain carried 551 slaves aboard the *Paula* and lost thirty during the voyage. After that, the *Paula* disappears from the available records.[16]

Rufino did not say where the *Paula* was bound when he shipped out on the schooner for the first time from Rio de Janeiro. All indications are that it was headed for the coast of what is now Angola—the ports of Benguela, Luanda, Molembo, Novo Redondo, Ambriz, and Cabinda, among others—the main region that exported slaves to Rio in those days, and in fact the transatlantic slave trade's most important supplier during that period, and three quarters of the total.[17] That long-standing connection is merely confirmed by the *Paula*'s previous voyages. From the sixteenth century until Brazil's definitive prohibition of the slave trade in 1850, the ports on the Angolan coast were the chief suppliers of slaves to that country. Between 1710 and 1830, the last year Brazil officially tolerated the legal slave trade, it is estimated that 1,822,949 slaves were embarked for Brazil from the ports of Luanda and Benguela alone, of whom 59 percent went Rio de Janeiro, 19 percent to Pernambuco, and 19 percent to Bahia.[18]

According to James Matson, an experienced naval officer who was involved in the suppression of the slave trade between 1830 and 1840, 1,033 of the 1,638 Africans he rescued from slave ships were children. He reported that nearly half had been sold by their own parents, and that the majority of slaves exported from Angola were not prisoners of war, as they claimed when questioned in Sierra Leone. They lied because they were ashamed of the circumstances of their enslavement. "A negro considers it a disgrace to have been born a slave, to be a debtor, or criminal, or to have been sold by his father; he will therefore always tell you that he has been taken in war."[19] Historian Joseph Miller explains that, in the first half of the nineteenth century, an increasing number of children were sold into slavery in parts of Angola, a region where militarist states had mostly become mercantile regimes that were an integral part of the Atlantic trade system. Most of the people enslaved during this period were, in fact, not

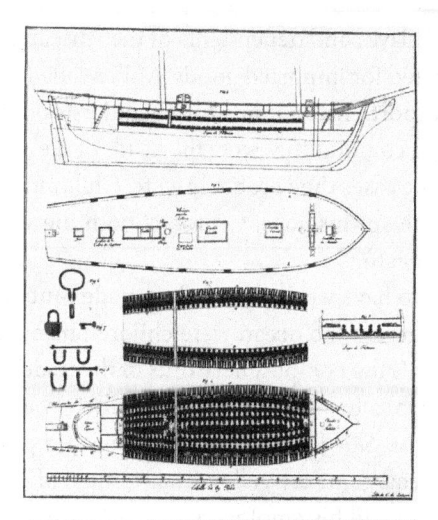

Figures 7.1a, 7.1b, and 7.1c From the end of the eighteenth century, images such as these were increasingly publicized in Europe to denounce the horrors of the slave trade. From *Affaire de la Vigilante, batiment négrier de Nantes* (Paris: Imprimerie de Capelet, 1823), Richard Drake, *Revelations of a Slave Smuggler* (New York: Robert M. De Witt, Publisher, 1860), and Johann Moritz Rugendas, *Malerische Reise in Brasilien* (Paris: Engelmann & Cie., 1835).

prisoners of war but slaves and dependents of the African elites who used them to pay debts contracted for imported goods. Miller called this trade the "release of dependents for export." Matson must have understood that the patriarchs of Angola's slaveholding communities were the heads of the families of the Africans sold overseas. In some cases they probably were. Children could be sold by their kin in times of famine, for instance, to protect both the seller and the enslaved from almost certain death.[20]

So Rufino seems to have worked on a slave trade route where at least half of the captives carried across the ocean were children below the age of 13.[21] The cook's next step reveals the complex networks of the trade in human beings that linked Brazil and Angola. Instead of returning to Rio aboard the *Paula,* he sailed to Pernambuco on the *São José,* a 78-ton, two-master patache, on which the freedman also took charge of the galley. That change of course may have been a maneuver by Rufino and his employers to avoid his return to Rio de Janeiro, from where he may have been deported to Africa by the powerful police chief Euzébio de Queiroz in 1839. In that case, ironically, a man deported on suspicion of being involved in an African uprising became a crewmember in the illegal trade in African slaves.

The *São José* belonged to a man called Brito, a name Rufino remembered in 1853 as being that of a trader whom he said lived in Africa. His full name was Joaquim Ribeiro de Brito, and he did live in Luanda in the 1840s. He owned several ships employed both in the transatlantic trade and coastal shipping in Angola, where he traded in slaves, textiles, oil, wine, and other types of merchandise. Joaquim Ribeiro de Brito was Brazilian, probably from Pernambuco, where most of his business interests lay and where his wife had lived in the 1830s. Nevertheless, at the time he was already a scion of Angolan society, holding the prestigious post of militia captain in the city of Luanda. Brito had been involved in the slave trade since at least the mid-1810s. He may have been a deported convict like so many others who became slavers and prosperous there. Besides the *São José,* he is known to have owned several ships, alone or in association with other traffickers, during different stages of his career: the brigs *Vulcano, Venus, Abismo,* and *Novo Abismo,* the corvette *Amizade,* and the schooners *Feiticeira, Josefa,* and *Maria Gertrudes,* among others. Often, to be sure, the same slave ship was given different names, and so the number of vessels Brito owned was probably lower. For instance, the *Abismo* became the *Nossa Senhora da Boa Viagem Abismo* (Our Lady of the Good Voyage Abyss), and the *Feiticeira* became the *Veloz Feiticeira* (Speedy Witch).[22]

Nine of Brito's slave-trade voyages can be identified between 1815 and 1848, during which period he shipped an estimated 2,900 slaves from Africa and delivered some 2,650 in Brazil, leaving a trail of around 250 deaths in his wake, a proportion (8.6 percent) that was within the average mortality rate for the business at the time.[23] Deaths were generally caused by overcrowding in the belly of the ship and associated with the shortage of food and water. The slavers were reluctant to change their ways because, despite the loss of life, they still profited handsomely from the sale of the slaves who survived the voyage. In 1814, for example, Brito and twenty other slave traders based in Angola signed a petition protesting a new law that reduced the permitted number of slaves on board and required that they receive better food and medical care. The slavers submitted their protest to the governor of Angola, claiming that this regulation would slash profits in half, even if it reduced the mortality rate during the Middle Passage— thus expressing the implacable reasoning of the slave trade. The governor caved in, temporarily suspending the enforcement of the law to allow the embarkation of a large number of slaves awaiting shipment in the port of Luanda. Many of those wretches probably belonged to Joaquim Ribeiro de Brito, who did business with Recife, Bahia, and Rio de Janeiro. He generally shipped slaves to all three cities during a single voyage, and purchased goods from those Brazilian ports—particularly fabric from Rio de Janeiro—for sale in Luanda, Cabinda, and the Zaire River estuary.[24]

The slaver Joaquim Ribeiro de Brito was still fully engaged in his trade when Rufino joined the crew of the *São José* in the late 1830s and early 1840s. At the time, Brito did business with other notorious slave traders from Pernambuco. When the British Navy captured one of his ships, the brig *Novo Abismo*, in 1840, one of his business partners, José Francisco de Azevedo Lisboa, better known as Azevedinho (little Azevedo), a resident of Recife, appeared before the Brazilian courts. On that occasion, there was just one slave aboard, but the previous year, the *Novo Abismo* would offload 444 in Pernambuco apparently scot-free. Azevedo actually appears as the owner of the *São José*, as well as in records of voyages undertaken in 1840 and 1841. During that same period, Henry Cowper, the British consul in Recife, the capital of Pernambuco province, identified him as the leading local slave trader and the owner of seven ships: the *São José, Rosa, Aracati, Leopoldina, Pernambucano, Francelina*, and *Temerário*. He was probably just the part owner of some of these vessels. At the time, Azevedo ran a major business enterprise focused on the slave trade that involved traders on both sides of the Atlantic.[25]

According to Rufino, the first time he set foot in Pernambuco he arrived on a ship, the *São José*, that belonged to a slave trader—possibly a company of slavers—that was highly active on the Atlantic circuit. However, Rufino did not say whether the *São José* had crossed the ocean laden with captives during that voyage. It probably had, since that type of business was Brito's main link with Brazil. We know that the *São José* made six voyages from Angola to Pernambuco between 1837 and 1841, and Rufino was aboard during at least one of them. At the end of each round trip, after secretly landing Africans on a beach, the *São José* would sail on to Recife. For one of those voyages, its manifest showed that the cargo it was bringing from Africa included a small and innocent supply of peanuts, starch, and straw mats, which were frequently used as beds for the slaves shackled in the hold. On another occasion, the ship dropped anchor under the pretext of a "forced landing," meaning that it required urgent repairs of some kind (to a torn sail, broken mast, or leaking hull). Everyone knew that ships never sailed on such costly expeditions as transatlantic voyages merely to transport peanuts, much less carrying nothing but ballast. The *São José* was a well-known slaver, and Rufino's statement merely confirms that.[26]

Rufino told the police in 1853 that, on his return from a voyage aboard the *São José*, the slaves were offloaded in Cabo de Santo Agostinho, a natural port south of Recife that the traders often used for that type of operation. We have identified another voyage of the *São José* in 1840, when Rufino must have been aboard as a member of a twelve-man crew. That year, the ship managed to evade the British blockade during a 166-day round-trip voyage, leaving Pernambuco on April 15, 1840, and returning on September 28 that same year. According to information gathered by the British, the *São José* transported slaves mainly collected near Luanda and deposited them on the beaches of Catuama and Maria Farinha, on the north coast of Pernambuco, before going on to Recife under ballast. On its return voyage, which lasted a long 42 days, Rufino cooked for twelve crewmembers and 291 captives, of whom he saw thirty-one die, representing 10.6 percent of the Africans imprisoned in the ship's hold. That may have been Rufino's last voyage aboard the *São José*.[27]

The late 1830s and early 1840s were a time of intense activity for the slave trade in the South Atlantic, despite the 1831 ban. The numbers speak for themselves: between 1837 and 1841, a conservative estimate shows that about 205,500 captives arrived in Brazil, of whom roughly 28,000 were taken to Pernambuco, over 90 percent from West-Central Africa, particularly Angola, which was precisely the route Rufino plied.[28] In July 1841, the British consul in Recife, John Goring, sent a report to his government on the slave traders' intense activities in that region, attributing it to lack of vigilance "by the superior authorities of the province," abuse of power by lesser officials, and the slavers' corruption of the justice system. As a result, many Africans were not only delivered in the outskirts of Recife but within the city itself, where the government could easily have combated human contraband if it had been so inclined. He reported that, in the first half of 1841, three ships about which he had information had embarked 2,167 slaves in Angolan ports bound for Pernambuco, of whom only 1,817 survived the overcrowding and insufficient water and provisions. In one case, on arrival just a few miles from the capital, "many perished on the beach from excessive thirst, weakness, and disease."[29]

Slave traders throughout Brazil also enjoyed the support of most of the press, which systematically attacked the operations of the British Navy cruisers sent out to pursue and capture slave ships. Regarding the prevailing Anglophobia, in his report the consul concluded that, weakened by the revolts that were springing up in several regions, "the Empire was never so little in a position to offer offense to any nation, much less to the most powerful in the world."[30] The report was addressed to Lord Aberdeen, then British Secretary of State for Foreign Affairs, who was responsible for introducing a stricter policy on the repression of the slave trade in the 1840s. Received from several Brazilian ports, as well as Lisbon and Havana, reports of this kind convinced him that diplomatic methods of persuasion would not suffice.

If, as Consul Cowper stated, Brazil was not in an ideal position to offend the most powerful nation in the West at that time, Brazilian slave traders defied it systematically and audaciously. In addition to relying on the collusion of Brazilian authorities and support from part of the press, they contrived a thousand ways to disguise the purpose of their voyages to Africa. Their ships usually carried false papers, fictitious statements of their routes and cargoes, and on their return, they dumped their human merchandise on deserted beaches. The slave traders' creativity knew no bounds. In 1830, the captain of the schooner *Destemida* swore that the fifty Africans found aboard his ship and rescued by the British on the Bahian coast had come from Ouidah to "learn trades" in Brazil, after which they would be returned to Africa. The slavers also used false flags and documents from countries that had not yet signed or ratified treaties with Britain banning the transatlantic slave trade. This was the case with Portugal until 1842 and Spain until 1845. Of course, Portugal had banned the trade in 1836, with punishments ranging from two to five years' hard labor, but the Portuguese authorities in Africa turned a blind eye to the contraband in human souls. There was perfect symmetry between the schemes of official connivance in the ports of departure and those where the captives arrived. As a result, the market still had a steady source of supply, and Pernambuco was one of the main destinations in Brazil.[31]

A Pernambuco newspaper in 1837 published a sarcastic report on something that was not even news:

> One day, not long ago, I was lying belly up in my hammock meditating... and saw a large number of armed folks pass by (because my house is on roadside in the area where I live), numbering over forty men, and in their midst some 200 African settlers, because that is how their drivers dubbed them; another told me that they had landed bound for the vicinity of the Bôto sugar plantation and that they had come on account, or belonged to a man who was so mild and peaceful that he was like a lamb[32]; and they further said that another Vessel had dumped

[more Africans] on another beach; but that many people were reluctant to purchase settlers from that Vessel because around sixty had already died, perhaps because they were stacked up too high: then I asked, so are you selling these settlers? They said yes, and they are so expensive that even sick with the scourge, no one could buy one for less than 300,000 [or] 400,000 réis.[33]

This report reveals the veritable military operations, high profits, and web of lies woven to make the slave trade thrive, and at the same time, exposes the human suffering it involved. This could well be the story of one of the landings of the *São José* when Rufino was the ship's cook. Between 1831 and 1850, many other vessels would offload captives—cynically called "settlers" (*colonos*) by the slavers—on that and other beaches in Pernambuco where planters, farmers, and merchants took delivery and sold them on the spot.

On the African side of the Atlantic, the main market that supplied slaves to Brazil at the time, and from where the abovementioned slaves probably came, was the Angola region, whose nerve center was Luanda.

8

Luanda, Slave-Trading Capital of Angola

São Paulo de Luanda, a Portuguese colony founded in 1575, may have been the most active port in the transatlantic slave trade when Rufino first boarded a slaver as a crewmember. Ceding to pressure from Britain, Portugal had banned the trade in 1836, but, like in Brazil, the law was not enforced there, and it did not contain a clause permitting the Royal Navy to seize or search suspicious Portuguese ships. Brazil's 1831 law was more effective, but not for long. Unlike the period when the slave trade was conducted legally, when the supply of slaves from Angola was concentrated in the hands of potentates in the hinterland–particularly the kingdoms of Kasanje and Matamba—the sources of supply were decentralized, "making access to slaves easier than in the past, so it was particularly difficult to put an end to the coastal trade," according to Roquinaldo Ferreira. In the mid-1830s, the slave trade rallied full force. As a result, roughly 77,000 captives were shipped from the vicinity of Luanda between 1837 and 1840, some of them aboard ships where they were fed by Rufino during the Atlantic crossing.[1]

The cook must have visited Luanda several times. Portuguese territory and the seat of the governor of Angola, the city had some 5,000 inhabitants at the time, about half of whom were enslaved. The German physician Georg Tams, who was there in early November 1841, left a rich description of the Portuguese colony. He had already visited some other ports along the Angolan coast, including Novo Redondo and Benguela, both of which—particularly the latter—were also actively involved in the slave trade.[2]

When he sighted Luanda from his ship, coming from the modest port of São Felipe de Benguela further south, Tams was heartened because he was arriving in a city that seemed more like those he knew in Europe. Viewed from the sea, he wrote that it had "a wonderful aspect," with numerous brick houses built "in the European style," painted in myriad colors topped with red roofs. This "European" city was the capital of the slave trade in the region.

The Story of Rufino. João José Reis, Flávio dos Santos Gomes, and Marcus J. M. de Carvalho, Translated by H. Sabrina Gledhill, Oxford University Press (2020) © Oxford University Press.
DOI: 10.1093/oso/9780190224363.001.0001

When he landed, Tams was amazed to see that there were just two paved streets, those which linked the upper and lower parts of the city, but he did not mind the other roads, paved with tamped sand, since they were more or less level. The German physician did not complain when his boots sank into them, unlike the American John C. Lawrence, a captain in the US Navy, who hated it when that happened four years after Tams's visit while he was there on a mission to suppress the slave trade. But both travelers praised buildings like the customs house and the chamber of commerce, describing them as well built and imposing, worthy symbols of the vigorous mercantile personality of a city whose economic dynamics were irrevocably linked to the transatlantic slave trade for the benefit of few.

Inside the European homes he visited, George Tams found the comforts and amenities of the civilized world. They were tastefully furnished and served English cheese, beer, and wine. Whites gathered there for lunches and dinners, following European table manners while closing deals on slaves in a most civilized fashion. Outside those homes, the city did not offer many attractions for European visitors. There were religious festivals, each in its own season, while daily entertainment revolved around a tavern, a pool hall, and a gin shop—at least these were what Tams had a chance to see—which were frequented by free residents, slaves, soldiers, and foreign sailors. A small theater also opened its doors from time to time.

Figure 8.1 At the end of the nineteenth century Luanda's commercial district still exhibited the wealth produced by the slave trade. Source: Postcard, unknown author. Private collection, courtesy of Roquinaldo Ferreira.

For the elite, the governor organized a ball every Sunday, with music provided by a military band whose talents left much to be desired and generally began the dance with a fandango. The great and the good who gathered there were, according to Tams, "a motley crowd of blacks, whites and mulattoes, all equally puffed up with pride at the honor they believed they were enjoying" by frequenting the official home of the Portuguese administrator—a local resident, Joaquim José de Carvalho e Menezes, described it as a "magnificent palace" with 21 windows. About the governor's guests, Tams concluded: "I doubt that there was a single one of them who was not a slave trader." They included the governor himself, who had replaced another who was brought down two years earlier because he attempted to enforce the ban on the Angolan slave trade. A large number of military men were also engaged in the trade. Carvalho e Menezes confirms and expands on Tams's impression, stating that in Luanda at that time, "the inhabitants in general seemed condemned always to live within the traffic." Most whites in the city were agents of slave-trading companies usually based in Rio de Janeiro and Lisbon, as well as Recife. The slave trade financed the good life of the guests at the ball. Outside the governor's palace, litters—called *tipoias* or *machilas* in those parts—and their bearers waited for their masters to tire of being entertained and to carry them back to their residences. Their passengers were often drunk.[3]

Every year, the same honorable governor took the same members of high society and European visitors on a crocodile-hunting expedition on the Bengo, the river that supplied Luanda with fresh water. Instead of crocodiles, Tams and other European adventurers faced dense swarms of mosquitoes in 1841. The winged pests not only robbed them of sleep but also infected most of the foreigners who went on the expedition that year with fatal diseases, probably malaria, yellow fever, or both.[4]

Luanda was a slave-trading city whose European inhabitants—many of them criminals deported there from Portugal—and some people of mixed race and local blacks not only engaged in the slave trade as their main source of livelihood but owned slaves that they employed in a variety of ways, as street vendors, artisans, farm workers, or household servants. Some owned as many as twenty slaves, particularly to flaunt their wealth, a deeply rooted local custom. According to historian Jill Dias "slave ownership was prized more for aggrandizement and protection" than for productive labor.[5] Even so, in 1840 there were reportedly one thousand enslaved artisans in the city. Captain Lawrence observed that the whites were "entirely dependent upon slaves for everything," even getting around, since they were carried uphill and down in sedan chairs, litters, and hammocks shaded with umbrellas.[6] Black servants always accompanied European merchants whenever they went out. Indoors, George Tams witnessed typically Brazilian scenes of household slavery like those depicted by French painter Jean-Baptiste Debret in Rio de Janeiro. At the home of a physician where he stayed as a guest, he noted that every day the lady of the house "reclined on a Brazilian rocking chair, [with] three or four black slave girls seated on the floor beside her, occupied with sewing." Whenever they missed a stitch, that lady, a beautiful and elegant Spanish woman, brutally punished the girls with a ferule, making the palms of those small hands swell and sometimes bleed. Then she forced them to get back to work. The physician thought that when they became masters, African freedmen showed less cruelty than the Europeans. In any case, bad experiences of slavery resulted in a typical repertoire of slave resistance wherever it is found: flight and occasionally—just as on the other side of the Atlantic—the formation of maroon communities.[7]

As in the Brazilian slave-owning cities, enslaved and free Africans predominated at open-air markets, where they sold imported and locally produced goods such as mats, baskets, pots, scissors, knives, weapons, fabric, ivory items, jewelry, pipes, fruit, vegetables, yams, bananas, and cooked food—including a tomato soup that was very popular among the locals. The German physician enjoyed it, too. The women who worked as hired-out slaves were decked out in gold chains and rings. It was said that they made a veritable fortune as merchants, although that might be an exaggeration.[8]

As he had already observed in Benguela, Tams mentioned the arrival in Luanda of several caravans bringing slaves from the interior, most of them

Figure 8.2 A caravan of captives from the backlands of Angola for sale on the coast. From David and Charles Livingstone, *Narrative of an Expedition to the Zambesi and its Tributaries; and of the Discovery of the Lakes Shirwa and Nyassa, 1858–1864* (London: John Murray, 1865).

carrying other kinds of merchandise, including ivory, gum copal, and orchella weeds, a lichen that was gaining importance as the source of a violet dye in the textile industry. Regarding other slaves, perhaps more rebellious ones, he wrote that "sometimes they arrived with their hands tied behind their backs or ropes around their necks, accompanying the convoy." The *libambo*– an iron chain that bound captives to each other by the neck—was also used. However, few slaves were taken to Luanda itself for sale to transatlantic slavers, because of Portugal's ban on such activities. Although the local authorities cooperated with the slave trade, they had to keep up appearances. Most of the captives were kept on rural estates which, according to Tams, had once been the summer homes of the mercantile elite. From there they were sent to Brazil. That is why there were few ships in port when the traveler visited that area. As he observed, "they were always dispatched as swiftly as possible by their owners residing in Luanda." According to the routine of the slave trade, ships arrived in Luanda, unloaded cargo brought from overseas, and immediately set out to put slaves on board on deserted beaches, just as they offloaded them in Brazil. Tams gave the example of a slave trader who had been active for many years, Arsénio Pompílio Pompeu de Carpo. This son of the Island of Madeira, somewhat cultured and even a poet, was exiled to Angola for a political crime committed in Portugal. Like many of his ilk in Luanda, he became a powerful slave trader, riding through the night for long distances to oversee the shipment of his slaves. "Considerable and repeated losses," wrote Tams, "had induced him to adopt the plan of embarking them in the dark of night, some way from Luanda."[9]

Officially, 22 ships left the port of Luanda in 1841, bound for the following destinations: fourteen to Rio de Janeiro, four to Lisbon, three to Pernambuco, and one to Bahia. But the previous year, twelve sailed for Pernambuco, ten for Rio de Janeiro, and thirteen for Lisbon. However, those numbers do not tally with the number of ships that actually left port. In 1842, for example, eleven ships from Lisbon anchored in Luanda, along with 22 from Rio de Janeiro, seven from Pernambuco, and six from Bahia. The erratic official statistics did not reflect the intense activity of slave traders in Angola during that period, because the slavers often sailed directly to other parts of the coast without even stopping in Luanda. Even so, the data at least confirms that Pernambuco and Rio de Janeiro were the chief destinations for Angola's trade with Brazil.[10]

Luanda was a cosmopolitan city, not only because of the presence of European residents and visitors but because Africans from many different lands and cultures along the coast and the interior of the continent also gathered there. Regarding the Africans who visited or lived there, Tams wrote: "This vast influx of people from different countries—and their myriad colors—the variety and abundance of their goods—their strange dialects and singular customs, presented an ever-changing spectacle and made the streets of Luanda very lively, especially on occasions when their merchandise was hotly disputed and those fortunate vendors, staying there for a few days, all spent most of their profits on spirits."[11] This is where a good part of the *cachaça* (sugar-cane brandy) brought in by the slave trade ended up, never reaching the interior from which most of the captives were obtained.

While he observed the behavior of Europeans and mestizos—their religion, gatherings, and social etiquette—Tams also had access, albeit limited, to aspects of the cultures of Africans living in Luanda. He devoted some pages to the "superstitions" of a group of skillful Cabinda rowers hired to transport goods from shore to ship. He was particularly impressed by the divination rites

Figure 8.3 A mid-nineteenth-century manipanso. Nkisi statue, wood carving, cloth, glass, vegetable fibers, etc. Fritz Klingelhöfer Collection (1875). Berlin Ethnological Museum.

performed with their personal idol-charms (*manipansos*), which he described as crudely carved dolls dressed in scraps of old cloth. He also commented on the political and social etiquette of other Africans, their songs, dances, and musical instruments, even describing the local version of the *berimbau* (the musical bow used in *capoeira*) and how it was played.[12]

Joaquim José de Carvalho e Menezes described marriage rites, or *lambamento*, that were common in Luanda, even among mixed-race individuals. Some of the most important aspects of the ceremony were the purchase of wives, the confinement of the bride for several days to purify her with the help of a "sorcerer," and her emergence, finely dressed, for the three-day festivities. Funerals, or *mutambi*, also followed a complex ritual protocol involving songs, dances, offerings, and the sacrifice of a pig. The funeral rites lasted eight days. A dish, a calabash, and a pipe belonging to the dead person were broken and thrown into the sea along with the pig's head so that "the *zumbi* (soul) would find eternal rest." Permanent contact between Luanda and the Angolan backlands was partly responsible for refreshing the city's African cultural expressions. In fact, Kimbundu was the most widely spoken African language in the Portuguese colony, as it was widely used even in the homes of "noble white families," as one governor complained as early as 1675.[13]

According to Tams, blacks in Luanda were all Catholics, but they practiced a form of Catholicism that the physician considered the result of a superficial conversion. The visitor was no different from other observers on both sides of the Atlantic who doubted the sincerity of the Africans' adoption of Christianity. The mindsets of those European prevented them from seeing the possibility of an Africanized but sincere and non-exclusive version of that religion, which could very well be embraced together with local creeds.

This was the Europeanized, cosmopolitan, mercantile Portuguese-African slavocracy that Rufino encountered more than once as a ship's cook. His travels in the pay of slave traders from Pernambuco confirm what Jill Dias writes about the close links those slavers maintained with most of the Afro-Portuguese families of Luanda—the "children of the country," not necessarily blacks—who were involved in that trade.[14]

9

Readying the *Ermelinda*

Rufino sailed to Angola on more than one voyage devoted to gathering "black diamonds," as slave traders used to call their precious human merchandise.[1] This time, the freedman cooked aboard the *Ermelinda*. A much larger vessel than the *Paula*, a schooner, and the *São José*, a patache, the Ermelinda was a two-masted barque that weighed 244 tons, was 53.12 feet long and 20 feet wide. It was designed as a cargo ship and built in the province of Alagoas in the shipyards of the port of Pedras. That site had been known since colonial times for its excellent timber and was used extensively by the Portuguese and Brazilian navies during the colonial era and after Brazil's independence. Rufino seems to have risen in the ranks of the slave trade, since his responsibilities had increased considerably: it was one thing to cook for about 300 slaves, as he had done on the *Paula* and the *São José*, and quite another to feed 400 or more, which was the maximum number of slaves the *Ermelinda* could carry.[2]

The helm of the *Ermelinda* was engraved with the name "Felinto Elizio," probably one of the ship's previous monikers, possibly in honor of the Portuguese poet, Father Francisco Manoel do Nascimento (1734–1819), who used that pseudonym. The tribute is explained by the priest's biography, as he was the son of a sailor, and his studies had been paid for by another, prosperous crewman. He hobnobbed with businessmen, probably involved in overseas interests, including the slave trade, while mingling with men of letters. "Felinto Elizio" belonged to a group of poets called Ribeira das Naus, which is what the Portuguese called their shipyards at home and abroad during the Renaissance and the age of overseas expansion.[3]

The *Ermelinda*'s name changed more than once, which was very common for slave ships, whether because they frequently changed owners, or to fool the domestic and foreign authorities who were combating the illegal slave trade. When ships were auctioned after being captured, it was not unusual for them to be purchased by slavers who then renamed them. Before it became the *Ermelinda*, Rufino's ship had been called *União*. A passport for the *União*, dated October 9,

The Story of Rufino. João José Reis, Flávio dos Santos Gomes, and Marcus J. M. de Carvalho, Translated by H. Sabrina Gledhill, Oxford University Press (2020) © Oxford University Press.
DOI: 10.1093/oso/9780190224363.001.0001

1838, shows that its owner was Elias Baptista da Silva, a major slave trader also involved in Pernambuco's illegal traffic.

According to British sources, when it was still the *União* the *Ermelinda* belonged to Angelo Francisco Carneiro. He handed it over to his nephew, Antonio Carneiro Lisboa Junior. He, in turn, sold it for 6,000,000 réis[4] in cash to his younger brother, Francisco Lisboa, who may have been starting out as an independent ship owner in the slave trade. In other words, official ownership of the vessel was passing within the same family of slavers, from uncle to nephew, and brother to brother. The *Ermelinda*'s current official owner was just nineteen years old. Despite his surname, Lisboa, and also according to the British, he was not related to the slave merchant José Francisco de Azevedo Lisboa ("Azevedinho"), the business partner of Joaquim Ribeiro de Brito, the owner of the *São José*, aboard which Rufino cooked on several voyages.[5] However, on the new ship, the cook was still on the payroll of the same group of slave traders, a partnership with several branches that included Azevedo Lisboa.

It is most likely that young Francisco Lisboa was just a figurehead for the slave-trading family enterprise and had lent his name for the purchase of the ship, since the other family members, long established in the business, would have caught the attention of the British authorities. It was also important to keep up appearances with Brazilian officials, at least the few not completely corrupted by the slave trade establishment. Francisco Lisboa was the youngest son of a family that was heavily involved in the slave trade.[6] He must have worked for his uncle, Angelo Carneiro, or his own father, Antonio Carneiro Lisboa. In the records of ships arriving in and leaving the port of Recife, Francisco's father is listed as the captain of the *Cacique*, which docked there in June 1836, arriving from Santos in the southeastern province of São Paulo. The following month it sailed for Le Havre with a cargo of cotton, and probably unloaded it in the French port to take on a cargo of cloth that would be exchanged for slaves in Luanda. This may have actually been an atypical triangular transatlantic slave trade voyage.[7]

We do not know much about the career of Antonio Lisboa senior, or the routes sailed by the *Cacique*, but the owner of that ship was none other than Elias Baptista da Silva, who also owned the *Ermelinda* when it was still the *União*. A well-known slave trader, Elias da Silva had transported people from Africa aboard the *União* before he transferred its ownership to Antonio Carneiro Lisboa Junior. According to the British, on one of its voyages across the ocean the *União* arrived in Recife on September 18, 1836, after offloading on Catuama beach the 480 survivors of the 520 Africans it had been carrying. Both when it left Recife in March and when it returned in September, the owner and consignee of its cargo was Elias Baptista da Silva. Portuguese consul Joaquim Baptista Moreira — no relation to da Silva — observed its arrival with a certain satisfaction, because it meant that Brazilian slavers were active in Pernambuco, consequently suggesting that their Portuguese counterparts were no longer involved in human contraband there.[8] Because the consul was a friend of Angelo, who loaned money to the consulate, and of Azevedo Lisboa, whom the consul had helped release from jail in 1832 when the slave trader was accused of taking part in the Abrilada—a Portuguese-led revolt that aimed at restoring D. Pedro I to the throne of Brazil—he may just have been seeking to cover for his friends with the authorities in Lisbon, as both of them were Portuguese nationals.[9] In any event, the consul was well aware of Azevedo's illegal activities, since he even took the slave trader to personally inspect a Portuguese vessel so that Azevedo Lisboa, a specialist in the subject, could attest to whether it was, in fact, a slave ship.[10]

Therefore, young Francisco was probably not just involved in the slave trade but belonged to a family that, together with their counterparts, would form a veritable organized crime syndicate after 1831, with tentacles spreading to both sides of the Atlantic. Both his father and his uncle were familiar with the Middle Passage. It was not uncommon for captains in the merchant marine to take their children aboard. It is very likely that the official owner of the *Ermelinda* had traveled on slave ships under the watchful eye of a relative or even ship captains employed by his uncle, father, or older brother. Without a doubt, that was the best kind of training for a future investor in the transatlantic slave trade.

In addition to changing its name and owner, the *Ermelinda* also changed its appearance, because the brig became a barque, probably with different rigging. The *Ermelinda*'s "Registration Certificate" shows that it was "square-rigged," meaning that yards and sails were set across the masts, from port and starboard, horizontally, and the ship had two masts, characteristic of a brigue. According to nautical experts, the main feature that distinguished one type of ship from another was the number of masts. A brigue has two, a barque, three. However, because it had just two masts, the *Ermelinda* was in fact a hybrid vessel—a "*brigue-barca*" (brig/barque), which was, in fact, precisely how it would be registered in the purchase and sale agreement that the two brothers signed on April 24, 1841.[11]

The brig *União* was already involved in the slave trade when it belonged to the brother of the young man who now owned, on paper at least, the *Ermelinda*. In October 1840, the *União* set sail from Pernambuco, bound for Luanda with a cargo of 217 barrels of *cachaça*, a typical product used to barter for slaves in that port. Then it loaded 683 Africans into its hold and returned to Brazil in March 1841—a forty-three-day voyage. The ship was overloaded and short of water: if slaves made up 100 percent of the *Ermelinda*'s tonnage, each individual would have been allotted just one square meter (275 inches) of space. However, they actually had much less room, subtracting the areas for the captain's cabin, the galley, the sailors' sleeping quarters, and the storage area for provisions and

Figures 9.1a and 9.1b Barque *Izabel* and brig *Tejo*, nineteenth-century Portuguese vessels with shapes and rigging similar those of the *Ermelinda*. From Telmo Gomes, *Navios portugueses século XIV a XIX. A memória do passado, uma referência para o futuro* (Lisbon: INAPA, 1995).

goods that were usually kept in the hold along with the Africans during the return leg. In other words, this is much less than one square meter per slave, which naturally contributed to the high mortality rate for that voyage. One hundred and eighty-three Africans died in the Middle Passage, 26.8 percent of the human cargo, and the 500 survivors were offloaded on Catuama beach, "many of them it is said in a weak and sickly condition from their previous severe privations," according to the conclusions of one British report. Soon after that horrific voyage, the brig *União* became the barque *Ermelinda*, but "in other respects she remained exactly as before," probably in addition to the new rigging.[12]

Between the date of its purchase and its departure a few weeks later, there was a great deal of activity aboard the *Ermelinda*. Boats and canoes plied to and fro, carrying cargo, equipment, and ship repair supplies, as well as sailors and artisans who were employed in a variety of tasks aboard the vessel before it weighed anchor. Repairing and equipping the barque required large quantities of sturdy cloth, canvas, cloths, sheets, cables, lines, pitch, tar (used as a disinfectant), paint, wood, copper and brass sheets, hinges, nails, rudder spokes, chains, tassels for the flagpole, wheels and hoists for the catheads, glass for the binnacle, a brass lamp with a reflector, a new dinghy, and other equipment. Elias Francisco dos Santos carried out "several tasks" as a pulley-maker; José Faustino Porto and his six-man team hoisted new sails—a spinnaker, mizzen, gaff-top, and jib—and repaired two topsails and three topgallant sails, among other tasks; the Mesquita & Dutra company took care of tinkering, working with copper and brass; Francisco das Chagas caulked the entire ship, Jacinto Elesbão did carpentry work, blacksmith Caetano José Coelho repaired or replaced the fixtures and fittings, and cooper Leandro José Ribeiro was hired to mend water barrels, casks, and do other jobs related to his trade.[13]

Some repairs made to the hull required turning it over at one point, and cables and other equipment had to be rented for that purpose. Two temporary cabins were installed on deck, probably for passengers on the outward voyage. Rufino the cook and other crewmembers must have been at their posts, because, besides other tasks, food was already being served on board. On land, agents hurried back and forth to obtain the papers required for the voyage, such as the cargo manifest, crew roster, ship's registration certificate, the Brazilian passport, health certificate, and a visa from the Portuguese consul to dock in Angola. Preparations for the voyage alone cost 10,162,863 réis, including a variety of materials, new equipment, manpower, and paperwork. That same amount could have purchased about twenty-five male slaves in the Pernambuco market in the first half of the 1840s. The bribes that were probably paid to government officials of course do not appear in the slaving operation's accounts.[14]

Another vital part of the preparations involved stocking the ship with food and water for the voyage. A small zoo would travel on board, including two horses, two cows, five goats, three pigs, three piglets, one hundred chickens, and twenty-four ducks, most of which were probably for the consumption of the crew and passengers. Except for the horses and perhaps the cows, the other animals ended up in Rufino's pots and pans. Wine, beer, champagne, coffee, tea, vinegar, olive oil, preserves, codfish, beans, corn, potatoes, onions, oranges, cheese, sugar, sausage, eggs, and other items were also put on board. It is hard to say exactly who ate what, but there was definitely a pecking order when it came to food that distinguished passengers from crew, and, among the latter, the higher-ranking members such as the captain (or master), the clerk, and the first mate. The captain's statement was clear about the division of the cook's tasks: "cooking for the cabin and crew," which suggests unequal rations for unequal mouths aboard the ship.[15] Very few chickens, if any, ended up on a healthy sailor's plate. Only the sick among them might be served some chicken soup. Champagne and tea were probably intended for the table in the captain's cabin and for a few of the passengers. Some of those amenities were probably destined for sale in Luanda or may have been ordered by specific individuals living there for their own consumption.

Thus, the *Ermelinda*'s larder and wine cellar contained a long list of more or less sophisticated items. Rufino certainly must have tasted a little of everything he cooked and served, or nearly everything. Some of the items in the larder and shipboard corral would have been ritually repugnant to the Muslim cook, such as the three crates of lard, pigs, and piglets. Several surahs of the Qur'ān regulate the food consumed by the faithful, particularly the types of meat that are banned because they are considered ritually impure. Muslims cannot eat animals that have "died on their own" (due to disease or an accident), or by strangulation, beating, or being killed by predators; they are also forbidden to consume "that on which hath been invoked the name of other than Allah" (the names of pagan gods, for example); and, particularly, they must not eat "the flesh of swine, because that is certainly impure."[16]

The *Ermelinda* inherited part of its crew from the *União*. The day after Francisco Lisboa purchased it in late April 1841, "rations" were paid to the crew. That list included not only the captain and first mate but also eight sailors and cabin boys. The captain received per diems for food valued at 800 réis; the first mate, 480 réis; and the sailors, only 120 réis each. More sailors were recruited in mid-May, reaching a total of fifteen by June 21. By that date, the crew that would sail aboard the *Ermelinda* had been almost entirely assembled.[17]

Sixteen other crewmembers traveled aboard the ship along with Rufino, including Captain Joaquim Antonio de Carvalho Coutinho, 39, a native of Rio de Janeiro. In addition to being the highest authority on the ship, the captain was responsible for safely delivering the cargo to its recipients, as well as finding, choosing, and acquiring captives, unless that had already been taken care of by the factors at the ship's destination. Coutinho was, in mercantile lingo, the ship's supercargo. The second most important person on board was the pilot and first mate, José Antonio Resende, 42, a Portuguese bachelor from Lisbon, who was responsible for steering the ship, taking over command from the captain when necessary, and supervising the equipment, the cleaning of the ship, and the discipline of its sailors. In addition to those two officers, the crew included three harbor pilots, each of whom probably specialized in entering and casting anchor in different ports and beaches of Brazil and particularly Africa; and a clerk responsible for drafting documents like the ship's log and reports of accidents, illnesses, deaths, and the loss or damage of merchandise, including slaves. Finally, there was the lower class of the crew, made up of four sailors, five cabin boys (apprentices), and a cook. There was no surgeon on board, but Rufino may have been partly in charge of that role. And there is also a noticeable absence of artisans such as a carpenter or cooper, who were essential for the ship's maintenance, but there must have been some crewmen, or even officers, with those skills aboard.[18]

The crewmembers not only took care of their own seafaring tasks but would also have to be the captives' overseers on the return voyage, because they were responsible for keeping those imprisoned on board under control. A slaver was a place of confinement—a prison-ship, as the English called it—ridden with anguish, tension, depression, disease, and death. But it was also a place of resistance, which wove a fine line between hope and despair and took on various forms: hunger strikes, suicide, rebellion. Over the hundreds of years in which the transatlantic slave trade went on, uprisings were responsible for the deaths of about 100,000 captives, counting both those staged at the points of embarkation and those aboard ships. The effort to control the human cargo increased the costs of voyages by an average of 18 percent, mainly due to the need to hire twice the usual workforce required by a conventional merchant ship. It was up to the crew, under the orders of tough captains, to watch the captives in shifts, especially to prevent them from rebelling during the night or when, during the day, a few times a week, they were brought up on deck to eat and, above all, dance—which they did under the threat of the lash—to keep their bodies minimally healthy while enduring the noisome squalor of confinement in the hold. Sailors were also responsible for punishing unruly captives with whippings and even crueler methods, torturing them to death or throwing them alive to the sharks to set an example for the rest.[19]

It was very likely as instruments of control that the *Ermelinda* had two nine-pound cannons aboard (capable of firing 4.5-kilo/9.9-pound projectiles), which were typically found on merchant ships in general, as well as about three kilos of gunpowder, half a dozen muskets, and another half-dozen cutlasses. According to the captain of the *Ermelinda*, those weapons were only to be used to fight off pirate attacks and quell mutinies. That was not true. The British authorities received a more honest statement in 1838 from a passenger aboard the *Veloz*—which also belonged to Rufino's employers—regarding the two cannons, gunpowder, and other weapons found on board, which he said were to be used, if necessary, to keep the slaves in submission. Ten years earlier, a captain whose schooner, the *Dona Bárbara*, was captured in 1828 in waters where the slave trade was illegal, stated that he carried few arms aboard, just enough "to defend the ship from a slave rebellion," revealing a common fear among those involved in that business. But they did not just combat shipboard uprisings with conventional weaponry. That was the case aboard the schooner *Dois Irmãos*, a 200-ton vessel belonging to Antonio da Silva & Co., one of Azevedinho's many partners. The ship had loaded 359 slaves in Mozambique, some stowed in the hold and others on deck. On the last day of 1829, the captives in the hold rebelled, and the captain ordered the crew to pour boiling water on them, forcing the slaves on deck to help—"a most horrible circumstance," wrote the shocked British consul in Recife, John Parkinson, who reported the incident to London. We do not know exactly how many captives died in combat, but they must have been among the seventy-eight of those who left Africa and did not reach their destination in Pernambuco—a considerably high mortality rate of twenty-two percent.[20]

The crew of the *Ermelinda* included individuals from varied backgrounds: eight Brazilians, six Portuguese, a Spaniard, and two Africans of the Mina nation. The Brazilians were from Rio de Janeiro, and the provinces of São Paulo (city of Santos), Alagoas (city of Maceió), Pernambuco, Santa Catarina, and Rio Grande do Sul—in other words, from the north to south of Brazil. The Portuguese came from Lisbon, Oporto, Aveiro, and Faial, in the Cape Verde islands. The Spanish sailor, Lourenço Francisco, 30, was actually born in Manila in the Philippines, so, besides Spain he represented Asia onboard. Unfortunately, there is no mention

Figure 9.2 African captives forced to exercise on the upper deck of a slave ship. From Amédée Gréhan, *La France Maritime* (Paris: Postel, 1837).

of the crewmembers' skin color, but most of the Brazilian sailors and cabin boys were probably black or mixed race. There were just two Africans in the crew, both freedmen and both registered as being from the Mina nation—the cook, Rufino José Maria, and the cabin boy, Duarte Martins da Costa, 38. Years later, in his will, da Costa identified himself as a *Saburú*, a variation of Savalu, an African state in northern Dahomey in today's Republic of Benin.[21] In other words, he was of the Mina-Savalu nation, just as Rufino was a Mina-Nagô. Therefore, the crew sailing aboard the *Ermelinda* was international and "multiracial," typical of the slave trade throughout the Atlantic. Sailors from Brazil and Portugal predominated, however, demonstrating that even after the colony's independence, Brazilians and Portuguese maintained a preferential partnership in that line of business.[22]

Rufino was not at all unusual aboard the slave ships on which he worked, because they employed large numbers of Africans. In addition to working as sailors, they were familiar with the regions that supplied slaves, acted as interpreters, and knew best how to convince, soothe, organize, and control the captives who spoke their languages. Generally, those seamen had been enslaved in Brazil and obtained their freedom there, like Rufino himself. The case of Musewo, or Toki Petro (possibly Pedro), was different. Of Songo ethnicity, he had been kidnapped at the age of fifteen and sold in Luanda. He lived there with his master, the Portuguese (possibly Brazilian) Henrique Gonsale (probably Gonçalves), a slave trader who used him when negotiating the purchase of slaves from the Songo nation. Petro was freed when his master died, perhaps in his will, and went to Brazil, where he worked in the slave trade for six years. He crossed the Atlantic seven times. On the eighth voyage, his ship was captured by the British and taken to Sierra Leone. He ended up living there and was interviewed in the middle of the century by Sigismund Koelle, the German linguist, to whom he told the story summarized here.[23]

Therefore, the crews of slave ships included Africans like Petro, who were responsible for negotiations for captives in the interior and coast of Africa—captives who could sometimes belong to their own ethnic group. Others did business in the slave ports, and a few became the supercargoes for the voyage, a post generally held by the ship captain. The African Joaquim Meireles was the supercargo aboard the *Nova Sorte*, a *sumaca* (a small two-masted schooner) owned by a Bahia slave trader that was seized by the British in 1822 for trafficking in the forbidden Bight of Benin. According to a statement from another African—Cândido Fernandes das Mercês, a sailor aboard the sumaca *São João*—Meireles was not just any crewman but "the cashier and in charge of negotiations." In other words, the ship captain, he went on, did not have "any power or command at all in the Sumaca, or in its business dealings, more than the said Cashier I mentioned, from whom he was to receive all orders except those related to handling and steering said Sumaca as first pilot and things related to his profession."[24] Cândido Fernandes also stated that he had been hired to work aboard the *São João* on Meireles's recommendation, suggesting that in addition to being the slave traders' "cashier," he was sufficiently familiar with the world of slaving to act as an intermediary when forming crews.

Therefore, African freedpersons could play the roles of sailors aboard slavers and interpreters in the slave ports, as well as being responsible for mediating the hiring of crews and negotiations on both sides of the Atlantic.[25] These characters, who were once victims of the Luso-Brazilian slave trade, went on to occupy several posts in the ranks of that same business once they were freed, and not just on the lowest rungs of the ladder. We have even found one slave ship captain of the Jeje nation, Antonio Nacizo, a freedman who lived in Bahia, and was responsible for several transatlantic slave voyages from the Slave Coast, Cabinda, and Molembo to Bahia, between 1812 and 1825.[26]

An additional advantage for using Africans in the slave trade was that they were more resistant to the often lethal tropical diseases endemic to the African coast—in some parts more than others—particularly malaria, yellow fever, and typhoid. Africans like Rufino must have had excellent immune systems. After all, besides the experience of slavery, they had also survived the Middle Passage in the holds of slave ships, where they could easily have caught a number of diseases. The survivors were either immune to them before the voyage or immunized as a result. It would be almost impossible for someone in poor health to survive the hardships that Rufino endured during his first Atlantic voyage on his way to enslavement in Brazil.

According to Jaime Rodrigues, seventeen percent of the crews of slave ships that sailed between Africa and Brazil from 1780 to 1863 were Africans, and of those, most (55 percent) came from West Africa, more specifically the regions in the hinterland of the Bight of Benin.[27] Rufino was from those parts, a native of Òyọ́. He probably came across other Nagôs in the slave ports, most of them crewmen like him, because there were no Yoruba-speaking settlements in the part of Africa he frequented—the Angolan coast. In Luanda, they put onboard many slaves obtained from local traders, both for coastwise sailing and the Atlantic crossing. The Portuguese authorities required the owner or factor of the ship to sign documents pledging to present the slaves within the period of the return voyage. The bureaucracy aimed to prevent the illegal slave trade from being carried on with the use of slaves as crewmembers. In October 1839, for example, Anna Francisca Obertally, a major Luanda slave trader who was a crony of the *Ermelinda*'s traffickers, shipped two slaves aboard the Brazilian brigantine *Flor de Luanda*, who were supposed to return within eight months after the ship arrived from Rio de Janeiro. In May 1840, José da Silva Rego was fined for not showing the authorities seven slaves within a mandatory six-month deadline. He had used them as sailors on a voyage from Luanda to Rio Janeiro aboard the brig *Ulisses*.²⁸ There were no enslaved sailors among the *Ermelinda*'s crew.

There is one strange detail: Rufino was listed among the crewmembers under a different name, Bernardo Almeida, possibly either an alias used for some unknown reason or an inexplicable clerical error. Could it be the name he adopted after being—if indeed he was—deported from Rio de Janeiro in 1839? Due to negligence, error, or fraud, the fact that this Bernardo is listed as being from the "Mina" nation coincides with Rufino's Afro-Brazilian identity, at least one of them. Furthermore, the crew list shows that Rufino was twenty-nine years old, of "average height," with a round face (he was also described that way when arrested thirteen years later), and received a salary of 40,000 réis for his work

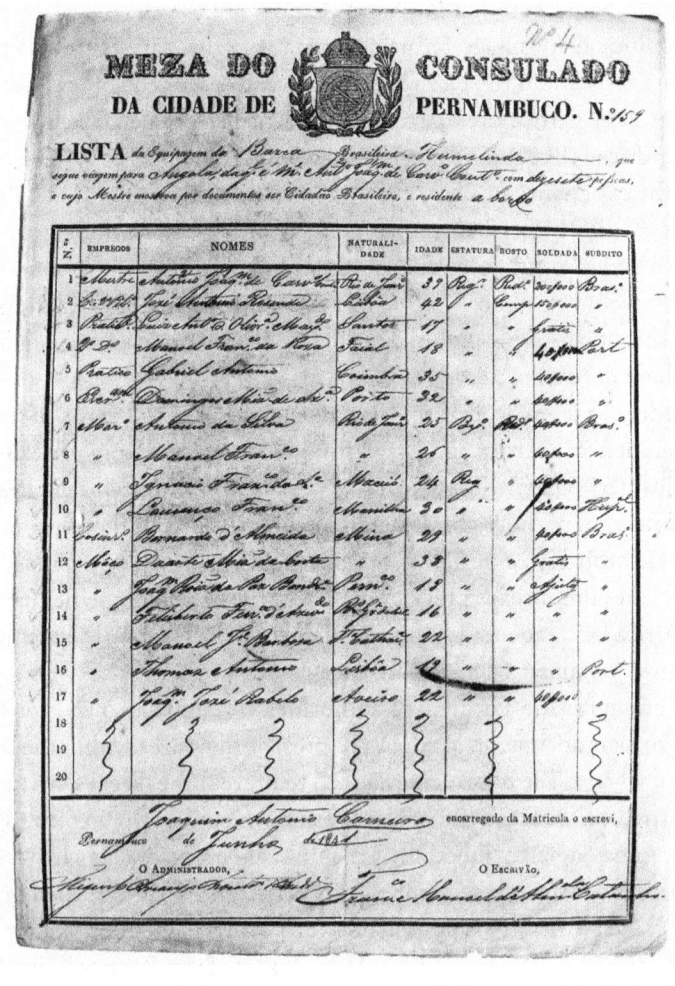

Figure 9.3 List of the *Ermelinda*'s crew, 1841. Arquivo do Itamaraty, Rio de Janeiro.

as a cook on that voyage. We have no doubt that the man named Bernardo was actually Rufino.

Rufino's registration errs again when it states that he was a "Brazilian subject," possibly meaning that he had naturalized as a Brazilian, which was unusual among Africans, particularly due to the official prejudice of those in power against former slaves born in Africa. It is likely, however, that employment in the country's merchant fleet was a passport to obtaining Brazilian citizenship, or at least facilitated the African sailor's travels on the Atlantic and his safe return to Brazil. We believe the latter to be Rufino's case, since other documents confirm he was never given Brazilian citizenship, having on the contrary been always described as "African." In any case, the slavers' political clout and the government's recognition of the slave trade's importance to the Empire's economic health, even during its illegal phase, helped ease restrictions on Africans' travel in and out of Brazilian ports. Lest we forget, after the Muslim uprising of 1835, laws were enacted to prevent freed and free Africans from entering the country, even those who lived and had families there and were merely returning from a voyage abroad.

Discriminated against on land, Africans received fairer treatment at sea, at least when it came to payment. Aboard the *Ermelinda*, Rufino received the same pay as the harbor pilots, sailors, and even the clerk, demonstrating that on that ship at least, intellectual work was not valued more highly than physical labor, seafaring knowledge, or culinary skills. The cabin boys, whose ages ranged from 16 to 38, did not have fixed wages at the beginning of the voyage, except for the Portuguese Joaquim José Rebelo, 22, who received the same pay as the sailors. The Mina cabin boy Duarte da Costa was there to work "for free," according to an observation penned next to his name. He may have paid for his passage to Africa by working aboard the ship, because he was also a small-time transatlantic merchant. As for the other cabin boys, the space on the form reserved for noting down their wages was filled in with "to be determined," that is, they would probably be paid according to how well they did their tasks, because they were still apprentice seamen. The highest wages aboard the *Ermelinda* went to Captain Coutinho—200,000 réis for the entire undertaking—and the pilot and first mate, José António Resende, 42 and single, a native of Lisbon naturalized Brazilian, who was to be paid 150,000 réis at the voyage's end. Two harbor pilots would receive the same pay as the sailors and cook, and a third was traveling "for free," like the Mina cabin boy.[29]

As an aside, the harbor pilot Gabriel Antonio was listed as a paid crewman, receiving 40,000 réis, just like the sailors. The same name appears in other contemporary sources as that of a major slave trader based in Pernambuco, a married planter and merchant but also Portuguese, like the *Ermelinda*'s crewman. The report about the landing of African "settlers" from the *Diário Pernambucano* was signed by "The Angel Gabriel." It would certainly be ironic if it refers to Gabriel the slaver, as we believe to be the case. However, Gabriel the crewman, who was sailing on the same ship as Rufino, stated that he was single, 35 years old, a native of Coimbra, Portugal, and made a living "as a sailor on the Barque *Ermelinda*, where he resides." And he was illiterate. That Gabriel Antonio did not own a share of the *Ermelinda*'s cargo. They must have been two different people with the same name employed in the same trade, but with radically different positions in its pecking order.[30]

The other Gabriel Antonio was not just any slaver. He was a major player. He seems to have got his start in the slave trade as a ship's captain. He had the tough personality generally associated with that post. On one occasion, shortly after his marriage, he tried to beat his own wife—just as captains generally treated crewmembers and slaves aboard their vessels—and would have done so if his mother-in-law had not come to her daughter's aid. On another occasion, he hit one of his father-in-law's cashiers with a stick, and another time he mercilessly beat a *cabrinha* (dark mixed-race child) boy. Some witnesses accused him of being violent and having a "quarrelsome temper." These incidents came to light during an investigation in which Gabriel was accused of whipping his neighbor's wife, in 1828. The type of whip was the same cat o' nine tails used aboard British ships to flay the backs of sailors and slaves, at least until Britain abolished the slave trade in 1807. However, witnesses in the slaver's defense said the neighbor's slaves had beaten him—that is, slaves, probably Africans, had beaten up the slaver, perhaps with a taste for revenge for the suffering inflicted on them by people like him, or even by Gabriel himself.[31]

At the time, he was actively involved in the slave trade. Before the 1831 ban, his voyages to Africa were advertised in the Pernambuco press so that anyone who was interested would know that blacks would soon be arriving for sale. In 1828 and 1829, he crossed the Atlantic twice as ship captain, and on one voyage he shared command of the brig *General Silveira* with A. J. Bronaio (the ship belonged to a major Pernambuco slaver, Elias Coelho Cintra); and soon afterwards he singlehandedly helmed the *Triunfo do Brazil*, a ship he also owned. It may be that the *General Silveira* and the *Triunfo* were the same vessel, because they shared the same description: both 231-ton bergantins. On those voyages Gabriel Antonio transported 1,033 captives to Pernambuco, thirty-one of whom died, a very small percentage given the number of Africans aboard— over 500 crammed together in the holds of each ship, or during each voyage of the same ship.

Gabriel Antonio is listed as the owner of several other vessels—the *Especulador, Livramento, Bonsucesso, Cospe Fogo, Francelina,* and *Mariquinha*— some of which may also have been the same ships with different names. He was also the consignee for the cargoes of other ships. Between 1828 and 1850, eight voyages in which the businessman took part as captain or ship owner transported to Brazil—particularly Pernambuco, but one shipment was offloaded in Bahia and another in Cabo Frio, a port in Rio de Janeiro province—a total of 2,918 captives, of whom 186 did not survive. This loss of human cargo was very low for the standards of that time. Of course, those eight voyages were not the only ones Gabriel Antonio organized or commanded. The Portuguese consul in Recife in 1835 called him the "main boss of those contraband undertakings" in a city where many vied for that title.[32]

If Gabriel Antonio the slaver was not aboard the *Ermelinda* in the flesh, he was well represented there by a letter from him to the wealthy Luanda merchant Manoel José Constantino, a Portuguese citizen who had been exiled for life in Angola. That name appears in lists of slave traders as the owner of the brig *Bonsucesso* in 1846, a ship that had been Gabriel's property seven years earlier. They must have been business partners. In the letter, dated July 4, 1841, Gabriel informed Constantino that a friend of his had equipped a ship to do business in Luanda, and asked Constantino to be his factor, for which he "would be forever grateful." Gabriel's friend was the famous José Francisco de Azevedo Lisboa.[33]

10
Rufino's Employers

José Francisco de Azevedo Lisboa was apparently the mastermind of the slaving business, at this time a criminal organization, for which Rufino worked. According to a lengthy report sent by the British consul in Pernambuco, Mr. Henry Augustus Cowper, to the British foreign secretary, Lord Aberdeen, on August 4, 1843, Azevedo Lisboa was better known as "Azevedinho," or "Little Azevedo," which is not a reference to his height but an expression of intimacy, affection, or informality. Given his pompous name, the colloquial nickname may reflect his considerable social dexterity, perhaps even expressing sympathy with its owner. However, that did not prevent Azevedinho from being cruel—from having the ice in the blood required by the slaving profession, as so aptly described by Alberto da Costa e Silva.[1] A native of Lisbon, Azevedinho requested, on October 3, 1825, a passport from King João VI to return to Pernambuco via other Brazilian ports. He was then 30 years old and residing in Boqueirão da Ribeira Nova Alley, in his hometown, where he had already been making a living as a businessman.[2] A few years later, he set up what was probably the best-organized slave trafficking company north of Bahia after the transatlantic slave trade was banned in 1831. The British made that clear in September 1837, when a contract and letters he had written to his subordinates on the Benin River were found during a disastrous operation by the British Navy to capture two slave ships, the *Veloz* and *Camões*.[3] This story would reappear during the court hearing on the *Ermelinda*. In his study of the same episode, João Pedro Marques observed that this would have been just one more slave ship captured by the British if it had not been for the confiscation of a rich and incriminating trove of documents.[4]

A ship built in New York, previously called the *Tobasco*, the *Veloz* (Speedy) – an audacious reference to its ability to escape British persecution – was leaving the Benin River with 228 captives on board when it was sighted by the British Navy schooner *Fair Rosamond*. Laden with slaves, the *Veloz* was forced to turn back into the river, which the *Fair Rosamond* did not dare enter this time because

The Story of Rufino. João José Reis, Flávio dos Santos Gomes, and Marcus J. M. de Carvalho, Translated by H. Sabrina Gledhill, Oxford University Press (2020) © Oxford University Press.
DOI: 10.1093/oso/9780190224363.001.0001

of the shallow draft. But the British ship did send a boat to board the slaver. The *Veloz* was armed with two cannons and used them to fight off the British vessel, killing two of its crew. For that reason, the commander of the *Fair Rosamond* took the risk of sailing upriver as far as the point where the *Veloz* was lying at anchor, almost side by side with the *Camões*. According to the British report, the *Veloz* had unloaded its cargo of slaves onshore while awaiting the right time to resume its voyage. The *Fair Rosamond* fired on the slaver, whose terrified crew jumped into the river.

The operation did not stop there. The *Veloz* was seriously damaged in the attack, so much so that it only arrived in Sierra Leone, taken as a legitimate prize, on May 26, 1838, eight months after it was seized. However, the *Camões* was not attacked. That ship had arrived in the Benin River in April 1837 and had already sold its cargo to the African merchants. With its sails still furled, it was awaiting the arrival of captives and the stowing of victuals to ready it for the voyage back to Brazil. At that point, the commanding officer of the schooner *Fair Rosamond*, Lieutenant William Brown Oliver, came up with what seemed to him to be an excellent idea. Once the ship was loaded, he could legally apprehend it. Somehow, whether with promises of freedom or death threats, the British got the slaver João Batista Cézar to write a letter to the head of a village two miles away (probably the area they called Bobim or Bobi in Ijebu territory, part of Yorubaland), asking him to send a pack of slaves for shipment. The interpreter for the conversation between Cézar and the British officer was Benedito, the African cook of the *Camões*, which demonstrates the versatility required of African crewmembers. Cézar's message was passed on by another sailor named José Maria, like Rufino, probably another African and from that same region.[5]

As ordered, 138 Africans arrived on the riverbank, where the commander of the *Fair Rosamond* loaded them onto the *Camões*. The Royal Navy vessel also mobilized two Britons, Mr. Hope and Mr. Millar, who were purchasing palm oil and ivory at a trading post, to provide the supplies required for the voyage to Sierra Leone, the British colony where confiscated slaves were taken. Having put dried meat, yams, and flour aboard, the slave ship sailed under the command of a Mr. Boys, first mate of the *Fair Rosamond*. The mortality rate during that voyage was very high—twenty-two slaves died before reaching Sierra Leone, and forty-five more perished after landing, a death rate well above the average in the Atlantic crossing to Brazil. We do not know how many more fatalities there were in the days that followed, but the survivors were in extremely poor condition. In addition to dysentery and dropsy, forty-five came down with ophthalmia, an eye infection that often caused blindness. The commander of the *Fair Rosamond*'s plan immediately cost the lives of at least sixty-seven of the 138 people put on board. According to the Royal Navy surgeon who examined the sick, the fatalities were caused by the extremely poor quality of the food served on board, which had been supplied by the British merchants involved in the so-called "legitimate trade" in Africa. It should be noted that most of the 138 Africans that the British put on board were boys (45) and girls (26).[6]

In Sierra Leone, the *Camões* was returned to its owners when the commander of the *Fair Rosamond*'s ploy came to light through his own testimony and that of his English crew. Lieutenant Oliver did not go unpunished. He was ordered to pay the court costs and compensation to the owners of the *Camões*, totaling 1,734 pounds and fourteen shillings.[7] We do not know if the sentence was carried out. That amount may have been deducted from the valuable prizes that British sailors received for capturing slave ships. However, Oliver paid no penalty for causing the deaths of sixty-seven Africans. His intentions were good, according to the authorities, as all he wanted to do was free them from slavery by taking them to Sierra Leone. Nevertheless, this entire episode aptly illustrates what historian Simon Schama has called "the brutally pragmatic world of the British Royal Navy."[8]

What most interested the Court of Mixed Commission was not the sad fate of those who died aboard the *Camões* but the documents found aboard the *Veloz*, which provide a glimpse into the modus operandi of illegal slave-trading procedures.[9] They named slave traffickers and described the business practices of Rufino's bosses, both on the African coast and in Brazil. In fact, it was unusual for such compromising papers to be confiscated. Slavers were canny about forging and destroying documents as needed. But all indications are that they had no time for that. The crew of the *Veloz* was taken by surprise because they did not expect a ship the size of the *Fair Rosamond* to dare sail upriver in shallow waters and arrive with guns blazing. The captain of the *Camões* and the slavers' factor from Pernambuco, who were aboard the *Veloz* at the time, panicked and jumped into the water stark naked, to the derision of the British.[10]

The business contract and letters seized by the Royal Navy disclosed the operations of the company for which Rufino would eventually work. Signed in Pernambuco on December 14, 1836, the contract established a commercial partnership among twenty shareholders whose names were unfortunately not listed in the document, each with a share of 4 million réis, totaling 80 million réis. Azevedinho was appointed treasurer, but his role went far beyond handling the company's accounts. He was quite the strategist: he would instruct the company's factors, have ships built, and run the entire venture. Joaquim Leocadio d'Oliveira Guimaraens and Manoel Alves Guerra were consultants, assisting the manager in the running of the firm, including the accounts. The explicit aim of the business was trafficking slaves. To do so, in addition to purchasing ships and merchandise, they would establish a trading post in the kingdom of Benin. Expectations were that they would purchase 200 to 250 captives per month, therefore approximately 2,500 per year. The profits would be divided into twenty-four shares: twenty for the investors and four more equal shares—one for Azevedinho, two for the company's factors in Benin (João Baptista Cézar and Manuel Delgado), and one for Joaquim Gomes Coimbra and Antonio Fernandes Vianna, who had boarded the *Camões* in Bahia. Vianna had established residence on the island of Principe where, thanks to his good relations with the Portuguese governor, he was able to establish a support base to supply victuals and water to the company's slave ships. Coimbra, in his turn, worked at the trading post under Cézar's orders.[11]

José Francisco de Azevedo Lisboa and his factors in Africa shared the profits without contributing their own investments—Azevedinho because he was directly responsible for the company's transactions, making contacts, passing on orders, and managing the company's operations, and the factors because they were risking their lives in "insalubrious climes." If the company's costs exceeded its earnings, Azevedinho and the factors on the African front would not feel the financial loss. However, the contract clearly established that the shareholders were the real owners of the ships. That must have been one of the first "capitalist companies" of that kind, adapted to the risks arising from the new circumstances of the Atlantic slave trade, which had become an illegal activity.[12]

Along with the confiscated contract, the British found a number of letters containing Azevedinho's instructions to the firm's factors on the Benin River, as well as correspondence between those factors and between them and Azevedinho and others in Brazil. The captain of the *Camões*, Antonio Gomes da Silva, collaborated with the factors João Baptista Cézar and Manuel Delgado to set up the trading post. Cézar was the senior factor. In his detailed instructions, Azevedinho showed in-depth knowledge of the slave trade and the ways in which the business of buying and selling slaves was conducted in that part of Africa. His letters are a veritable how-to manual for a modern business. The difference is that the merchandise was men, women, and children.[13]

According to his instructions, the trading post's staff should behave in a dignified fashion to ensure that the Africans respected the company. The factors were supposed to exert their authority over their local subordinates with civility, and not just through their power of command. By the same token, regarding the "natives," Azevedinho emphasized that, although they lacked the refinement of more civilized peoples, they were fully capable of judgment. If the factors set an example of good behavior, Africans would respect and try to imitate them. Therefore, it was essential to avoid licentiousness and drunkenness, cultivate moderation and affability, and above all, avoid conflicts with the local elite. Azevedinho also advised that, although he could not interfere with anyone's "conscience," it was important for the factors to be seen to follow some form of religion to help keep up the firm's good reputation with the Africans.

The general manager emphasized that, when it came to doing business, they would have to follow local customs, but they should carefully evaluate the products offered by the company, especially those that did not yet have a fixed price. The merchandise should be amply presented in a suitable setting that prevented potential buyers from entering the warehouses so as not to awaken their greed. It was important to convince the king and other chiefs that the trading post always had the best spirits and tobacco in the region, an attempt to monopolize the local trade with foreigners.[14] To ensure the king's support, he would always receive gifts from the trading post—a common practice in dealings with African chiefs. However, nothing was to be sold on credit to avoid problems when the bill came due.

The ever-zealous manager also ordered that a flagpole should be set up at the highest point near the trading post with a view of the sea to exchange signals with the company's ships. The codes would be kept secret and only available to the senior factors. The ships always sailed with someone in the crow's nest so they could immediately spot other ships and avoid unpleasant surprises. The codes would also be used to communicate with slavers on land when they arrived in Brazil. There, before casting anchor, all the shackles and other implements that could raise suspicion were to be thrown into the sea. The secrecy surrounding the signals and the company's objectives extended to the Europeans working at other coastal trading posts. When asked about their activities, they were to say that they were doing business with Havana and never let anyone see the dispatch papers for their merchandise. Although the company aspired to a monopoly on the slave trade in that area, Azevedinho predicted that other factors might require one of the company's ships to transport cargo. They would be charged no less than thirty carefully selected slaves for the charter of the vessel.[15]

The instructions set down by Rufino's employer showed that, for security reasons, the ships were to stay off the river. To avoid looting, they were not supposed to dock on the riverbank. The company's boat, commissioned in Bahia from the Duarte & Warren firm, would go out to meet the ship to transport merchandise to the trading post. Once the ship had been spotted and its identity confirmed with the coded flag signals, the African captives would immediately be taken to the chosen site so they could be embarked as quickly as possible. Speed was so important, emphasized Azevedinho, that a ship that could carry 300 captives should not delay its departure for want of fifty, for example.[16]

Rounding out the paperwork, Azevedinho also sent a document ready to be signed by the entire crew and presented to the port authorities in Brazil after the Africans had been offloaded. It gave a detailed account of how pirates had attacked and looted the ship on the high seas, which explained why it was arriving without any cargo.

An efficient manager, Azevedinho was not just concerned about ensuring that the company ran smoothly, with employees who were motivated, well paid, and adapted to his leadership, but also familiar with the finest technology of the day. Thus, in a letter to João Baptista Cézar, his senior factor in Africa, he explained that if a "telegraph" station installed by the British was too far away, two men from the trading post should be sent to live near it.[17] If it was close by, the telegraph would be visited regularly. The slave traders knew how to make good use of the Britons' modern methods of communication to ensure that they escaped more easily from the British themselves.

In fact, their relations with the Britons who were legally trading in palm oil, ivory, hides, copal, orchil, and other products were far from poor. Tensions on the coast of Africa were constant, and there was a real risk of death due to the epidemics that were usually fatal for Europeans and their descendants. It may be that those risks, or the fact that they were white and mixed-race people living in isolation in tropical Africa, made for greater solidarity among the foreigners at the trading posts. At least, that is what we gather from the reports of individuals employed in this transatlantic model of organized crime, who were thoroughly familiar with the well-stocked British warehouses. The relationship between them was so friendly that, at least twice, the Britons played a prank on the Brazilians by raiding their ships, pretending to be the Royal Navy. They were drunk on both occasions. Once, the Britons arrived in a boat from a Royal Navy ship that was anchored nearby. Mr. Hope and Mr. Millar, the two merchants who helped the commander of the *Fair Rosamond* obtain provisions for the *Camões's* voyage to Sierra Leone, performed in one of their pranks.[18] Of course, there was no harm done, and the episode probably ended up in a good laugh on both sides and several friendly drinks. According to Cézar, Mr. Millar had been aboard the *Aracati*, the slave ship owned by Azevedinho that was captured on its way to Angola in 1842, regarding which a letter was found on the *Ermelinda* a year earlier.[19] We do not know what a Briton was doing aboard a slave ship. He may have been supplying it with victuals, as he would for the *Camões*, making good money in the bargain. All this shows that the British did not form a united front among themselves against the slave trade and that many would rather profit from their dealings with the same people their government was relentlessly pursuing.

Furthermore, Antonio Gomes da Silva, the captain of the *Camões*, stated that one of the *Fair Rosamond*'s officers had dined with him at Mr. Millar's home in September, a few weeks before the same officers arrested him.[20] Given Gomes's, Mr. Millar's, and the British officers' shared taste for spirits, they must have got along very well. Joaquim Gomes Coimbra, another of Azevedinho's agents, had also dined at Mr. Millar's home. We do not know if it was on the same occasion. Millar supposedly told him that Mr. Hope would be jealous because they had not yet paid him a visit.[21] When Cézar came down with extremely high

Figures 10.1 and 10.2 Slave barracoons in Sierra Leone, 1849. From *The Illustrated London News* (April 14, 1849).

fevers—possibly malaria—to the point of delirium, the captain of the *Veloz* sent for a British physician. Therefore, there is abundant evidence of fraternal relations between the slave traders and the British. Again, the true "brothers" of the British in those parts were other whites, even though they were slave traders, and not the enslaved blacks who were the "brothers" of the abolitionists in far-away Britain.[22]

Azevedinho was also intent on producing the foodstuffs used to supply his ships. Therefore he recommended that the trading post have a steady supply of yams, the main food staple of the peoples in that region, which was often used to feed the captives during the Middle Passage. He also ordered his minions to plant trial crops of beans and other legumes and vegetables. Cézar must have planted cassava, because he received the equipment needed to make flour, another product used to feed both captives and crew aboard Brazilian slavers. And there was more. Perhaps due to their enforced coexistence with the British, the general manager was in tune with the legal trade in African products. Seeing an opportunity to make a profit, Azevedinho ordered Cézar to diversify the company's activities, not only buying people but also gold, ivory, and cloth wrappers, the latter being highly valued by African women in Brazil. Azevedinho almost forgot, but he added a postscript to his letter to Cézar asking him to investigate whether there were traders sourcing copal and orchil in the vicinity, from whom he could buy those products.[23]

Last, and perhaps most important, at the time of purchase the firm's representatives were supposed to choose the best "merchandise." Slave traders gave priority to buying young men, and the manager insisted that Cézar stick firmly to that principle. He should refuse to buy old men rejected by the domestic African market. Perhaps with some condescension, Azevedinho recognized that Cézar was thoroughly familiar with the "tastes" of the African market, which most valued people between the ages of twelve and twenty. However, he should not reject women with fully developed breasts, which indicated not just an aptitude for work but for procreation.[24]

These were the management plans that Rufino's boss set down for his trading post on the Benin River. The vast knowledge of the business that he displayed greatly impressed the British authorities. But business did not always go well. Everything started out as planned. His factors met with the king of the major kingdom of Benin and the local nobility, whom they also called kings of the cities that paid tribute to Benin—in this case Oery (or Oere, Warri, Iweri, Ode Itsekiri) and Gotto (or Ughoton, Gwato). The king of Benin trusted Cézar enough to send one of his own slave boys to Brazil to learn about seafaring. Cézar emphasized the importance of guaranteeing the boy's safety and ensuring that he returned on the same ship. Otherwise, he could incur the wrath of the African chief.[25] His report to Azevedinho shows that the initial business dealings were successful. The king of Benin, accompanied by his counterpart in Oery, personally took Cézar to see the other four trading posts in the vicinity, where the African ruler recommended that everyone treat the trafficker very well. Even the British went to visit the slave traders, probably because they knew that they had the support of the local elite, without which no trading post could prosper.[26]

Aside from the diseases that afflicted everyone, other problems gradually began to emerge.[27] In João Baptista Cézar's detailed report to Azevedinho regarding the company's activities and difficulties, the factor openly criticized the captain of the *Camões* for failing to obey his orders, overspending, distributing unauthorized promissory notes, and generally getting into trouble. He had paid a visit to the king of Oery while intoxicated and became known among the local Africans as a *moxaquori*—a drunkard, according to Cezar's own translation of the local language.[28] Some merchandise had gone missing as a result. On another occasion, two of the company's factors had the gall to visit the king of Benin without taking gifts. One of them had to remain behind as a hostage until the slight was remedied.[29] The African traders also demanded high-quality products when making their purchases. A load of spoiled tobacco from Bahia made the African buyers wary. These episodes demonstrate that the company's employees were not following the traffickers' code of ethics.

The reports from Cézar and his subordinates indicate that the various ranks of the African hierarchy charged high taxes, which required the company's factors to be well aware of the complex codes of etiquette and deference. Competition was also fierce. The African traders and the nobility had several suppliers of European and Brazilian goods, as well as other channels for exporting their precious human merchandise. They had been trading with the Atlantic world for centuries. It was from Gotto, the nearest river harbor to the kingdom of Benin, that the Portuguese took slaves in the late fifteenth century to trade for gold on the Gold Coast in what is now Ghana.[30] Africans knew what they wanted from the slave traders, sometimes very specific things to which they had long been accustomed. For example, the king of Benin in 1837 sent a girl for the specific purpose of exchanging her at Azevedinho's trading post for ham, assorted crackers, butter, sausages, sugar, and tea.[31]

As the manager of a large and highly profitable international business that was also risky and speculative, Azevedinho had administrative problems that went beyond simply sending ships to Africa to bring captives back in chains. Nevertheless, it was possible to leave the business or just transfer it to another part of the African coast.[32] The thirteenth clause of the company's founding contract only required the investors to stay on for three years as of December 1836. However, for the British, the firm not only still existed but was also active in other waters when the *Ermelinda* was sent to the Angolan coast in 1841.

They were right. The names of the likely owners and consignees continued to appear in the years that followed, as the case of the *Ermelinda* clearly demonstrates. The *Camões* itself, before sailing for the Benin River, where it would be seized by the *Fair Rosamond*, had taken captives from Angola to Pernambuco, going on in ballast to Recife with a passport issued in Luanda saying that it had stopped in Ambriz, also on the Angolan coast. Its consignee at the time, July 1837, was Manoel Alves Guerra, one of Azevedinho's two board members, according to the company's charter. When it left Recife in ballast to meet its fate in Benin, it was carrying a passport to visit Cape Verde, stopping in Bahia and several

African ports. Its consignee then, finally, was Azevedinho.[33] The trading post on the Benin River was therefore just part of the company's activities in Africa.

Not even the *moxaquori* Antonio Gomes da Silva lost his job after his mistakes on the Benin River. Cézar advised Azevedinho not to give the bonus being offered by the company to the captain of the *Camões*.[34] Nevertheless, da Silva's career in the slave trade continued. It was well known that nobody became the captain of a slaver overnight. Furthermore, no matter how well they were paid, not all good navigators were willing to get involved in that activity. For that very reason, it must not have been difficult for an experienced slave-ship captain like him to get a job, despite his taste for alcohol. He was probably the "A. G. da Silva" who appeared in Recife as the captain of the *Luendal* (or *Quendal*), which arrived in Angola on October 5, 1839. The ship belonged to Joaquim da Silva Regadas, also a well-known slave trader in Angola who moved to Pernambuco in pursuit of better business opportunities.[35] It is even safer to assume that he was the "A. Gomes da Silva" who commanded the *Cospe Fogo*, a 64-ton *escuna* that sailed from Recife laden with spirits and sugar to exchange for slaves in Angola on November 6, 1839. The small ship belonged to another familiar name, Gabriel Antonio.[36] Antonio Gomes da Silva reappeared in Pernambuco at the helm of the *Cospe Fogo* on May 23, 1840, after unloading his cargo on a beach north of Recife. According to information furnished by the British, the ship carried 145 people in its hold, but the mortality rate was extremely high due to overcrowding, and only seventy to seventy-five survived.[37]

Rufino was a contemporary of all these people and may even have sailed with Captain Gomes da Silva, whose drinking habits must not have gone down well with an observant Muslim. We know that the firm still existed after 1837 and was also active in other parts of Africa because the names of Rufino's bosses are frequently found in the paperwork for the slave trade to Pernambuco and because Azevedinho himself reappears under different circumstances. In January 1839, the *Andorinha*, a small 76-ton vessel owned by Azevedinho (or, more accurately, the company he managed) anchored in Recife in ballast. According to the captain, it had been attacked by pirates as soon as it left Cabinda.[38] The captain of the 220-ton *Josefa* made the same claim and had the audacity to claim that the pirates had taken 400 slaves from him as soon as he left Angola in late 1839. However, the British consul in Pernambuco suspected that the *Josefa* had offloaded 320 captives on a beach south of Recife a short time before. That ship also belonged to Azevedinho.[39]

For these reasons, among others, we have concluded that the operation on the Benin River was just one branch of the slave trader's business. Azevedinho had long-standing connections with the Angolan market, as demonstrated by his partnership with Joaquim Ribeiro de Brito, the owner of the *São José*, aboard which Rufino worked as a cook. However, their relationship must have soured, because Gabriel Antonio sent a letter via the *Ermelinda* recommending Azevedinho to his agent in Luanda, Manoel José Constantino. Gabriel told Constantino that the *Aracati* would be leaving Pernambuco in forty days and asked him, in the slavers' code, to prepare "many bars or cakes of wax, enough to fill the vessel." The *Aracati*, which had once received Mr. Millar on board, belonged to Azevedinho. The details of the operation were sent aboard the same ship that carried the order he had dispatched to Constantino. Seven years later, Gabriel's agent had problems with the law because of the illegal slave trade and fled from Luanda to Brazil where, it seems, there was no lack of people willing to give him aid and shelter.[40]

The *Aracati* would actually begin its slaving voyage in early September 1841, laden with kegs of cachaça and sacks of sugar valued at £1,245, according to the British authorities. In late March of the following year, the ship unloaded, onto a beach a few leagues south of Recife, 358 of the 410 Africans embarked on the coast of Angola. The fatalities were primarily due to lack of water, the captives having died of thirst. A day after the survivors were put ashore, Azevedinho's *Aracati*, which was lying at anchor off Cape Santo Agostinho, was captured by a Brazilian man-of-war schooner, the *Fidelidade*, and sent to Rio de Janeiro for trial.[41]

The slave ship's crew had climbed into a longboat and fled before the vessel was boarded. There were no more Africans on board the *Aracati*, but there were clear signs of its recent mission. The main one was the terrible stench that came out of its hold. The mixture of sweat, excrement, vomit, and blood spilled during weeks spent in a hot, humid, enclosed space created a pestilent atmosphere and a foul odor that took a long time to fade and could be smelled from far away. Even the sailors had a hard time dealing with the smell of death and pain that accompanied the crossing. They used tar to disinfect the ship—a product also purchased for the *Ermelinda's* voyage. There was also a great deal of mud on the ship, attributed to the movement of a large number of people on the deck, another indication of a recent clandestine disembarkation. Added to that was the large amount of fresh fruit on board—watermelon, mangoes, oranges, and passion fruit—probably left over from the provisions distributed among the captives to prevent or combat diseases like scurvy. It is reasonable to suppose that, when the *Aracati* was captured, its crew was trying to clean the ship before taking it into a larger port like Recife or even Salvador, where it would probably be fitted out for another voyage to Africa. The ship's owners naturally spun elaborate arguments in their defense, denying that the ship was a slaver. One of the sailors said the fruit had been purchased from a passing barge and tried to explain the source of the foul smell. He said it was from "rotten fish."[42]

Two letters dealing with the slave trade would be used as evidence in the case against the *Aracati*. One of them, written in Luanda on February 3, 1842, and addressed to Joaquim Pereira de Mendonça, recounted the misadventures of a commercial representative of the Brazilian slave traffickers. Joaquim do Couto Lima said that he had been caring for twenty captives purchased between June 15 of the previous year and July 17, 1842. At the time, he was awaiting the ship owned by the slave trader Arsénio Pompílio Pompeu de Carpo, with whom he had arranged to continue on his voyage to Brazil. However, de Carpo ended up breaking the deal with Couto Lima and doing business with Luis Antonio de Carvalho e Castro instead, going on to the Dande River to put "his people" aboard. In addition to being a slave trader, de Carpo was known to be shady in his business dealings. Couto Lima had no choice but to sell off one of the captives under his care and sought out "Mr. Constantino" (certainly Manoel José Constantino, Gabriel Antonio's correspondent) to negotiate the shipment of the remaining slaves to Brazil. However, the best he could manage was a small *lancha* to take him and his cargo to Rio de Janeiro. That vessel could carry a maximum of 100 people, but there were 150 aboard. It was intercepted by the British, who arrested Couto Lima and confiscated all nineteen of his captives. According to him, the bearer of the letter (probably Manoel José Fernandes, 24, the young commander of the *Aracati* from Pernambuco) got Couto Lima out of that tight spot. However, the contretemps did not persuade him to give up that criminal life, and he continued to work in the slave trade. He managed to send eleven captives to Rio de Janeiro aboard an American ship sometime in the 1840s. Of the 824 Africans in its hold, 320 died during the Middle Passage. Just five of the writer's eleven captives survived the voyage. In fact, just four survived because one died after going ashore. At the end of his complicated financial report, after so many adventures and deaths, Joaquim do Couto Lima would only make 1,200,000 réis when, in his estimation, he could have racked up some "six million."[43] This was just another slaver's account and more evidence of the human trafficking networks found aboard one of Azevedinho's ships.

On September 19, 1843, Azevedinho announced in the press that, "his disease having worsened," he was leaving his post as treasurer of the lottery of the parish church in the Boa Vista district, one of the many charitable activities in which slavers were customarily involved.[44] Two weeks earlier, the 54-ton ship *Furão* had left Recife bound for Luanda under the command of J. R. Dias. That was the last time Azevedinho's name appeared as consignee of a slave ship from Pernambuco.[45] In April of the following year, 1844, he announced that due to his "serious illness" he was handing over the business to his bookkeeper and retiring "wistfully" to Lisbon.[46] He died at the age of fifty on March 1, 1845. He did not live long enough to fully enjoy the wealth he built up through the slave trade. He left no children. Except for a few bequests to relatives and extended family, his widow inherited everything. Probably concerned about shortening his wait for Heaven, Azevedinho stipulated in his will that he wanted 100 masses sung for his soul, 100 for his father's, 100 for his mother's, and another 100 for the soul of his "Uncle Silvestre." He did not leave money to celebrate any masses for the hundreds of his slaves who were buried in the Atlantic; he may have believed that they had no souls to save. His coffin was to be carried by four poor men, who were to be given alms of 1,400 réis for their efforts.[47] Rich and possibly radiant with joy, his widow remarried in 1849. Her new husband, Mr. Antonio Bernando Ferreira, represented her in a lawsuit in which Ribeiro de Brito, one of Azevedinho's former partners, was trying to regain two captives he claimed to be his—the remnants of a slaver's deal with the dead man.[48]

11

Passengers, Shippers, and Cargo

Fourteen passengers boarded the *Ermelinda,* paying different fares to cross the Atlantic depending on the accommodations assigned to them. There were nine passengers in the stern who paid between 60,000 and 100,000 réis, and three in the bow, who paid just 40,000 réis, the equivalent to Rufino's salary. Most of them maintained steady relations, commercial or otherwise, with Angola and, more often, specifically with the Port of Luanda. At least half of the passengers were traders or their employees who owned shares or were responsible for the cargo aboard the ship. Without a doubt, they were engaged in the slave trade typical of that Angolan city.

Some of the passengers are not listed as shippers. One of them was a lieutenant in the Portuguese army in Africa, and it would be interesting to know what he was doing in Pernambuco on that occasion. Was he just stopping there on his way to Luanda from Portugal? Regarding Portuguese military officers based in Luanda, historian Anne Stamm wrote, "They are ambitious and eager to make their fortune but often dedicated and patriotic."[1] We do not know about the lieutenant's ethical compass, but he must have known that he was aboard a ship that defied Portuguese and Brazilian laws banning the slave trade. Perhaps he learned his first lessons about how to "make his fortune" while sailing to Angola.

At least two of the passengers, both white, were born and lived in Luanda: Bernardo José da Silveira, 34, a widower, and Antonio Gonçalves de Carvalho Vieira, 31, a married man. Augusto César, 21, was white and unmarried. He was born on the Island of Madeira but lived in Angola. These men were not shippers either. The last two, in addition to the Brazilian Thomas Pinto de Caldas, were the passengers who established the closest relations with the captain during the voyage because theirs were the only names he could recall—although he mixed up Thomas's surname—in a statement given to the British authorities a few months after the *Ermelinda* set sail.[2]

A "floating marketplace"—this is how historian Stephanie Smallwood refers to slave ships bound for Africa.[3] The *Ermelinda* was one of those floating marketplaces. It carried rolls of tobacco, crates of cigars and sugar, barrels of *cachaça* (sugar-cane brandy), sacks of rice and cassava flour, as well as a variety of manufactured goods, including 150 "bundles of different re-exported textiles." The cloth came from Europe, most of it made in England, a lucrative way for that country to participate in the trade that it was trying to suppress in the South Atlantic. The British officers charged with combating the slave trade played their role in this mercantile scheme. Henry Wise addressed this matter as a representative of the United States at the Imperial Court of Rio de Janeiro, in a serious charge leveled against the British policy of enforcing its ban on the slave trade: "British manufactures are shipped by British subjects on board of Slave vessels at Rio de Janeiro; when these vessels arrive thus loaded on the coast of Africa, the British cruisers allow them to pass unmolested, to the end that they may land those goods, buy a cargo of slaves, which are afterwards captured, and sent as apprentices to the possessions of Great Britain, and for which the Government pay a bounty of so many pounds sterling 'per capita.'" Wise even wrote that the British avoided destroying the slavers' trading posts on the African coast because, they said, "we would burn our own merchandise."[4] Although the charges were not entirely fair, they were not misplaced, partly because relations between Brazilian slave traders and British merchants on the coast of Africa were generally friendly.

But most of the cargo that the *Ermelinda* was carrying was actually produced in Brazil, particularly tobacco and *cachaça*. These two products and the textiles were articles traditionally used in the slave trade all along the African coast, although *cachaça*—or *jeribita*—had played a key role specifically in the Angolan trade since the mid-sixteenth century. In 1699, of all the *cachaça* legally imported in Luanda, 11.4 percent came from Rio de Janeiro, compared with 57.4 percent from Bahia and 31.1 percent from Pernambuco. Nearly a century later, in 1785, it was said that Angolans had developed a "distinct preference" for *cachaça* from Rio de Janeiro, but they continued to buy the product from other regions, as the *Ermelinda*'s cargo confirms.[5]

Only three of the *Ermelinda*'s crew had their own merchandise aboard: the clerk Domingos Martins de Souza, the cabin boy Duarte José Martins da Costa, and the cook Rufino José Maria. The first was a Portuguese from Oporto, aged 32, who declared in his name miscellaneous items worth 2,409,340 réis, including a crate of textiles—calico and *madapolão* (white cotton cloth, something between calico and percale) —and forty casks and two barrels of spirits, totaling eight percent of the value of the cargo on board. (This explains why the clerk was happy to receive the same wages as a cook: that pay was small change for him.) The cabin boy Duarte Martins, who along with Rufino was one of the two Africans among the *Ermelida's* crew, brought cargo aboard that included two and a half casks of spirits, 209 crates of sweets, and nine crates of cigars, worth a total of 737,667 réis, the equivalent of 2.4 percent of the ship's cargo.

As for Rufino, the *Jornal do Commercio* described him as a "small shipper." On that voyage, he took 180 crates of guava sweets in two large caskets. Several shippers put a wide variety of sweets aboard, in addition to Duarte and Rufino. It is not surprising. Sweets had been commonly found on the list of Brazilian exports to Angola since at least the eighteenth century, and the tradition continued into the following century. During his visit to Luanda in 1841, Dr. Tams enjoyed "a table covered with wine and sweets from Brazil" at a bazaar he visited.[6]

Being a cook, Rufino may have made the sweets himself. They were worth 598,332, which was not a paltry figure. That amount was enough to buy a good slave in Brazil and perhaps even seven captives in Luanda in 1841. That year, it would also purchase the freedom of an adult slave in Rio de Janeiro, and in Bahia it would manumit a slave woman worth two-thirds that sum. That was the amount that Rufino said he paid for his own manumission in Porto Alegre in 1835. In other words, about five years after he became a freedman, he had at the very least earned back the price of his freedom paper. And he would not have been able to do that if he earned nothing but his cook's wages. That money came from trade, probably the slave trade. This gives us an idea of how lucrative that venture could be, even for a "small shipper," despite the risks involved—the dangers of disease, death, shipwreck, piracy, and being captured by the British, among others. We now know that Rufino was not just a cook aboard a slave ship but the owner of a small portion of its cargo.[7] But the freedman may have just been getting started in that business because, unlike the other shippers, he had not marked his property—generally with letters (sometimes the owner's

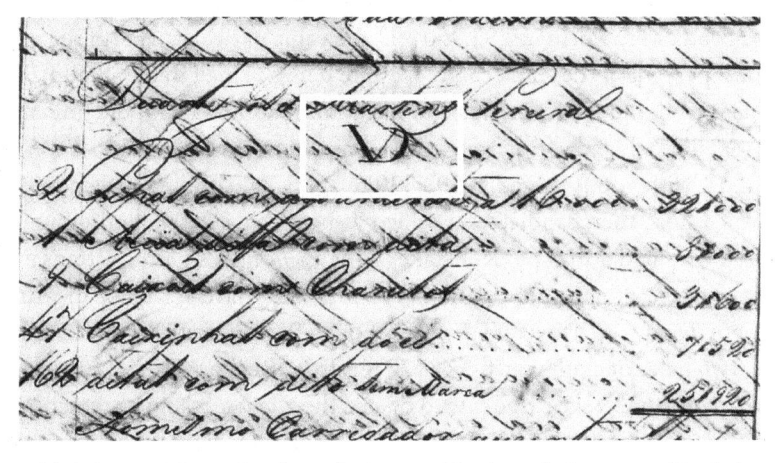

Figure 11.1 Duarte Martins' trademark. Arquivo Histórico do Itamaraty, Rio de Janeiro.

initials) branded on crates and bundles of merchandise. On the way back, the same branding irons would be used to mark the bodies of the captives that shipper had purchased. The other African on board, Duarte Martins Pereira (or da Costa), already had his own brand, something like VD—perhaps a combination of his initial (D from Duarte) and that of another business partner unknown to us.[8]

Duarte and Rufino were both Africans, crew members, and small-time transatlantic traders who jointly owned 4.4 percent of the *Ermelinda*'s cargo. They were not unique. It was relatively common for African seamen to put their own cargo aboard the slave ships on which they worked or to act as intermediaries for small investors seeking specific products sold on the African coast, including captives. Another example of such maritime workers is Vicente Francisco Camacho, a widower born on the Mina Coast who lived in Cais Dourado in Salvador and had shipped out as a "barber and bleeder" (barber surgeon) on the *Vencedora*, a schooner that plied "the route to the African Coast." When his ship was captured in 1836, he declared that on that voyage he had "taken his cargo to barter for cloth and palm oil."[9] Since the slave trade was illegal at the time, Camacho would naturally omit that the merchandise he intended to buy on the African coast included slaves.[10]

Slaving expeditions were not always monopolized by one or two investors, but rather by a broader association that included members both large and small. The *Ermelinda*'s cargo was valued at 30,450,007 réis, Brazilian currency, and the freight, 4,273,040 réis, Angolan currency.[11] Thirty-one shippers owned all the merchandise on board, several of whom owning a very small share. There were ten individuals whose cargo was worth less than 400,000 réis, totaling 2,688,130 réis, or nearly 9 percent of the entire cargo. They shipped all kinds of effects: cologne bottles, earrings, soap, fabric, grease, rice, sweets, and mainly tobacco and spirits. The smallest trader was Bento Botelho Pinto de Mesquita, whose goods were worth just 92,960 réis, the value of twenty cans of sugar and a mere 0.3 percent of the ship's cargo. Despite being a small trader, Bento already had his own brand, BM, perhaps an indication that he was not unfamiliar with transatlantic trade.

Rufino, with goods valued at 598,330 réis, was one of the thirteen middling shippers whose merchandise was valued at between 500,000 and one million réis, and who had a 27.5 percent stake in the *Ermelinda*'s business transactions on that voyage. That group of investors may also have included the African cabin boy Duarte Martins and Antonio Lopes Pereira de Mello. The latter was taking two bales of cloth worth 554,110 réis from Recife to Luanda for Joaquim Ribeiro de Brito, the slave trader who owned the *São José*, a ship on which Rufino had also worked.[12] The biggest investors included the eight who owned goods worth over one million réis, whose cargo was worth a total of 19,326,926 réis, or 63.5 percent of the value of that trading expedition.

Although it had several investors, the *Ermelinda*'s voyage was mainly a family enterprise, very much like those seen in other Brazilian slave ports, particularly Rio de Janeiro, the largest of them all.[13] The official owner of the barque was young Francisco Lisboa, but the man responsible for registering the crew at the Consular Office in Pernambuco in June 1841 was a relative of his, Joaquim Antonio Carneiro, perhaps a cousin. The biggest shipper and consignatory of the *Ermelinda* also belonged to their family. Angelo Francisco Carneiro, the ship owner's uncle, was the man responsible for preparing, loading, and expediting the cargo on that voyage. A commander of the Brazilian Empire and future Viscount of Loures in Portugal, Carneiro may have been the *Ermelinda*'s real owner. Theirs was a respectable slave-trading family, and on that particular expedition the investment would be shared by the young man, who theoretically paid six million for the ship, and his uncle, who spent an additional ten million to prepare it for the Atlantic crossing. Angelo Carneiro's goods were marked with a large and stylish letter A.[14]

The cargo of African "settlers" alluded to by the Pernambuco newspaper belonged to "a man who was so mild and peaceful that he was like a lamb [*cordeiro* in the original]," a coded reference to *Carneiro*, which means sheep in Portuguese. The year was 1837. Angelo Cordeiro, that is, Carneiro, was no novice when it came to the slave trade. His name frequently appears on lists of similar folk between the late 1810s and the beginning of the following decade. On at least two occasions, in 1818 and 1822, he was identified as the captain and owner of the ship at the same time, which gives the idea of how deeply involved he became in the transatlantic trade in human beings. In 1818, he commanded the *D. Domingos*, a ship he owned in partnership with Antonio

Figure 11.2 Angelo Carneiro's trademark. Arquivo Histórico do Itamaraty, Rio de Janeiro.

Ferreira de Faria. On that occasion, it was carrying 310 slaves from Benguela, only 279 of whom were still living when the vessel reached Pernambuco. During the 1822 voyage, commanding the same ship, Angelo Carneiro put most of the 629 slaves purchased on board in Luanda. Only 561 reached Pernambuco alive. Carneiro was Faria's business partner in at least one other ship and had a stake in other slave ships. In 1821, he co-owned the schooner *Feiticeira*, along with Elias Baptista da Silva, the former owner of the *Ermelinda*, but a few years later it belonged to Joaquim Ribeiro de Brito. On the voyage undertaken that year, the *Feiticeira* carried 255 captives from Luanda and the surrounding region, thirty-three of whom died during the Middle Passage. In 1822, according to the British, Carneiro shared ownership of the schooner *Velha de Dio* with his crony Francisco Antonio de Oliveira, later the Baron of Beberibe, who loaded a cargo of 280 slaves in Luanda, 254 of whom survived the crossing. Among many other business dealings with the slave trader Joaquim Ribeiro de Brito, Carneiro sold him the hull of the schooner *Maria Gertrudes* in Luanda. During eight of the voyages he is known to have made between 1818 and 1823, the commander of the Empire carried 2,823 captives, 351 (12.4 percent) of whose dead bodies were thrown to the sharks.[15]

We have been unable to find any information about Carneiro's slave-trading activities during the remainder of the 1820s and the following decade. However, it is abundantly clear that he did not give up the trade in human beings after 1823, as the allusion to his name in that newspaper in 1837 attests. Another indication is his investment in the *Ermelinda* and other ships in the following decade. Carneiro was named as the owner of the *Flor do Tejo*, a barque formerly Azevedinho's *Andorinha*, which in May 1841 landed 650 to 670 of the 720 slaves loaded in Angola on Catuama beach in Pernambuco. Four months later, the same ship left Recife with a crew of nineteen bound for Luanda, carrying forty-six casks of *cachaça* worth 413 pounds. Carneiro was also named as the owner of the 248-ton brig *Viajante Feliz* (Happy Traveler) —slave traders' names for their ships revealed a vile sense of humor—which set sail with a crew of twenty-seven on December 11 of that same year. The ship's manifest states that its destination was a Pacific port—Lima, Peru. The *Viajante Feliz* was actually bound for an Atlantic port, Benguela, where 730 slaves would be put aboard. They were offloaded on a beach south of Recife after a failed attempt to disembark in Bahia. This also indicates that the dealings of Pernambuco slave traders extended to other Brazilian provinces. Angelo Carneiro may have been the biggest slave trader operating north of Bahia. At least, Mr. Cowper, the British consul in Pernambuco, believed that he was "the most successful, and the most notorious slave dealer in northern Brazil, and every vessel which he sends to Africa is engaged in the slave trade."[16] Historian José Capela confirms Carneiro's reputation as a slave trade baron based on evidence from the other side of the Atlantic, when he says that the man was "the greatest slaver of his time in Luanda."[17]

And Angelo Carneiro still maintained his links with his homeland. While he lived in Recife, he collaborated actively with the Portuguese consulate, sending letters of credit as advance payment for expenses, even for ships from the Portuguese squadron that stopped in Recife. In 1848, he advanced funds for the maintenance of a brig and a schooner, both, ironically, involved in the suppression of the slave trade by Portuguese naval forces.

Like other slave traders, Angelo posed as philanthropist and regularly contributed money to help people affected by natural calamities in Portugal. The Portuguese crown rewarded these gestures by bestowing upon him the hereditary title of Viscount of Loures when he returned to his country after 1850.[18]

In 1841, Angelo Carneiro loaded the *Ermelinda* with twelve casks of spirits, six bundles containing 640 pieces of fabric, two horses, and a dismantled *berlinda* (a small four-wheeled carriage), totaling in value 9,756,410 réis. Since the fifteenth century, horses had been part of Portuguese trade with Upper Guinea—for military, ceremonial, and ostentatious use—and were exported more or less regularly to Angola as an integral part of the slave trade from at least the mid-1600s. In the following century, horses specifically from Pernambuco came to be considered the best for use in the Angolan climate, but it is unlikely that that reputation should have continued to influence the demand for those animals in the mid-nineteenth century. In Rufino's time, horses in Luanda were used to transport the city's elite, who were followed on foot by young slaves or pages who had to run to keep pace with the often rapid trot of the horse, holding onto its tail so as not to be left behind.[19]

Angelo Carneiro's carriage and two horses—which altogether were worth an astronomical 5,124,880 réis, 17 percent of the value of the entire cargo—had been ordered by the wealthy slave trader Arsénio Pompílio Pompeu de Carpo. Some time had passed since Carpo maintained business relations with the slave traders based in Pernambuco, for whom he had worked as a factor and facilitator with the Luanda authorities, whom he handled with dubious cordiality and fat bribes. One of his biographies, published in 1846 in Rio de Janeiro—where he had been active and left victims of his business deals—said that he began accumulating wealth with the help of none other than Angelo Francisco Carneiro. Carpo had spent long periods in several parts of Brazil. One of them may have been Recife, which he visited along with his wife in 1829, prosaically as a passenger on a slave ship that left Angola with 304 Africans on board, only nine of whom died in the Middle Passage.[20]

About a decade later, Arsénio Carpo was back in Angola, having returned there from Brazil in 1837 to live the life of a prosperous slave trader. Regarding carriages, when he was in Luanda in 1841, Dr. Tams observed that the only ones in that city were "just the governor's small carriage and those owned by two or three private parties who could enjoy that commodity."[21] Arsénio de Carpo was one of them. He already owned several carriages and he wanted to add the *berlinda* brought over by the *Ermelinda* to his fleet. He perfectly fits Jill Dias's judgment of Luanda's elite slave traders as conspicuous consumers with a lifestyle that displayed a penchant for exhibitionism.[22] In Carpo's case, the ostentation was even more significant because he was a mere nouveau riche, unlike those who belonged to the old slave-trading lineages. Historian João Pedro Marques explains the slaver's obsession with exhibitionism as a pathological idiosyncrasy and even symptomatic of megalomania.[23]

But the old business associates Carneiro and Carpo did not just deal in luxury goods. The barrels of spirits that the slaver from Pernambuco put aboard the *Ermelinda*—products more typical of the slave trade than carriages—were also for the slaver from Luanda. The recipient of Angelo Carneiro's textiles was a famous slaver, also based in in Luanda, the good-looking, well-educated Anna Francisca Ferreira Obertally, a woman of mixed race *(mulata)*. Both she and Carpo were probably the main suppliers of the slaves that the *Ermelinda* would pick up in Angola. Commander Carneiro's goods would be the main bargaining currency, since he owned 32 percent of the ship's cargo, followed by that of the clerk Domingos, with his modest 9 percent.[24]

Unfortunately, the *Ermelinda*'s records do not allow us to ascertain the value of all the merchandise on board. The most eye-catching numbers are the 191 casks, nine half-casks, and twenty-two barrels of various sizes, all full of spirits, which confirms the historic preeminence of *jeribita* as a product used as barter currency for slaves in the Angolan market. The cargo also contained other types of goods traditionally used in the slave trade: sixty-three rolls of tobacco and 209 crates of cigars, eleven bundles and three crates of cloth, and twenty-six pieces of

Table 11.1 **Breakdown of merchandise aboard the *Ermelinda*, 1841 (in mil-réis)**

Value	Shippers	Total	%
<400	10	2,688.00	9.0
400–1000	13	8,435.00	27.5
>1000	8	19,327.00	63.5
Total	31	30,450.00	100.0
Angelo Carneiro	biggest	9,756.41	32.0
Rufino José Maria		598.33	2.0
Bento Mesquita	smallest	92.96	0.3

denim. Based on the available data, we have only managed to calculate the value of just a few of those goods.

Spirits were once again in the lead. Each cask was worth 55,340 réis, altogether totaling 10,569,940 réis, roughly one-third of the ship's cargo. Each bundle of cloth cost 277,000 réis, totaling over three million réis. A crate of fabric was declared at 361,721 réis, totaling 1,085,160 réis. As a result, we have calculated a total value of nearly fifteen million réis in fabric and spirits, practically half the value of the *Ermelinda*'s cargo. If we deduct Carneiro's carriage, an exceptionally expensive item and unusual for the slave trade, the spirits, cloth, and tobacco made up somewhere between 65 and 70 percent of the cargo's worth.[25]

12

The *Ermelinda* Goes to Sea

On June 21 1841, the *Ermelinda* left Recife, bound for São Paulo de Luanda on the Angolan coast. This was not the first time it had sailed to that port. The ship had visited it previously, possibly several times, under a different name, the *União*, rigged as a schooner. This time, the voyage got off to a bad start. After twenty-three days at sea, when reaching 19°5' latitude south and 38°48' longitude east, a serious leak was found in the hull. It was a sign that the ship was aging and had not been properly repaired in Pernambuco, although a great deal of money had been spent on repairs before it departed. Two hand pumps failed to remove the water from the ship's hold, leading Captain Joaquim Antonio Coutinho to call in "the top men in the crew" to consult them about the damage, with the passengers as witnesses. He then decided to head for the first port that was better prepared to handle the emergency.

As a result, the *Ermelinda* hobbled into the Bay of All Saints in Salvador, Bahia, where it cast anchor on July 19, 1841, to undergo repairs. As soon as he arrived, the captain had a document drafted—a "letter of protest to whosoever's jurisdiction it may be" —explaining the decision to stop in Bahia. That document was required to protect him in case he was sued for damages in the future by the owners of the ship and its cargo. The letter of protest was also written into the ship's log. The following day, the captain, helmsman, pilot, and three sailors, as well as eleven passengers, signed the letter in the presence of the municipal judge of Salvador, Luis Maria Moniz Barreto, in his home. When asked, they all confirmed the captain's story and the urgent need for the repairs to safeguard the lives and goods on board.[1]

Two days later, experts inspected the vessel and confirmed the damage. Here, particularly for the seafaring reader, is the technical diagnosis recorded by the official city clerk:

> ... going on to examine the said Barque, they found the bolts completely ruined, and the planks fitted in place, and unable to continue

The Story of Rufino. João José Reis, Flávio dos Santos Gomes, and Marcus J. M. de Carvalho, Translated by H. Sabrina Gledhill, Oxford University Press (2020) © Oxford University Press.
DOI: 10.1093/oso/9780190224363.001.0001

the voyage, needing to bring in new planks and so that it should not happen again, it is necessary to use dowels to reinforce the bolts; likewise the entire ship would require caulking outside and in the gunwales as well as other details so as not to require further repairs, which all told is estimated at six hundred and fifty thousand réis for the fees of carpenters and caulkers, wood, burlap, nails, tar, and other materials necessary for such repairs.[2]

On July 30, another judge, Theodoro Praxedes Froes, issued an order stating that the captain had taken the right decision to make the forced stop for repairs ten days earlier.

The *Ermelinda* spent a few weeks in the City of Salvador while its hull was being mended. The cost of the repairs (materials and manpower), transportation, inspection, drafting and registration of the letters of protest, and expenses with the crew totaled 844,754 réis. Rufino received 100 réis per day to cover his expenses, the cost of his "rations," totaling 1,800 réis for eighteen days' anchorage in that city—half the pay he would receive as daily wages at sea.[3] Given the amounts paid for the daily on-land expenses of the captain/master (800 réis), the boatswain (400 réis) and the pilot (200 réis), they certainly ate better than the cook.[4]

There is no record of where Rufino stayed during that sojourn in the city where he had first set foot in Brazil twenty years earlier and spent eight years as a slave. He must have seen old acquaintances, and may even have visited his young master Francisco, who had traveled with him to Rio Grande do Sul and sold him there. His former master, the apothecary João Gomes, and his wife, had died four years before.

Life in the province of Bahia went on much as usual. During the time Rufino was there, and a little before and for some time afterward, one Braz Cardoso published an advertisement in a local newspaper seeking to purchase a female slave with "good habits" who could "cook and starch perfectly." He did not state a preference for a specific ethnic background. A dark-skinned mixed-race male slave was for sale. He was a carpenter and cabinetmaker, in addition to being "lazy." He was useless, at least according to his current master. There was also a Jeje man, "a very good blacksmith for sale," age twenty-eight, advertised along with "genuine *musgo* chocolate." Both were offered for sale at a shop on the docks, from where one could easily see the *Ermelinda* lying at anchor. Chocolate and slaves were merchandise, but the slave had a mind to think with and legs for fleeing. One day he would escape. Like the twenty-three-year old Creole tailor Luiz, "well known for being accustomed to asking for alms every Saturday for the lamp oil of Our Lady of Aparecida, erected in Pelourinho Plaza," where slaves used to be punished by whipping on a pillory (*pelourinho*). The devout slave burned whale oil for the saint, and must have asked her to protect him by shining a light on his escape routes.

Of all the Africans, the *ladino* slaves were the best at fleeing. One of them, also named Luiz, about twenty years old, who "looks Creole," escaped wearing a ragged white shirt and an old pair of trousers, limping because he had jiggers in his feet, and bearing a recent scar on his face—a husk of a man who had nevertheless retained his strength of will. Luiz also took the millet in which he sold the bread baked by his owner, a baker, who thought him "very *ladino*, lazy and crafty" for wanting to be rid of his master. Another African, Joaquim, this time from Angola, was about sixteen years old. He spoke "a little more intelligibly" and therefore was "*ladino*, seemingly Creole." He had been on the run for over six months, so the reward was high: 200,000 réis, the same amount as the salary paid to *Ermelinda*'s captain. Some of those escapees, among others, could have run into Rufino in the City of Bahia.[5]

The cook did not stay long in Salvador, which, in some ways, never changed. On August 6, 1841, after eighteen days of repairs, the *Ermelinda* resumed its voyage to Luanda. Unfortunately, we have not been able to find the ship's log for the *Ermelinda*. Assuming it has survived, it would have enabled us to follow its voyage before and after it left Bahia. Even if we had been able to locate it, it would not be a true record because slavers' logs often contained false information about their routes and incidents along the way to hide evidence of the illegal trade from the police, customs officials, and, above all, the British, who were making strenuous efforts to suppress the slave trade in the South Atlantic. However, the ship's log could either confirm or add more substance to information found in other sources.

In any case, there is no record of the *Ermelinda*'s voyage until it was intercepted off the coast of Luanda (9° 20' latitude South and 9° 40' longitude East) on October 27, 1841, by the British brig *Water Witch*. Armed with ten cannons, that vessel was attached to the Royal Navy's station in Luanda. There were three more ships assigned to that station, the *Brisk*, the *Fantôme*, and the *Bonetta*— too few to guard Angola's long coastline, according to the Royal navy's report to Parliament. The same report complained about the difficult task of suppressing the slave trade along its main artery because the "slave trade vessels are well known to be built expressly for speed; they are remarkable for their sailing qualities," in contrast with the British ten-gun brigs, which were "proverbial in the service for the dullness of their sailing." The Royal Navy brigs were not just slow of sail. Small, with stifling accommodations that were unhealthy for the tropics, they were known as "floating biers" But it was one of those coffin ships that managed to intercept the *Ermelinda*, which was not one of the fast slavers more typical of that time.[6]

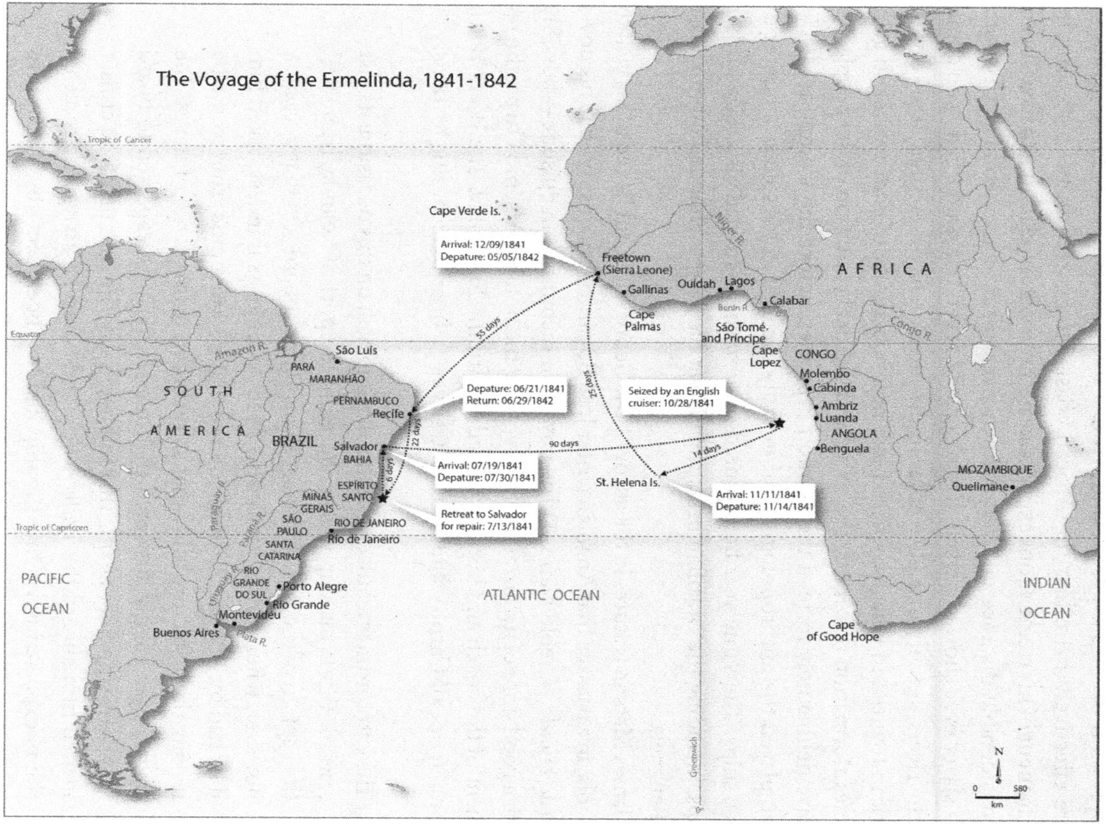
The Voyage of the Ermelinda, 1841-1842
Tropic of Cancer
Cape Verde Is.
Arrival: 12/09/1841
Depature: 05/05/1842
Freetown
(Sierra Leone)
Gallinas
Ouidah
Lagos
Calabar
Niger R.
Benin R.
A F R I C A
Cape
Palmas
São Tomé
and Principe
Cape
Lopez
CONGO
Congo R.
Molembo
Cabinda
Ambriz
Luanda
ANGOLA
Benguela
Seized by an English
cruiser: 10/28/1841
Equator
São Luís
PARÁ
MARANHÃO
Amazon R.
S O U T H
A M E R I C A
BRAZIL
PERNAMBUCO
Recife
Depature: 06/21/1841
Return: 06/29/1842
55 days
25 days
22 days
90 days
14 days
6 days
Salvador
BAHIA
Arrival: 07/19/1841
Depature: 07/30/1841
St. Helena Is.
Arrival: 11/11/1841
Depature: 11/14/1841
MOZAMBIQUE
Quelimane
ESPÍRITO
SANTO
MINAS
GERAIS
Retreat to Salvador
for repair: 7/13/1841
Tropic of Capricorn
SÃO
PAULO
RIO DE JANEIRO
Rio de Janeiro
SANTA
CATARINA
RIO
GRANDE
DO SUL
Porto Alegre
Rio Grande
Montevideu
Buenos Aires
Plata R.
Paraguay R.
Paraná R.
Uruguay R.
PACIFIC
OCEAN
ATLANTIC OCEAN
INDIAN
OCEAN
Cape
of Good Hope
Greenwich
N
0
580
km

The ship that captured the *Ermelinda* was commanded by Lieutenant Henry James Matson. An active participant in the British anti-slave trade campaign in the South Atlantic, he was something of a legend in those waters. Matson served four years aboard the *Water Witch*, capturing forty slave ships. He gave a statement as an expert witness before the British parliamentary committee on the suppression of the slave trade and wrote a book asserting that British cruisers were effectively patrolling the African coast. He boasted in his testimony in Parliament of his tremendous experience in those waters, claiming to have "been a considerable distance up every known river, from Sierra Leone as far south as a slaver ever showed herself, having passed several days and nights on some of the rivers, seventy or eighty miles in the interior, having visited many dozen African towns and villages, where I lost no opportunity of endeavoring to gain some information respecting the social and political condition of the people, — I have deliberately formed the opinion expressed before the Committee."[7] He even played the anthropologist, but he truly excelled in his role as a hunter of slave ships. The same year he captured the *Ermelinda* he had also seized other ships, including the Brazilian brigantine *Dona Elena*, apprehended off the coast of Benguela.

James Matson features in the account Dr. Georg Tams published of his visit to Angola, in a passage that Angolan writer José Eduardo Agualusa used in his novel *Nação crioula* (Creole Nation). The physician recounted an episode—possibly with a good dose of fiction as well—involving the notable Arsénio Carpo, the recipient of the coach and horses shipped aboard the *Ermelinda*. The *Water Witch* captured one of Carpo's ships with 400 slaves on board. According to Tams:

> The extraordinary audacity of this Arsénio had, on this occasion, its just reward. While his ship was anchored in the port of Loanda, he invited the captain of the British cruiser *Water-witch* aboard. On that occasion, however, when lunch was almost over, Arsénio, as if in jest, asked him if he had by any chance been advised that his [Arsénio's] ship would be leaving the coast, probably that same night, with a cargo of slaves. The Englishman calmly answered that in a few days he expected to board that same ship once again. That following day, the captain of the cruiser invited him aboard the *Water-witch*; and when he arrived he received the unexpected news that his ship had just been sent [by Matson] to Sierra Leone.[8]

Tams was probably unaware that there was nothing unusual about that dinner, because Carpo, with his engaging personality and mastery of Matson's language, was engaged in all sorts of business dealings with the British. In fact, since 1839 he had been the contractor who supplied coal to one or two steamships employed by the Royal Navy to suppress the slave trade. The slave trader's relations with the British establishment went even deeper, to the point where he felt free to begin a correspondence with the foreign minister, Lord Aberdeen, about ways of combating the slave trade and developing legitimate trade. In fact, Aberdeen—the man who, later in that decade, decided to blockade Brazilian ports to force an end to the slave trade—held him in high esteem.[9]

In this context, if it actually occurred, the episode Tams recounted might have been nothing but a friendly wager, this time won by Matson, who was reputed to be one of the most active officers in the war on the slave trade.[10] We have not found other sources that confirm the details of this story, but one of Arsénio Carpo's ships was in fact captured by the British—probably by James Matson—in April 1841, a few months before the *Ermelinda* fell into his hands. The schooner *Euro* was taken to the island of St. Helena to be tried by the Vice-Admiralty court. The ship had sailed from Rio de Janeiro and put captives aboard in Ambriz, a slaving port north of Luanda. It had 308 slaves in its hold (not 400, as Tams indicated), of whom just 272 reached St. Helena alive. Most of them died while in the hands of the British.[11]

Tams wrote that, in 1841 alone, the *Water Witch*, *Fantôme*, and *Brisk* had helped capture thirty-three ships, from whose holds they are said to have rescued 3,427 captives. Those numbers may have been inflated, as we will see, but not the rest of the account. According to the physician from Hamburg, the captives were "corralled in a horrible manner" in those ships. He also commented that one of the slavers, whose name he failed to mention, carried 105 children younger than eight years old, "piled up like bales of cotton"; the other, the brigantine *Corisco*, was captured by the *Water Witch* with 392 slaves "stacked" in it, most of whom "looked like living skeletons, most of them suffering from smallpox and scabies." Matson dispatched them to St. Helena and is said to have written on that occasion, "With great trepidation I am sending an officer and some men aboard that lazar-house." Since the eighteenth century, when the British became the greatest slave traders in the Atlantic, they had coined the term "marine lazar house" to refer to slave ships for their own ships. That is how they expressed the high death rate aboard those vessels, for which the Portuguese had an equally funereal name: *tumbeiro* ("floating tomb").[12]

The capture of another ship mentioned by Tams, the *Corisco*, is reported in Foreign Office documents. That vessel, which weighed sixty tons and was carrying a piece of artillery, left Rio de Janeiro and embarked slaves on the coast of Angola, from where it set sail on August 3, 1841. Seized twelve days later, the *Corisco* was taken to St. Helena by Matson's crew with 382 captives on board, of whom 366 left it alive. Ten died en route and the remainder perished while in quarantine. The dead were no more than 4.2 percent of those embarked as slaves, a number that would have been much higher if the ship had managed to cross the Atlantic on its way back to Brazil. The voyage would have taken no less than a month, with nearly 400 slaves occupying a maximum of 150 square meters. The reader can estimate the traumatic experience they endured on board. British data confirms Tams's observation that most of the cargo consisted of children, who made up nearly 60 percent of the survivors.[13]

The *Water Witch* was involved in an even worse tragedy off the coast of Ambriz, "where the slave trade absorbed all interests," according to Tams. A few weeks before the physician arrived there, a ship laden with 500 captives was pursued by the British cruiser, and its captain ran the ship aground. There were no survivors among the Africans in the hold. While their captives drowned, the captain and his crew escaped in boats after firing at their pursuers, who were in the launch sent by the *Water Witch*. Some British sailors were wounded. The captain of the slave ship took refuge aboard Tams's vessel, the *Camões*, whose captain hid him from the British, preventing them from arresting him in flagrante. The slave-ship captain then sailed as a passenger aboard the *Camões* as far as Luanda. The human cargo that had drowned in Ambriz apparently belonged to Anna Obertally, the agent of the *Ermelinda's* main shipper, the respectable Commander Angelo Carneiro. Soon after the incident in Ambriz, Obertally put the helm of another ship in the hands of that same cruel captain.[14]

British launches like the one we have just seen in action made up a significant part of the fleet that was combating the slave trade. They were small, fast sailboats with a cannon in the prow. Each launch was linked to a mother ship—the *Water Witch*, for example—from which it was dispatched to patrol the shallower coastal waters and sail upriver to pursue African slave traders' canoes and locate the barracoons where they kept their African captives.

Georg Tams described another episode involving the launch from the brig that captured *Ermelinda*. Soon after his ship anchored off Ambriz, the physician saw "a vessel with dark sails," a somewhat sinister boat that was rapidly approaching and which they soon saw was flying the British flag atop its mast. "That vessel," he wrote, "was one of the large war launches sent by the *Water Witch* to patrol [the coastal waters]; it was on its way to join the ship stationed off Luanda at the end of a four-week cruise," he explained regarding the routine British patrols. The launch carried forty armed sailors aboard, four of them black, as well as an officer and a doctor. In addition to hunting slavers, they also treated both natives and Europeans arrogantly, as if they were all criminals. Tams's ship was boarded and carefully searched for signs of any intent to engage in the slave trade. The British sailors were only doing their job, of course. However, Tams accused them of being drunken louts who not only boarded slave ships but confiscated other people's liquor for their own use. On land, the same men who had boarded his ship, according to Tams, attempted to loot gin from a tavern. However, that

Figure 12.1 English boats preparing to board and take over a slave ship. From *Le Magasin Pittoresque* (1844).

establishment was defended by its slaves, who managed to send the Englishmen packing.[15]

Based on the writings of the traveler from Hamburg, we have been able to sketch out some aspects of the activities on the African coast of the ship that captured the *Ermelinda*. Although it was written by a critic of the slave trade who sought to promote legitimate commerce between Europe and Africa, many aspects of his account can be confirmed by other sources. Rufino was involved in a business where brutality was the norm, and we have just presented shocking new evidence of that. That, in short, was the world in which Rufino moved and helped recreate every time he crossed the Atlantic.

13

The Equipment Act

All of the incidents involving the *Water Witch* recounted in the previous chapter took place very close to the time when the British cruiser captured the *Ermelinda*. However, in all of them the Royal Navy pursued and seized ships laden with slaves. This was not the case with the *Ermelinda* or many other Brazilian vessels captured during that period.

Rufino's ship was apprehended in the afternoon of October 28, 1841, nearly four months after it left Recife, under the accusation of being *equipped* to transport slaves. It was therefore considered a "good prize," according to the concept arising from the anti-slave-trade treaty signed by the Brazilian and British governments in 1826. However, Britain had unilaterally enacted the law that was now being used to confiscate the ship. It was the Equipment Act of August 1839, also known as the Palmerston Act, named after Henry John Temple, 3rd Viscount Palmerston, better known as Lord Palmerston, the British Foreign Affairs Minister who conceived it. The Brazilian government did not recognize that law.

The Equipment Act had the immediate aim of charging ships sailing under the Portuguese flag with the crime of engaging in the slave trade after the British government had made numerous attempts to force Portugal to sign an anti-slave-trade treaty to replace the 1817 convention banning the trade north of the Equator. The Portuguese were reluctant because they feared it would conflict with the interests of residents of its African territories. There was even a fear that, in certain circles, the local elite might emulate Brazil and declare independence. In 1823, for example, there was a movement in Benguela, with repercussions in Luanda, to unite that colony with independent Brazil. This is because, as the historian José Capela observed, the Angolan slavers' true dependence "lay in their relations with Brazil and had relatively little or nothing to do with Portugal."[1] In other words, the slavers' dealings in Luanda, Benguela, Mozambique, and other ports may not have been determinant factors, but they weighed heavily against any decision on Portugal's part to restrain the slave trade. However, the

The Story of Rufino. João José Reis, Flávio dos Santos Gomes, and Marcus J. M. de Carvalho, Translated by H. Sabrina Gledhill, Oxford University Press (2020) © Oxford University Press.
DOI: 10.1093/oso/9780190224363.001.0001

Portuguese government's official claim was that the problem lay with Brazil, not in Africa, and much less in Portugal. In his analysis of the British law of 1839, Viscount de Sá da Bandeira, who had been the Portuguese Foreign Affairs Minister until shortly before, wrote that the "only way to suppress the Slave Trade is the total abolition of slavery in the Americas and other countries where it exists, and that import slaves." By the Americas, he primarily meant Brazil and Cuba, which were practically the only importers of African slaves in that region at that time. The British certainly did not think like Sá da Bandeira, because they believed that their maritime might could discourage and even completely extinguish the slave trade with or without the blessing of diplomacy. There was much less pressure to abolish slavery, so that would be left for a future stage.[2]

The British overlooked international laws in the name of combating the infamous trade. In the meantime, according to a British historian, "The legality of so drastic a measure might be disputable, but its efficacy was not."[3] In fact, a large number of Brazilian slavers fell into the net of the 1839 act. Ruling the seven seas since Napoleon's defeat, and with its hegemony virtually unchallenged, Britain's aggressive diplomacy may have reached its height at that time. As historian David Eltis suggests, it was a short step from arrogance to chauvinism. Years later, Lord Palmerston wrote in a private letter, "The Portuguese are . . . the lowest in the moral scale and Brazilians are degenerate Portuguese, demoralized by slavery and slave trade, and all the degrading and corrupting influences connected with both."[4]

Figures 13.1a and 13.1b Lord Palmerston and Viscount de Sá da Bandeira. From www.gutenberg.org.images and Biblioteca Nacional de Portugal.

The suppression of the slave trade, a mission with an indisputable moral basis, gave the Royal Navy a pretext to occupy or blockade African ports, seize ships, attack and burn trading posts, and threaten local chiefs. On one occasion, in 1851, Palmerston wrote to a subordinate on the ground that he should make the pro-slave-trade Oba (king) of Lagos understand that his kingdom was located on the coast, and the British ruled the nearby waves with their ships and cannons.[5] That sums it up well. Although the repertoire of threats varied, the people who received that treatment were not limited to African potentates. To varying degrees, they also included Brazilian and Portuguese heads of state. The fact is that the suppression of the slave trade gave Her British Majesty's government an excellent ideological instrument for justifying its imperial stance with states on three continents. At the same time, British belligerence and disdain for international law—and now the Equipment Act, an important factor—ended up serving the interests of slavers who, by denouncing them, also acquired their own instrument in the political disputes, both in Brazil and Portugal. In both countries, few dared openly and directly to defend the slave trade, but it became commonplace in the press and Parliament to protest against the arrogance of the Royal Navy's imposition of its government's views. The nationalist, jingoist, Anglophobic narrative gained more and more supporters, but the British did not give a fig.[6]

The Equipment Act primarily aimed to restrict the slave trade to Brazil. However, as we have seen, Brazilian ships often unfurled the Portuguese flag to confound the Royal Navy. The law defined the equipment used in the slave trade, much of which was already covered by the Anglo-Brazilian treaty of 1826. The boxed excerpt that follows is from the relevant chapter of the act that served, whether or not the Portuguese flag was flown, to justify the capture of many Brazilian ships, including the *Ermelinda*. According to that ship's captor, James Matson, it was only after the Equipment Act "that the maritime police of Great Britain had any real powers to suppress the Slave Trade." Accordingly, between 1840 and 1842, the Royal Navy seized over 200 ships, 192 of which were condemned.[7]

Chapter Iv Of The Equipment Act, August 24, 1839[8]

IV. And be it enacted, That every such Vessel shall be subject to Seizure, Detention, and Condemnation, under any such Order or Authority, if in the Equipment of such Vessel there shall be found any of the Things hereinafter mentioned; namely,

First – Hatches with open Gratings, instead of the close Hatches which are usual in Merchant Vessels:

Secondly – Divisions or Bulkheads in the Hold or on Deck more numerous than are necessary for Vessels engaged in lawful Trade:

Thirdly – Spare Plank fitted for being laid down as a Second or Slave Deck:

Fourthly – Shackles, Bolts, or Handcuffs:

Fifthly – A larger Quantity of Water in Casks or in Tanks than is requisite for the Consumption of the Crew of the Vessel as a Merchant Vessel:

Sixthly – An extraordinary Number of Water Casks, or of other Vessels for holding Liquid, unless the Master shall produce a Certificate from the Custom House at the Place from which he cleared outwards, stating that a sufficient Security had been given by the Owners of such Vessel that such extra Quantity of Casks or of other Vessels should only be used for the Reception of Palm Oil, or for other Purposes of lawful Commerce:

Seventhly – A greater Quantity of Mess Tubs or Kids than are requisite for the Use of the Crew of the Vessel as a Merchant Vessel:

Eighthly – A Boiler of an unusual Size, and larger than requisite for the Use of the Crew of the Vessel as a Merchant Vessel, or more than One Boiler of the ordinary Size:

Ninthly – An extraordinary Quantity either of Rice or of the Flour of *Brazil*, Manioc, or Cassada [sic], commonly called Farinha, of Maize or of *Indian* Corn, or of any other Article of Food whatever beyond what might probably be requisite for the Use of the Crew; such Rice, Flour, Maize, *Indian* Corn, or other Article of Food not being entered on the Manifest as Part of the Cargo for Trade:

Tenthly – A Quantity of Mats or Matting larger than is necessary for the Use of the Crew of the Vessel as a Merchant Vessel:

Any One or more of these several Circumstances, if proved, shall be considered as *prima facie* Evidence of the actual Employment of the Vessel in the Transport of Negroes or others, for the Purpose of consigning them to Slavery, and the Vessel and Cargo shall thereupon be condemned to the Crown, unless it be established by satisfactory Evidence on the Part of the Master or Owners, that such Vessel was, at the Time of her Detention or Capture, employed on some legal Pursuit, and that such of the several Things above enumerated as were found on board of such Vessel at the Time of her Detention, or had been put on board on the Voyage on which, when captured, such Vessel was proceeding, were needed for legal Purposes on that particular Voyage.

The Equipment Act explains the increase in the number of slave ships captured by British cruisers *before slaves were embarked*. Soon there was a substantial decline in the number of captives rescued at sea—from 7,188 in 1839 to 2,364 in 1840, when the law came into effect. However, it did not take long for that figure to rise again and vary until the Brazilian slave trade was definitively abolished in 1850, reaching an average of nearly 5,000 in the last five years before the British law came into effect, when there was a new boom in slave trading activities. Therefore, the number of slaves rescued reflected the traffickers capacity to adapt to different circumstances and break through the British blockade to embark human cargo. In other words, the increased number of captives rescued reflected the increase in the number of slaves. But that story comes after the capture of the *Ermelinda*. Let us focus on that time.[9]

The year when the *Ermelinda* was seized, 1841, the British and Brazilian Mixed Commission for the Suppression of the Slave Trade in Sierra Leone tried and convicted ten Brazilian ships. Each of their stories broadens our understanding of the slaving business after the enforcement of the Equipment Act began, situating the incident involving the *Ermelinda* in the context of the tougher British policy on suppressing the slave trade. The capture of those ships is recounted in a report written in late 1841 by Michael Melville, the British judge on the British and Brazilian Mixed Commission Courts in Sierra Leone, which sums up the circumstances of their capture, the evidence found, and other details justifying their conviction for engaging in the illegal commerce. None of the ships was seized with slaves on board, but in the judgment of the British authorities all of them were equipped to embark captives. Three ships sailed from Bahia and seven from Rio de Janeiro, but two of the latter also stopped in Bahia before crossing the Atlantic. They may have done so to take on a load of tobacco, Bahia's main product used in the trade with Africa.

Once condemned, each ship was auctioned off and the money shared between the Brazilian and British governments. The sale price varied greatly, depending on the size and condition of the vessel and the value of the merchandise it carried. Generally speaking, because there was a small number of bidders, ships and merchandise ended up being sold at very low prices. The British physician Harrison Rankin observed in 1834 that the money invested in their purchase could often be recovered in the freight charges for a single voyage to England.[10] That said, the following is a summary of incidents involving British cruisers and Brazilian slave ships in the South Atlantic in the early 1840s.

We begin with the *Feliz Ventura* (Good Luck), a 123-ton brigantine owned by Francisco José da Silva, an active slaver since the period before the trade was first banned in 1831. The slave ship sailed from Rio de Janeiro in September 1840, with the stated destination of São Tomé and Príncipe, under the command of José Mariano da Costa e Silva, with a crew of thirteen men. It stopped in Bahia, where it took on a load of tobacco and *cachaça* before continuing on its voyage to Africa on the 22nd of October. It also carried textiles, gunpowder, muskets, iron bars, sheets of lead, and glass beads, the latter being greatly in demand in African communities for personal adornment and ritual use. The ship was captured on November 29 by the Royal Navy brig *Rolla* in Cape Mount, off the coast of Liberia, 1,200 nautical miles (2,222 km) from the destination recorded in its official papers. The cargo of the *Feliz Ventura*, like that of the *Ermelinda*, belonged to several shippers from Rio and Bahia, including a sailor who embarked seven barrels of biscuits and one of preserves. The captain himself and his first mate shipped tobacco and *cachaça*. Three African freedmen were traveling as "passengers." Actually they had boarded the vessel in Bahia, after being expelled by the provincial government with an order to be put ashore in any West African port.

The *Feliz Ventura* arrived in Sierra Leone on December 10, and a month later was convicted on suspicion of intending to engage in the slave trade, because one hundred tin measures, or cups, were found on board, presumably to provide the captives with food and drink on the return voyage. But the main piece of evidence, as with most of the ships seized without slaves on board, was the presence of barrels capable of holding 1,433 gallons of water (473 gallons would have been enough for the passengers and crew), a larger than necessary kitchen apparatus—a cabouse "lined with tin, and provided with a grating whereon a slave boiler could be used"—two wooden bowls large enough to hold six to seven gallons "adapted for feeding slaves"; large quantities of cassava flour and dried meat, "in addition to as much biscuits and beef as the crew could possibly use," according to the British commissioner Michael Melville. Other factors taken into consideration when condemning the ship were ongoing preparations to build a "slave-deck" as well as the wages paid to the crew, which were considered exorbitant: 16,600 réis per head (much less, by the way, than what the crew of the *Ermelinda* received, 40,000 réis). The *Feliz Ventura* was judged a good prize in the decision handed down on January 11, 1841. The ship and its cargo were sold at auction for £911.[11]

The 100-ton schooner *Belona* was the property of Manoel Antonio Ferreira da Silva, a merchant from the city of Rio de Janeiro. Commanded by Francisco Pedro Ferreira, the *Belona* was captured off the coast of Angola with "an unusually large cooking apparatus, and an amount of provisions [...] much more than requisite for the use of the crew."[12] It was not the ship's first slaving voyage, having plied that route at least three times prior to 1840, according to available records. On one such voyage, in 1838, it sailed from Rio de Janeiro to the Angolan coast, where it embarked 416 slaves who were kept in a hold measuring less than 260 square meters. As a result, forty-two of them died during the Middle Passage to Bahia.[13] Flying the Portuguese flag and bearing that country's passport, as on its previous voyages, the *Belona* left Rio de Janeiro on November 7, 1840, claimed by its owner to be a whaling ship. According to the documents found on board, the whale oil the ship produced was to be sold in Bahia and Lisbon. This was no doubt written for the Royal Navy's benefit—or just *"para inglês ver"* (literally, "for the English to see"), as the saying went. The captain claimed that ill winds had blown him directly onto the coast of Angola, making him cross the entire Atlantic in an easterly direction! His shipboard diary had become a fictional .tale

"These excuses," wrote a skeptical English commissioner "appeared in the form of a series of very lengthy protests, which set forth in great form and prolixity, that gale after gale of winds sprung up forced them away their intended

Figures 13.2a and 13.2b The capture of slave ships, a constant theme of the abolitionist campaign. From *The Illustrated London News*, vol. 17 (Dec. 14, 1850) and *The Illustrated London News*, vol. 36 (April 28, 1860).

course, and that on one occasion when they had actually harpooned a whale, another gale came on which forced them to allow the said whale to escape carrying off all their fishing tackle." It was therefore decided that the *Belona* should sail to the closest port, "which proved, conveniently, to be Angola," said the commissioner with heavy irony. There, the ship ended up being captured by the *Fantôme*. Confiscated evidence of intent to engage in the slave trade included barrels large enough to hold 5,400 gallons of water, twenty-eight tin measures and mugs, and a 62-gallon cauldron. In the pantry, they found a large quantity of cassava flour, dried meat, and beans, much more than needed for use by the crew. The prize was condemned on January 11, 1841, and sold for just £307, probably because the ship was in poor condition and its cargo of little value, if any. It is also possible that the *Belona* was being used as bait, another ruse the slave traders used to distract the British by sending out a worthless vessel carrying little or no cargo while the real slave ship was lying safely at anchor, waiting to be supplied with slaves.[14]

The brigantine *Nova Inveja* (New Envy), which sailed from Rio de Janeiro, was a real slave ship. Captained by Francisco Antonio de Oliveira and owned by Antonio Fernandes Coelho, the *Nova Inveja* was captured by Her Majesty's sloop *Persian* on January 20, 1841, at the entrance to the port of Cabinda, located north of Angola, another major source of slaves sent to Brazil.[15] Its officially declared destination was São Tomé, where it was supposed to engage in a modest trade in salt, urzella, wax, and ivory, aims carefully planted in letters to supposed consignees and the captain. Large quantities of food and water were found on board (maize, cassava flour, and biscuits). Among other suspicious arrangements, it also had a "hatchway unlawfully fitted," meaning that it was grated and enlarged, which allowed more air to enter the hold while preventing the captives from reaching the deck. The brigantine was condemned on March 2, 1841, and sold at auction for the goodly sum of £2,422, which indicates that it was a very fine ship carrying valuable cargo.[16]

The schooner *Bom Fim,* meaning literally *good end*—referring to the resurrection of Christ, a common, devout name for slave ships for obvious reasons—also sailed from the port of Rio de Janeiro, helmed by José Pinto de Araujo. The British commissioner described its owner, José Bernardino de Sá, as "notoriously engaged in the slave trade," and he actually had dedicated himself to that business for more than a decade.[17] There is data that indicates that he organized fifty slaving voyages between 1829 and 1851. On nineteen of them, carried out between 1829 and 1840, his ships disembarked 9,164 slaves, and 793 died during the Middle Passage—a massacre. On one of those voyages, in 1839, 667 slaves were crammed into the hold of the brigantine *Espardate,* resulting in less than 7.75 square inches per person, possibly less than six square inches for some. Sixty-seven perished.[18]

The documents for the *Bom Fim*, which was seized in 1840 state that the purpose of its voyage was to trade in São Tomé and ports in southern Africa, for which purpose the ship was laden with cloth and spirits (*jeribita*). It also carried large quantities of cassava flour, beans, dried meat, and water barrels, and had suspicious "divisions" on deck. According to the British report, "[t]here were several consignees for the bale goods and spirits, but the bill of laden did not appoint any place of delivery; neither was there a letter on board for anyone of those gentlemen." The *Bom Fim* ended up on the coast of Cabinda instead of São Tomé, once again due to bad weather and ill winds, as the captain claimed in a letter of protest dated November 22, 1840. It was captured there two months later by the *Persian*, pronounced guilty on March 13, 1841, and sold for £716.[19]

The schooner *Juliana*, commanded by Quirino Antonio, had made a profitable voyage the previous year. In Bahia in late October 1840, it had disembarked 330 of the 367 slaves put on board alive at Ouidah, the slave port in the kingdom of Dahomey where Francisco Félix de Souza, the famous Chachá, and his sons controlled a good deal of the trade with Brazil.[20] The ship was soon sent back to the same African port by its owner, Joaquim Rodrigues Pinto, with a new captain, Daniel Coelho. Its manifest stated that it was sailing to Fayal Island in the Azores, but on February 12, 1841, the brigantine *Buzzard* captured it far from its destination, off the coast of Ouidah. The captain of the *Juliana*'s explanation for its presence in such suspicious waters was, according to Melville, "the invariable excuse, in such cases, of the currents, calms, and contrary winds having set the vessel towards this coast"; and the reason why the vessel was preparing to cast anchor in Ouidah was said to be a lack of provisions. The first excuse, according to Melville, was "unprobable," and the second, "untrue," because sufficient provisions for the crew were found on board. Evidence of slave trading included a deck prepared to receive captives, barrels holding up to 4,640 gallons of water, two large cauldrons, and "a large quantity" of cassava flour, maize, and beans. The explanation given by the captain was that the equipment and provisions were to be used by free immigrants traveling from the Azores to Brazil, but the Court of the Mixed Commission was not convinced. The *Juliana* was condemned on April 6, 1841, resulting in the booty of £235.[21]

The Brazilian brig *Orozimbo* left the port of Rio de Janeiro in September 1840. Helmed by Matias José de Carvalho, it was bound for Luanda and Benguela. The ship's name was probably an allusion to gold (*oro*, in Spanish) and *zimbo*, the shells used as currency along the entire West African coast, known in other parts as cowries. The *Orozimbo* was captured when en route to Cabinda or a neighboring port, although its papers stated that its final destination was Montevideo, Uruguay, as it was supposed to be on a return voyage to the Americas. The evidence presented to justify its capture included the usual suspects: too much food, large water barrels, and a deck prepared to receive slaves, as well as (and this was new) "a large quantity of mats suitable as substitutes for the prohibited second or Slave deck." The feeble excuse that the cassava flour and beans had been taken on board in Luanda to be sold in Uruguay was unconvincing. The *Water Witch,* under the command of James Matson, and two other British ships took part in the capture of the *Orozimbo* after a lengthy pursuit. It was finally boarded by the *Fantôme* on January 8, 1841. The *Orozimbo* was condemned on April 6, 1841, and sold for £521.[22]

The brigantine *Firme* left the port of Salvador, Bahia, on April 24, 1841, commanded by Captain Silvério de Brito. Its owner, José Maria Henriques Ferreira, had declared that it was bound for Valparaiso, Chile—at least he was original—but instead of sailing for the Pacific, the ship crossed the Atlantic, heading straight for Ouidah, where it was captured on May 30. Its crew fired muskets at the two British boats sent by the brigantine *Dolphin* to capture the slaver, resulting in the deaths of two crewmen of the British vessel. Four Britons were wounded, including the officer in command of the boarding operation, who was put out of combat in serious condition. The slave traders held out for fifteen minutes according to the British report. The *Firme* was taken to Sierra Leone and condemned for attempted slave trading on July 8, 1841, given "the clearest evidence of actual equipment" for it. It was auctioned off for the handsome sum of £2,169, the highest amount obtained during that period.[23]

The brigantine *Nova Fortuna,* owned by José Joaquim de Almeida, also began its voyage in Bahia, under the command of Francisco José da Rocha. Its papers stated that its destination was the West Coast of Africa, with the intent of acquiring gold, ivory, palm oil, and salt. It stopped at the Fort of Elmina in what is now Ghana, and after doing business in several ports along the coast, reached the British area in Accra, where it was captured on June 6, also by the *Dolphin.* The *Nova Fortuna* was on its way to the port of Ouidah. Evidence of intent to engage in the slave trade were four movable sleeping berths on the deck, alongside the typical accommodations found in legitimate merchant ships; an unusually wide hatchway for such vessels (so as better to ventilate the hold); one hundred African mats on board, which more recently had been commonly used instead of the so-called "slave deck" made of planks; numerous water barrels, "but temporarily filled with cowries," and a kitchen equipped to accommodate a "slave boiler," an expression the British employed to refer to the huge pot used to cook for the generally large number of captives carried aboard slave ships.

According to the manifest, most of the cargo of the *Nova Fortuna* on the return voyage to Brazil was supposed to be salt, but as the British report explained, "the word salt was meant to apply to something else"—to slaves, of course. Further evidence was found, including letters referring to the Spanish slaver *Picón,* later confiscated with a cargo of captives. Other letters from Bahia, addressed to residents of Ouidah, clearly dealt with matters related to the slave trade. The owner of most of the cargo on the *Nova Fortuna* was believed to be a notorious slaver, and the captain "had also been for years in the slave-trade, having belonged to three vessels condemned here." The ship was found guilty on June 20 and sold for £1,713.[24]

The *Flor da América* (Flower of the Americas), a schooner with a lovely name on a vile mission, was from Rio de Janeiro, belonged to Manoel Nunes Pereira and sailed under the command of Manoel José Pereira, possibly members of another trafficking family. It was captured by the British sloop *Persian* on the Congo River on June 29, 1841, again intending to pick up slaves at Cabinda. The usual evidence that it was attempting to engage in the illegal slave trade was found, but there was a peculiar explanation for the findings. The numerous water barrels, according to its captain, were to be used to quench the thirst of sailors involved in the Cabinda slave trade who had been captured by the British squadron and would be returned to Rio de Janeiro aboard the *Flor da América*. Incredibly enough, he claimed to be on a philanthropic mission! There are further interesting aspects regarding the owner and consignees of this ship. One of the documents confiscated on board indicated that Guimarães, the owner of the cargo, and Pereira, the captain, "had been profitably connected in slaving adventures for some time previous to this voyage." Evidence of a slaving operation included a large hatchway, a kitchen built for a slave boiler, two bunks, barrels holding up to 1,040 gallons of water (whereas 460 would have sufficed for the crew), and a larger than necessary quantity of firewood, among other clues. The *Flor da América* was condemned on July 31, 1841, and sold for £219.[25]

Finally, the brigantine *Dona Elliza* was seized while lying at anchor off São Felipe de Benguela, undoubtedly awaiting cargo from that port, another active supplier of slaves at the time. Its captain was Antonio da Silva Monteiro, who could not be found to take responsibility because he had left the ship. The only officers aboard were the boatswain and first mate, but the boatswain was so ill that he was dropped off in Benguela, probably under the care of the only doctor who resided there, and the first mate was the only officer available to testify about the voyage of that slave ship, which was taken to Sierra Leone like the others.[26] There was no proof that it was a Brazilian vessel except the flag on its mast. The first mate, Joaquim José de Azevedo, said he had boarded in Benguela, but the captain lived in Rio de Janeiro, where the vessel had been built, and that himself was a Brazilian subject, and the crew was part Brazilian, part Portuguese. The *Dona Elliza* was captured on June 30, 1841, by Lieutenant James Matson. It was condemned on August 3, 1841 and auctioned off for just £175.[27]

In 1841, the British claimed that they had disembarked just 306 slaves in Sierra Leone, a small fraction of the 5,139 rescued in several parts of the Atlantic. The captives taken to the British colony were removed from two ships: a Spanish vessel flying the Portuguese flag, and a confirmed Portuguese slave ship. The first was loaded in Ouidah and was probably bound for Cuba. The second received slaves in Cape Lopez and probably headed for Brazil.[28] As we have seen, none of the ten Brazilian ships mentioned in this chapter was captured with African captives aboard. Accused of being equipped for the slave trade, they were all condemned before the *Ermelinda* was captured, and for the same reason. Therefore, 1841 was a bad year for Brazilian slave traders, who no longer sailed as often as they used to due to the pressure from the lords of the seas. A small-time African slaver who lived in Bahia wrote picturesquely about that topic in a letter to a business partner in Ouidah, dated April 1841: "It seems that one does not pray so hard to go to Heaven as one does to press for the coast" of Africa. A month and a half after it was written, that same letter was confiscated by the British Navy on the *Nova Fortuna,* whose adventures we have just recounted.[29]

All of the ships that sailed through this chapter were tried and convicted by the British and Brazilian Court of Mixed Commission based in Sierra Leone, where Rufino José Maria would undergo an experience he could hardly have expected when he sailed on the *Ermelinda* toward that most interesting part of the African continent.

14

Sierra Leone

Soon after boarding the *Ermelinda,* James Matson had six barrels of cassava meal and six sacks of rice transferred to the *Water Witch,* justifying the order because his sailors had been on half-rations for several days. Then, except for the captain, Joaquim Antonio Coutinho, and the cook, Rufino José Maria, the crew and passengers were put into a boat and sent to the British ship. All except the cabin boy, Manoel Barbosa, were deposited in an unspecified port on the coast of Angola, probably Luanda, where the *Water Witch* was based. No preparations had been made to receive them, except perhaps what was offered by the slave traders who were partners of the *Ermelinda*'s consignee. In cases like theirs, the British authorities predicted that most crewmen— abandoned, unemployed, homeless, often sick and hungry—would once again find employment in the slave trade, "turn[ing] pirates in desperation" as they replaced sailors of others ships who were dying in droves, felled by tropical diseases.[1]

Meanwhile, crewed by twelve British sailors under the command of boatswain Richard Burstal, the *Ermelinda* was taken to St. Helena. Located 955.7 nautical miles from the African coast, it was a small, 47-square-mile volcanic island that was uninhabited when the Portuguese discovered it in the early sixteenth century and named it after the saint of the day. Briefly occupied by the Dutch for about twenty years until the mid-seventeenth century, it became a British possession in 1659 under the aegis of the East India Company.[2] In 1813 James Prior, a Royal Navy officer, described St. Helena as follows:

> ... a vast mass of rock, rising abruptly from nearly the centre of the great Atlantic ocean, jagged and irregular, cut and slashed as it were into pieces by the great hatchet of nature—too large to be passed without examination, and too small, and unfruitful, and badly situated, to be of much use; – seems like a great sign-post of providence that would say of its divine architecture, "My hand has been here."[3]

The Story of Rufino. João José Reis, Flávio dos Santos Gomes, and Marcus J. M. de Carvalho, Translated by H. Sabrina Gledhill, Oxford University Press (2020) © Oxford University Press.
DOI: 10.1093/oso/9780190224363.001.0001

In addition to being an entrepôt of some importance on the route between the Atlantic and Indian oceans, particularly for taking on water, St. Helena would soon go beyond the utility sought by Prior and gain a reputation on the international political stage as the place where Napoleon was imprisoned from 1815 to 1821, after the British won the Battle of Waterloo. A place where African slavery had already existed, albeit on a small scale, it became the site of a British base for the suppression of the slave trade. In 1839, a Court of the British Vice-Admiralty was established on the island to help police the seas, judge slave ships, and deal with other matters related to British expansion on the Atlantic and the neighboring Indian ocean. St. Helena was a reception center for captives rescued from the ships judged there—captives who, once freed, were primarily sent to serve as hired laborers in the British colonies in the Caribbean and South Atlantic. Between June 1840 and September 1847, 9,133 Africans landed on the island, of whom 63 percent were removed to Jamaica, Trinidad, Guyana, and the Cape Colony (the Cape of Good Hope) in what is now South Africa. Another 32 percent died before being so distributed.[4]

Rufino's *Ermelinda* spent just two days on that small island in the middle of the vast Atlantic while it awaited the arrival of the *Water Witch* from the Angolan coast. In the meantime, it took on a supply of water, which was in fact the reason its captors gave for stopping there. But it also got down to business. The British sold the two horses carried on board for Arsénio Carpo's carriage. Possibly because they were debilitated by the long voyage, they went for £17 each despite the protests of Captain Coutinho, who claimed that they were worth at least twice that. More supplies were also put on board the *Water Witch*, in addition to cordage and hides.[5]

Rufino was chosen to stay aboard the *Ermelinda* along with the captain and a cabin boy, who was transferred to the *Water Witch* after it returned from Luanda. The captain was expected to stay at his post, since he was responsible for the fate of the ship and its cargo. Like it or not, people in his position always accompanied the slave ships the British seized. But why the cook and the cabin boy? Besides the practical aspects—cooking and serving the Brazilian captain and the British officers aboard the *Ermelinda*— under similar circumstances the British usually chose members of inferior rank. This may have been in hopes of getting more compromising statements than those that could be obtained from higher-ranking crew members such as the boatswain, first mate, and pilots, men who were generally more experienced and committed to the slave trade. An African like Rufino, who had once experienced what it was like to be a captive in the hold of a slave ship, would presumably have been more inclined to help the British out of solidarity with the victims of that trade. However, the British already knew very well that that was not the case.

In fact, African sailors usually went along the other crew members in confirming fantastic tales, duly memorized and rehearsed, of winds and tides that allegedly pushed ships off the courses stated in their travel documents. Here are some examples from the time when the slave trade was only banned above the Equator, prior to 1831. During that period, almost invariably, the ships that sailed to ports on the Slave Coast in the Bight of Benin—Little Popo, Ouidah, Porto Novo, Badagry, Onim (Lagos), and so on—and other forbidden shores, stated that their destination was the Angolan coast, mainly Molembo, north of Cabinda. The ship that transported Rufino from a port in the Bight of Benin to Bahia in the early 1820s probably declared Molembo as its point of disembarkation in the customs documents. When they were caught, slave traders and crewmen alike repeated something of a mantra: they were on their way to Molembo when the currents swept them into the illegal zone. Historian Alexandre Ribeiro Vieira has found that, of the fifty-four ships taken to Sierra Leone for trial between 1822 and 1830, forty (74 percent) declared Molembo as their destination.[6] Under interrogation, the crew of the brig *São João II Rosália*, captured in 1825, harped on the same string. Marcelino Ferreira and Alexandre Moreira, both "Mina" Africans, stated that while in the port of Onim, where the ship was seized, they were merely "unloading" rolls of tobacco that they "traded for African wrappers and other types of cloth."[7] The same situation allegedly occurred with the schooner *Tentadora*, which left Salvador in November 1826 "bound to make slaves in Molembo." Captured in Ouidah in March of the following year, its crooked course was justified by sailor and African freedman Joaquim José, also of the "Mina" nation, who lived in Salvador. He claimed that the ship "had only stopped in the port of Ouidah to take on water and supplies and trade, as it had been trading some goods from its cargo for others suitable for trade and consumption in Molembo."[8] Ironically, Joaquim José himself may have been sent to Brazil as a slave through Ouidah, possibly the busiest of its kind in the region twenty years prior to his statement, before Onim/Lagos surpassed it in the 1820s. In fact, Ouidah is the port where the vast majority of slaves from the Slave Coast were embarked during the entire transatlantic slave trade period—nearly a million, which was about half the total number for the region.[9]

Because this sort of business would gradually become illegal in an ever-broader swath of the Atlantic, the crewmen's loyalty to their employers and protectors was a highly valued asset. Therefore, it is understandable that so many gave statements favoring the slave traders, and there were sailors who were small-time slavers themselves. This obedience to a kind of code of silence, typical of organized crime, was not just a characteristic of freedmen but of everyone involved in the trade in human beings, including those who were still enslaved. This was the case with Joaquim, a Mina slave and sailor on the sumac *Novo Destino*, which left Iguape, Pernambuco, in 1835, bound for Angola laden with rice, and was intercepted by the British. Questioned about conversations he might have overheard between the sailors and ship's captain about their dealings in African ports, Joaquim simply replied "that he could say nothing about it because they conversed in the stern, and he was in the prow of the vessel."[10]

Therefore, the British must have known that they could not expect Rufino, the cook, to collaborate merely because he was an African who had once been enslaved and presumably sympathetic to the cause of suppressing the slave trade. After all, it was the slave trade that had given him a job as a freedman. Rufino may have been chosen to stay aboard the *Ermelinda* for a very simple reason: the new British crew needed someone to cook for them on the way to St. Helena, as well as during the next stage of the voyage. This is because, after stopping in St. Helena, Rufino went on to Sierra Leone, where the *Ermelinda* arrived on December 8, 1841, forty-one days after it was captured in Angolan waters. He had probably never set foot in that part of Africa before.

Sierra Leone was founded in 1787 by a group of British philanthropists, including the legendary Granville Sharp, who had fervently embraced the cause of abolishing the transatlantic slave trade and would soon organize an impressive mass movement to pressure his country's Parliament to do so. Originally called the Province of Freedom, the colony was intended to receive poor blacks who lived in Great Britain and were beginning to be viewed as a danger to society. Many had fought alongside the British during the recent American War of Independence and had gone to live in the United Kingdom after the war. The creators of Sierra Leone wanted to show the world that blacks were capable of living in freedom, governing themselves, prospering, and becoming civilized in the process. That meant introducing or improving Christianity among them so they could abide by the Protestant work ethic, and increasing their desire to engage in commercial activities that would eventually displace the trade in slaves, which was very active in that part of the African coast. The idea was to transfer the heavy weight of the white man's burden onto the backs of the black settlers.[11]

The first group of 411 settlers included at least some white men and women. The men included artisans, merchants, and medical practitioners, called surgeons at the time. Some of the women were married to black settlers. Others were believed to be prostitutes (there are good reasons to doubt that) who later accused the expedition's agents of plying them with drink and forcing them to set sail. The settlers arrived in Sierra Leone aboard three ships, and the captain of the expedition soon acquired a piece of land from a local chief to establish the colony. The voyage was poorly planned. They arrived in May, during the rainy season, which made it difficult to build shelters and plant crops. The supplies they had brought with them from Britain soon ran out, and many of the settlers died of hunger and endemic fevers. By mid-September the colony was reduced to just 276 people, including twenty-nine women, less than half the number that sailed there. One settler described his tremendous disappointment in a letter to Granville Sharp, the chief mastermind of the project: "It was really a very great pity ever we came to this country . . . for we are settled upon the very worst part. There is not a thing put into the ground . . . quite a plague seems to reign here among us. I have been dangerously ill myself but it pleased the Almighty to restore me to health again and the first opportunity I have I shall embark for the West Indies."[12] In other words, the man was thinking of setting off for the slaveholding heart of the British empire, abandoning the dream—turned nightmare—of the Province of Freedom.

Thinking like him, other settlers, including the surgeons, left the colony to find employment in the slave-trading posts in the surrounding region to improve their chances of survival. To make matters worse, the colonial town would be destroyed by a local chief in retaliation for a disastrous British military operation that resulted in a native African's death. Before and after this episode, some of the settlers were kidnapped and sold to French slave traders. Soon the number of settlers would be reduced to just sixty-four survivors who had taken refuge in the village of another local chief. To revive the colony, its masterminds in the United Kingdom founded a philanthropic shell firm, the Sierra Leone Company.

Other, more numerous groups followed that ill-fated handful of pioneers. In 1792, Sierra Leone welcomed 1,131 blacks (of the 1,192 who sailed from Britain) who had also sided with the British during the American Revolutionary War. Most of them had escaped the thrall of slave owners who rebelled against the Crown; after the British lost the war, they had been taken to Nova Scotia, Canada. They were not only promised the confirmation of their freedom but a reward in the form of land to farm and the resources they needed to begin a

Figure 14.1. The widely publicized motto of British abolitionism.

Figures 14.2a and 14.2b Granville Sharp (1735–1813) and Olaudah Equiano (c. 1745–1797): interracial alliance for the abolition of the slave trade and slavery. National Portrait Gallery, London and frontispiece of *The Interesting Narrative of the Life of Olaudah Equiano, or Gustavas Vassa, the African, Written by Himself* (London: Printed for and sold by the Author, 1789).

new life. However, they were betrayed. While white refugees received land immediately, their black counterparts had to endure a long wait. Some received no land at all, and those who did got the worst plots. Many were so desperate that they began working for white landowners as indentured servants in conditions very close to the slavery from which they had escaped. Some employers even re-enslaved them and sold them to the slave-owning colonies in the Caribbean and United States. Racial discrimination and violence, harsh winters, failed crops, poor housing, hunger, and disease characterized the experience of the black refugees in Nova Scotia and led many of them to emigrate to Sierra Leone, this time lured by promises of land and protection extended by the eponymous company. That new wave of immigrants arrived in a fleet of fifteen ships after a difficult voyage due to bad weather.

In 1800, a new group of refugees arrived in Sierra Leone—550 maroons from Trelawny Town, Jamaica, including women and children. They had initially been taken to Nova Scotia after the suppression of the so-called Second Maroon War, a bloody uprising that took place on Jamaican soil in 1795–1796. Despite an agreement with the British that they would not be deported if they laid down their arms, the maroons were sent to the Canadian colony. After the first winter there, they begged to be transported to Sierra Leone as loyal subjects of the

British Crown. Their request was granted three years later. They arrived in Sierra Leone during an uprising by the black settlers against the colonial administration that the maroons helped put down with the efficiency of the good warriors that they were.

A year after Britain's abolition of the slave trade in 1807, Sierra Leone ceased to be a private enterprise and became a colony of the British Crown, which began governing it through officials appointed in London. The change came at a good time because the Sierra Leone Company was virtually bankrupt. From then on, that place would be used to receive Africans from a wide range of ethnic backgrounds rescued by British cruisers from ships that plied the illegal slave trade under a wide range of flags.

Mixed Commission Courts for the Suppression of the Slave Trade were established in Freetown, the capital of the colony of Sierra Leone. They were courts made up of British commissioners on one side and, on the other, their counterparts from the countries with which Britain had signed bilateral treaties to combat the slave trade in the absence of an international law capable of banning it altogether. The number of countries reached forty-two in 1840, including Argentina, Chile, and Bolivia, which were barely affected by the slave trade at the time. However, not all of those countries appointed commissioners—just the nations that were more directly involved.[13] The only commissions that operated effectively in the 1830s and 1840s were those established between Britain and, individually, Portugal, Brazil, and Spain. The latter represented the interests of Cuba, its main slaveholding colony, where the slave trade fueled a vigorous sugar economy boosted in the first decades of the nineteenth century by the debacle in Haiti, which had been the world's main supplier of sugar until the slave revolution of 1791. Due to the importance of the Cuban connection to the slave trade during that period, Havana was the base for an Anglo-Spanish Mixed Commission, while the other was based in Freetown. Similarly, Brazil, the biggest importer of slaves during the period when the trade was banned, was represented on two mixed commissions, one in Rio de Janeiro and the other in Freetown. They were established in 1825, three years after Brazil gained its independence from Portugal. As for the latter country, its enclaves in Angola continued to be the main exporters of captives, and until Portugal accepted to sign a treaty with Britain, its flag was routinely flown by Brazilian slave ships.[14]

Between 1819 and 1841, 59,837 captives were seized and taken to Sierra Leone, including just 306 in 1841, the year when the Royal Navy captured the *Ermelinda*.[15] The state in which many of those captives arrived in the colony gives an idea of the dramatic and torturous conditions they endured in the holds of the slave ships, which did not immediately end after they were liberated by the British. The following statement is from a British physician, Robert Clarke, who

Figures 14.3a and 14.3b Sierra Leone at the time of Rufino. From Johnson U. J. Asiegbu, *Slavery and the Politics of Liberation 1787–1861: A Study of Liberated African Emigration and British Anti-slavery Policy* (New York: African Publishing Corporation, 1969).

worked in the hospital for the freed slaves and witnessed appalling scenes like this one more than once:

> Great numbers of individuals landed from the slave-vessel, arrive at the Hospital, so deplorably emaciated, that the skin appears to be tensely stretched over, and tied down to the skeleton. The expression of the countenance indicates suffering, moral and physical, of the most profound and agonizing nature. Occasionally among the newly arrived group, all sense of suffering is found to be merged in melancholic or raving madness. The wizened, shrunk, and skinny features, are lighted up by the hollow, jetty and sparkling eye. The belly is, as it were, tacked to the back, whilst the hip bones protrude, and give rise to foul sloughing and phagedenic ulcers. The hand and skinny fingers seem much elongated, by the great and neglected growth of the nails, which in such cases resemble talons. The squalor and extreme wretchedness of the figure is heightened, in many cases, by the party-colored evacuations with which the body is besmeared. The legs refuse to perform their functions, and with difficulty support the emaciated, tottering and debilitated body. Many of them labor under extensive gangrenous ulcerations, situated on the extremities, often detaching the soft parts from the bones, which becoming carious are exfoliated. This truly pitiable state of the newly arrived Liberated African, must have been observed by every member of the profession, who has had any opportunity of seeing them.[16]

The brutality of the slave trade was entirely, irrefutably revealed with each disembarkation in the British colony. The doctor's words also bring to light the failure of the British system of suppression to give adequate care to the captives between the time the slave ships were boarded and cast anchor in Sierra Leone. Nevertheless, despite the skeletal state in which the Africans arrived there, most managed to survive and reinvent their lives in assisted freedom.

Two years after Rufino's arrival, the colony had a population of 40,060, of whom 56.8 percent were men. The Creole population (descendants of the first groups of settlers that arrived there from Britain and the Americas) and, above all, freed slaves from many parts of Africa, formed the majority, including 21,754 men and 17,280 women. The floating contingent of Africans who lived outside the colony and passed through there was entirely male—927 men. The European minority consisted of just seventy-five men and twenty-four women. However, it is unlikely that those numbers, which are the official figures, accounted for the local demographic makeup. For example, a doctor who lived there calculated that the number of Africans from outside the colony was actually 2,800.

Figure 14.4 The Liberated African Office building in Freetown. From Johnson U. J. Asiegbu, *Slavery and the Politics of Liberation 1787–1861: A Study of Liberated African Emigration and British Anti-slavery Policy* (New York: African Publishing Corporation, 1969).

The fates of the Africans who disembarked in Sierra Leone from slave ships seized by the Royal Navy varied greatly. Most were employed in the colony as apprentices in a range of trades, or as farmhands, generally under the tutelage of the few European residents, locally born settlers, and other long-established Africans. It should be recalled that Sierra Leone was also planned as a testing ground for a civilizing experiment, which included a new work ethic. Nevertheless, it frequently became an experiment in the exploitation of cheap— if not unpaid—labor.[17] In 1820, João Altavilla, the Brazilian representative on the Mixed Commission, wrote that when the slave ships arrived in the colony, "any resident who needed servants generally goes aboard and chooses those he wants, and it is expected that that individual will clothe and instruct them, either to become the perfect servant or [in] any trade." The younger "recaptured" captives, or "recaptives" were instructed in religion and taught English before being trained to become carpenters, bricklayers, and so on. The adults were temporarily employed in the "service of the State" in activities such as cleaning streets, felling trees, and "clearing the interior," until they were granted small plots of land to farm. Both the youths and adults received government support until they could make their own living, a period calculated at roughly two years from the time of disembarkation. The girls were "sent to schools run by Creole black women" and generally became domestic servants. However, the fate the British authorities considered to be the most suitable for them—as for all the women disembarked—was to become the wives of the large number of unmarried emancipated men. Altavilla also wrote about that subject: "Because there is a great lack of women in this colony, they immediately have many (black) suitors, but since the government wants them to know something of Religion before they enter into the State of matrimony, they place them in the care of several older black women from the Colony to so instruct them." In the 1840s, this system also included the forced migration of Africans rescued from that time on, who were deported to the British colonies in the Caribbean, where slavery had been abolished in 1833, and the period of "apprenticeship" ended in 1838.[18]

The proportionally large male population of Sierra Leone coincides with what we know about the characteristics of the captives tossed into the slave ships' holds: a much larger number of men than women, who, on average, made up just one-third of the human cargo. Obviously, the results were reflected in the population of the British colony, forming a favorable marriage market for women, as João Altavilla observed. This may explain why they left their husbands more often than men did their wives. It did not strike a death blow to the patriarchal system, but it must have hit it very hard. In 1827 a British traveler, James Holman, wrote that he had witnessed an encounter between a British vicar and a man who had apparently sought him out for consolation and advice in one of the Emancipated Africans' villages. "During our short stay, a poor fellow came to complain to Mr. Davy that his wife had gone to live with another man, and that when he went to demand her restoration, the guilty paramour and his friends turned him off with a sound beating." This seems to have been an unusual occurrence, since the more experienced Dr. Robert Clarke, in turn, stated that women accused of adultery were harshly punished in most of the African communities established in the colony.[19]

Sierra Leone and the surrounding areas constituted a veritable patchwork of African peoples who formed clearly defined ethnic communities. Some were natives of the region or had lived there for centuries, such as the Bulom (or Sherbro), Temne, Limba, and Kru peoples. Originally from the coastal region further to the south of the British colony, the so-called Grain Coast between Cape Mensurado and Cape Palmas, the Krus were renowned for their skills as sailors and canoeists and therefore played an important role in the transportation of captives from the shores and inland rivers to the slave ships. They were distinguished by the ethnic marker of a perpendicular line tattooed from the middle of the forehead to the tip of the nose. The Susus, Yalunkas, and Fulani lived to the north of the colony, having formed the kingdom of Futa Jalon in the early eighteenth century under the leadership of Fulani Muslims. Wolofs and "Mandingos" (or Mandinka, Malinke) and other Mande-speaking groups could also be found in Sierra Leone. Individuals belonging to all those groups had settled in or regularly visited Sierra Leone, generally on business. Groups of Mandingos had established themselves in the interior of Sierra Leone since at least the mid-eighteenth century, therefore prior to the creation of the British colony. In the 1810s, a neighboring district of Freetown was called Mandingo Town.[20]

However, in the year when Rufino arrived there, most of Sierra Leone's residents were made up of captives "recaptured" from slave ships and belonging to numerous ethnic groups—"more than two hundred different tribes and nations," according to Sigismund Koelle, the German linguist who studied the colony in the mid-nineteenth century.[21] Foreigners with a less scientific outlook left even more interesting impressions of the Tower of Babel that Sierra Leone had become. Elizabeth Helen Melville, the wife of Michael Melville, a member of the Mixed Commission that would judge the *Ermelinda,* wrote a journal about her life in the colony between 1840 and 1846. Therefore, she was there when Rufino arrived in Freetown. According to the Scottish lady, the emancipated Africans spoke "nearly forty languages" and, not without some mistakes, she listed some of the "tribes" she knew by name: "Congoes, Coanzos, Coromantins, Calabars, Bonnys, Bassas, Mokoes, Eygies, Tapuas, Kossoes, Pawpaws, Eboes and Akus or Eyoes."[22] From her perspective as an upper-class European woman, but one with a keen sense of observation, she wrote about some of the national and social African groups that she came across on a daily basis in the streets of Freetown and her own home, noting their outward signs of identity and the tensions among them:

> ... the negro carries his badge of nationality in his face, all of one tribe being marked in the same manner by cuts or tattooing. On notes and messages being brought to the house, when I ask my little waiting-woman "who been bring this?" it surprises me to be answered "one Aku man," "one Kroo boy," as the case may be, or by her saying "one settler girl" or "one Maroon woman" wants to speak to me, though the individuals she thus distinguishes may be personally unknown to her, for, excepting the Jollofs and Mandigoes, all the black people seem alike to me. But it is by their national marks that she can so readily tell one countryman from another. It is only the Kroomen and liberated slaves who have the additional features of tattooed or carved figures upon their faces. The settlers and Maroons are totally different from all the rest of the community of Sierra Leone – hate each other cordially, and look down with utter contempt upon the liberated Africans.[23]

Another resident of Sierra Leone from Rufino's time confirms the feeling of superiority of the settlers and Maroons, mainly Creoles descended from those original groups—Creoles both because they were born in the colony and because they were more assimilated into a hybrid, predominantly British, culture. That included taking the first steps in creating their own language, Krio. Dr. Robert Clarke was surprised that the Christian schools for children from those groups were not the same as those in which the children of liberated Africans studied. "This distinction," he observed, "inspires the Creole children with ideas of their own superiority . . . and to such an extent is this feeling fostered, that I have often heard the Creole boy or girl when they quarrelled with one of the liberated African children, call them *niggers,* which is to the latter the most opprobrious of all opprobrious epithets."" As in the British Americas, the term "*nigger*" was used offensively by whites to refer to blacks, whether enslaved or otherwise. In the Sierra Leone of Rufino's day, the two "classes"—Creoles and liberated Africans—did not share common interests, the British doctor concluded. To remedy the tensions between the two groups, he prescribed that they should be taught together, without separation or discrimination, with an emphasis on practical instruction in farming and "mechanical trades." Clarke had in mind the creation of a single class of rural and urban proletarians, presumably better suited to serving the Crown and its metropolitan British subjects.[24]

Separate schools merely reflected what was going on in the surrounding society. With the exception of the Freetown elite, Sierra Leone's residents lived in separate ethnic communities in the many towns established in the outskirts of the capital. According to Captain J. F. Napier Hewett, who visited the colony in the 1850s,

> Freetown is divided into several quarters, the best of which is occupied indiscriminately by Europeans, half-castes, "Nova-Scotians" or settlers, some few descendants of liberated slaves; together with certain immigrants who have naturalized themselves and settled here for the purposes of trade, – all of whom are the tradesmen and artificers; but the remaining black population, swayed by that peculiar clannish sentiment which is so conspicuous a trait in the African character, has divided itself spontaneously into distinct communities, each consisting of the members of one particular tribe, who congregate together in their special portion of the city, and hold themselves as much aloof from other races which inhabit other parts as each would when dwelling in its native wilds.[25]

The latter were the groups of liberated Africans. Each of these ethnic communities, according to Hewett, was "a nation in miniature" where one could "familiarize himself almost with the history and the manners and customs of each people." Given this strange world, and ignorant of who its occupants had been in their homelands, the British captain failed to understand the changes the emancipated Africans had had to undergo in order adapt to that new way of life. The very awareness of belonging to a specific group—although generally reconfigured in that new land—must have become more extreme as an imperative for self-defense and survival among foreign peoples in an unfamiliar setting. In fact, the British did much the same, because they developed their own social habits in foreign lands in a failed attempt to keep their values intact. Even the English language underwent fundamental changes within the British community. For example, Elizabeth Melville mentioned the need to set aside her aristocratic English and speak the "broken English" of the colony in order to make herself understood to the natives, which included giving orders that her servants could comprehend.[26]

The ethnic communities formed by the various groups of liberated Africans made their living mainly by growing yams, cassava, and bananas, among other crops, in the towns of Kissey, Wellington, Hastings, Hamilton, Waterloo, Wilberforce, York, and others. However, many of the freedmen who were not necessarily part of Freetown's elite lived there and engaged in other occupations, such as boatmen, canoers, fishermen, porters, and street vendors, for example. The Creoles dominated commerce, selling their wares from established shops, and refused to do farm work, which they considered to be beneath them. Some were part of the British colonial apparatus, employed as minor officials, or served in the Royal African Corps, the colonial army. The Kru's livelihood came mainly from maritime occupations such as canoeing, sailing, and fishing, as well as working on boats that carried lumber felled in the forests flanking the rivers in the region and exported to Britain. Many also worked as domestic servants, particularly the younger individuals. Women from the Kru group were extremely rare in the colony. A Kru man's dream was typical of most immigrants—building up enough savings to return to his homeland, start a family (preferably with several wives), and live there until the end of his days.[27]

As for the Islamized groups—Wolofs, Fulanis, and Mandingos—they engaged in trade and held a virtual monopoly over blacksmithing, goldsmithing, and leather making, in which they employed young people rescued from the slave ships and handed over to them by the British as "cheap apprentices," according to a contemporary observer. However, many were herders. Mrs. Melville, who blushingly appreciated the beauty of the men from those predominantly Muslim nations, observed that they were not identified by facial scarification, which they did not practice, but by their form of dress, which "consists of a wide flowing mantle... with loose hanging sleeves; very ample trousers drawn full round the ankle; a high peaked cap of blue cloth embroidered in gaudy colours, or else of plain scarlet or white stuff." They also wore one or more amulets called "'gree-gree,' usually formed of a scrap from the Qur'ān, hid in a mass of black paste or sewed up in small leather pouches," hanging from their necks. They wore

Figure 14.5 A Fulani smith in Freetown, 1836. From F. Harrison Rankin, *The white man's grave: a visit to Sierra Leone, in 1834* (London: Richard Bentley, 1836), vol. 1.

amulets similar to those worn in Brazil by African Muslims like Rufino. "They have also rosaries, sometimes of common glass beads, or little balls of polished wood, with, in the middle, two or three larger beads of an opaque yellow stone," noted the observant Elizabeth Melville about the Muslim *misbaḥah*. Some of them who came from the interior, outside the colony's borders, to trade, also carried a sheepskin pouch containing a copy of the Qur'ān. The few women in these Muslim groups wore "a wide scarf, generally white, being thrown over the head, and allowed to fall in ample folds round the whole figure." According to both Mrs. Melville and Dr. Clarke, the women were elegant and lovely.[28]

However, there were ethnic and class divisions among the Muslims. Those who belonged to the various groups of liberated Africans dressed more simply, as Clarke observed, and they included the Aku. The next chapter focuses on that group.

15

Among Akus and African Muslims

Speakers of Yoruba—or Yarribah, as Mrs. Melville learned to call them—were known as *Aku* or, less common, *Oku* in Sierra Leone. The ethnonym derived from greetings in that language, such as *Ẹkú àárọ!* (Good morning!) and *Ẹkú alẹ!* (Good evening!). Several generations of Akus had lived in the British colony and become a growing presence during the last decades of the transatlantic slave trade, increasing at the same rate that war spread to the four corners of Yorubaland.[1]

The largest group of emancipated Africans in Sierra Leone at the time was the Akus, most of whom came from the kingdom of Ọ̀yọ́, Rufino's homeland. An 1848 census showed that over 50 percent of the freed slaves in the colony were of Yoruba origin. In a way, when Rufino arrived in Sierra Leone he was returning home. At the very least, many things about it must have been familiar to him. His was the most widespread language among the many locally spoken tongues, the Yoruba owned most of the drums that beat insistently through the humid nights in the British colony, and the food would also be familiar, not only because it originated in Ọ̀yọ́ but also because of Rufino's Brazilian experience: yams, coconuts, cassava, *àkàrà* (bean fritters), and even a variation of the Bahian dish known as *caruru*, a stew made from okra, palm oil, chili peppers, and smoked fish, which received a tasty name in Sierra Leone—"palaver sauce." In fact, palm oil seasoned just about everything people ate there, including food for patients at the emancipated Africans' hospital.[2]

Robert Clarke noted that the traditional Yoruba religion was alive and well in Sierra Leone, despite British attempts at intense Christian indoctrination. Africans could be seen in the streets wearing bead necklaces in the colors that symbolized their *orișa*, including the Yoruba thunder god, Ṣàngó, the chief divinity of Ọ̀yọ́. Clarke described priests wearing what he considered extravagant clothes and carrying a fly whisk, a symbol of spiritual authority. The drums sounded, the devotees danced, and the gods came down to earth. "The movements of the body are generally slow, and in many cases highly indecent," wrote the British doctor, thus interpreting the spirit possession ceremony he witnessed from the viewpoint of prudish Victorian Britain, which was in the

The Story of Rufino. João José Reis, Flávio dos Santos Gomes, and Marcus J. M. de Carvalho, Translated by H. Sabrina Gledhill, Oxford University Press (2020) © Oxford University Press.
DOI: 10.1093/oso/9780190224363.001.0001

throes of full capitalist expansion, a culture of industrially disciplined bodies. Clarke described what he saw as "The Devil dance." He also observed priests of Ifa, the god of divination, in full activity, casting sixteen half-palm nuts to investigate the designs of the gods and the future of their clients. The latter's most frequent requests to the gods were for wealth and children, "barrenness bearing a stigma with these people."[3]

The connection between the Akus and their past in Yorubaland stubbornly persisted. When the American missionary Thomas Bowen arrived in the British colony in 1856 after a long sojourn in the Akus' native land, they sought him out to get fresh news. "So soon as the Yórubá and Egbá people discovered that I had come from their country, they gathered around me like bees. Every one had something to say and something to ask, if it were only for the sake of hearing me speak their native tongue," wrote the preacher, showing a touch of pride in his language skills.[4] The fact that he was able to distinguish the Egba from the Yoruba suggests that the Aku maintained the internal ethnic divisions they had brought from their homelands. Those whom Bowen described as Yoruba were specifically from Òyó, while the others were from the kingdom of Egba, which was one of the most war-ravaged parts of that region in the 1830s. Most missionaries considered all Yoruba speakers to be Yorubas, including the Òyó and Egba, as well as the Ijebu, Ilesha, Ketu, and so on. The linguist Sigismund Koelle criticized the designation of all Akus as Yorubas, a generalization practiced by many Christian clerics. He observed that, thanks to the missionaries, that term was sometimes used specifically for the Òyós and at other times to designate the entire "Aku nation." While in Sierra Leone, Koelle interviewed refugees from Ota, Egba, Ilesha, Yaba, Ekiti, Ife, and Ondo.[5] However, there was no denying that the representatives of those peoples were grouped together under a single umbrella identity as Aku, based on a common language that came to be called Yoruba. Nevertheless, Koelle preferred to speak of an Aku language that covered the numerous dialects spoken by different ethnic groups in Sierra Leone.

The Europeans took a fancy to classifying the "tribes" that lived in the British colony according to certain supposedly characteristic traits. Not everything they included in their classifying endeavors should be taken seriously, but stereotypes often say something about national character. Mrs. Melville considered the Akus as the most "painstaking and industrious amongst all the Liberated population." Dr. Robert Clarke agreed with the Scottish lady that they were "the most industrial and enterprising" among the Africans in Sierra Leone, and compared them to the Scots and the Swiss. Furthermore, the Akus were, also according to Clarke, "pre-eminently distinguished for their love of trading, and occasionally amass large sums" of money, which led the British to consider them the "African Jews." However, for all their drive to engage in trade and accumulate property, the Akus, like the Jews, were not individualists. They joined forces to form credit unions and buy European merchandise for a good price and then sold their wares in the streets of Freetown, including auctioned goods seized from slave ships. In the 1850s, some of the best shops in the colonial capital belonged to the Akus, whose proverbial politeness charmed many loyal customers.[6]

In the British colony, the Akus were not only divided by class and specific ethnic backgrounds but also into Christians, Muslims, devotees of the Òrìsà and those who moved freely among the different faiths. Religious divisions were often sharp among the Akus. The missionary schools and Christian churches established in the villages and Freetown strove to win the souls of the hundreds of emancipated Africans who arrived in Sierra Leone every year. Many Akus became ministers, and a few gained even higher positions in the religious

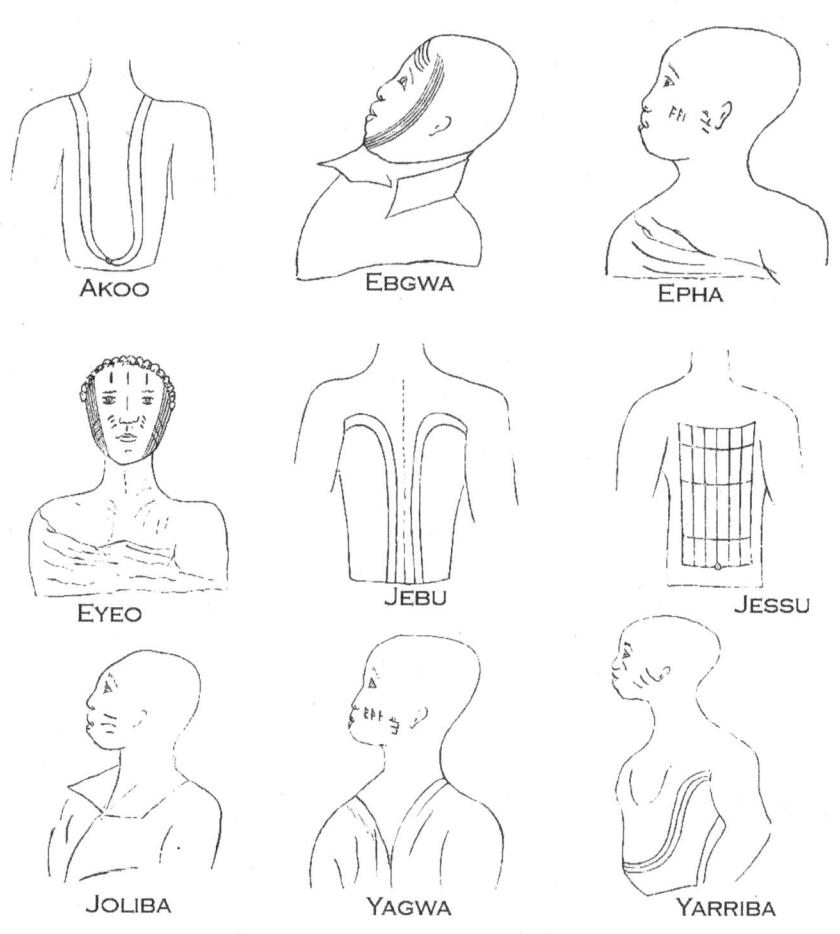

Figure 15.1 "National marks" of liberated Africans in Sierra Leone, according to Dr. Robert Clarke, c. 1840. From Robert Clarke, *Sierra Leone, A Description of the Manners and Customs of the Liberated Africans with Observation upon the Natural History of the Colony, and A Notice of the Native Tribes* (London: James Ridgway, 1846).

hierarchy. Samuel Ajayi Crowther, who arrived in Freetown in 1822, the year Rufino probably disembarked in Bahia, would become the first African bishop in the Anglican Church. Both men came from dependencies of the kingdom of Òyọ́ and were victims of the same conflicts that scourged that region.[7]

While Crowther, who came from a family of Òrìṣà worshippers, became a Christian in Sierra Leone, Rufino José Maria, or Abuncare, remained a Muslim in Brazil. When he arrived in the British colony, which had a significant Muslim presence, Rufino not only sought out other members of his faith but went even further. Dissatisfied with his knowledge of Islam, he seized the opportunity of his sojourn in Sierra Leone to improve his religious education and knowledge of Arabic. In his statement to the Pernambuco police in 1853, Rufino said he had attended a Qur'ānic school in a place called "Farobê," where, in his words, "I continue[d] speaking Arabic, whose basics I already knew, from a black man who taught there."[8]

A witness to Rufino's interrogation reported to the *Jornal do Comércio* what he understood ("Farobê"), but the African really meant Fourah Bay.[9] Located near the rural Aku town of Kissey, not far from Freetown, Fourah Bay was the main hub for Aku-Yoruba Muslims like Rufino in the 1840s. The area where they lived and built a mosque was donated by William Henry Savage, a lawyer and wealthy businessman who was born in England to an African father and a European mother. One of the prosecutors of the mixed commissions in Sierra Leone, he died in 1836 or 1837. In 1833, Savage defended the Akus when they were prosecuted for rebelling against the colonial government. The conflict started when the Aku Muslims rejected a series of edicts that restricted the movements of residents in rural towns, established a stricter (Protestant) work ethic, and required attendance at Christian services. A group of Muslims who had left their towns some time before and settled in a place called Cobolo, outside the British colony, was attacked on the grounds that they were planning to storm and seize Freetown. By the time the British troops arrived in Cobolo it had been evacuated, but many Aku Muslims were arrested in several parts of the colony and charged with the crime of lèse-majesté.

The governor of Sierra Leone at the time was Lieutenant Colonel Alexander Findlay, who was waging a personal holy war against the Muslims. However, after winning the armed conflict the governor was defeated in the legal battle by William Savage, the lawyer appointed by the government itself to defend the accused. After the trial, Findlay continued to persecute Muslims, insisting on restricting their freedom of movement and preventing foreign Muslims from entering the colony—most of them Fulas and Mandingos who went there to do business and took the opportunity to spread the Islamic faith. Findlay's proclamation went so far as to ban liberated Africans "from assuming any other dress than that usually adopted by Europeans." In addition, African soldiers who retired from the colonial militia were prohibited from converting to Islam on pain of losing their pensions.[10]

Despite this persecution, for five years after William Savage's donation of the land, the Fourah Bay Muslim community flourished and attracted followers and converts from the districts of Hastings and Waterloo. Some moved there permanently, while others stayed in their own villages and walked there on Fridays to attend religious services. In Fourah Bay, they gathered around religious leaders or *alfa* like Alfa Kassim, Alfa Musa Ojay, Alfa Amara, Alfa Aliyu Badara, Alfa Dowdoo, Alieu Thomas, Sumanu Othman Ajibode, Mohammed Badamasie, and Mohammed Yadalieu. At first, Mandingo and Fula missionaries helped the Muslim Akus establish mosques and schools, where some worked as religious instructors. "Recognizing their superior knowledge and training," wrote Harrell-Bond, Howard, and Skinner, "the Aku had relied on Fula and Mandingo *alfa* to provide them with religious education and spiritual guidance."[11]

However, by the time Rufino arrived there, the Akus had already established their own religious leadership. Mohammed Yadalieu—also known as *Alfa Momodu Yadda*—was the first *alimami* (political-religious chief) in Fourah Bay, bearing the title of Imam Ratibou, which means a minor imam, a local leader in a more limited community, such as a block or a small town.[12] Yadalieu helped build the Aku mosque in 1836, a hub that attracted many people to the community, and his leadership lasted until 1849. Therefore, Rufino must have heard him preach. The *Ermelinda*'s cook also met at least some of those preachers, one of whom was the "black man" he mentioned who taught him Arabic in Sierra Leone. Most of them were probably prisoners of war taken in conflicts like that which led to Rufino's enslavement and who, like him, had become human merchandise for the Atlantic slave trade. Unlike Rufino, however, the British had helped those Muslims escape enslavement in the New World, mainly Brazil. Some even prospered in Sierra Leone. Mohammed Yadalieu was a wealthy merchant when he became the leader of his fellow Aku Muslims.

Fourah Bay was also the battleground for an interesting cultural war between Islam and Christianity. The Muslims of Yoruba origin lived alongside Fourah Bay College, a Christian institution of higher learning established in 1827 to train African missionaries. The future Bishop Samuel Crowther studied there. The Anglican college was founded by the Church Missionary Society (CMS), of which it was the intellectual and ideological arm in Sierra Leone. The CMS saw its Muslim neighbors as prodigious adversaries of its evangelizing mission. At that time, the British still maintained a relatively tolerant policy that recognized the Islam professed by emancipated Africans. For example, in criminal investigations and legal proceedings, Muslims could swear on a copy of the Qur'ān to act as witnesses. In 1822, Ali, an Aku who was a sharecropper in the town of Lichfield, swore on "the Al-Koran" to faithfully translate the statements

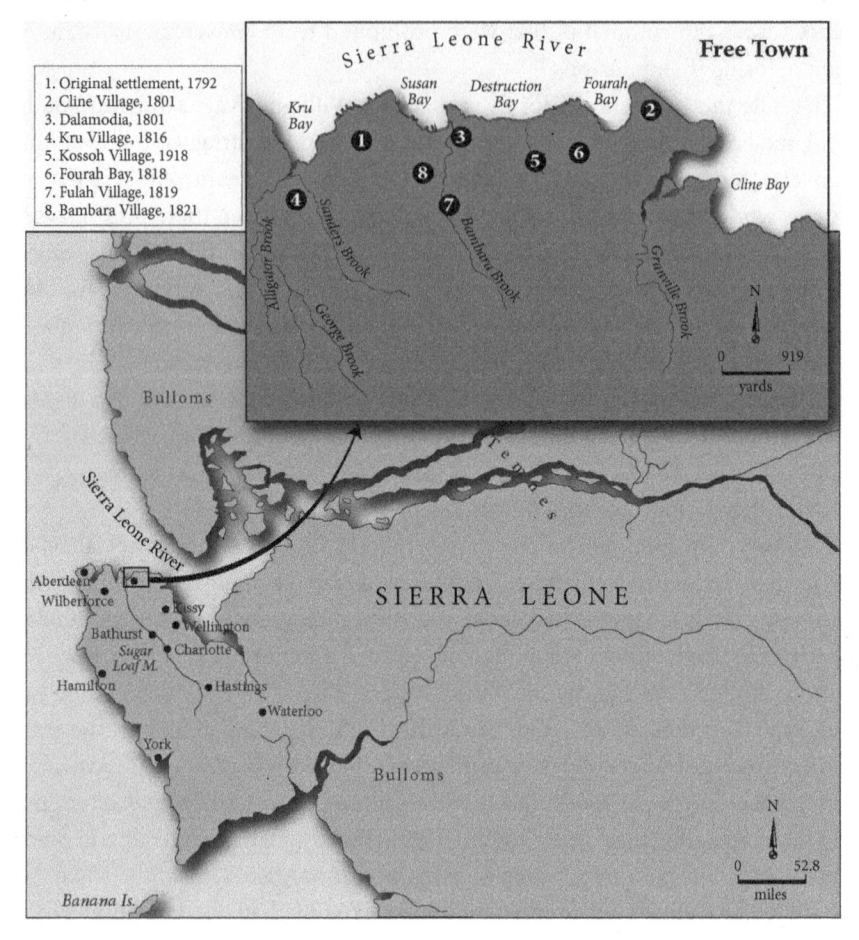

Figure 15.2 Ethnic communities in Freetown, including the Akus. From B. E. Harrell-Bond et al., *Community Leadership and the Transformation of Freetown* (The Hague: Mouton, 1978).

of Africans from his homeland rescued as victims of the illegal trade from the Brazilian ship *Esperança Feliz* (Happy Hope). Along with him, for the same purpose, Guilherme Pasca, a Catholic Hausa, swore "on the Holy Gospels."[13] However, some of the stricter Christians felt a growing sense of unease about what they considered a privilege that was inappropriate in a colony founded as a Christian project with missionary aims. It was in this context that the so-called Cobolo War erupted, whose ramifications went beyond the trial that led to the acquittal of the Akus involved.

In the late 1830s, the new governor of Sierra Leone, Richard Doherty, revived the persecution of Muslims in response to an appeal from CMS missionaries frustrated by the difficulties they found in converting the Africans in the colony to Christianity, while Islam was visibly gaining ground. In 1827, a British official observed that Muslim preachers were more successful in their ministry than Christian missionaries because they negotiated the elements of their culture better, and knew how to adapt their religion to the "spirit" of the local people. For example, the liberated Africans were more inclined to distinguish and dignify themselves with the outward symbols and ritual procedures of followers of Islam, such as their characteristic clothing, amulets, prayer beads, and methods of divination. The amulets and oracles fit like a glove with African traditions in vast swaths of the continent, where they were used to find solutions to everyday problems involving health, fertility, love lives, and financial difficulties. Christians had little to offer in this regard except holding up the Bible and promising salvation after death—and, of course, a small dose of respectability in the equally small but powerful world of the whites in Sierra Leone.[14]

The CMS's complaints were joined by those from the African Christian leaders, who submitted a petition to the colonial government accusing the Muslims of practicing witchcraft, believing in incantations and amulets, and failing to keep the Sabbath on Sunday, among other serious violations of Protestant doctrine. Doherty and some previous governors stubbornly refused to believe that most of those Africans had not converted to Islam in Sierra Leone but were born into that faith or had converted to it in their homelands. In short, they were already Muslims when they first arrived in the British colony. This was certainly the case with most and perhaps all of the Muslim leaders in Fourah Bay who had come from Yorubaland. It was true of Rufino himself.

As for the Aku Muslims, the governor tried to drive them out of Fourah Bay on the false pretext that the land they occupied belonged to the British Crown. To show his intentions, he ordered the destruction of a mosque in Fula Town, a predominantly Yoruba Muslim community near Fourah Bay, although the name suggests a Fulani ethnic association. Fulani Muslim teachers regularly served a large Aku religious clientele. Following in Findlay's footsteps, Doherty planned to drive all Muslims out of the colony, thereby paving or at least broadening the way for the CMS's evangelizing mission.[15]

However, when Rufino arrived in Sierra Leone in December 1841, a year had gone by since Richard Doherty had been replaced by Sir John Jeremie. An active abolitionist and a judge, in March 1841 Jeremie famously banned domestic slavery in Sierra Leone for all British subjects, including black settlers and emancipated Africans. At the same time, he signed a treaty with the Temne (or Timmanees), who controlled the Bullom Coast north of Freetown, on the opposite side of the Sierra Leone River estuary, "to encourage innocent and useful trade" in the region in exchange for payment of 4 percent of the import tariffs levied in the colony. Two months later, Jeremie defended the establishment of small British fortresses in the nearby regions where the slave trade was still thriving on the Nuñez and Gallinas rivers, and further down in Liberia.

While he was combating the slave trade and slavery, Jeremie introduced—or better yet, restored—a policy of tolerance toward followers of Islam. Ironically, Muslims—particularly the Mandingos and Fulas—were suspected of being the most active slave traders in the region. The governor's decision was based on political economy. Muslim merchants were a vital factor in the distribution of British products through the caravans that penetrated the interior of Africa, a way of encouraging legitimate commerce, with which Britain was striving to replace the slave trade. The Mandingos and Fulas brought small quantities of gold to Freetown, which they exchanged for a varied range of merchandise including muskets, gunpowder, lead shotguns, flints, swords, daggers, Indian cotton fabric, Indian red silk taffeta, other types of red cloth, beads, and tobacco used to make snuff. They also sold amulets. In the early 1860s, the erudite adventurer Richard Burton visited Mandingo stores that sold spears, bows, and horse saddles, and harness, as well as Muslim amulets.[16]

Rufino José Maria was one of the beneficiaries of the policy of détente that Sir Jeremie represented. This new environment enabled him to attend the Qur'ānic school in Fourah Bay in peace while he awaited the Mixed Commission's judgment of the *Ermelinda*. This new situation better explains what the *Jornal do Commercio* published about the relationship between Muslims and the British government in Sierra Leone. According to its correspondent in Pernambuco, the Rio de Janeiro newspaper reported that "The British, in their project to civilize Africa, gave land to teach those blacks who did not prefer to indoctrinate themselves in the Protestant faith."[17] As we have just seen, on the whole they were not that tolerant when it came to religion because they considered civilizing to be synonymous with Christianizing, and the freedom from slavery offered to the emancipated Africans must have been just the first step on the path to religious conversion. However, perhaps more than that, the British were interested in doing good business, and for that they needed to make partners of the Muslim merchants.

By the time Rufino visited Sierra Leone in the 1840s, the Fourah Bay community already had well-established Muslim institutions that followed models learned from other Muslims who had settled there, or from occasional visitors. Fourah Bay had a supreme leader, the alimami, who exercised political, judiciary, and religious powers. He represented the Muslim Akus in the colonial government and Sierra Leone's other ethnic and religious communities. He was additionally responsible for hearing and judging disputes between members of the community with the assistance of judges called *alkali*. Personal and religious matters were also discussed by a council formed by the *alimami* and the community's elders, called *sheikhs* under the inspiration of Sufism, which was widespread among West African Muslims. Religious leaders performed marriage rites and levied taxes like the *zakat* (Muslim alms-giving) to maintain the mosque, pay the imam, feed the poor, and finance religious festivals.[18]

Rufino fit into this structure of religious and political power during his sojourn in Sierra Leone. It was a new experience, but he was not among strangers. In fact, he sought out a community that closely reflected the life he had left behind in his homeland nearly twenty years before: Muslims like him, who were mostly from Ọ̀yọ́. Rufino may even have come across acquaintances or members of families he had once known—at any rate, people who had been captured in Ọ̀yọ́ long after his enslavement and could provide fresh news about his homeland and even his kin, if any of them had escaped being captured and sold to transatlantic slave traders. The Aku Muslim community in Fourah Bay, especially, would somehow lead him to take up a life he had left behind along the way, such as continuing his Arabic studies, as he himself observed, as well as other religious ideas and practices that he preferred to conceal from his interrogators in 1853. In short, it was not by chance that Rufino chose to spend his time in Sierra Leone with that particular community. His choice expressed an individual identity that, while inevitably transformed by his long experience in several parts of the Atlantic world, was in many respects still closely linked to his roots in Yorubaland and his life in Islam there. In Fourah Bay, he could be Abuncare.

16

The Trial of the *Ermelinda*

Coincidentally, Michael Melville, the judge who presided over the trial of the Muslim Akus after the Cobolo War in 1833, was one of the members of the British and Brazilian Court of Mixed Commission that tried the case of the *Ermelinda*. Thus, the histories of the Aku Muslims and the Brazilian slave trade converged in the person of a British magistrate in Sierra Leone. The *Ermelinda*'s trial only began on January 19, 1842, forty-one days after the ship arrived in the colony. The delay was caused by an illness ("a strong country-fever and an irritation of the intestines") that had afflicted the Brazilian judge, Hermenegildo Frederico Niterói, since he landed in Freetown a few weeks earlier. However, it was also due to his disagreements with the British commissioners about the Brazilian ship's capture and trial.[1]

It cannot be said that there was an irrefutable charge against the *Ermelinda*, because neither manacles nor shackles, considered the strongest evidence of intent to engage in the slave trade, were found aboard the ship. However, the British applied the Equipment Act to the case and found that it was enough to point out the presence, among other things, of chains (which the captain claimed were used to hold up the masts), siphons (supposedly to give the captives drinking water), four barrels to serve as latrines for the prisoners, and a small cabin to house the enslaved women. In fact, Lieutenant Matson wrote that the hold, prow, and stern had been prepared to set up a slave deck.

The ship also carried vast quantities of food (such as 158 bushels of rice and twenty of cassava flour) and barrels of water that would presumably be used for the captives to drink when they were put on board. Furthermore, there was a considerable supply of flour that was not listed in the ship's manifest, and a large quantity of firewood for Rufino's stove. According to the captain of the *Water Witch*, they also found a large amount of kitchen equipment. It was set up for large boilers, and there were more boilers than necessary for the use of the crew of a conventional merchant ship. As we have seen, according to the British, these were classic signs of activities associated with the slave trade.[2]

The Story of Rufino. João José Reis, Flávio dos Santos Gomes, and Marcus J. M. de Carvalho, Translated by H. Sabrina Gledhill, Oxford University Press (2020) © Oxford University Press.
DOI: 10.1093/oso/9780190224363.001.0001

Boilers like those which would be used in Rufino's kitchen struck terror in the captured Africans. Over the centuries that the trade endured, its victims believed they would be cooked as food for the whites, whom they viewed as cannibal sorcerers—even the British who rescued them from the slavers, putting them aboard ships with names like *Water Witch*. In the eighteenth century, surgeons on French slave ships were prohibited from dissecting the cadavers of Africans during the Middle Passage to prevent disturbances due to the widespread fear among captives that whites engaged in cannibalism.[3] This is clear in the statement by Olaudah Equiano, a victim at the age of eleven of what was then the highly active British slave trade. He became an enslaved sailor for a number of masters on the routes across the North Atlantic and Caribbean, and managed to use the profits from small business deals to purchase his manumission. He settled in England and joined the abolitionist movement—he was even involved in the original plan to establish the colony of Sierra Leone, of which he eventually became a critic. In his autobiography, an instant bestseller when it was published in 1789, he wrote that when he first set foot on a slave ship he believed he had entered a "world of bad spirits, and that they were going to kill me." ". . . When I looked round the ship too," he continued, "and saw a large furnace of copper boiling, and a multitude of black people of every description chained together, every one of their countenances expressing dejection and sorrow, I no longer doubted of my fate; and, quite overpowered with horror and anguish, I fell motionless on the deck and fainted." Upon their arrival in Barbados, seeing their potential buyers, Equiano and his companions in misfortune thought that "we should be eaten by these ugly men, as they appeared to us."[4]

Even if they are fictional, as some authors claim them to be, Equiano's words express a feeling of despair that can also be found in non-literary sources.[5] In 1823, for example, Makua captives from Mozambique rebelled aboard a slave ship off the coast of Bahia because they thought the time had come for them to be plunged into the white men's boiler. A similar story was told by the African Augustino, the slave of an Englishman in Brazil, who testified before the British Parliament about the horrors of slave ships, including the fear of being cannibalized. According to him, the fitter youths and adults were crammed into the hold in chains, where many died quickly, while the adolescents and children were kept on deck, unfettered. Frightened out of their wits, they had no idea what they were doing there. Many believed they were being fattened up to be devoured in due course, and jumped overboard to escape that fate. Samuel Crowther also shared the fear of being cannibalized by the Royal Navy. He and other children, his shipmates, believed that their British rescuers were going to eat them because they thought the parts of a hog hanging on the deck were human flesh. Naturally, they were heartily relieved when they realized their mistake.[6]

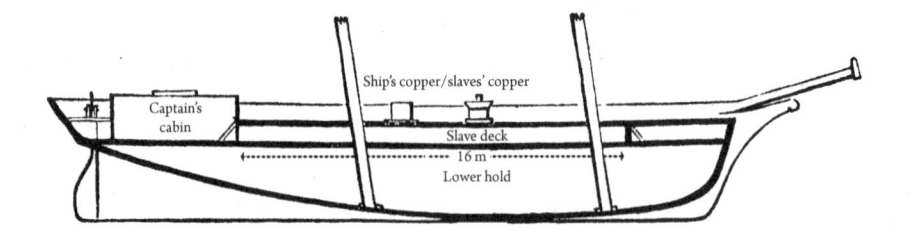

Figure 16.1 Most of the ship's slave boilers were located in the center of the ship, between the prow and stern, near the entrance to the hold, as shown in this 1857 drawing. From *The Illustrated London News* (September 19, 1857).

We can just imagine what was going through Rufino's mind when he first saw a boiler aboard the ship that transported him as a slave to Bahia. And now, as the cook of the *Ermelinda,* he may have seen the same terror in the slaves he fed aboard the ships on which he worked. Rufino's boiler was an excellent allegory for the predatory machine of the slave trade, which at the very least evoked a symbolic cannibalism. Saidiya Hartman has observed that Africans used the metaphor of witchcraft, giving a sensible interpretation of what was at stake in the operation that victimized them. "The slave was the prey hunted and the flesh eaten by the vampire of merchant capital," concludes Hartman, using a similar metaphor to portray the role of slaving mercantilism in the gradual formation of the modern world.[7]

In addition to the equipment required for the boiler, the *Ermelinda* also contained indirect evidence that the British considered significant: the name of the ship's owner. The commissary judge, William Ferguson, then interim governor of the colony, and the commissioner of arbitration, Michael Melville, wrote to Lord Aberdeen about the ship:

> In her papers, however, we find the notorious name of Francisco Lisboa as her owner: this person has already been reported from these Commissions . . . ; he is there stated to be the treasurer of an extensive Slaving Company established in the Brazils, and it is also there remarked that an arrangement had been made by the parties forming that Company, for Lisboa's name to appear in the papers of all vessels belonging to them as the ostensible proprietor: accordingly he appears in that capacity in the Imperial passport of the "Ermelinda."[8]

Suspicions about Francisco Lisboa's activities were groundless, because it was unlikely that a nineteen-year-old who was still cutting his teeth in the slave trade could have held the position attributed to him by the British, even if he were a financial prodigy. The "treasurer" was actually José Francisco de Azevedo Lisboa, also known as "Azevedinho," a figure well known to the British authorities. He was, in fact, the leader of a consortium of slave traders active on the African coast. Ferguson and Melville either took a shot in the dark—or mistook the name—but hit their target, because Azevedinho had recently done business, and probably still did, with the family of the *Ermelinda*'s owner, particularly with his uncle and the factor for that voyage, Angelo Carneiro. We should also recall that the *Ermelinda* was carrying a letter from the slave trader Gabriel Antonio, in which he placed an order of slaves for Azevedinho from his associate in Luanda. However, the British authorities missed that connection.

Further indirect evidence of the *Ermelinda*'s involvement in the slave trade, which the British did not mention but was attached to the trial records, included a letter from a slaver from Pernambuco, Luis Augusto, to his associate in Luanda, Manoel Matoso da Silveira:

> I arrived in this country after a fortunate voyage, although it proved [a] tedious twenty-eight days, fourteen of which was passed on half-rations. One hundred and upwards of the slaves died, but not one of mine, and I sold all of them for 300 to 360 Dollars each. Some [slave traders] suffered great losses, but fortune favored me. I am sending you a tin box with a variety of seeds, which I hope will grow at your beautiful place.

Illegal business deals and gardening amenities were openly discussed in the same friendly missive. The transatlantic conversation included other expressions of warm feelings between the two slave traders. Luis Augusto promises to buy a gold chain for a woman called Zefinha in Lisbon—possibly Manoel's wife or daughter—and asks him "to remember me most kindly to" her "and the rest of the family," as well as sending his "best regards" and a request to deliver 400 dollars to a nephew of his associate, with whom he also did business. The letter, seeds, money, and good wishes sent aboard the *Ermelinda* never reached their intended recipients in Luanda.

The *Ermelinda*'s crew were interrogated on December 27, 1841, seventeen days after the ship arrived in Sierra Leone. In his deposition, Captain Coutinho duly stated that he vehemently denied any involvement in illegal activities. He reported on the ship's voyage, stop in Bahia, and capture by the British, "but does not know under what pretence." He said the *Water Witch* was first sighted at 8:00 a.m. on the day his ship was seized (she was boarded some time in the afternoon), that there was no pursuit, and that he even approached the British vessel to ask about provisions, this last point probably being a misunderstanding on the part of the court interpreter, since, on the contrary, it was the *Ermelinda* that served food to its captors.

Coutinho said that he had received the ship he commanded directly from the hands of its owner, and that it should be returned to him, most likely in response to a question regarding the common practice among slave traders of using frontmen to keep out of sight of the authorities. The captain was careful not to state the name of the ship's factor and main shipper, Angelo Carneiro, saying that he only recalled the name of one shipper, who was not a passenger, Mr. Borges, who had consigned merchandise to the passenger Antonio Felix Machado. Coutinho also described the ship's cargo without mentioning the expensive carriage that belonged to Arsénio Carpo, who was well known to the British. However, he did recall "a general assortment of French and English manufactures," clearly implicating British subjects in the dirty business of slaving, in case the commissioners decided the voyage was illegal. He also stated that he had orders to return to the port of Santos, in the Brazilian province of São Paulo, with a cargo of salt from Cape Verde. Luanda, on whose shores the *Ermelinda* was captured, was merely the final destination for the merchandise and passengers that embarked in Recife. He contested the charge that the ship was equipped for slaving, claiming that its characteristics, utensils, rigging, and provisions were appropriate for the number of crew and passengers it carried. He denied the existence of large boilers aboard, as they were typically used to prepare food for large numbers of captives held aboard slave ships.[9]

The cook, Rufino José Maria, and the steward Manoel José Barbosa, the only two crewmen taken to Sierra Leone along with the captain, were also interrogated. According to the British clerk, their statement, "in regard to every point of any importance of which they professed any knowledge whatsoever, was a mere echo of the master's testimony." If the British hoped they would obtain a statement from the African that would be of any use to them, that ship had sailed. Instead, the two crew members complained of mistreatment by a British officer, Richard Acheson Burstal, the boatswain of the *Water Witch* and "prize captain" of the *Ermelinda*, who was responsible for taking the ship to Sierra Leone from the point where it was captured. Furthermore, Rufino and Manoel complained to the Mixed Commission about the disappearance of "trifling articles"—in the opinion of the British—from the ship. The accused had become the accusers.[10]

There were two separate incidents, about which we unfortunately only have Burstal's version, because the British reports do not contain a transcript of the victims' words. The episode involving Manoel Barbosa took place two days after the ship arrived in Sierra Leone. Barbosa allegedly ran from the poop with an iron bar in his hands to attack a Kru sailor who had left the crew of the *Water Witch* and was trying to disembark from the *Ermelinda* with a chest of clothes

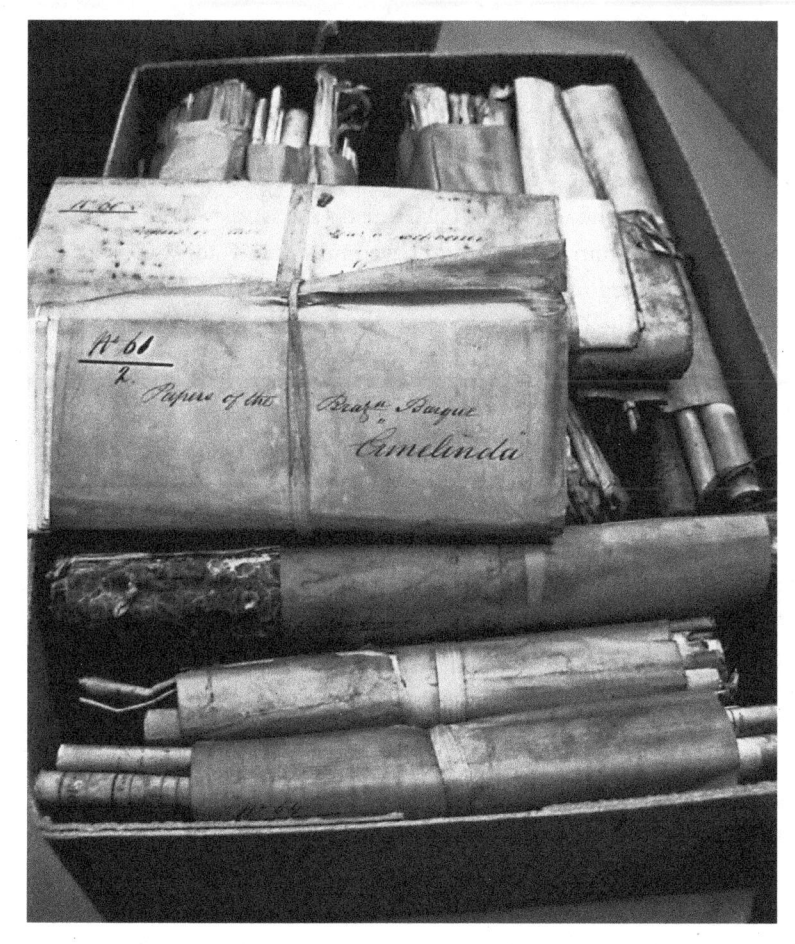

Figure 16.2 Records from the trial of the *Ermelinda*. From the National Archives of Great Britain. Photo by Mariângela Nogueira.

belonging to Barbosa. Burstal claimed that it took a great deal of effort to prise the iron bar from the plaintiff's hands, and that he had merely pushed him into a corner to prevent the assault. The English officer also stated that, after he learned of the theft of the chest, he "immediately ordered the Krooman to return it or to pay the steward for it."[11]

Rufino accused the British officer of beating him and hurting him with a stick, in addition to falsely accusing him of stealing kitchen utensils from the ship. Here is Richard Burstal's version, which even the British judges deemed "unsatisfactory":

> ... this deponent respecting the complaint of the cook says, that having been informed by one of the Prize crew (a Krooman) that the said Cook

had given away some of the saucepans belonging to the said Barque, this deponent went forward to ascertain the correctness of his statement, and as the said Cook refused to let this deponent see the number of saucepans in the galley, this deponent then taxed him with being the Thief, when the Cook called this deponent a dog. This deponent then told him if he did not at once muster the whole of the saucepans he would send him on shore and have him put in Gaol, and as he still refused, this deponent sized him by the shirt to pull him out of the Galley, when the Cook laid hold of this deponent, and this deponent did then strike him with his hands, and not with a stick as stated by the said Cook and that in the scuffle the said Cook's head struck against the corner of the Galley, which caused a slight cut, and further that upon counting the number of saucepans in the Galley two were missing.[12]

The British records state that Rufino, Captain Coutinho, and Manoel Barbosa were the only officer and crewmen left aboard the *Ermelinda* who were taken to Sierra Leone. The rest were deposited on the Angolan coast. That Kru man was therefore not a member of the *Ermelinda*'s crew, but probably came from another captured slave ship. It is not clear what he was doing aboard the Brazilian vessel. The most plausible explanation is that he was the same *Water Witch* crewman who was involved in the altercation with Manoel Barbosa.

We do not know how the case of the stolen saucepans ended. Was Rufino jailed for theft? Did he actually steal them? It is likely that the charges were groundless, which explains how he could freely attend the Muslim school in Fourah Bay.

Although clearly skewed in favor of the aggressor, the British officer's testimony shows us something of Rufino's character—he was not easily intimidated and was capable of standing up to overbearing treatment, even from a representative of the British empire. It is no less important to note that the only verbal abuse he hurled at the officer was to call him a dog, one of the worst insults for a Muslim. According to Islamic tradition, dogs are ritually impure. Therefore, the *Risala*, a tenth-century Maliki text that was widely read among Muslims in West Africa, recommends not keeping dogs inside the house. An Afro-Muslim contemporary of Rufino in Recife, whom we will discuss further on, set down in his memoirs that his Pernambucan master once insulted him by calling him a dog, a recollection that shows how mortifying that episode was for him. Therefore, it was not Rufino the sailor, the Yoruba cook, who responded to the English Christian's insult, but Rufino the Muslim. In fact, it was not even Rufino, but Abuncare.[13]

It is possible, however, that the language in which they quarreled was the pidgin spoken in the trading ports on the African coast. Then again, Rufino may have managed some broken English and Burstal some Portuguese, because in the mid-nineteenth century, Portuguese was the most widely spoken of the two European languages along the slave-trading coast. It was also a basic element in the formation of a local pidgin. The fact is that, according to the British officer's testimony, in the course of that misunderstanding they understood each other perfectly. However, the dispute did not affect the trial of the *Ermelinda*. It merely served to reinforce the Brazilian judges' opinion about the British authorities' arrogance and prejudice.[14]

The *Ermelinda* would become a cause celebre in the annals of the Brazilian slave trade as it was, at the time, the only suspect ship to have been acquitted by the Mixed Commission in Sierra Leone. According to the British commissioners, the trial was postponed due to the delaying tactics of the Brazilian judge, Hermenegildo Niterói, who did not consider the *Ermelinda* a good prize because it had not been captured with slaves aboard. Judge Niterói and his aide, commissioner of arbitration Joaquim Thomas do Amaral, had been recently appointed by Brazil's conservative government, whose policy toward the illegal slave trade was tolerance and often even support. Thus, Niterói was carrying out the orders he had received. In the case of the *Ermelinda*, he also rejected the charge that the equipment and provisions found aboard were conclusive evidence of guilt, and would continue to do so in future slave trade trials.[15] Amid all the bickering between the commissioners from both sides, Niterói fell ill. However, Melville

Figure 16.3 The Mixed Commission building in Freetown. From Johnson U. J. Asiegbu, *Slavery and the Politics of Liberation 1787–1861: A Study of Liberated African Emigration and British Anti-slavery policy* (New York: African Publishing Corporation, 1969).

believed his illness to be feigned in order to disrupt the process, an accusation Niterói strongly denied.

The anti–slave trade treaty called for a summary judgment within twenty days after the ship arrived in Sierra Leone, which did not occur due to the delay in starting the trial. It finally started on January 19, 1842, and the *Ermelinda* was acquitted due to a procedure in that court in which, when the parties disagreed, the decision was made by lot, a game of chance won this time by the Brazilian arbiter, Joaquim Thomasdo Amaral. The judgment of acquittal was handed down on January 20, 1842, the day after the trial began.[16]

The British members of the commission were furious at the decision and accused the Brazilians of partiality from the outset of the case against the *Ermelinda*. In a letter to the British Foreign Secretary Lord Aberdeen, commissioner Michael Melville accused Niterói, the Brazilian judge, of irregular behavior. According to Melville, when a statement was being given at a session where he should not have been present, Niterói sat—at the same table where the clerk and interpreter were seated—beside the witness, the steward Barbosa, and spoke to him in Portuguese, a language the clerk, C. B. Bidwell, did not understand, and perhaps even the interpreter did not speak very well. Bidwell accused Niterói of disrupting the interrogation and even implied that he had instructed the witness. The Brazilian commissioner was said to have corrected the interpreter several times. According to the British commissioners, the interpreter was "a man of humble origin and very limited education, but under the existing system sufficiently qualified for his office, is capable, when quietly seated with only the witness and Registrar, of doing what is required from him; of giving a rough, certainly, but yet a faithful interpretation of the questions and replies passing between the Registrar and the examined . . . "

The interpreter was Jan van Luyek, a Dutchman, probably a sailor who had somehow learned the rudiments of Portuguese (or sailor's Portuguese) in some or several parts of the Atlantic, possibly aboard slave ships. He was then living in the British colony, where he may have arrived aboard a convicted ship. "Neither can we anticipate" the British commissioner concluded, not with a touch of irony, "that the Interpreter's plain sailor-like interpretations, though right well adapted to the Foreign witnesses, would prove so acceptable to the more refined ear of the Foreign Judge," namely Niterói. A little later, however, Melville mentioned the "imperfect knowledge of English of most Foreign Commissioners," without directly accusing Niterói of speaking broken English.

However, the problem was clear: the fact was that Niterói suspected the detainees' words might be twisted. The Brazilian judge said that he wanted a fair trial, giving that as his reason for taking part in the interrogations. The British accused him of acting as a defense attorney for the slavers, although they couched the charge in the most diplomatic terms. According to the minutes of a tense meeting of the Mixed Commission, Niterói maintained that "no alteration had taken place in his opinion that the Commissary Judges should themselves interrogate the witnesses, whilst the Registrar attended to record such proceedings; and further that the duties of the Registrar should be strictly limited to the simple registration of the acts of the Commissioners." His colleague, Amaral, agreed. The Brazilian judge protested that he was under no obligation to follow the procedures of the other foreign commissions, and was merely required to obey the terms of treaties with Brazil, while the British based themselves on the court's traditions. In the end, Niterói agreed to follow the Commission's modus operandi until their respective governments could reach an understanding and take a stand on the subject.

The prisoner who caused the commotion, Manoel Barbosa, the sailor from Santa Catarina, actually believed that Niterói was the Brazilian consul from Sierra Leone and initially refused to sign his statement unless that official was present. At the time, he also accused Richard Burstal of mistreating him, which led Niterói to make the ironic observation that "it was very brave" of a British naval officer to strike a defenseless prisoner. In short, the investigation and trial of the *Ermelinda* were in a welter of confusion. There was much more to come.[17]

Whatever the motivations on either side, this is an interesting story about the language—or communication—problems involving the people who gathered in that Atlantic port to decide the fate of slave ships (and their crews) captured by the British. We get the same impression from the conflict between the boatswain Burstal, on one side, and Rufino and Barbosa, on the other. In Sierra Leone, the Tower of Babel was not just a characteristic of the emancipated Africans, who, in fact, had already invented their own tongue by that time—Krio. At the audiences of the Mixed Commission, they apparently also spoke a kind of pidgin, which was the language of the statements interpreted by van Luyek, whose English was probably rudimentary and his Portuguese even worse. Clearly, the Brazilian judge had good reason to doubt the transparency of that ritual.

In addition to the incident in the interrogation room, Niterói was accused of another breach of communication. This time, it was conversing with the captain of the *Ermelinda* as soon as he arrived in Sierra Leone, on which occasion he advised him about the procedures he should take, according to the British commissary judge. Niterói denied it. Melville informed his government that the judge was behaving in that manner because he contested the guilt of the *Ermelinda* and other Brazilian ships, more recently the *Galiana,* and opposed the terms of the Equipment Act. The captain of the *Ermelinda*, Joaquim de Carvalho Coutinho, indeed declared that as soon as he anchored in Sierra Leone he was allowed to disembark, and he had then sought out Niterói, believing him to be the Brazilian consul, not a judge on the Mixed Commission. The Brazilian judge was alleged to have instructed him to return to the ship immediately and keep an eye out for the approach of any boats, particularly at night, to prevent incriminating evidence from being planted on the *Ermelinda*. According to the British, that contact between the captain and the Brazilian judge was irregular, to say the least.

Meanwhile, the charges against the *Ermelinda* were being filed by Robert Dougan, Lieutenant Henry James Matson's representative, who handled his affairs, and, in particular, ensured that his client received the prize money due him for capturing slave ships that were condemned and sold at auction. This is because combating the slave trade was not just a humanitarian mission making the rounds in the Atlantic. It was also a profitable business. Philanthropy went hand in hand with the prospect of profit, aptly expressed by the Reverend Robert Walsh. The Anglican minister who wrote harrowing pages on the brutality of the slave trade did not fail to celebrate the prize money to be pocketed if the *North Star*, the British warship on which he served as chaplain, should capture the slave ship *Veloz*: "We were, therefore, all on the alert, exulting on the prospect of liberating so many fellow-creatures, and bartering and bargaining for our share of the ransom-money, for it seemed almost certain that she could not escape us." And the vessel did not escape. The monetary reward, Walsh calculated even more clearly, was "10£. a-head on all recaptured slaves; and in the case of success in this instance, would share 1,600£ prize-money," which led him conclude: "an inducement which the government most judiciously add to other incentives, in this great cause of humanity." The British ship rescued 562 slaves found aboard the *Veloz*, so the prize, if paid, must have been even higher than what Walsh had calculated.[18]

Again, the captains and crews of British cruisers were richly rewarded for capturing ships and confiscating slaves. In Rufino's day, officers and sailors received £4 per slave rescued from a fully laden ship (which would be reduced to just £2 if the slave died before reaching the port of disembarkation in Sierra Leone or another British base). In his book, Matson himself gave an example of the financial advantages of capturing a ship with a full hold: the prize for a 50-ton slave ship without human cargo was £200. If that same ship carried 400 captives, its maximum capacity, it would be worth £2,000. The British officers were even accused of allowing slaves to be put on board the ships so they could be more profitably rescued at sea—a charge that Matson considered outrageous.[19]

In 1841, the year the *Ermelinda* was captured, £25,744 were paid out in prizes for rescued slaves, £30,931 per ton of the ships captured, and £9,865 deducted from the sale of ships and confiscated goods that were also distributed to the captors. According to Sherwood, those amounts were the equivalent of over £30,300,000 in 2005. Between 1839 and 1843, Matson himself pocketed the not-inconsiderable sum of £2,629 in prize money, the equivalent of about £120,000 in 2005. Under Matson's command, the *Water Witch* captured at least sixteen ships, most of them Brazilian, by 1845. In the case of the *Ermelinda*,

Matson did not receive any prize money because the ship was acquitted, but the Mixed Commission paid him £201 for expenses he claimed for the operation to capture and transport the slave ship. The Brazilian commissioners voted against that payment, but this time they were out of luck. If the 244-ton *Ermelinda* had been convicted, Matson and his men would have received £976, in addition to the proceeds from the sale of the goods it carried.[20]

We are not saying that the British officers combating the slave trade did not include sincere abolitionists. But it is a fact that that self-proclaimed humanitarian mission gave Her Britannic Majesty's government an ideological tool—or "moral capital"—to impose its imperial rule over the waves.[21] The Royal Navy's abuses even benefited the major slave merchants who, by denouncing them, gained their own tool in the ideological debate. Defenders of the slave trade in Brazil appropriated a nationalist discourse according to which the Brazilians had a right to engage in the trade and should not submit to the British Empire. Few in Brazil dared to defend the "infamous trade" openly, but it became routine for the press and Parliament to protest the arrogance of the Royal Navy. That nationalist, jingoist, anti-British discourse gained a growing number of supporters, particularly after the Aberdeen Bill of 1845 permitted British cruisers to hunt slave ships off the Brazilian coast.[22]

17

Dirty Tricks

Niterói had a good reason to alert the captain of the *Ermelinda* to the possibility of fraud. Although he had recently arrived in Sierra Leone, it is possible that the Brazilian judge was aware that unorthodox practices were the norm there when it came to ensuring that captured ships were condemned. As we have seen, there were numerous interests at stake, especially those of the officers and crew of the Royal Navy, as well as those of Sierra Leone merchants who were keen to buy not only the seized ships but the merchandise they carried. One method commonly used to convict slavers was planting incriminating evidence. In a letter to the president of the province of Pernambuco, Niterói noted that Brazilian, Spanish, and Portuguese ships were being condemned "through this and other similar crimes."[1] He was right, and that is precisely what happened with the *Ermelinda*.

On January 6, 1842, thirteen days prior to the date the ship went on trial, the Aku merchant Joseph Reffell planted chains, bolts, and shackles aboard the vessel to provide evidence of its involvement in the slave trade. The slave irons were taken from another ship, the *Açoriana Oriental*, which had been condemned a few months earlier and kept in a public warehouse on the docks from where they could easily have been taken. Customs officers and Mixed Commission officials seem to have collaborated with Reffel, at least indirectly and discreetly, by turning a blind eye to his scheme.[2]

To better understand this story, let us take a look at the procedures to which captured ships were subjected upon arrival in Sierra Leone. The Mixed Commission's official boarded the prize to ascertain the details of its capture and make a general assessment of the ship, the state of the cargo it carried, and the presence of slave-trading equipment on board. Naturally, he also checked to see if it carried slaves and if so, how many, to whom they belonged, their physical condition, and where they had embarked. Then, the official sent a report to the customs office with copies to the Mixed Commission members. He also ordered the ship's captain and crew to appear at the commission court, which the official also attended, to give their statements.

The Story of Rufino. João José Reis, Flávio dos Santos Gomes, and Marcus J. M. de Carvalho, Translated by H. Sabrina Gledhill, Oxford University Press (2020) © Oxford University Press.
DOI: 10.1093/oso/9780190224363.001.0001

The official was responsible for safeguarding the captured vessel by hiring a shipkeeper to oversee its maintenance and security. In his turn, that shipkeeper employed his own team of assistants. Canoers were also hired while the ship was anchored in the port to take ashore any equipment considered suspicious and any rescued captives (however, pursuant to the treaties, the latter were only disembarked if and when the ship was officially condemned). The canoers also took merchandise from ship to shore so it could be sold to cover the day-to-day expenses of the ship and its crew. Later, if the ship was condemned, the canoers took the entire cargo to the docks to be auctioned off along with the ship. Joseph Reffell had been hired as a canoer to work with the *Ermelinda*.[3]

Reffell's plot was uncovered and he was arrested. The British members of the Mixed Commission deemed that there could have been two different motives for his criminal behavior, one worthy and one base. The worthy motive would be his desire to ensure that justice was done to the slave ship, since he was an African who had been rescued from a slaver. In this case, he would have a moral motive, even a political one. However, Commissioner Melville believed that there was a less noble motive for the crime: the Akus' knack for commerce, love of a good bargain, and esprit de corps. Or, in Melville's words:

> Reffell is an Ackoo, one of a tribe who have made themselves remarkable here for their fondness of money, and who are closely united amongst themselves, especially in mercantile transactions: these people are in the habit of clubbing together and by that means raising large sums, enabling them to purchase extensively at prize sales; the prisoner's own name often appearing in the list of buyers. Prize goods were scarce in the market at the time and Rum, in particular, which composed a chief portion of the "Ermelinda's" cargo, high in price: the consequence of the condemnation of the vessel would be an opportunity for Reffell and his associates to speculate to any extent they wished, or their funds enabled them, with the means then, as they supposed, of having the vessel condemned put into their hands, by the negligence of those whose duty it was to take care that such articles as slave-irons were not left open to the public, it can hardly be matter of surprise ... that persons ignorant and uneducated as they are, had availed themselves of the facilities afforded them for carrying their wishes in effect, and that Reffell had been prevailed upon to become an instrument for effecting that purpose.[4]

Therefore, Reffell was of Yoruba origin, like Rufino. The Aku merchant was involved in schemes for selling off the spoils of the ships captured by the Royal Navy and condemned by the Mixed Commission. But he also made a living as a canoer. He was hired by the court clerk, Mr. C. B. Jones, to unload the *Ermelinda* to permit a more thorough inspection of the hold. It was a routine procedure for all captured ships. Seeing that the goods stored in the ship's hold were valuable, Reffell apparently succumbed to temptation and devised a plan to plant the irons there. This was probably not the first time he had done so, as it was a well-known practice in Freetown. Apparently, Mr. Jones had allowed the canoer to commit the crime and may even have collaborated actively, perhaps in exchange for future rewards. However, the British official died shortly before the incident, another victim of the local fevers, so he could not tell his side of the story.

Other Britons also colluded with Reffell's operation, which only came to light a month later. On February 6, 1842, a man named Richard Lawrence sought out the Mixed Commission's proctor, John Dawes Thorpe, to report the scheme. An American citizen, auctioneer, and merchant in Sierra Leone, Lawrence had been appointed by Captain Coutinho to represent the *Ermelinda*'s interests in the colony. His duties included ensuring the integrity of the cargo and the ship as well as getting it ready to go to sea if it was acquitted. During his meeting with Lawrence, Thorpe admitted that he had been aware of the illegal introduction of the shackles onto the *Ermelinda* from the start but had done nothing because, in his words, "he had nothing to do with the vessel." A feeble excuse. To redeem himself, Thorpe decided to give Lawrence a note from an employee informing him, Thorpe, that the shackles had been transferred from the docks to the ship.[5] The author of the note was James Williams, the wharfinger (keeper of the wharf). It read: "They have taken about two dozen shackles and shackle bolts to day (sic) from under the shed, and gone to put it on board of the Brazilian barque 'Ermelinda.'" The message was dated January 6, 1842.

As he later confessed, Thorpe ignored the whistleblower's report. In his statement, James Williams confirmed having sent the note and stated that on the day he had written it, he had seen Reffell

> ... take a lot of shackles and hand them to a man on board his canoe, who hid them in the bows of the canoe: the shackles were taken from under the wharf shed, and there were about two dozen of them ... ; the shackles were wrapped up in an old broken mat, but the ends were open, which enabled him to see them. ... saw the canoe leave the wharf and go alongside the Ermelinda; he told Mr. Thorpe the same day; ... never saw such a thing before. ... When the shackles were put on board it was about seven o'clock in the morning. ... About nine o'clock that morning a boat belonging to the barque came ashore, and a boy named Billy who was in her said he came to call the surveyor, as slave irons had been found on board the barque under the forecastle. ...[6]

One of the men in Reffell's employ had planted the shackles under a stack of firewood in the hold of the ship.

Sam Williams, a wharf constable, confirmed the story and added that the items in question were "handcuffs, neck irons and waist irons." He said that he "asked [the] prisoner [Reffell] what he was going to do with them; he replied in the Akoo language that he was going to carry them on board the prize barque Ermelinda" and that he had received orders to do so from the late Mr. Jones and Thomas McFoy, Jones's assistant, who were also frequent bidders at auctions of condemned ships. When the schooner *Galiana* was judged a good prize on January 11, 1842, for example, McFoy purchased four barrels and 36 gallons of *cachaça*, the Brazilian sugarcane spirit. It is possible that he colluded with Reffell in the plot against the *Ermelinda*. Reffell was so confident of his protection by the British that, when Constable Williams asked him why he was removing the slave irons from the warehouse, he coolly replied that he was doing it so "that they might get the vessel condemned."[7]

The irons were "accidentally" found the next day by Augustine, an employee of Anthony Mason, the shipkeeper appointed by the commission to watch over the *Ermelinda* while it awaited trial. Young William "Billy" March, who also worked for Mason, told the surveyor that the shackles had been found. Mason counted fifteen full pairs of handcuffs and one incomplete pair, in addition to two barrels of slave irons. Another man who worked aboard the *Ermelinda*, Samuel Boyle, accused Reffell of telling him that he wanted to ensure that the *Ermelinda* was condemned and that anyone who found illegal irons aboard the ship would receive a £5 reward. The offer of a bribe is clearly apparent in Boyle's statement. He also saw one of Reffell's men plant something that he thought was "cassava" wrapped in mats in the hold of the ship.[8]

Two witnesses who worked for Reffell gave statements that sealed the canoer's fate. Thomas Bucknor, the crewman for his canoe, confessed that he had been following Reffell's orders when he placed the irons in the ship's hold. He also said he had asked what it was all about, but when he got no answer he simply did as he was told. That same morning, when he was in the canoe, he heard shouts from the *Ermelinda*: " 'they find irons,' and his heart then told him that the bundle he had carried below in the bows of the ship were irons." Soon afterwards, a boat was sent ashore to inform McFoy about the discovery. Another employee of Reffell who testified, Abraham Cole, said he was hired to unload the *Ermelinda*, saw the stack of irons, and confirmed Bucknor's statement. Like Reffell, both Bucknor and Cole were captives emancipated by the British. When asked if he recognized the irons shown him, Cole said he did and that they were of the type used to "fasten slaves." According to the trial records, the witness "has had irons on his hands and feet and therefore knows them."[9]

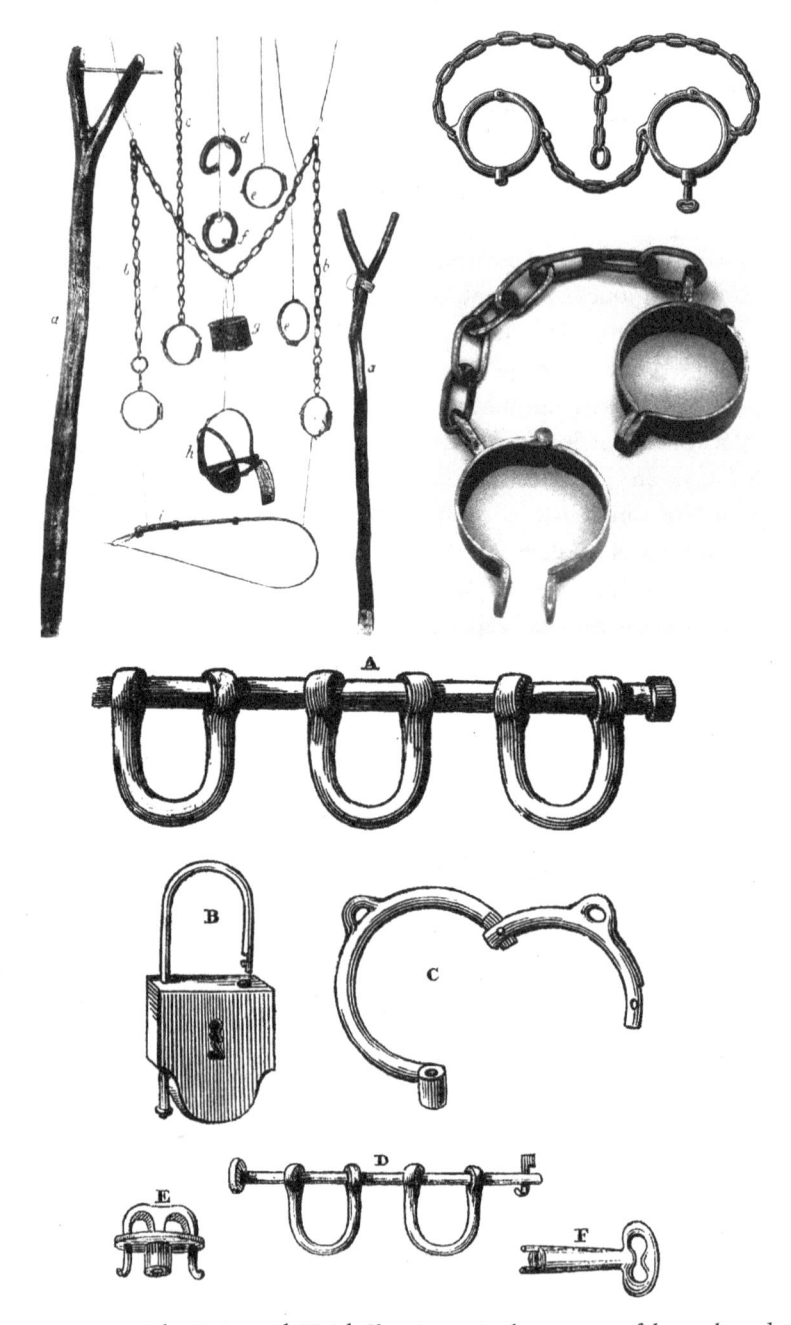

Figures 17.1a, 17.b, 17.1c, and 17.1d Slave irons similar to some of those planted aboard the *Ermelinda*. From Arthur Thomas Quiller-Couch (ed.), *The Story of the Sea* (London: Cassell and Co., 1895–1896); Société de la Morale Chrétienne, *Faits relatifs a la traite des noirs* (Paris: Imprimerie de Chapelet, 1826); Anthony Tibbles (ed.), *Transatlantic Slavery: Against Human Dignity* (London: HMSO, 1994); and Société de la Morale Chrétienne, *Faits relatifs a la traite des noirs* (Paris: Imprimerie de Chapelet, 1826).

The worker who found the irons gave an excellent statement. Augustine was a fisherman but had been hired by Anthony Mason to work aboard the *Ermelinda*. He said the irons had been placed there by Reffell's men, and he was surprised to find them when he went to fetch firewood because he went there every day and had never seen them before. Aside from Reffell, he was the only witness to mention that a certain Anthony Hamilton was present at the scene of the crime. When the irons were planted on the *Ermelinda* and Augustine suspected that something untoward was going on, Hamilton asked him: "'Do you know what we come for?'" and added "'You do not wish to see the vessel condemned." According to Augustine, he replied that Hamilton was "not the judge." In short, several witnesses testified during the trial. Even the man responsible for the *Açoriano Oriental* appeared at the police office because he had heard that Reffell was arrested for using irons originally confiscated from that ship to incriminate the *Ermelinda*.[10]

Joseph Reffell was arrested on February 8, 1842. In his defense, he accused Anthony Hamilton of being the true mastermind of the plot and said that Thomas Bucknor, who had put the irons in the hold of the *Ermelinda*, was following Hamilton's orders, not his, Reffell's. He further stated that Hamilton was present on the barque on that occasion, as was McFoy. Hamilton allegedly asked him if he should plant irons aboard the vessel to get it condemned, to which McFoy reportedly replied: "'No,' and 'if he did he would get into trouble.'" The charge against Hamilton did not stick. He was heard and released. After the investigation, on February 11, 1842, Joseph Reffell was indicted for stealing the slave irons and planting them on the *Ermelinda*. On March 17, a little over a month after the investigation ended, the prosecutor dropped the charge of fraud and Reffell was only sentenced to two years in the galleys—in other words, hard labor in the colony's penitentiary for theft. Reffell would labor in chains on public works, mainly doing road construction and maintenance. Nobody else was punished for collusion or negligence. However, pursuant to the recommendation by British representatives on the Commission to London, John Thorpe lost his job.[11]

In short, the slave irons were planted on the *Ermelinda* on January 6, and the following day the British authorities were happy to include the evidence in the proceedings. However, it all came to naught because the Brazilian commissioners acquitted the vessel. In his statement, Richard Lawrence said that after the ship was freed, when carrying out his duty to get it ready to go to sea, he spoke to Captain Coutinho several times, even on his deathbed. On that occasion, said Lawrence, "The affair of the slave irons seemed to press heavily on his mind, and he said, 'As a dying man I never knew there were slave irons on board the vessel.'" Lawrence asked Mr. Thorpe to investigate the case and received the note from James Williams that exposed the fraud. It was then that Lawrence decided to request the arrest of the accused.[12] Rufino was apparently unaware of all of this, as it transpired while he was in Fourah Bay, studying the language of the holy Qur'ān.

·18

Back to Sea

While the *Ermelinda* was waiting to embark on its return voyage to Brazil, the barque *Gentleman* arrived in Sierra Leone on January 13, 1842. The two ships lay at anchor at the same time in the same Freetown bay, possibly side by side. The *Gentleman* came from New York, having departed in late November of the previous year, carrying the thirty-five survivors of the schooner *Amistad,* the Cuban slave ship that was the backdrop of a mutiny staged by illegally traded slaves. The fifty-three rebels took over the ship but ran adrift until they were intercepted off the coast of Long Island in 1839. The trial of that case focused on the Africans' fate—whether they should be returned to their alleged owner, the Catalan slaver Ramón Ferrer—and mobilized abolitionists and religious groups, local and national politicians, including a former president, and even the Supreme Court. That heated legal battle put a strain on relations between the US government and the Spanish Crown, under whose flag the *Amistad* was sailing. In the end, the court decided that the Africans had been the victims of contraband and they were returned to the region where they had been embarked, near Sierra Leone. The *Gentleman*'s mission was very different from those of the other ships, particularly the Brazilian vessels that usually cast anchor in Freetown bay, including the *Ermelinda*.[1]

A total of six Brazilian ships were tried in Sierra Leone in 1842. All but the *Ermelinda* were condemned: the schooner *Galiana;* the brigs *Santo Antonio, São João Baptista,* and *Resolução;* and the barque *Ermelinda Segunda.* Of those six, three were from Bahia. The rest came from Rio de Janeiro, Pernambuco, and Santos, the main port city in the province of São Paulo.

The only slave ship anchored in Sierra Leone while the *Ermelinda* was in that port was the *Galiana,* a swift 114-ton schooner that arrived a day after Rufino disembarked. It was built in the United States, the trademark of light slave ships in those days. Previously called the *Hugh Boyle,* for about two years the schooner had been sailing under its Brazilian name on the Gallinas River near Sierra Leone. On that occasion, it is reported to have taken the powerful Spanish slaver Pedro

The Story of Rufino. João José Reis, Flávio dos Santos Gomes, and Marcus J. M. de Carvalho, Translated by H. Sabrina Gledhill, Oxford University Press (2020) © Oxford University Press.
DOI: 10.1093/oso/9780190224363.001.0001

Blanco to the Americas—probably to Havana, where it stopped for supplies. Blanco dominated the slave trade on the Gallinas River, and his barracoons had been recently been bombarded and razed to the ground by the British in a famous episode in the annals of the repression of the trade on that coast. The fact that that ship went into service in the Brazilian slave trade is further evidence of the Atlantic and international network formed by that kind of organized crime.[2]

Now sailing as the *Galiana*, the schooner left Bahia on September 1841, reportedly bound for the Island of São Tomé and Príncipe to take on a load of palm oil; after that, it claimed to be going on to the Azores to pick up immigrants to be transported to Bahia. Of course, that was a complete fabrication. The ship carried a crew of nineteen to twenty-three men—sources vary—commanded by the ship owner himself, José Pedro da Silva Senna, a resident of Bahia. After a hot pursuit that lasted twenty hours, during which Senna made strenuous efforts to change the ship's course, the *Galiana* was captured without a fight on November 23, 1841, in the Bight of Benin by the brig *Signet*, commanded by Lieutenant Edmund Wilson, and arrived in Sierra Leone on December 10.

Like the *Ermelinda*, the *Galiana* was not carrying any slaves, nor was there any merchandise in its hold. It anchored in ballast in Freetown. The ship must have already sold its cargo and was getting ready to put slaves on board. The British considered it to be equipped for the slave trade, but the Brazilians on the Mixed Commission disagreed. The British believed that the ship belonged to the famous Brazilian slave trader Francisco Felix "Chachá" de Souza, based in Ouidah, and claimed that he was traveling aboard it as a passenger when the ship was seized, but that was probably a case of mistaken identity. Condemned on January 11, 1842, the *Galiana* was auctioned off for a little over £506.[3]

The *Galiana*'s story is closely linked with that of the *Ermelinda*, not just because the two ships dropped anchor side by side in the port of Freetown, but because the captain of the former was appointed the captain of the latter. As we have seen, just two weeks after Rufino's ship was tried, on February 6, 1842, Joaquim Antonio de Carvalho Coutinho, the captain of the *Ermelinda*, died at the age of 40, felled by one of the many tropical diseases that commonly afflicted visitors to those shores.[4]

It is appropriate here to open a parenthesis about a popular topic at that time—the unhealthy conditions in Sierra Leone, particularly for Europeans. In a book published in 1823, Captain John Adams wrote: "The insalubrity of the air of Sierra Leone is almost become proverbial, and those going there are considered by many as embarking for the next world."[5] Indeed, among other evidence there is a long and impressive roster of British governors and other civil servants who died in that colony, one after the other, felled by the "country fevers." A visitor to that region, F. Harrison Rankin, wrote in 1836 that "it is quite customary to ask in the morning, how many died last night." Nevertheless, he was one of the few who believed that the European mortality rates in those parts of the tropics were greatly exaggerated, sometimes to justify the high wages paid to civil servants in the colony due to its dangerous health conditions. Rankin, however, titled his book on Sierra Leone *The White Man's Grave*. The term "grave" was also used in 1788 by the abolitionist Thomas Clarkson, one of the founders of the Sierra Leone colony, referring to the extremely high mortality rate among the British sailors then employed in the slave trade, who died at an even higher rate than the slaves, whose immune systems were better adapted to the local diseases. That term was a recurring theme in the rhetoric of British abolitionism.[6]

As for Sierra Leone, its reputation as a European sepulcher was confirmed by many other visitors and residents, some of whom saw death first-hand during the daily life of the colony. Robert Clarke, for example, wrote about people who went there to get ahead, "But as they arrived, flushed with hope and expectation, one by one they dropped into an untimely grave, or perhaps have lingered out an existence, stamped in their sallow, pallid or jaundiced looks, emaciated limbs, and tottering gait."[7] Captain John Lawrence observed in 1844 that it was "that most pestilential bower from which so few white men return ... or if they return, they only reappear as shadows and phantoms of their former selves." Lawrence was one of the whites who never returned. He died on the Liberian coast a little over a year after writing those prophetic words, and the Atlantic was his grave.[8]

Two years later, a report from the British government indicated that yellow fever and "remittent bilious fever" (malaria) were the main causes of death among Europeans, and that Sierra Leone was a typical "white man's grave" in Africa. This made tropical diseases a hot topic for everyone who visited or lived in the colony. According to the statistics, three out of four Europeans admitted to the hospital in 1840 died. In 1842, both the Brazilian judge and the arbiter on the Mixed Commission, Hermenegildo Niterói and Joaquim Thomas do Amaral, fled to safety in London due to illness.[9]

Thus, in that context, there was nothing unusual about the death of the *Ermelinda's* captain. A week later, on February 19, 1842, the Brazilian commissioners appointed a new commander, José Pedro da Silva Senna, the owner of the *Galiana* and the only Brazilian qualified for the post in Sierra Leone. Senna soon got down to work. There were court costs to pay as well as the expenses of repairs to the ship, and the wages and recruitment of a new crew. Therefore, he requested and obtained—but not without some delay—permission from the Mixed Commission to sell off part of the ship's cargo, from which he received £711, more than the amount obtained for his ship when it was auctioned. Then, Senna submitted a request for compensation for damages caused by the seizure of the *Ermelinda*. However, the British judge did not consider him legally qualified to represent the ship's owner. The Brazilian

Figure 18.1 Frontispiece of Rankin's book, *The White Man's Grave*. From F. Harrison Rankin, *The White Man's Grave: A Visit to Sierra Leone, in 1834* (London: Richard Bentley, 1836), vol. 1.

commissioners, Amaral and Niterói, disagreed, a decision that was once again made by lot and once again put the British on the losing side.

Senna's request for compensation to the Mixed Commission reached an astronomical £6,362.19, including, among many other items, expenses and wages for the crew and maintenance workers. For example, the tally included daily allowances and other small expenses incurred by Rufino, which totaled less than £10, paid by Richard Lawrence. Then there was payment for repairs to the damage done to the ship since it was captured; a long list of spoiled goods, such as sugar, spirits, tobacco, and cassava flour; wear and tear to equipment, including sails, ropes, and cordage; payment of port taxes and customs tariffs in Sierra Leone, which were levied despite the fact that the ship was taken there against its captain's will; the theft or loss of navigation instruments—such as a compass and a binnacle lamp—as well as boilers, saucepans, teapots, crockery, and cutlery. The list even covered Captain Coutinho's funeral expenses. The damaged merchandise included nineteen crates of "marmalade" worth £1.18, probably part of Rufino's cargo. The missing saucepans most certainly comprised those which the cook had been accused of stealing. Of course, the British commissioners contested almost all the items in Senna's request, as well as insisting that they did not recognize the captain's authority to represent the interests of the owners of the ship and its cargo, because they considered him "a mere sailing master of the vessel, a person placed there for expediency's sake alone."[10]

On April 17, having fallen ill himself, José Senna resigned from his post and fled to the Canary islands to find healthier climes, abandoning the ship and the demand for damages, according to the British report, which underscored that the captain had left Sierra Leone "<u>clandestinely</u>," as underlined in the original document.[11] Three days later, a new captain was hired. Because there were no Brazilians in the colony who were qualified for the job, this time the post went to a Briton, Thomas Wilkinson, a man of good reputation and an experienced professional, who, according to Niterói, was "recommended by respectable local merchants whose ships he had commanded." Wilkinson received £50 (about 450,000 réis)[12] for his services, half paid in Freetown, most likely with money obtained from the sale of more of the ship's cargo, and the other half to be paid when he arrived with the vessel in Recife. The captain's nationality weighed in his favor, because the British officials could trust a fellow citizen not to take the risk of incurring stiff penalties by turning the helm toward another West African port in an attempt to engage in the slave trade, as Senna or another Brazilian with a similar background might have done. However, as the Brazilian commissioner Niterói explained, the only reason the newly acquitted *Ermelinda* would not continue its voyage to Luanda, its original destination, was because the late Captain Coutinho was the "only supercargo and consignee of the ship and its merchandise, and since the Imperial commissioners had not discovered whom in Luanda was to receive the ship and dispose of its cargo, they therefore resolved to return it to the port of its registration and ownership." That meant Recife.[13]

Under the command of Thomas Wilkinson, the *Ermelinda* left Sierra Leone for Pernambuco on May 5, 1842, still carrying most of the cargo it had been taking to Africa, including Angelo's carriage and Rufino's guava sweets. Rufino had rejoined the ship's crew as its cook. He had spent precisely 139 days in Sierra Leone, which does not coincide with the account he gave in 1853, when he said he had spent seven months in the British colony, not less than five. However, it is possible that he was including the time spent at sea.

On the return voyage, Rufino and the steward from Santa Catarina, Manoel José Barbosa, were the only crewmembers who had traveled from Brazil aboard the *Ermelinda*. The others were hired in Sierra Leone—a total of ten, including the captain and a British assistant, Charles Toye.[14] Now reduced to twelve men (on the outward voyage there were seventeen), most former crewmembers of condemned ships, with wages of 25,450 réis per month (40,000 on the outward voyage), and two passengers who were obliged to do all the work of the ship's regular crew in exchange for their passage, the ship returned to Recife in fifty-six long days, a voyage that usually took one and a half months. It arrived exactly one year and nine days after it had left that port in June 1841.[15]

A curious postscript about the barque called the *Ermelinda Segunda* (*Ermelinda II*) would be fitting here. It was a larger ship, weighing 271 tons, and belonged to the slave-trading family that employed Rufino. Its owner was the same Antonio Carneiro Lisboa Junior who owned the first *Ermelinda* when it was still called the *União* and was classed as a brig. Calling the new ship the *Ermelinda Segunda* could have been a way of mocking the British one more time—a demonstration of the slave trader's power—because it was fitted out after news of the capture of Rufino's *Ermelinda* had reached Brazil. Having a ship seized would not make a slave trader give up that lucrative business. According to British calculations, while a Cuban slaver could not withstand the loss of 50 percent of his ships, in Brazil a trafficker could lose four out of five vessels and still make a profit. This was because the voyage to the Caribbean took over twice as long and was much more difficult due to the strong winds, including seasonal hurricanes. To withstand them, the ships that carried captives to Cuba required larger crews to handle the ropes and sails. In addition to more crewmen, they also needed more water and supplies. The ships therefore ended up carrying fewer slaves, and their voyages were less profitable than those to Brazil.[16]

While Rufino's ship was sailing back to Recife, the *Ermelinda Segunda* was crossing the Atlantic in the opposite direction. Its route confirms how far the tentacles of the Pernambuco slave-trading family's enterprise could reach. The *Ermelinda Segunda* did not set sail from Recife, Pernambuco's capital, but from Santos in southeastern Brazil, on May 10, 1842, with a crew of fourteen, including Brazilians, Portuguese, and Spaniards. Each of the sailors received 20,000 réis per month (half the amount paid to the crew of the first *Ermelinda*, a sign of the declining profits of the trade in human beings). The destination stated in its passport was the Île Bourbon (now Réunion) in the Indian Ocean, with stops (never made) in the ports of Paranaguá and Montevideo. It carried water barrels "as ballast," 150 sacks of cassava flour, 180 of beans, 20 of rice, 35 bushels of dried beef, and 5.5 meters of "flooring" (possibly planks used as dividers for slaves)—in other words, provisions and equipment required to ply the slave trade.

The *Ermelinda Segunda* was apprehended on July 12 while resting at anchor in the mouth of the Kwanza River, south of Luanda, after rival slave traders reported it to the British. Its capture sparked a diplomatic incident. According to the Governing Council of Angola, the ship had actually been seized by a Portuguese force whose commander suspiciously relaxed his vigilance, giving the British the chance to take the prize. The council protested to the commander of the British cruiser about the incident. The captain of the *Ermelinda Segunda*, Joaquim Maria Cordeiro, and his crew also protested, claiming that they had been forced to stop there due to a sudden gust of southeast winds, and that they had had to replace the rotten wood in masts and other parts of the ship. Set out in a letter of protest signed by eleven crewmembers (probably those who could read and write), that explanation held no water.

The ship was taken to Cabinda, where the British embarked 118 emancipated slaves, apparently rescued while still on dry land and awaiting passage to Sierra Leone. The *Ermelinda Segunda* was supposed to take them to St. Helena, but it had to stop at the island of Príncipe for repairs, confirming its captain's claims about the damage to the slave ship. It was leaking profusely. However, it managed to reach Fernando Po, where it was declared unfit to sail. The "black passengers" —the British term—disembarked. The schooner did not leave that port. It was tried in absentia in Sierra Leone and condemned on December 21, 1842.[17]

PART III

They tell me he is a Mohammedan, and very articulate, so much so that when someone contests his religious dogmas he contradicts them in such a way that he allows one to see the oppression of his soul, profoundly enslaved by an unshakable faith.
    Correio Mercantil, Rio de Janeiro, September 21, 1853

Pernambuco, where everything becomes a tool of anarchy...
    José Bento da Cunha Figueiredo, President of the Province,
    Diário de Pernambuco, May 7, 1856

19

Counting the Costs

From the business standpoint, the voyage had been disastrous for Rufino José Maria and other investors in the slave-trading expedition. The *Ermelinda*'s remaining cargo had been returned "in a tremendously ruined state," according to a Brazilian government report written many years later.[1] They included Rufino's guava sweets, which were not allowed to be sold in Sierra Leone. By the time they got back to Recife, they were spoiled. His merchandise was put ashore along with other goods and deposited in Angelo Carneiro's warehouse—formerly a building that was part of the Old Customs House in Recife—for inspection and instructions on the intended suit for damages. Indeed, Rufino's sweets were not included in the merchandise that survived the long voyage and was sold at auction for three million réis—about ten percent of the cargo's declared value when it was first shipped two years earlier. The barque would be auctioned off for another three million in early November 1842. The municipal judge in charge of the case ordered the British consul, Henry Cowper, to be present at the auction, but he refused, claiming that it had nothing to do with his diplomatic duties.

However, Cowper had been following the case of the *Ermelinda* since it returned to Recife. One month after it arrived, he informed his government that the local slave-trading community was heartened by the slave ship's acquittal in Sierra Leone. The consul advised London that Angelo Carneiro was taking steps toward suing for damages, raising expectations among slavers that thenceforth the British would have to pay for the financial losses inflicted on their business. Cowper had been informed that a so-called Slave Trade Society, a confraternity of slavers that was anything but secret—perhaps the business headed by Azevedinho (see chap. 10) had decided that if its distinguished member Angelo Carneiro won the lawsuit, ships should be sent to the coast of Africa with the specific intent of being seized so as to wrest money from their bitter foes, the British. Cowper therefore recommended to his superior, Lord Aberdeen, that they prevent the slave trader from succeeding. He promised that if Carneiro did win, he would "endeavour to collect effective evidence in proof of the undoubtedly

The Story of Rufino. João José Reis, Flávio dos Santos Gomes, and Marcus J. M. de Carvalho, Translated by H. Sabrina Gledhill, Oxford University Press (2020) © Oxford University Press.
DOI: 10.1093/oso/9780190224363.001.0001

illegal object of the voyage."² That letter merely served to strengthen the British government's resolve to resist the compensation suit.

The *Ermelinda*'s official owner, young Francisco Lisboa, had died of an unknown, sudden illness on July 22, 1841, shortly after the barque set sail from Recife. As he was unmarried and childless, his estate went to Antonio Carneiro Lisboa, his father. Because Carneiro Lisboa lived in Lisbon, on Rua Direita de São João da Praça, his brother, Angelo Francisco Carneiro, the consignee and the biggest investor in the failed business venture, spearheaded the efforts to make the British government pay for the illegal capture of the *Ermelinda*.³

In early August 1842, Antonio Carneiro Lisboa had made a power of attorney in Lisbon appointing some individuals as his legal representatives and granting them broad powers to handle the claim. In Sierra Leone, the list included Richard Lawrence, Joaquim Pinto Menezes Campos, and none other than the Brazilian commissioners Hermenegildo Frederico Niterói and Joaquim Thomas do Amaral, all of whom were residents of the colony; in Recife, his representative was his brother, Angelo Francisco Carneiro, who had the most at stake in the suit for compensation for the lost cargo.⁴

Lest we forget, the late Captain Coutinho had entrusted the American Richard Lawrence with getting the *Ermelinda* ready to sail back to Brazil, and Lawrence did not fail to send the bill for his services and expenses: in 1842 he received £250 from Angelo Carneiro through a London firm, Foster & Brothers. It was therefore natural that he should continue to represent the stakeholders

Figure 19.1 The port of Recife in 1875. Photo by Marc Ferrez. Instituto Moreira Sales, São Paulo.

in the lawsuit. And so he did. However, Lawrence was also a businessman, so he attempted to expand his partnership with Angelo Carneiro. In mid-1843, he encouraged the Brazilian slaver to send *cachaça*, coffee, and sugar for sale in Sierra Leone, describing it as a highly profitable venture. Carneiro probably had no interest in that sort of merchandise, preferring the "black diamonds" Lawrence could not supply. Their partnership did not go beyond the case of the *Ermelinda*.

In early September 1845, we find Lawrence asking the British commissioners to recognize the heir of the *Ermelinda*'s late owner as the ship's legitimate proprietor and to accept the documents—sent two years earlier—regarding the compensation suit. On that occasion, the American wrote that no efforts had been spared to condemn the barque, and he even underscored that "a man of the name of Reffell was *instigated* to put *Slave-Irons* on board of her, to effect her condemnation" (emphasis in original). It was a veiled accusation levied at the British officials. In another letter, he charged them with using subterfuge and complained of "the same determined spirit of opposition, which has been manifested throughout the whole Proceedings, in the case of the Barque *Ermelinda*."[5] This time the problem was that they had refused to accept the translation of the power of attorney that appointed him as the representative of the principals in that lawsuit, but Lawrence did not want it to be done by the official translator, Joaquim Pinto Menezes Campos. This was because, despite being on the list of Carneiro Lisboa's legal representatives, Campos had allegedly expressed an opinion contrary to the interests of the owner of the vessel. Furthermore, Lawrence implied that he could not trust Campos because he had been the supercargo of the *Guiana*, a ship condemned for slaving. In other words, to defend his own slave trader, Lawrence was accusing another one of being untrustworthy.[6]

The reader might suppose that we believe the *Ermelinda* was innocent. Of course not! Not only were most of the ships that plied that route involved in the slave trade, but we have shown that the owner and consignee of the barque belonged to a family with strong ties to powerful slave traders from Angola and Pernambuco, in particular, as well as from other Brazilian provinces. We also have Rufino's statement, given in 1853, to support the accusation. Supposing that absolutely no evidence of slave trading had been found in 1841, the intentions of the men involved in the *Ermelinda*'s voyage were suspect at the very least. At the same time, we must recognize that the actions of the British were irregular, if not illegal. Taken with a view to condemning the ship, they ranged from allowing slave irons to be planted on board to contesting legal representatives and using delaying tactics whenever possible to stall the lawsuit until the statute of limitations had been exhausted.

The Mixed Commission's decisions were reached partly due to the fact that the Brazilian representatives disappeared from Freetown soon after the *Ermelinda*'s departure. Both Hermenegildo Niterói and Joaquim Thomas do Amaral were in London in mid-1842, escaping the unhealthy conditions in Sierra Leone. In his dramatic request for sick leave, Niterói claimed to be "in such poor health, and so enfeebled, that he would certainly succumb if the rainy season [when disease was rife] found him in that country, desiring to go to a healthier place to gain some strength to resist the insalubrity of the Commission's seat." He sailed to rainy London after a brief stop in Tenerife. While in the United Kingdom, he received instructions from the Brazilian Empire's Foreign Affairs Minister, Oliveira Coutinho, to seek out the Brazilian representative in London to officialize his status. Otherwise, he would have been jobless. He was appointed as an aide at the embassy. We do not know which work he performed there, if any, but Niterói was still on the Imperial government's payroll. Later, the government would decide on "your final destiny, as deemed convenient," wrote Oliveira Coutinho, clearly displeased. Minister Oliveira Coutinho himself would lose his post for opposing the illegal slave trade, dismissed by a government that was becoming more and more tolerant of human contraband from Africa with each passing day.[7]

Amaral soon joined Niterói in London, but he left Sierra Leone in haste, without official authorization, because he thought death would not await the slow-moving diplomatic mail. He was therefore dismissed for abandoning his post but would soon be reinstated. Oliveira Coutinho instructed him to await new orders in the United Kingdom.[8]

In their absence, the British handled the Commission's business on their own and as they pleased until the Brazilian government decided to take action. In late January 1843, Minister Coutinho wrote to Niterói, who was still in London, demanding that he set off immediately for Sierra Leone so that the Mixed Commission would not "continue to do its work without the interference of the Brazilian Commissioners, because the interests of citizens of the Empire may not be upheld." Several months went by before Niterói sailed back to the British colony, where he would only arrive in mid-June. Amaral decided not to return at all. Manoel de Oliveira Santos replaced him as commissioner of arbitration.[9]

Rufino would continue to be linked to the fortunes of the *Ermelinda* and its owners in many ways. However, he was not idle when he returned to Pernambuco. In his 1853 statement he declared that he "spent some months selling cloth"—probably the wrappers that were very popular among Africans in Brazil, particularly women.[10] Meanwhile, the freedman continued to live aboard the *Ermelinda* and eat the rations set aside for its crew until the ship went to the auction block a few months later. Furthermore, on several occasions he received a total of 35,000 réis from the consignee of the barque, Angelo Francisco Carneiro, "for having tarried in this City [Recife], for going on to Sierra Leone, by order of that same gentleman, in order to testify, if necessary, in the case of the claim for compensation for the Brazilian Barque 'Ermelinda,' on which I was the cook," according to a receipt for Rufino issued on April 5, 1843.

According to a letter dated shortly after the *Ermelinda*'s departure from Sierra Leone, from Richard Lawrence to Francisco Lisboa—who was dead by that time—testimony from Rufino and Captain Wilkinson was included as evidence in the suit for damages. In another letter, written two days later, Lawrence was even more emphatic about the need for Rufino to return to Sierra Leone, when he wrote: "I must repeat to you it will be highly necessary for you to secure Capt.ⁿ Wilkinson and the Cook, and if possible the former mate of the Ship that was on board at the time of the capture for their Evidenes [sic] will be of essential service to you in the recovery of your claims here." Captain Thomas Wilkinson received 153,600 réis for spending time in Recife while awaiting the paperwork for the compensation suit. His food and lodging in the home of a fellow Briton, Luke Roberts, were also covered.[11]

This explains Rufino's next steps: Two days after signing the receipt he issued to Angelo Carneiro, Rufino sailed aboard the *Santo Antonio Flor do Brasil*, a name he had forgotten by 1853, although he recalled that it was a yacht, a light, two-masted vessel. Santo Antonio (St. Anthony) was a very popular name for slave ships because the saint was considered the patron of slavers, both Luso-Brazilian and Spanish. *Flor do Brasil* (Flower of Brazil) was also a common name for such ships. However, the combination of the two was unusual.

According to its papers, the yacht was supposed to sail to Benguela, stopping in São Tomé and Príncipe, but it changed its route to include a stop in Sierra Leone. Therefore, Angelo Carneiro arranged the payment of 850,000 réis with its owner, Henrique José Vieira da Silva. That amount included the conveyance and delivery of the documents for the *Ermelinda* lawsuit to Richard Lawrence, as well as transporting and feeding the Nagô cook Rufino José Maria and the English captain Thomas Wilkinson. We do not know if Rufino once again took his own goods to sell in the British colony, but the records show that he was again sailing as the ship's cook.[12]

The registration papers for the *Santo Antonio Flor do Brasil* filed with the Consulate of Pernambuco provide further interesting details. In addition to showing that Rufino was sailing as a cook, it gives his age in 1843—thirty-four—which does not tally (although it is close) with the age of twenty-nine that he had stated two years earlier. This is no surprise, for an imprecise age was the norm for African slaves as well as freedpersons in Brazil. The list also contains the names of nine other crew members: a master, a pilot, a boatswain, and six sailors. Their ages ranged from fifty-six (the Portuguese boatswain, José Ignacio de Oliveira) to twenty-six (the master or captain, José Rodrigues Dias, from Santa Catarina, a province in southern Brazil). It was not a young crew. Just two were in their twenties, four in their thirties, three in their forties, and one was in his fifties.

In the section set aside for recording the crewmen's birthplaces, Rufino is once again identified as being of the Mina nation. The boatswain and pilot were Portuguese. The remainder were Brazilians from several parts of the country, as were the crew of the *Ermelinda*. One was from Santa Catarina, another from Porto Alegre, two were from Rio de Janeiro, and three were from Pernambuco. Their wages were listed as follows: 200,000 réis for the master and 100,000 réis for the pilot for the entire voyage; 37,000 réis per month for the boatswain, and 25,000 réis per month for the rest, including Rufino, to be paid in each port where the ship cast anchor. The master and pilot would be paid in Benguela in the local currency, which would enable them to convert it more easily into goods—possibly slaves—to be sold on their return to Brazil. The other crew members were to be paid in Brazilian currency. Except for Rufino and Wilkinson, none of them had recently sailed aboard the *Ermelinda* from Sierra Leone to Recife. Rufino's contract with the slave-trading venture covered payment for all his expenses, including those for the return voyage.[13]

We have not found any information about Rufino's testimony in the lawsuit for compensation for the *Ermelinda's* illegal seizure. It is likely that no statement was taken, because the British did not allow the suit to be brought. That situation dragged on for at least twenty years, and we do not know the outcome. The British quashed the suit at each of the several attempts to bring it before the Mixed Commission court in Sierra Leone. In September 1845, they declared that the principals had missed the deadline, which the Brazilian authorities refused to accept. The death of Captain Coutinho, the flight of Captain Senna, the death of the owner, Lisboa, and the delay before his father and heir (who was in Lisbon) could take the case to court were all factors that enabled the British to reject the claim. However, the main factor was British stonewalling, which is clear in the abovementioned letters from Richard Lawrence.

In 1846, Francisco Lisboa's father, Antônio Carneiro Lisboa, calculated the damages at exactly 141,186,928 réis, which included 3,316,947 réis in interest of 1.5 percent per month until August 28 of that year. In 1867, when the suit was still in progress, the Brazilian rapporteur suggested deducting half the six million réis at which the plaintiffs had valued the barque—the amount received when it was sold at auction in 1842. The rapporteur also valued the cargo at a mere thirty million réis, reducing the amount of damages claimed by one hundred million. He also concluded that just thirty-three million should be paid for all the damages, including those incurred by Rufino José Maria's ill-fated sweets.[14]

The same report listed all the ships seized between the Convention of 1826, when Brazil undertook with Britain to abolish the transatlantic trade within four years, and the Aberdeen Bill of 1845, when Britain decided unilaterally to pursue suspected slave ships off the coast of Brazil. The owners of fifty-three vessels confiscated by the British over the course of those twenty years demanded compensation totaling the astronomical sum of 7,341,843,744 réis, although just

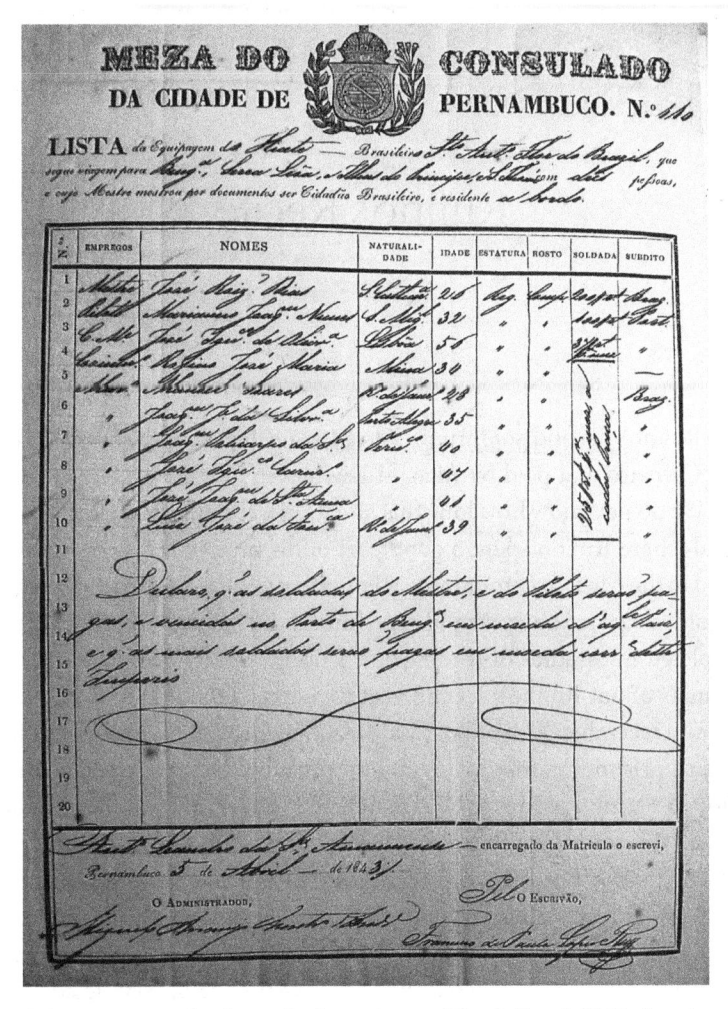

Figure 19.2 Crew roster for the yacht *Santo Antonio Flor do Brasil*, 1843. Arquivo Histórico do Itamaraty, Rio de Janeiro.

809,749,000 réis underwent arbitration. Also listed were fifteen Brazilian ships seized before the Convention of 1826 and twenty-five caught after the enactment of the Aberdeen Bill. Most of the ships captured during that period were speedy brigs—twenty-six all told—followed by schooners, which numbered eighteen. There were just five barques like the *Ermelinda* among the ninety-three ships flying the Brazilian flag that the British seized in the first half of the nineteenth century, and whose owners or their heirs attempted to win compensation for damages. They joined another sixty-two whose judgments were uncontested. These numbers suggest that the owners of the vast majority of ships captured by the British contested their confiscation. It is even more astounding that those losses were fully compensated by the profits amassed through long years of illegal slave trading.[15]

20

Rufino's Recife

During Rufino's second sojourn in Sierra Leone, his expenses were covered by Angelo Carneiro and paid by Richard Lawrence while he waited for events to unfold. We do not know how long that situation went on. We do know, however, how and where Rufino spent a good part of his time in the British colony: he returned to the Muslim community in Fourah Bay, where he once again attended a Qur'ānic school for one year and seven months. During that time, in his words, "I completed my studies of reading and writing Arabic." Unfortunately, that is all we know about Rufino's second visit to Sierra Leone. He returned to Brazil in around December 1845, aboard a barque owned by a Brazilian trader who had been a prisoner in the British colony, probably for slave trading. The ship's first stop in Brazil was Rio de Janeiro, where it stayed for two months and seventeen days, according to Rufino's precise account of his time. We do not know what he did there, but it is very likely that he received a warm welcome from the local Muslim community, people he may have known during his brief stay there after leaving Rio Grande do Sul a few years before. He certainly had much to share with his fellow Muslims about his experience of Islamic education in Sierra Leone. During his nearly four months' stay in Rio, he may have taught Africans who were in the early stages of conversion to Islam, discussed matters of doctrine with long-time Muslims, and practiced Islamic divination, medicine, amulet making, and other less orthodox aspects of the religion.

He started preparing for his trip north within three months of his arrival. On March 12, 1845, he paid 160 réis for a passport before going on to Recife, probably in mid-April, when the Rio de Janeiro police finally issued the document. On his passport, which was signed by Rio's chief of police, Rufino was identified as a freed black man from the Mina coast, age 35, with an oval face, gray hair, dark eyes, a flat nose, and "average" height, mouth, and beard. No identifying ethnic marks were observed on his face, which suggests that he either did not bear the facial markings characteristic of the Nagô (Yoruba) nation or they went

The Story of Rufino. João José Reis, Flávio dos Santos Gomes, and Marcus J. M. de Carvalho, Translated by H. Sabrina Gledhill, Oxford University Press (2020) © Oxford University Press.
DOI: 10.1093/oso/9780190224363.001.0001

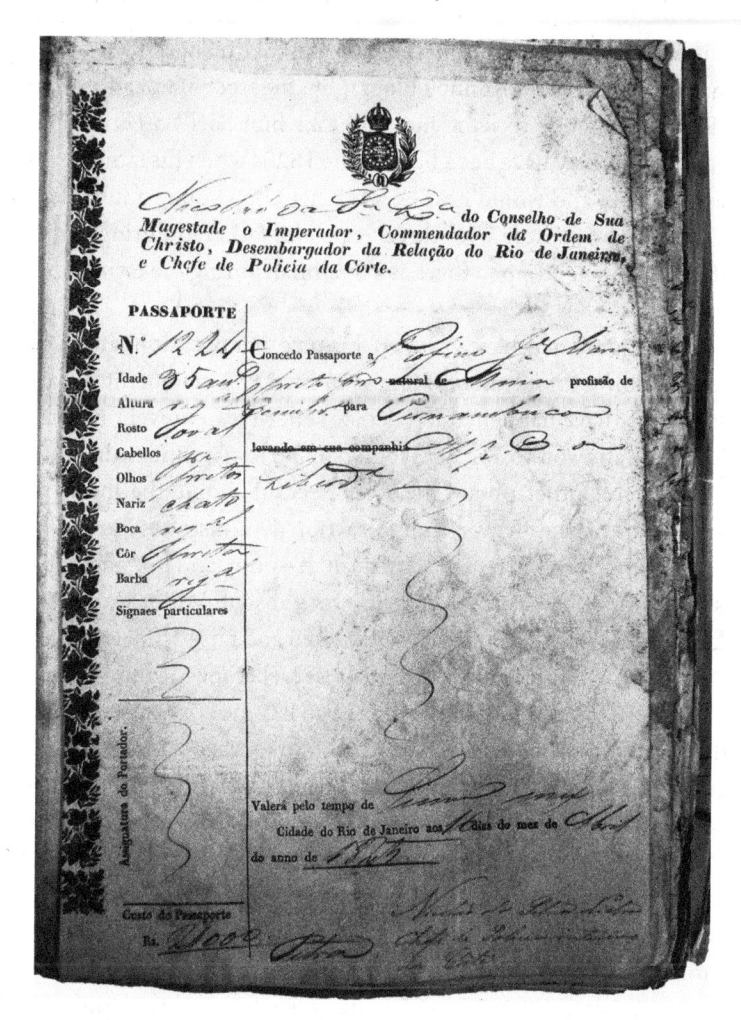

Figure 20.1 Rufino's passport issued in Rio de Janeiro, 1845. Arquivo Público do Estado da Bahia.

unnoticed. The African had presented the authorities with another piece of paper to obtain that one—his letter of manumission.[1]

Rufino traveled to Recife, where he stayed for three months before visiting Bahia. According to his recollection, we are in mid-1845, and that is confirmed by a customs certificate from Salvador stating that he arrived there aboard the yacht *São João,* coming from Recife, in August of that year. The ship's roster lists him as a "deckhand" with wages "to be determined," stating that he was 40 years old just five months after the Rio de Janeiro authorities had given his age as 35.[2] This time, Rufino did not sail as a cook, nor did he receive wages, a sign that he was falling in the ranks. On that voyage, however, his terms of employment were the least important factor.

This is because, at this point of the story he told his interrogators, we come across another key item in Rufino's biography: the freedman had a son in Bahia, where Rufino had gone to fetch him and take him back to Pernambuco. That son, Nicolau José, may have been born in the 1820s when his father was living in Bahia as a captive, and would now be a teenager or a young adult. He may also have been a child of a little over three years old, fathered during Rufino's brief stay in Bahia when he stopped there as a freedman during the *Ermelinda*'s voyage to Angola in mid-1841.

Of course, Rufino may have visited Bahia on other occasions after he received his manumission without mentioning it in his 1853 statement. In any event, something must have happened to Nicolau's mother to prevent her from going with the father and son to Recife. Would she be joining them there later? Had she died? Did the father obtain the son's freedom, while the mother was still enslaved? Whatever the answer, Rufino's action demonstrates the importance of father figures in communities in the African diaspora, and possibly the function of those communities when the parents were absent. We believe that Nicolau was taken in by a group that may have protected and raised him in the absence of not only his father but possibly his mother as well. Since Rufino was a Muslim, his son may have found shelter in Bahia's large Islamic community. It could have been the same group which welcomed Rufino, perhaps as an *alufa* and minister, during his stay in Bahia that time. There was a good market in Bahia for the former cook's ritual skills, especially after his studies and observations in Sierra Leone. Thus, religious matters must have kept him in Bahia during his stay there, which lasted much longer than it would have required him just to deal with family matters.

Regarding his family, Rufino does not mention anyone else aside from his son, perhaps to protect them. In 1853, the police found three manumission letters in a tin box in his home, two of which may have belonged to his son and his wife—whether or not she was Nicolau's mother. The third would have been the one that Judge Peçanha issued to Rufino eighteen years earlier, which he always took with him on his travels. Unfortunately, those documents were not transcribed during the investigation.[3]

Rufino's passport application confirms that he was not accompanied by a woman when he traveled from Salvador to Recife. In December 1845, he followed the usual procedure of requesting the document from the Bahia police chief in order to "return to Pernambuco, taking with him his son Nicolau José, a Creole," and no one else. At the time, a passport was required not only for African freedpersons but for anyone traveling within Brazil. On December 22, the police ordered him to submit a background check from the criminal courts before issuing him the passport, but he claimed there was not enough time to do so. Instead, he asked if he could present a merchant– "with a wet goods shop behind the nuns' wall," that is, the Clarite convent in Salvador—as a guarantor of his good behavior. It seems that Rufino had Bahian connections beyond those he must have established with the Yoruba-speaking Muslims and other Africans. In this case, it was someone who may also have helped him spend several months in Bahia, as he had on that occasion. Thanks to the merchant's signature, he was granted permission to travel with his son. Unfortunately, there are no details in his passport regarding the child or young man—nothing about his age, appearance, status (free or freed), or birthplace, the kind of data usually found in such a document. However, since Nicolau did not have his own travel document he was probably still under 16, the age after which one was required to hold a passport and the other identity papers needed to go from place to place.

A report on port activity in the *Diário de Pernambuco* newspaper states that Rufino traveled from Bahia to Recife aboard the steamer *São Salvador*. This may not have been the first time he had sailed aboard that kind of vessel, as he had been familiar with them since his days in Rio Grande do Sul. An advertisement in the newspaper *O Mensageiro* published in late 1835 shows that the steamship *Liberal* ran between the capital of that state, Porto Alegre, and the city of Rio Grande, stopping in Pelotas. The steamer aboard which Rufino was now traveling with his son came from Rio de Janeiro, stopping in Salvador and Maceió before casting anchor in Recife, from where it went on to the ports of Fortaleza, São Luís, and Belém. The steamers of the Companhia Brasileira de Paquetes a Vapor had followed that route since 1836, when the company was established for the main purpose of ensuring that official correspondence traveled more quickly from one province to the next, an important step toward modernizing political control by the Imperial State. A privately owned company, it required a generous government subsidy to operate because it obtained very little return from carrying private mail, goods, and passengers. Rufino's voyage confirms that: he and his son were the only passengers who disembarked in Recife on January 16, 1846. In fact, that date establishes that they both arrived in Recife six months later than the time he had given—mid-1845. It also suggests that his stay in Bahia was not as brief as his statement would have us believe, but lasted several months, from August 1845 until January of the following year.[4]

More than four years had gone by since the capture of the *Ermelinda*. However, that incident continued to overshadow Rufino's life. In late May 1846, he and twenty-five other shippers who had suffered a financial setback due to the loss of their merchandise got together in the office of a notary. All residents of Recife, they belonged to the group of investors in the *Ermelinda*'s ill-fated voyage. They included everyone from the smallest shipper, Bento Mesquita, with his tiny investment of 92,096 réis, to Domingos Martins de Souza, and his 2,409,340 réis. The men who gathered there signed a power of attorney granting "unlimited powers" to Commander Angelo Francisco Carneiro in Pernambuco and to

Foster & Brothers in London to represent them in the legal battle with the British government. According to that document, those agents were supposed to "seek and demand all their rights and justice in all of their lawsuits and claims, both criminal and civil, brought on their behalf in the Audiences and Courts in one or the other jurisdiction, hearing the verdicts and favorable decisions, and have them removed from the process, ensuring their due fulfillment, and for those which are unfavorable, to appeal, aggravate and seize everything, follow and renounce, until the highest level of the Supreme Senate," and so forth.[5] We do not know if Rufino or any other stakeholder in the *Ermelinda*'s voyage ever received his share of the compensation—just that it still had not been paid by 1867.

That group of twenty-six people, in addition to Angelo Carneiro, must have been important figures for Rufino in Pernambuco. We can see him asking one or the other of those shippers for news of the lawsuit. Rufino must have had business dealings with one of them, Duarte José Martins da Costa, the Mina steward on the *Ermelinda*'s disastrous voyage. Duarte was present at the meeting of those who lost money due to the capture of the barque, and his name appears alongside Rufino's—and last—on the list of those who signed the power of attorney for Carneiro. Eight years later, in 1854, Duarte dictated his will, in which he recalled being a sailor and shipper on the *Ermelinda* (which the scribe understood and wrote first as *Melindroza*, and then as *Melindra*), which "was seized... in Angola by the British," declaring that he expected to receive compensation of "nine hundred and seventy-eight thousand two hundred réis" including interest. Then he listed other outstanding debts: "I hereby declare that the said cook of the same barque owes me thirty-two thousand réis, the remainder for a slave I gave him to sell, which black man lives on Rua da Senzala."[6] Without a doubt, he was referring to Rufino José Maria: the barque seized by the British in Angola, a cook from that ship who lived on Rua da Senzala Velha ... it all fits. That document is the only one that clearly states that Rufino bought and sold slaves. However, we do not know if his dealings with Duarte took place before or after the voyage of the *Ermelinda* discussed here, or if the transaction occurred in Brazil or Africa. This is because, in addition to Rufino's debt, Duarte indicates that one Jorge Lima owed him "the price of two slaves who remained in his power in Luanda in order to sell them." This is interesting information, because it suggests that the sailor was buying slaves in the interior or more likely the coast of Africa to resell them in Luanda—a little-known kind of commercial dealing for petty slavers based in Brazil, but well suited to a small investor who preferred not to risk losing his investment during the Middle Passage. Rufino himself had probably done this occasionally, possibly in partnership with Duarte.

However, that incident on the Angolan coast changed Rufino's life, inducing him to stop working as a slave-ship's cook and perhaps small-time slave trader, and embark on the religious career for which he was trained in Sierra Leone.

There is nothing in his 1853 statement that indicates that he stopped dealing in slaves due to a moral objection to that activity, but it is possible that he was overwhelmed by doubts about the trade in human beings during his stay in Sierra Leone. After all, the British colony was a refugee camp for victims of the traffic, where intense anti-traffic propaganda and the repression of those involved in it and in slavery itself were an integral part of the Christian doctrine preached there. British subjects in Sierra Leone faced the death penalty for the crime of slave trading, a harsh law enacted to discourage a business that was so lucrative that its residents—even former captives—continued to practice it right under the British officials' noses.

However, the opinion that must truly have influenced Rufino would have been that of his fellow Muslims and teachers in Fourah Bay, and we do not know their thoughts on that subject. Mandingo and Fula Muslims, in particular, were said to be the chief agents of the slave trade in the interior, even within the British colony, as we have already shown. Perhaps the Aku Muslims, Rufino's people, did not engage in that practice, however. The fact that he did not return to his former occupation—if we believe his statement—raises at least the suspicion that he may have learned in Fourah Bay that it was not a worthy way to make a living. In principle, this had nothing to do with Islamic doctrine because, strictly speaking, it did not prohibit the sale and enslavement of human beings, except for its own followers. And even among those, depending on the circumstances, the doctrine was not followed in practice: all it took was to view the other as a heretic, one who did not follow the true Muslim path. We should recall that Rufino himself was the victim of other Muslims, and he himself may have at some point enslaved a child of Allah.

Whatever the reason, Rufino decided to settle permanently on dry land after more than a decade of dangerous Atlantic crossings. He chose to make his home in Recife, a growing city of nearly 50,000 in the mid-1840s. According to one official census, the population of the central districts alone grew from 25,678 in 1828 to 40,977 in 1856. Together with residents of outlying districts, the figure would reach roughly 100,000 by the middle of the century. During that period, free and freedpersons were the fastest-growing segment of the population— Rufino and his son made their small contribution to this growth—having risen from 17,743 to 33,270 between 1828 and 1856. The number of slaves fell slightly, from 7,935 to 7,707. Rufino had settled down in a city where slavery was dwindling due to the decline of and definitive ban on the transatlantic slave trade, an increase in inter-provincial traffic to the southeast of the country, and the sale of slaves from the provincial capital to both the southeast of Brazil and the cane and cotton fields in the interior.[7]

If Rufino had been a fictional character, it would have been hard to make up a street that was more closely linked to his life's path than Rua da Senzala Velha

(Old Slave Quarters Street), where our real-life protagonist lived when the police came to arrest him. After a career tied to the transatlantic slave trade, Rufino was living in a street whose name was derived from a former slave quarters used to imprison and resell captives recently arrived from Africa during the first century of colonization in Brazil. It was probably the first large slave warehouse in the future city of Recife, and thus one of the oldest urban slave quarters in the former Portuguese colony. It was already old during the time of the Dutch occupation (1630–1654), when "Rua da Senzala Nova" (New Slave Quarters Street) was built, according to the inventory of arms and equipment that the Luso-Brazilian forces seized from the Dutch.[8] By the time Rufino was arrested in 1853, the street had lost that landmark. It was just one of many in the port district, frequented by sailors, stevedores, hired-out slave men and women, store clerks, soldiers, and port workers. The *Folhinha de Algibeira*, a sort of almanac of Recife at the time, listed in 1853 the varied number of businesses on Rua da Senzala Velha. In addition to seven taverns, a bar, and the ever-present warehouses in the port district, there were at least one drug store, two barbershops, and seven bakeries, establishments where Rufino may have worked—especially the drug store, as he had been an apothecary's slave—if he wanted or needed to. Since demolished, the Church of Corpo Santo also stood a few yards from his street, but frequenting that address was probably of little interest to a devout Muslim like Rufino.[9]

In fact, if he wanted to live within the bubble of his own African nation, Rufino did not have far to go. As a Nagô, he was an exception in Pernambuco where, like Rio de Janeiro, only a minority of Africans came from Yorubaland and the surrounding regions. The clear majority came from the Congo-Angola line of the slave trade. However, the Nagô of Recife may have formed a significant minority, as we have been able to find some other members of the Nagô nation in that city at the time of Rufino's arrest.

For example, the police investigations of 1853 searched the homes of "free blacks," Africans from "several nations of Angola" and "free Africans" in the São José district, a typical low-income neighborhood.[10] In the case of the "free Africans," they were captives who had been confiscated as contraband by the authorities after the 1831 ban on the transatlantic slave trade. Unfortunately, except for the Angolan groups, there is no mention of the nations to which the victims of those police raids belonged, but we do know that there were Nagôs like Rufino among the free Africans living in Recife. One of them requested his manumission in 1862, claiming that he had worked at the War Arsenal since 1849, when he was 21, before going on to the local Orphans' College in 1852, where he continued working.[11]

Nine other "free" Nagôs were distributed in 1850 as follows: four to work in the administration of the orphanage's assets, and five in charitable institutions.

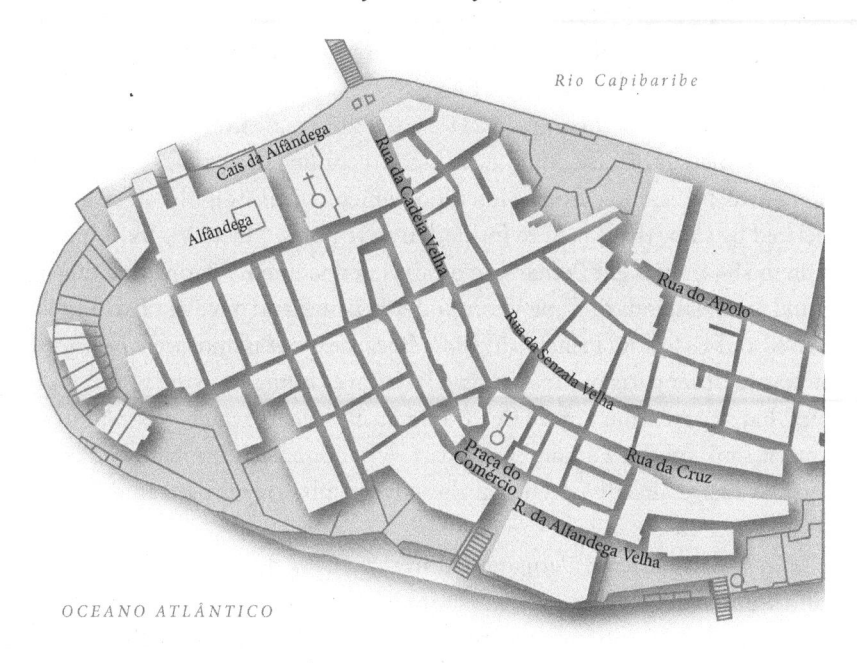

Figure 20.2 Map of Rufino's neighborhood in Recife, showing the Rua da Senzala Velha where Rufino lived when arrested in 1853. Map drawn by Eliziário Mamede based on an 1854 original reproduced in José Luiz Mota Menezes, *Atlas Histórico Cartográfico do Recife* (Recife: Prefeitura da Cidade do Recife/Fundaj, 1988).

The entities that benefited from their services were obliged to "support them, dress them and treat them with all humanity," as well as indoctrinating them with Christian principles, according to the instructions of November 19, 1835 regarding free Africans. At least one of the Africans employed in 1850 did not yet have a Christian name, which indicates that he had been recently "seized."[12] However, this was not the case with the Africans apprehended at the time of Rufino's arrest. According to the report on the 1853 raids, most of them were older men; at least they looked old, like Rufino, who at the age of about forty-five was described in the press as an "old black man" and a "fat old man."[13]

It is therefore possible that some of those Africans had arrived in Pernambuco prior to 1831, when the slave ships supposedly arriving from Angola could still land their cargo legally in the port of Recife, although they were carrying people from regions north of the equator, where the slave trade had been banned since 1815. There are records from the late 1820s of at least two ships transporting captives from Bahia to Recife, where thousands of Yoruba were imported during the first half of the nineteenth century. The *Maria Thereza* carried 260 in 1827, and the *Nossa Senhora da Guia* (which the British would capture near Lagos in 1830) landed another 147 in 1828. As we have seen, ships officially returning to Brazil from Molembo, in Congo, actually came from Onim, Badagry, and Ouidah—all ports in the Bight of Benin.[14]

In 1829, the *Borboleta* brought 218 captives to Recife from the Bight of Benin. None had died during the Middle Passage. According to its papers, the schooner claimed to be coming from Molembo, which, again, was the port generally declared by ships that sailed to forbidden slave ports.[15] In 1839, 1840, and once again in 1844, ships left Pernambuco carrying documents stating that they were bound for the islands of Cape Verde and São Tomé, and once again to São Tomé in 1840 and 1844, and Príncipe in 1846. Because those islands were just stops on the way to other parts of the African coast, slaves brought on the return journey could have come from anywhere. The yacht *Bom Jesus,* which was captured because it sank off the Pernambuco coast, was bound for Príncipe—at least on paper. We have already noted that these were subterfuges used to disguise the illegal slave trade.[16]

More Nagôs entered Pernambuco in the 1840s due to the brief period of traffic from the Bight of Benin that started up to avoid the Angolan coast, which was being closely watched by British cruisers—the capture of the *Ermelinda* confirmed that they were indeed vigilant. According to the Portuguese consul in Recife, in 1844 Brazilian ships were diverted to the ports of Onim, Benin, and Ouidah. They were "ships of small lot" in his description, less visible from a distance, easy to maneuver, and fast in a getaway—in short, swift of sail. Because they could not carry much human cargo they spent less time on the African coast, which made them better able to avoid the British Navy and tropical fevers. It is true that smaller cargoes meant lower profits, but their greater speed made up for it, both because it reduced the length of the Middle Passage, which meant a lower death rate among the captives and made it easier to escape their British pursuers. At least six such ships unloaded slaves in Pernambuco in 1844.[17]

However, the trade in African captives from Yorubaland and the surrounding area was generally slight, which is reflected in the escaped slave notices: few of the reported fugitives were said to come from those parts. In 1844, Inácio, the slave of a merchant, fled when he was being forced to board the patache *Pelicano*, probably to be sold in another province. According to his master, he was a Nagô and bore the "marks of his nation": two or three crossed scars on his face. In 1848, it was the turn of the Nagô Joaquina to flee into the streets of Recife. In his study of hundreds of escaped slave notices, Gilberto Freyre gives just two examples of West African slaves, one being Teresa from the Benin nation, who fled in 1834, and the other being Inácio, mentioned above. The advertisements Freyre describes confirm the small number of slaves from West Africa. Most escapees were from Angola, Benguela, Cabinda, Congo, Mozambique, and their respective hinterlands. It is likely, however, that the large number of slaves described as being "*do gentio da Costa*" ("from the heathens from the Coast") or "*de nação da Costa*" ("from the nation of the Coast") embarked in one of the ports in the Bight of Benin where the Nagô/Yoruba usually embarked.[18]

There were Muslims among the captives exported from those ports. Although he was a Nagô, it is worth recalling Mohammah Gardo Baquaqua, who came from the city of Djougou in what is now the Republic of Benin. A contemporary of Rufino in Pernambuco, he embarked for Brazil in the port of Ouidah, probably in 1845. In his memoirs, Baquaqua recounts that when he reached Pernambuco, the ship that had brought him there as a captive from Africa sailed up and down the coast all day and only landed its human cargo at night. Once on dry land, the African was taken to a farmhouse that served as a slave market, where he was purchased by a trader who resold him to a baker. He was employed in a range of activities, from carrying building stones to selling bread in the neighborhood. Displeased with his work, the baker sold him to a slave trader who sent him to Rio de Janeiro, and there he was purchased by a ship's captain who sailed the coastal route along the south of Brazil, including the southernmost province of São Pedro of Rio Grande do Sul, where Rufino had lived. While on a voyage to New York, when his master was shipping coffee for an English merchant, Baquaqua fled the vessel under the protection of a local abolitionist society and gained his freedom.[19]

While in the United States, Mohammah Baquaqua became a Baptist. Muslims and Baptists shared something in common: opposition to the use of human figures, which are so dear to the religious traditions of Catholic Brazil. Baquaqua scornfully described the religious services he was forced to attend daily when he was a slave "near the city of Pernambuco," as he calls it in his memoir. His master's house contained what he called "some images made of clay" before which everyone knelt, the family in front and the slaves in back. The prayers and hymns were accompanied by a whip, ready at hand to discipline the inattentive.

As members of a small minority among the African population of Recife and the vicinity, Muslims like Mohammah and Rufino (better yet, Abuncare) may have crossed paths in its streets and recognized each other. Although sparse, the local Muslim community was highly active, as we will see. Just as he was not the only Nagô there, as a Muslim Rufino was not entirely alone in Pernambuco.

21

A Man of Faith and Sorcery

All we know about Rufino's life during the eight years after his return to Recife is what he said, when he was arrested in 1853, about his activities in the market of faith. At that time he declared that he was just forty-five years old, although the unnamed author of the report published in the *Jornal do Commercio* described him as an "old man." The writer who had witnessed his interrogation by the police observed that Rufino had an "intelligent forehead . , . .""His nose [was] hooked and very flat," the physiognomist continued, "[with] two deep lines around his mouth, given that he had a round, fresh face, lending his physiognomy a certain something that attracts attention and impresses anyone who looks at him." At the time of his interrogation, although Rufino spoke with a heavy accent he communicated easily in Portuguese and made himself understood very well.[1]

Despite being under pressure, Rufino was not cowed by the authorities' veiled and explicit threats and taunts. During the interrogation, he was sometimes clearly distressed by his inquisitors' disrespectful behavior. Otherwise, he remained calm. The silent movements of his lips showed that he was constantly praying. At times he was ironic, and at others he responded with a "bitter smile."[2]

Rufino answered all the questions put to him without evasion and even "calmly and frankly," in the words of the *Jornal do Commercio*'s correspondent. It was soon established that he was a respectable "and very obvious" Muslim— a Muslim preacher, a Yoruba *àlùfáà*, or *alufá* in Brazilian parlance. At the time of his arrest, he was wearing his *agbada*—the ritual white tunic typically worn at home by African Muslims in Brazil at the time. He also wore an African cap and was found surrounded by his manuscripts and other religious articles. That was how he received his clients and acolytes, a scene that must have involved some calculation as to how to make a good impression. When questioned about his work, he left out details about an *alufá*'s activities and his participation in an organized Muslim group. This showed how clever he was, because in those circumstances, any African with a following was a dangerous African. However, an excerpt from the report published in the *Correio Mercantil* describes him as a

The Story of Rufino. João José Reis, Flávio dos Santos Gomes, and Marcus J. M. de Carvalho, Translated by H. Sabrina Gledhill, Oxford University Press (2020) © Oxford University Press.
DOI: 10.1093/oso/9780190224363.001.0001

Muslim preacher: "his followers were obliged to provide him with everything, because he says that an *alufá* does not work."[3] That also described the relationship between initiates and Muslim teachers in Africa—the former generally paid the latter for their lessons with work and gifts.

However, the *alufá* himself confessed that his dealings went beyond "his followers." He said that his clientele was not just made up of members of his nation and religion but included other Africans, people of mixed race, and even some whites, for whom he predicted the future and cured a range of ailments, even removing evil spells from their bodies and minds. According to the statement he gave during his interrogation, he received one cruzado (four hundred réis, approximately three pounds sterling) in advance for his services, and the remainder payable after the desired result was obtained, according to his "merit." Of course, Rufino also made a point of observing that he did no harm to anyone. He used his knowledge to fulfill the requests of those who sought him out, as long as they asked for "good things." He made a living from that beneficent activity. He said he knew how to cast evil spells but did not do so because he was a God-fearing man—"even though he knew how to do so, he did not make medicine to harm anyone, since he would have to account to God, whom he feared."

What can four hundred réis (or one cruzado) buy?

With the amount he received as an advance payment for his services, Rufino could take a short walk to the bakery on 30, Rua da Senzala Nova (New Slave Quarters Street), and buy "lovers' biscuits," which cost exactly four hundred réis, or twice as many "small English biscuits," which cost two hundred réis. Unfortunately, we do not know what the bakery's measures were (if it was in a box, weight in pounds, etc.), because that is how they were vaguely advertised in the *Diário de Pernambuco* on September 9, 1853. The prices current at the time of Rufino's interrogation also enabled him to buy "guava sweets" (like those he took to sell in Luanda) for two hundred réis (probably per box, but of what size and weight?). The prices of basic foodstuffs were advertised more precisely. A bushel of "ordinary beans" cost 3,000 réis, about 230 réis per liter, and cassava flour cost 2,500 réis, or about 192 réis per liter. If the *alufá* drank alcohol, his cruzado would be worth a *canada* of sugarcane spirits, the equivalent of a little over half a liter of the local rum. If he wanted to charm an African lady with a gift of *"riscadinho francês"* (French pinstripe fabric), he would find it on

> sale for 200 réis per cubit at 42, Rua Nova (New Street) in the district where he lived. Food was expensive. Had he visited Bahia that year to meet up with other *alufás*—a possibility—Rufino could have stopped at the shop of the Hausa Candomblé priest Cipriano José Pinto on Ladeira do Carmo (Carmo Hill) and used his one cruzado to buy a chintz shirt or denim pants, and even receive some change, because they only cost 320 réis each. By the way, in 1853, the year of Rufino's arrest in Pernambuco, Cipriano was also jailed in Salvador, Bahia. He was found with papers written in Arabic as well as other religious items. A few days later, by pure coincidence, rumors spread about an imminent slave revolt in that city and the authorities believed that Muslim rebels were awakening from a long-dormant state. Cipriano, who was already under arrest, stayed in jail until he was deported to Africa eighteen months later. They played hardball in Bahia.[5]

In other words, he did not place curses but, as he said, "cured spells." This part of his statement is not necessarily credible.[4]

Unfortunately, we do not know how familiar Rufino was with Arabic and the Qur'ān when he arrived in Sierra Leone for the first time in 1841 or the level of knowledge he had achieved when he left the British colony for the second time, in 1845, after completing his studies. Depending on his qualifications, he would initially have studied at an Islamic religious school or madrassa that taught Arabic reading and writing. In Fourah Bay, madrassas were known as *Ile Kewu* (Qur'ānic schools), just as in Yorubaland—and were generally located in the homes of Muslim teachers. According to Gibril Cole, the length of study in those schools was not pre-established and varied according to the student. However, its objectives included the training of Muslim clerics, who had to memorize the verses of the Qur'ān.[6]

In addition to the madrassa, Rufino must have attended the local mosque (built in 1839, shortly before his arrival) where, as in other Muslim communities in the British colony, "the ongoing education of young and adult Muslims was provided through sermons and rituals and where the message of Allah was reinforced and rejuvenated."[7] It is unlikely that he underwent more specialized higher study—in Islamic law and theology or Arabic literature, for example—which was also available in Sierra Leone and chiefly in the neighboring Muslim states, such as Futa Toro. When Rufino was a student in Fourah Bay, the local Muslims were not educated within the more orthodox tradition that was introduced shortly thereafter by religious leaders trained in Futa Toro.

Dr. Robert Clarke observed that Muslims in Sierra Leone "believed in witchcraft, incantations and amulets," which was also the case with Rufino. They used an infusion made from pieces of tree bark on which passages of the Qur'ān were written and then washed. The liquid was bottled and sold to be used for bathing "before asking for favors." Other sources indicate that these preparations were also supposed to be drunk, as they were believed to protect the body and soul against evil spells and spirits. Captain Hewett not only confirmed the general use of Muslim amulets in Sierra Leone but observed divining methods such as astrology used by marabouts who claimed to have the power to "read the sky." Furthermore, among the Aku, as in their country of origin, Islam tolerated the traditional Yoruba culture, including aspects of its religion, to the point where Muslim Yorubas belonged to secret societies such as the Gẹlẹdẹ, which celebrated female ancestors, and the Egungun, which was devoted to worshiping the dead, the *eguns*. In short, the Muslims with whom Rufino interacted in Sierra Leone bore little resemblance to the orthodox jihadists about whom we wrote in the first chapter.[8]

In fact, Rufino's version of Islam in Brazil was similar, in many ways, to the form practiced in a vast swath of West Africa, both on the coast and in the interior, including Ọ̀yọ́ and Sierra Leone. In the British colony, Muslim teachers, in Skinner's succinct description, "used prayer, divination, magic potions (*nasi*), and magic tablets to identify wrongdoers and to protect and cure people."[9] Rufino must have known something about this before he went to Sierra Leone, but he honed his knowledge there. One of the main activities of an *alufá*, both in Africa and Brazil, was preparing amulets containing passages of the Qur'ānic, powerful non-Qur'ānic prayers, incantations, cabalistic figures, or other inscriptions written on sheets of paper. They were carefully folded in a ritual manner and placed in a small pouch made of cloth or leather that was hung from the neck or other parts of the body, as we have seen in Sierra Leone. For example, at the time of his arrest and during his interrogation, Rufino wore a cap with four amulets attached. A string of amulets was also found in his possession that he probably wore around his neck. Two typically Muslim writing boards—which the Yoruba called *patako*—were also confiscated from him.

Rufino's skills also included helping people with their love lives, a service that should always be part of the practice of any good witch doctor. To do so, he wrote the young man's name facing that of the girl on one side of his board for prayers and spells and "prayed" on the other side—that is, he wrote formulas to bring and keep couples together. The water that washed the words written on the *patako* had protective and healing powers and improved the luck—even in love—of those who drank it.

To convince the skeptics present at his interrogation, the *alufá* guaranteed that *"When God wills it, cold water is medicine,"* which was probably reported word for word and therefore italicized by the author of the article published in *Jornal do Commercio*.[10] That expression, which we have been unable to link to any orthodox Muslim traditions, was popular among black Catholics (even if they were more than just Catholic) in nineteenth-century Brazil. Cândido da Fonseca Galvão, the famous Dom Obá II d'África, used a similar expression in one of the numerous articles he published in Rio de Janeiro's newspapers in the 1880s.[11] In Rufino's case, it was probably a proverb he learned in Brazil.

He also seems to have adapted other aspects of Brazilian popular Catholicism to his magical-religious arsenal. This was probably the case with the procedure for "binding" couples together described above, which may have been inspired by magical charms used with Catholic saints like Anthony and John, both of whom were well-known matchmakers. It should be added that, as the former slave of an apothecary in Bahia, Rufino may have learned about certain drugs from his former master and added them to his healing arsenal. His other practices and beliefs, as well as the divining methods Rufino claimed to know, were not unfamiliar to the West-African Islamic world where the freedman received his education.[12]

One of the main differences between Rufino and non-Muslim African religious leaders was his use of the written word. In addition to writing boards, rosaries, sheets of paper, and books handwritten in Arabic, the police seized quills and black, blue, and red ink in his house. The red ink was used to emphasize sections of devout writings, a person's name (that of the amulet's owner, for example), or drawings considered important from a mystical perspective, as well as to highlight the beginning of copied verses of the Qur'ān. In 1853, Rufino—better yet, Abuncare—was ordered by his interrogators to explain the contents of the manuscripts, including one that he identified as being a well-worn copy of the Qur'ān that he had brought back from Sierra Leone, and a more recent copy that he had begun to transcribe. Furthermore, "he had books for prayers, others that taught remedies, others that taught his language," in this case, Arabic, as well as some that he himself had written, including "prayers, songs and other things, and even a sermon"—this last bit of information identified him as a preacher. But Rufino's life was not all about religion. He said that the songs he wrote were his way of passing the time when taking a break from his spiritual endeavors. If the freedman was not hiding the function of that specific part of his writings, the apparently non-ritual or non-magical use of the language of the Qur'ān makes him a rarity among the literate Yoruba-speaking Muslims in Brazil.[13]

The authorities tried to ascertain whether the *alufá* was telling the truth about the manuscripts found with him, but failed to find anyone in Recife who could translate them. We have come across the same difficulty among officials in Porto Alegre and Rio de Janeiro. On the day of Rufino's interrogation, the *Diário de Pernambuco* published an advertisement stating that there was "great interest in finding in this city a person who understands Arabic, Chinese or Hebrew writing or even some of the languages spoken in Central and Southern Africa."[14] Note the confusion caused by Rufino's linguistic world. A Jewish man, who lived in the city and had also resided in Morocco and Egypt, appeared at the police station to attempt to make some sense of it. He said "something in Arabic" to Rufino but failed to translate the documents he was shown. The *Jornal do Commercio* reporter speculated that they were either written in a "dialect" with which the Jewish man was unfamiliar or in classical Arabic, which he also did not understand, as he only spoke its "modern" form. Pure speculation. However, the Jewish man helped make things go easier for the Muslim, while pointedly labeling as "witchcraft" much of what he had seen in the Islamic world of North Africa. According to the newspaper, he saw Rufino as "someone who was entirely devoted to his religion, [while also] telling amazing tales about the things he himself had seen Saracen sorcerers perform."[15]

A very small part of the mystery surrounding Rufino's writings would be solved in Rio de Janeiro. At least one of the documents found in his possession has survived. The president of the province of Pernambuco sent it to the minister of justice to be translated in the nation's capital. The minister wanted to solve the puzzle as soon as possible, so on September 27, 1853, writing his instructions in the left-hand margin of the first page of the Muslim manuscript, he ordered the chief of police of Rio de Janeiro to "spare no efforts to obtain a translation of the attached Arabic document found among the papers of a black man of the Nagô Nation arrested in the City of Recife due to rumors of insurrection that had arisen there." The chief of police must have had a hard time carrying out his mission, because he only returned the "writing in the Arabic language" a week later—a month after Rufino's arrest—accompanied by "its translation into the vernacular."[16] We do not know who produced the translation, which has since been lost, but the Portuguese version must have reassured the minister that it contained no grounds for charging its owner as a dangerous conspirator. The president of the province of Pernambuco agreed when he read a copy of the translation that was sent to him two days after the minister received it.[17]

Rufino's Arabic manuscript seems to have been part of his collection of sermons, and contains instructions on marriage. It was written in well-drawn

---

The *alufá* Rufino's notes for a sermon on marriage[19]

Blessing! Blessing!

"Also [prohibited are] women already married except those whom your right hands possess:[20]
Thus hath Allah ordained [prohibitions] against you.
Except for these, all others are lawful provided ye seek

> [them in marriage] with gifts from your property, desiring chastity, not fornication.
> Give them their dowry for the enjoyment you have of them as a duty; but if, after a dowry is prescribed, ye agree mutually [to vary it], there is no blame on you.
> Surely, Allah is All-knowing All-wise." (Q. 4:24)[21]
>
> Blessing! Blessing! Praise be to Allah Who permitted the permitted and forbade the forbidden, and forbade fornication and adultery, and brought about marriage between the sons of Adam and the daughters of Eve without pressure [?].[22] And Allah bore witness, and the angels bore witness[23] and they bore witness to what is lawful. Praise be to Allah Who imposed
>
> **PAGE 2:**
>
> Who imposed on us the marriage and the dowry [?].[24]
> In order [to perform] the witnessing correctly, two trustworthy witnesses and, in the ʿaqd [marriage certificate], "X[25] son of Y."[26]
> Blessing! Blessing! Oh Allah, bless us in the marriage. Praise be Allah, Lord of the Universe.[27] The end."

letters, probably set down by the *alufá* himself, in Maghrebi Arabic, which was used by Muslims in West Africa. Here is the full translation of the manuscript. The original in Arabic can be seen further on.[18]

The sermon seems to be a good supplement to the magic spells Rufino invoked to make people fall in love. He not only brought couples together, he married them! Above all, this document represented his activity as a leader in a Muslim community whose members married in accordance with Islamic law, and probably also followed the same law when subjected to other rituals in the cycle of life, for instance at birth and death. In his marriage sermon *alufá* Rufino (now probably revered by his Muslim fellows as Abuncare) instructed the desirable behavior of a good Muslim in relation to his future wife. The man should avoid adultery—this is the meaning of the recommendation of chastity in the sermon—and negotiate an appropriate dowry from his wife (or her family). The text was clearly written from a male perspective and addressed to him, but clearly the woman could also demand such fidelity to the Qur'ān, if not to herself.

The Qur'ānic surahs Al'Imran and An-Nisa (Women) serve as a guide to conjugal behavior in this sermon. The first celebrates the family of the mother of Isa (Jesus in the Christian tradition), Maryam or Mariam (Mary, to Christians), whose father, Imran, gives his name to the surah. It deals with the honorable

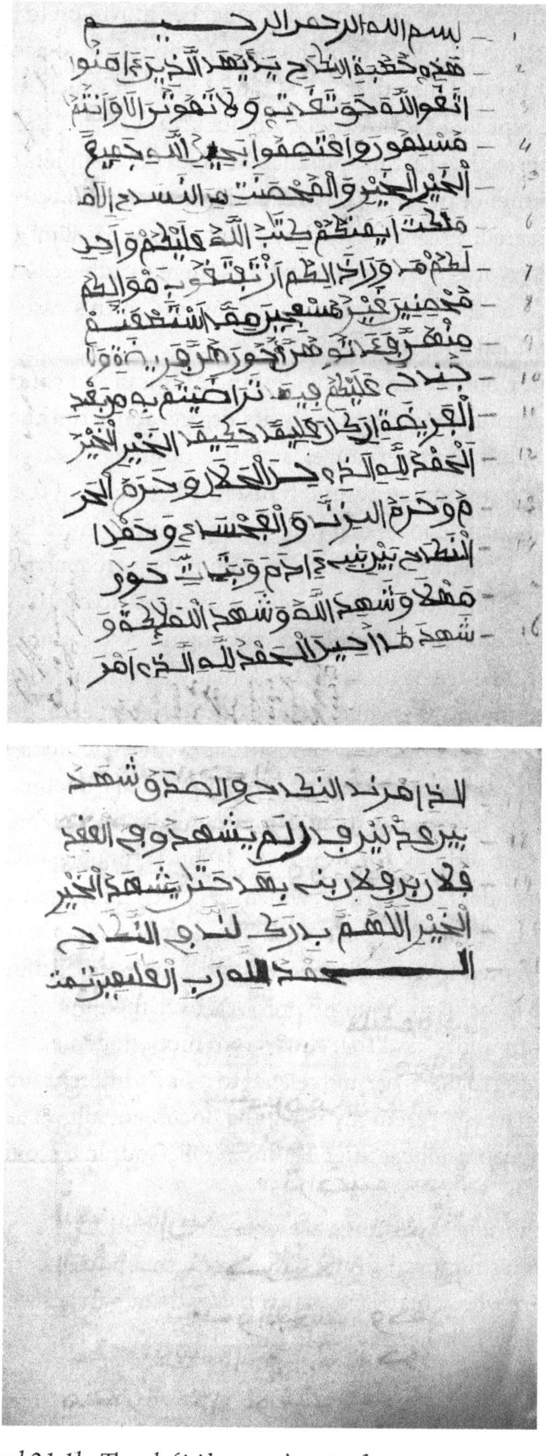

Figures 21.1a and 21.1b The *alufá* Abuncare's notes for a sermon on marriage confiscated by the police in 1853. Arquivo Nacional, Rio de Janeiro.

place that families occupy in Islamic doctrine, but moves on to harshly criticize Jews and Christians (the People of the Book) who refuse to accept the religion of the Prophet. In this regard, it is a surah of jihad in which threats of eternal damnation are repeated for those who do not accept Islam. The passage Rufino quoted fits in perfectly with this spirit. It combines the complete text of verse 102 with the first sentence of verse 103 of the Al'Imran surah. It warns believers that Allah is to be feared, a reason why they should die as Muslims (verse 102) and then, in the first words of verse 103, exhorts them to adhere to the Qur'ān (the "rope of Allah") as the binding force for Muslims, in this case particularly between the betrothed couple.

The surah on women comes right after the Al'Imran and contains the essence of Qur'ānic doctrine about the family, its organization, the choice of spouses, their rights, including inheritance, and the desirable behavior for married couples, among other topics. Rufino transcribed verse 24 of the surah in full, as it deals with the man's choice of a wife. Always written from the man's perspective, permission to marry slave women, even if they are married in their home communities, is often interpreted as being a reference to captives taken in a holy war whose husbands' whereabouts are unknown.[28] We cannot know if Rufino interpreted that passage of the holy book that way, but his choice makes sense in a Muslim community in which many African freedmen had female slaves—with whom, in the eyes of a now pious Rufino, they had illicit relations out of wedlock. These enslaved wives, by definition uprooted from their original family structures, did not have to pay the dowry ordered by the Qur'ān.

The document written (or transcribed) by Rufino insists on an Islamic moral code of conduct in marriage, which, in given circumstances, included the transfer of a man's property to a woman. And to be valid, that contract had to be public and signed by two witnesses. It is possible that Rufino's sermon was simply a script to be used when he presided over the nuptials of couples from his Muslim community, and that there were more documents regarding other matters pertaining to marriage and related to it or to different subjects. However, regarding the marriage ceremony itself, the document allows us at least to hear the bride and groom repeat after Rufino: "Oh God, make our marriage very good."[29]

Although the *alufá's* writings were neither politically or socially subversive, they were far removed from Catholicism, the official state religion of the Brazilian Empire whose marriage, baptismal, and funeral rites were the only ones recognized by law. In other words, in Imperial Brazil, no one was considered to be legally wed unless they had been married by a Catholic priest. The only exception made was for Protestants, whose marriages celebrated by their own ministers were recognized after a decree issued in September 1861.[30] If he married people in accordance with Islamic law, the *alufá* Rufino was clearly breaking the laws of both the Catholic Church and the Brazilian State at once.

Rufino showed sincere Muslim conviction—"unshakable belief," according to the *Correio Mercantil*. He told his interrogators that he followed the religion of the "prophet that God sent to earth, called Mahammoud [sic] who was born in Mac-Madeira," as the police clerk noted with a hefty dose of cultural perplexity.[31] "Mac-Madeira"? It is possible that Rufino actually said—but the clerk failed to understand—Maka or Makka, meaning Mecca, and Al Madinah, Medina, the two holy cities of Islam, the first being Mohammed's birthplace and the second, the haven to which he fled when he was pursued by "idolaters." The Qur'ān is said to have been revealed to Mohammed in both cities.

According to the *Jornal do Commercio* reporter, Rufino's explanations demonstrated "great knowledge and intelligence about the entire doctrine of that religion." And the African went even further, saying categorically that he would not abandon his beliefs, "even if they sent me to the gallows." In the face of such defiance, the deputy chief constable, José Joaquim d'Oliveira, his interrogator, decided to provoke him, saying that Muhammad was nothing but a "knave" and that Catholicism was the only true faith. But Rufino was not intimidated. He patiently and diplomatically explained that people embraced different religions—was the deputy chief constable unaware of this?—and "regarding which was best, this was *a question that will only be decided when the world ends,*" said Abuncare, this decisive statement apparently reported word for word in italics by the newspaper. However, he also openly criticized Catholic priests. When his interrogator asked who had made him a "priest" of his religion, he replied that *"here* [in Brazil], *priesthood is an office that is learned deliberately; but in his homeland, it was wisdom; the wisest led the rest."* Once again, a verbatim transcription. The African admitted that he was an *alufá,* just as his father had been in Africa, and that if he returned to his Yoruba homeland he would also teach it to others. When asked why he did not use his skills to get rich, he replied that "some ask God for wealth, but he had only asked for wisdom; that the two precepts do not fit in the same bag"—a principle that is foreign to Islam, which does not condemn wealth in and of itself, recognizing it as a gift of Allah, although it strongly recommends honesty and charity.[32]

On this subject, the surah on women contains several passages dealing with the right way to spend one's own wealth, and sounds dire warnings for the avaricious and arrogant:

> 29. Do not consume your wealth falsely, but trading is permitted by mutual consent...
>
> 36. Allah certainly does not love the proud, boastful...

37... 0. those who are avaricious, and exhort people to avarice, and conceal what Allah has given them from His bounty. And we have prepared a disgraceful punishment for unbelievers.

38. And Allah does not love those who spend their money ostentatiously, and believe neither in Allah nor in the Last Day. Whoever is accompanied by Satan – what an evil companion he has![33]

Rufino certainly knew his religion. And it must have helped him get through troubled times in his adopted home.

22

Tense Times in Rufino's Recife

> However, because of that rogue, this city walked in fear, for there were widespread rumors that an insurrection was planned; and even today those fears have not been entirely abated, because in the countryside some slaves have been somewhat disobedient, and it has been necessary to mete out harsh punishment.[1]

A Pernambuco correspondent of the Rio-based newspaper *Correio Mercantil* made this observation regarding Rufino's arrest a few days after it occurred. There were several misrepresentations in his report, such as the idea that Rufino's arrest had sparked rumors of insurrection. Actually, the arrest was motivated by a rumored slave rebellion, specifically on plantations near the towns of Pau d'Alho, Nazaré, and Jaboatão on the outskirts of Recife. To understand this drama and its repercussions, we must bear in mind the political situation in Pernambuco from the time Rufino settled there in the mid-1840s until his arrest in 1853. Since it seemed to be his lot to live in turbulent places, the Muslim Nagô or Malê may not have been a protagonist, but he was at least a witness to a period of tremendous unrest, including anti-Portuguese movements in 1845, 1847, and 1848, as well as the Praieira insurrection, a liberal and anti-Portuguese revolt against the imperial government in Rio de Janeiro that broke out in November 1848, staged by a faction of the Pernambuco elite with the backing of popular support.

Once peace had been restored in the province in the first half of 1849, some of the large landowners who were arrested for involvement in the Praieira rebellion soon received an amnesty. However, a guerrilla war ensued for over a year in a densely forested area close to the border with the province of Alagoas, for which the movement's leader, Captain Pedro Ivo, was immortalized by the poet Castro Alves as a symbol of liberal resistance.[2] As for the poor souls who took up arms at their bosses' behest during the Praieira uprising, those who were caught were beaten and forced to join the army or navy and sent off to serve far from home under wretched conditions. During the post-Praieira era, fear reigned among the poor, both freed and free alike.

The Story of Rufino. João José Reis, Flávio dos Santos Gomes, and Marcus J. M. de Carvalho, Translated by H. Sabrina Gledhill, Oxford University Press (2020) © Oxford University Press.
DOI: 10.1093/oso/9780190224363.001.0001

It is therefore not surprising that the so-called *Ronco do Marimbondo* (Roar of the Wasp) erupted in January 1852: a violent protest against the government's attempt to conduct a census and introduce civil registration of births and deaths (imperial decrees 797 and 798 of July 18, 1851). To make matters worse, the press gangs had returned to recruit men by compulsion for a war against Argentina. No one knows exactly how the rumors started, but it was said that the government had decreed the enslavement of free blacks and mixed-race people. And they fully believed this to be true, which demonstrates the general perception of the precarious freedom enjoyed by people "of color" in slaveholding Brazil. Their fear was fully justified because black individuals, particularly women and children, were often kidnapped and sold to slavers who exported them to the southern part of the country, where they were lost forever to their families. It was easy to believe that fresh sources of labor were being sought after the recent (September 1850) termination of the transatlantic slave trade. Regardless of the degree of collective elaboration that fear may have reached, in just a few days crowds made up predominantly of black and brown people quickly mobilized. Armed with knives, hoes, and guns, they stormed into city halls and churches, demanding information about the law that enslaved "people of color." The rumor spread throughout the countryside, terrorizing villages from Minas Gerais to the interior of Pará.[3]

Despite strenuous efforts, the Pernambuco authorities could not find the culprits responsible for spreading the rumors of 1852, but they suspected that the scuttlebutt had begun in the churches, where parish priests were unhappy with the sudden demotion of ecclesiastical registration of births and deaths. The hotbeds of the uprising were precisely in the parishes of Pau d'Alho and Nazaré, where the rumors of the slave rebellion that led to Rufino's arrest would spread in 1853. The previous year, during the Ronco do Marimbondo in Pau d'Alho, the authorities were pursued by a crowd of "600 to 700" people, according to the president of the province. In Nazaré, government troops were ambushed on their way to the São João plantation, which had been occupied by the rebellious crowd. Clearly, force was not enough. It would be necessary to mobilize an army of priests and missionaries to convince the "people of color" that rumors of enslavement were groundless. The public protest was so intense that the imperial government gave up on conducting a census and introducing civil registration that year.[4]

That level of tension is not easily abated. The following year, 1853, armed bands continued to roam the countryside, including some who had taken part in the protests of January 1852, bandits and deserters from the Praieira, and even rural landowners' henchmen charged with maintaining the seigneurial order.

However, an even more serious problem arose in the town of Nazaré, one of the hotbeds of the Ronco do Maribondo. In April 1853, rumors of a slave rebellion spread on the local plantations. Two hundred men were sent to search the Pedregulho plantation and surrounding forests. According to the officer in charge of the investigation, local slaves were planning a rebellion in conjunction with "partial leaders" from other plantations. The reason for the revolt was a rumor that the slaves had been freed, and some parish priests held their letters of manumission but had failed to distribute them. Two free men were charged with spreading "such dangerous ideas." However, in the course of the investigations, the suspects were cleared and released. During the inquest, witnesses confirmed that the "false idea and obsession of having free status" was spreading among the slaves, but that no weapons had been distributed nor were there any other "external acts" of insurrection. If a conspiracy had been underway the rebellion was quashed, and therefore no one was indicted.[5]

One detail of these rumors made the authorities particularly nervous. The people they questioned reportedly said that the radical liberal Borges da Fonseca, one of the main leaders of the Praieira uprising, had promised aid from Recife. He was a known leader of the opposition to the status quo in the province, who had been arrested in 1845 for stirring up the masses against the Portuguese. When the Praieira uprising broke out three years later, he joined in and was responsible for the most radical aspect of the revolt. Although he accepted the racist ideas then in vogue, he is known to have been an activist in "*A Popular*," a secret society that supported the gradual emancipation of slaves. Later on, in the 1860s, he flirted with the nascent abolitionist movement. If he was not an outright abolitionist, he was a liberal and at least supported the rights of free and freed blacks, publicizing that support in the radical press.[6]

Borges da Fonseca was the last of the chief Praieira leaders to receive an amnesty, and only regained his freedom in August 1852.[7] Clearly, the Conservative Party had a powerful interest in putting him back in jail. Implicating him in a slave uprising would be the perfect pretext. The suspicions cast on Pernambuco's foremost liberal agitator may have been yet another political scheme against a man who, speaking from his jail cell in Recife in 1848, had incited the crowd to kill the Portuguese. A man like that posed a danger. If those interrogated were telling the truth when they said that Borges had promised aid from Recife for the slave rebellion, there was good reason to believe it was a credible threat and to send out two hundred armed men in search of suspects.[8]

It is clear that what the seigneurial class feared in 1853 was not just a slave protest but the possibility of a broader rebellion involving social agents that the authorities called—with a combination of contempt and fear—the "populace": the same free and freed "people of color" who had stormed the churches and public buildings in January 1852 and joined forces with the Praieira four years prior. Thus, the authorities were alarmed when, in August 1853, one month before Rufino's arrest, fourteen armed black men went to the home of Agostinho

Tinoco, who lived on a plantation in Pau d'Alho, "stormed it and stole a blunderbuss, a machete, two pistols, and four hundred and five thousand réis in notes." According to an official report, the insurgents' motivation lay in the violation of a custom: the reduction of the number of saints' days—therefore holidays for slaves—from thirty-five to fourteen that was ordered in two briefs issued by Pope Pius IX in 1851 and 1852. Once again, there was a truly unsettling factor, namely, that there were two free men among those involved, Demetrio José Pinto and Manoel Duarte Ribeiro. Once again, rumors were rife about a general uprising involving not only the enslaved but free and freed blacks from the interior of the province and even the city of Recife. Troops were swiftly mobilized to raid the local plantations and arrest any suspects hiding in the surrounding forests.[9]

Even before the arrival of the provincial government troops, local masters had captured four slaves and a freedman and handed them over to the authorities for summary punishment. The public prosecutor was taken aback by the slave owners' request: they wanted to punish the slaves with "whips on the prison bars" but not to prosecute them. For the prosecutor, that was highly irregular—a pretrial that gave criminals the same status as the innocent, preventing the fair application of the law.[10] From the masters' perspective, it was ideal because those involved would be punished without making them unavailable for work, which they would have been if they had received jail sentences for the crimes of theft or rebellion.

Once again, it should be stressed that the raid on the plantation in Pau d'Alho was not an isolated incident but a move linked to rumors of a broader rebellion. According to one official, if steps had not been taken immediately the plot would have spread to include "many freedmen" and not just slaves.[11] José Pacheco de Albuquerque Maranhão, the owner of the Papicu plantation, reported that one of his workers had uncovered a plot to kill the masters, concocted by "the populace of Pau d'Alho county." According to the captain in charge of the police investigation, the owner of Papicu was so terrified by the report that he sent his family to the city of Goiana, near the border with Paraíba province, adjacent to Pernambuco. The movement was said to be "in defense of the faith," presumably to maintain the endangered religious holidays.[12] In an official letter to the justice minister, the president of the province confirmed that information: "In Pau d'Alho, some slaves rebelled on the 24th last [of August 1853] and committed some robberies, complaining of the suppression of holy days."[13] Therefore, it was a protest with a limited objective and not, say, an abolitionist revolt.

Rumors of slave uprisings also circulated in the neighboring county, Nazaré, soon after the incidents in Pau d'Alho. The commander of the local detachment visited the plantations, warned the residents about what was going on, and searched several suspicious areas. However, when questioned, some landowners said that they were astonished by the news because they believed that their slaves were calm. Although the Pipacu plantation owner's charges were not confirmed, the commander recommended that local landowners "be as vigilant as possible, not just on their own plantations but also of their residents, banning *maracatu* dances and gatherings."[14] We can see that the Pernambuco authorities were wisely suspicious that the festival was not just an escape valve—it could also be a pressure cooker for social revolt.

When reporting these incidents to the minister of justice, the president of Pernambuco stated that during the same period, in Jaboatão, there arose a "movement in a sense possibly more serious than that in Pau d'Alho, were it not for the timely measures taken and the presence of the force that I sent there." The rebellion was planned to start on September 3, 1853, but the authorities had moved quickly. By the first of the month, they had already arrested two of the slaves involved, both of whom came from a plantation that belonged to a widow from the highest ranks of Pernambuco society, Dona Francisca Severina Cavalcanti de Lacerda. A freedman was also arrested. According to the president, they confessed that there was a "premeditated plot for an insurrection that was supposed to break out in the Capital and spread to the Plantations, whose owners were to be killed." Regarding military tactics, the rebels planned to destroy bridges to isolate the base of the rebellion and then rally slaves from the local plantations and farms. A police force of eighteen cavalry troops was dispatched and raided a house where rebels were allegedly gathering, but they had already fled into the woods. The local authorities suspected that some freedmen had joined forces with the slaves.[15]

We do not know what happened to the slaves who were involved in the rumored uprising in Nazaré and Jaboatão. The previously mentioned report in *Correio Mercantil* may have alluded to some of them when its author wrote that, because they were "disobedient," it had been "necessary to inflict harsh punishments upon them." However, aside from domestic punishment of slaves who may have been roused by rumors of rebellion, the government's reprisal was swift and brutal for those who took part in the raid on the plantation house in Pau d'Alho: three were condemned to 600 lashes, two to 500, four to 300, and one to 200. Two were acquitted.[16]

Unfortunately, we do not have the statements of the individuals who were involved in the 1853 plot recounting everything that was left out from the sources produced by the provincial authorities who arrested Rufino on suspicion of being one of the links between the rebels in the countryside and those in Recife. The other black men investigated were accused of taking part in illegal gatherings and vagrancy. The police also suspected that they were hiding fugitive slaves. Rufino had three letters of manumission in his home. If they did not belong to him and his family, they could well have been used by slaves on the run.[17]

23

A Free Man

Rufino drew the attention of the authorities and the press in Pernambuco because he was suspected of conspiracy, but that was not the only reason. He also raised bad memories of the 1835 Muslim slave rebellion in Bahia and an episode that had taken place in Recife in 1846. The latter incident, like the 1835 revolt, involved blacks who were considered both rebels and religious fanatics by the agents of law and order. According to the Brazilian constitution, non-Catholic faiths would be tolerated as long as their houses of worship did not look like a church, at least on the outside. Of course, that rule did not apply to all faiths or all the faithful. For example, the Anglican church in Recife occupied an imposing church on Aurora street, the site of the residence and businesses of the local Catholic upper class. Strictly speaking, the law required that the British be arrested and Rufino be protected, as he practiced and preached his religion in his own home. However, when it came to black people a different policy prevailed.

The same thing happened to a group of black Christians arrested on the charge of harboring escaped slaves and, chiefly, of plotting a rebellion in 1846, a few months after Rufino settled in Recife. Rufino certainly knew about that case, which was widely reported at the time. The suspicions raised about that Christian group were similar to those which would fall upon him seven years later.

The leader of that Christian faith community, which opposed the Catholic church, was Agostinho José Pereira, better known as the Divino Mestre (Divine Teacher, an epithet of Christ) because he taught his followers to read and write while preaching his new religion, a type of Evangelical sect. There does not seem to have been any doubt about the black leader's rebellious mindset. The key evidence against him was an "ABC" found in his possession. A common type of *cordel* chapbook, a form of folk literature meant to be read aloud, it was written in verses beginning with a letter of the alphabet in their natural order. In this case, it communicated a form of Christianity that was truly revolutionary for its time.

Agostinho's "ABC" celebrated the dignity and political potential of blacks, who were portrayed as "*morenos*" (brown people) or people of "the noble color

The Story of Rufino. João José Reis, Flávio dos Santos Gomes, and Marcus J. M. de Carvalho, Translated by H. Sabrina Gledhill, Oxford University Press (2020) © Oxford University Press.
DOI: 10.1093/oso/9780190224363.001.0001

moreno."[1] The first *moreno* was said to be Adam. Then, the *moreno* Moses freed his brothers-in-color from Egyptian bondage. Christ himself, the "true Messiah," chose to be born among *morenos* like himself. In 1846, the time had come for the liberation of the *morenos*, which might not be a peaceful one. It all depended on the white masters. Several passages of the "ABC" contained threats against them:

> *Men without humanity*
> *Remember the future*
> *Give freedom to the morenos*
> *And fear a dark cloud*

The "ABC" promised Brazil a Haitian-style slave revolution if freedom was not granted peacefully:

> *Oh! Great is the blindness*
> *Of these Brazilian folk*
> *Do not look at Haiti.*

Just as Haiti had become a black monarchy, so in Brazil, "The color brown will remain/With crown and scepter in hand." God, of course, fully approved of this:

> *The Voice of God and His promises*
> *Still are not rescinded*
> *We must declare to all Nations of the World*
> *That the moreno will rule*

Father Agostinho seemed to be forming a messianic movement with all the letters of the alphabet. Despite the use of a somewhat surprising term—"*moreno*"—the movement expressed a very clear racial and anti-slavery message, because the Divino Mestre wanted to turn the world on its head, forming a new one in which blacks governed whites. This was because, as he promised, "They will easily be subjugated/By those who were once their masters." In other words, the *morenos* had once ruled and would rule once again, so this was, ideologically speaking, a restorationist movement.[2]

One of Pernambuco authorities' main concerns about Agostinho was whether he had contacts in other provinces. Therefore, he was asked about his travels and whether he had been in Bahia during the Sabinada rebellion in 1837–1838. The Sabinada was a movement organized by liberal-federalist rebels and led by the "mulatto" (a contemporary term) physician Francisco Sabino, hence the name of the revolt. The rebels occupied Salvador for a few months, with widespread support from the local black population.[3] The police had similar views regarding Rufino José Maria, who was also asked if he had been in Bahia "in 1837." However, in that case, the year the clerk wrote down may have been mistaken, as he should have written 1835, the year of the Muslim rebellion in that province. Rufino understood what they were asking about, and replied that "at that time [1835], he was in Porto Alegre," although he was no longer there two years later, during the Sabinada.[4] The authorities' fears were exacerbated not only because they knew that rebels in Bahia had documents written in Arabic in their possession, like those found with Rufino, but also, according to the reports circulating in the country at the time, many of the 1835 rebels had been freed Africans and Nagôs like him.

Because he was also a black man who could read, write, and indoctrinate others, the press referred to Rufino as the "Divino Mestre II," (Divine Teacher II) despite the fact that he was a Muslim. A Rio newspaper summed up the alarming news published in Pernambuco newspapers taken aboard the steamer *Brasileira* to the imperial capital as follows: "Propaganda from African followers of Mohammed has just been discovered. The police have made several arrests, including that of an inculcated prophet, as well as many writings in Hebrew."[5] However, it soon became clear to the Pernambuco police and political leadership that this "prophet's" religion had nothing to do with the rebellious form of Christianity preached by Agostinho, as well as being different from the militant Islam practiced by the Malês in 1835. Besides, his manuscripts were not written in "Hebrew."

The poise shown by Rufino and other Africans during the 1853 investigation led the police to conclude that their suspicions of conspiracy were groundless, particularly regarding Rufino's alleged connection with the a slave conspiracy in the countryside. A week after his interrogation, the chief of police wrote to the president of the province to report that the manuscripts found with Rufino did not constitute sufficient evidence to consider him a threat to law and order: "It seems to me that this fact, in the absence of other more significant evidence, in no way corroborates the suspicions against the said Rufino José Maria." The statement from a black man named José, arrested for being a "comrade" of Rufino, does not seem to have sufficed.[6] Less than two weeks after his arrest, the *alufá* would be released, although he was required to report weekly to the officer in charge of the case. According to a newspaper report, it had been proven that he was nothing but a harmless old man who was a "sectarian of the Muslim religion" and earned a living from his spiritual calling and ritual skills.[7]

The religious aspect of the matter remained to be dealt with, however, since the practice of African religions was still viewed as a criminal activity throughout Brazil at the time. In addition to preaching a different faith from the nation's official religion, which strictly speaking was not a crime, as we have just seen, Rufino appears to have officiated Muslim wedding ceremonies in Catholic Brazil. Even so, the Pernambuco police apparently decided that religion was not within their jurisdiction, and on September 16, 1853, the president sent the local Catholic bishop a copy of Rufino's interrogation transcript "to consider it from the religious aspect." Unfortunately, it is not known what the prelate decided in this case, if he reached a decision at all. However, this procedure echoed the one followed seven years earlier with Agostinho Ferreira, the first Divino Mestre, who was taken to the episcopal palace to be personally admonished by the same bishop, the Augustinian Dom Friar João da Purificação Marques Perdigão, a man reputed to be extremely pious.[8]

By September 17 or 18, Rufino was a free man after spending nearly two weeks behind bars. News of his release was reported by the *Diário de Pernambuco*, which had covered the case since the alufá's arrest.

> The black African José Maria (the second *divino mestre*) has been released . . . albeit with the obligation to appear weekly at the police department. Nothing was found that could substantiate the charge that he was the provocateur of a criminal movement among his peers; but it was recognized that being a sectarian of the Mahomedan religion, as he stated under interrogation, he lived in his home without any other trade than telling the fortunes of those who sought him out, using for this the power or science that comes to him from the prophet, without knowing which path. To such an extent were the hidden money exploited by the divino mestre that we always conjectured and wrote that the wise live at the expense of fools, and rogues at that of simpletons.[9]

Rufino was forced to submit to weekly police checks – for how long, we do not know – and perhaps to sign, as often as circumstances permitted, a document promising good beha¬vior and finding in a "licit" way of making a living. This latter suggestion, however, is undermined by the absence of any mention of the subject in the *Diário de Pernambuco*, which had also taken an interest in that angle of the story. In other words, the newspaper summarized with a strong dose of prejudice everything that Rufino had stated frankly and in detail to his interrogators regarding his livelihood. The report, however, does not fail to portray an interesting circumstance—the specific relationship between Islam and Rufino's "power or science" remained a mystery, because they did not know precisely "which path" he followed in his faith.

The final announcement that the case was closed came from a statement by the president of the province of Pernambuco during the opening session of the Provincial Legislative Assembly in 1854, a few months later. After summing up the events that occurred in Pau d'Alho, namely a slave conspiracy, and mentioning the investigation he had ordered in the capital, President José Bento da Cunha e Figueiredo introduced Rufino:

> ... among those [prisoners] one from the Nagô nation is particularly noteworthy, said to be an oracle among his peers, and he was found in a cassock, surrounded by some books written in Arabic and some trinkets, which he said pertained to religious ceremonies, of which he was a priest. Called in for questioning, he revealed nothing that raised suspicion: and even the translation he gave in my presence of an excerpt from one of his books agreed with another obtained from Rio de Janeiro. Finally, as fears of an insurrection had dissipated, the public eased [its call for] police action.[10]

This report reveals yet another significant aspect of Rufino's arrest—that he was personally interrogated by the president of the province. Now we also find that the document the president had sent to Rio de Janeiro for translation had previously been translated by Rufino in that official's presence, and that the translation from Rio matched that done in Recife. We can also observe that although he called the prisoner's religious objects "trinkets," unlike the *Diário de Pernambuco* the president did not harp on his moral disapproval of the *alufá*'s activities. He called him a "priest," while the press accused him of being a "rogue." It must be recognized in the words of Pernambuco's most senior authority that Rufino had won a certain moral victory.

It is possible that the Malê cleric was not let off because he had established his innocence but because he served a clientele whose protests at his arrest may have echoed in a veiled manner among the police and politicians of Recife. Rufino's clients included not only Muslims but other Nagôs, Africans from other nations, Creoles, mulattoes, and even whites. In fact, the trust that whites placed in him dated back to the time when, as a cook, he had helped feed the engine of the slave trade. Some of his clients in 1853 might have known him since those times. His network of contacts—which could have included investors in the *Ermelinda*—gave him access to resources, information, and personal experiences that Africans rarely enjoyed in Brazil or other plantation societies in the Americas.

However, although the Pernambuco police had released Rufino, many were uneasy about that decision. A Pernambuco correspondent to the Rio de Janeiro newspaper *Correio Mercantil* labeled the Muslim an "improvised prophet," "idle schismatic" and "knave," applauded his arrest, and criticized his release, suggesting that he should be deported back to Africa, among other civilities.[11] The call for deportation was not an idle threat, because that was how many African freedmen were treated by provincial governments for committing

> **Newspaper report in the Rio de Janeiro press about rumors of a slave uprising in Pernambuco, 1853**
>
> The *Brasileira* [steamer] has brought us [news] from Pernambuco up to the 13th and from Bahia up to the 16th of this month.
>
> In Pernambuco, the authorities continued to use all their powers to punish crimes, arresting major criminals in several districts, particularly in that of Goyanna. Detachments of the 1st line are staging raids in the city center, putting pressure on the most cunning evildoers.
>
> A political association that was to be established on the 9th, in the Navy arsenal, did not go into effect because it was prevented from doing so by the chief of police, who did not approve of political gatherings in public buildings.
>
> Propaganda from African followers of Mohammed has just been discovered.
>
> The police have made several arrests, including that of an inculcated prophet, as well as many writings in Hebrew.
>
> Because of a similar occurrence, the public has been terrified by rumors of insurrection; but when the steamer left [Pernambuco], peace still reigned supreme, and in the district of Pageú an individual involved in the rebellion of 1843 was pursued, the result being that, not wishing to be subjected to oppression, perhaps premeditated against him, that individual resisted three police raids, there being injuries and deaths on both sides, without managing to arrest him.
>
> There is little news of interest from Bahia.
>
> The letters from our correspondents, which will be published in the appropriate section, will inform our readers of everything that has occurred.
>
> *Correio Mercantil*, September 21, 1853.

minor infractions, not having the right job, or participating in African religious practices.[12]

Rufino may have been spared that punishment because in Pernambuco, unlike Bahia, Islam was not seen as a dangerous doctrine. The newspaper *O Echo Pernambucano*, for example, portrayed Rufino as a combination of a conman and religious fanatic whose aim was to profess his faith without breaking the law.[13]

By this time, Rufino's fame had spread beyond Pernambuco. His story became known throughout Brazil, disseminated in different ways, not just aboard the ships on which he sailed. Within the government bureaucracy, one of his manuscripts mobilized the justice minister and the chief of police of Rio de Janeiro to translate it, and far from the back rooms of officialdom, news of his arrest and interrogation circulated nationwide in the pages of the *Jornal do Commercio,* published in Rio de Janeiro. The same report was republished in Rio Grande do Sul by the *O Riograndense* newspaper on October 19, 1853, and some of its readers may have remembered the African who had lived there twenty years earlier as a slave of the police chief of that distant province. Two years later, the *Chronica Nacional: Folhinha dos Bons Costumes para o Anno de 1855* (National Chronicle: A Leaflet on Good Customs for the Year 1855) thought it appropriate to introduce in its section on "curious and interesting news" an entry for September 5, 1853, regarding the "terrifying rumors" that led to the arrest of Rufino, "the celebrated Alufá (a priest and schoolteacher), [in whose home] were found books and documents in unknown writing, which were confiscated and their owner, arrested."[14] In other words, two years after that incident, the press was still bringing up the arrest of the *alufá* Rufino as an example of bad behavior.

24

The Malês of Recife and a Doctrinal Dispute

The traces Rufino left in the documentary record vanish in 1853, but we have been able to retrieve some information about the Muslim community in Recife a few years later.

In 1865, the imam 'Abd al-Raman al-Bagdádi arrived in Rio de Janeiro with a Turkish squadron in which he served as chaplain. When he went ashore in religious vestments—including an imam's tunic and turban—the Muslim Africans living in Rio identified him as an authority and insisted that he preach to them. After some reluctance, partly because he suspected that the Africans were not true followers of his religion, the priest gave in and spent a few days among them. However, the Muslims, most of whom were Nagô (therefore, Malês), felt that this gesture was not enough. They wanted to receive more teachings from the imam and begged him to stay on longer in Brazil. Al-Bagdádi hesitated at first, but on consideration he began to look on the proposal more favorably. He discussed it with the commander of the squadron, who initially rejected the idea because he feared causing a diplomatic incident, as he had been informed that there was a thinly veiled ban on the practice of Islam by Africans in Brazil.

However, having made up his mind to stay, the chaplain of the Turkish squadron argued that he wanted to preach to the Africans in order to "set this community right, because they are relying on us." The commander eventually gave way, although they agreed that the cleric's preaching would be considered something of a secret mission. The Brazilian authorities would be informed that the imam was staying there as a foreign visitor—one of many—who was curious about the wonders of that land. It was not far from the truth. Al-Bagdádi remained there for nearly three years, an experience he described in a travelogue entitled *The Foreigner's Delight in Everything that is Amazing and Wonderful*.

In addition to Rio de Janeiro, al-Bagdádi visited Muslim communities in Salvador and Recife, where he was also invited to preach. The imam's travels in

The Story of Rufino. João José Reis, Flávio dos Santos Gomes, and Marcus J. M. de Carvalho, Translated by H. Sabrina Gledhill, Oxford University Press (2020) © Oxford University Press.
DOI: 10.1093/oso/9780190224363.001.0001

Brazil and the speed with which word of his presence spread in advance indicate that African followers of Allah moved about and corresponded with each other, forming a truly national network of co-religionaries instead of isolated groups. And they all had a similar way of practicing Islam. In all the communities al-Bagdádi visited, he came across Muslims who, in his view, had a rudimentary understanding of the basic tenets of his religion and a lifestyle that was far removed from those principles. They drank alcoholic beverages, married non-Muslim women, charged fees to accept converts into their groups, were barely able to recite the Holy Book, did not offer alms, pray at the right times, or follow the Muslim calendar, particularly the exact time when they should celebrate Ramadan. They were also excessively attached to amulets, divining, and other practices that the imam considered impure and superstitious and therefore truly reprehensible.[1]

Recife was the third city al-Bagdádi visited during his mission in Brazil. Coming from Bahia, he also went there at the invitation of local Muslims. In his view, the Malês of Pernambuco showed ritual and doctrinal deficiencies similar to those he had found in the other communities he visited in Brazil, but what most caught his attention were their divination methods. This is what the imam wrote about them:

> Their behavior in prayer and fasting is like the situation previously mentioned. And they have a strong inclination toward magic squares, geomancy, numerology and the mystical meaning of Arabic letters. Because of this, they are less hidden than [the Muslims] in the first cities, because the Christians trust them implicitly and believe their expressed intentions. Thus, they offer them money and do their bidding in all situations, although they know nothing of what they evoke except the name. Sometimes, however, the decree of fate coincides with [what they say], and they attribute this to their doing.[2]

It was as if al-Bagdádi were writing about Rufino's life at the time of his arrest. The imam mentioned "magic squares," "geomancy," "numerology," and the magical use of Arabic letters, all of which were widespread methods of divination and protection used by Muslims in western Africa, including Yorubaland, where Rufino grew up, and Sierra Leone, where he trained to become an *alufá*. The Malês of Bahia also engaged in this type of ritual practice. The documents confiscated by the police in 1835 included magic squares filled with Arabic numbers and letters.[3]

The use of these divination methods by Yoruba Muslims followed the arc of time until recently. For example, Patrick Ryan gives a detailed description of them based on research done in the 1970s. He came across magic squares, sand (hence "geomancy"), and divination with a *tessubá* (called a Malê rosary in Bahia), whose oracular use he describes. Ryan observes how far these arts are removed from the basic tenets of orthodox Islam in that region. Uthman Dan Fodio, the supreme leader and ideologue of the early nineteenth-century Fulani-Hausa jihad, vehemently condemned divination because, in his view, only God could know the future. Imam al-Bagdádi must have been singing from the same hymn sheet.[4]

Al-Bagdádi offers us one of the keys to understanding some of the religious tolerance that still prevailed with regard to the Malês in Recife. According to him, that city was more tolerant than Salvador and Rio, probably because the local *alufás* had managed to attract a large clientele from outside the Muslim community with a broad range of divinatory practices. Those clients had become their allies. As a result, the Malês not only earned their daily bread but gained protection from high-ranking individuals, both white and mixed-race, who, despite being Catholics, generally had the same world view as the Muslims. Just like Africans of various origins, many Brazilians (and probably some Europeans) believed that divination could find the causes and solutions to their problems, aiming to achieve success in their love lives, financial prosperity, maintain and restore their health, and win political campaigns. Using divination, they also discovered whether their ailments and misfortunes were the result of witchcraft. Al-Bagdádi's report thus confirms what the *alufá* Rufino José Maria had revealed a little over ten years earlier when he was arrested in the capital of Pernambuco. That is, he had a socially and racially varied clientele among the residents of that city, who sought him out to solve their everyday difficulties. In short, "he was seen as an oracle by those who visited him with religious observance," according to report from the president of the province of Pernambuco to the justice minister. Thus, Rufino did not pose a threat to law and order. To that official, the *alufá* was not as dangerous as the band of "criminals" who had occupied the streets in a rural village and killed two soldiers, and he suggested the creation of a permanent flying squadron to keep them and similar bands of outlaws in check.[5]

Rufino was just a Muslim who wanted to increase his knowledge in order to better practice his religion, and in this he was not unlike the numerous children of Allah whom al-Bagdádi met in Brazil and to whom he preached. However, all indications are that in Sierra Leone, Rufino' was trained to read, recite, and copy sacred texts while he was learning divination, protection, and healing methods that were widespread among the Islamized Aku, practices of which the imam from Baghdad took a dim view. For Rufino, al-Bagdádi represented a new kind of evil spawned by the ocean—the chaplain of a foreign naval squadron imbued with the mission of purifying ideas and practices that were part of the *alufá* Abuncare's way of life and livelihood.

Al-Bagdádi may have met our protagonist in person and learned about those reprehensible activities (in which Rufino also engaged) through the *alufá* himself during his stay in Recife. According to the imam, the local Muslims were divided into two groups led by men who were apparently not on good terms. After meeting so many Muslims from other parts of Brazil, the imam finally remembered to write down their names—José and Salomão. He praised the former—the younger of the two—calling him "wise," probably because he accepted al-Bagdádi's doctrinal and liturgical reforms. He described the latter, an older man, as "the opposite" and reproached him for rejecting the new fasting period he had recommended since he began his ministry in Rio de Janeiro.[6]

Could the older man have been Rufino, now aged about sixty-five? We can reasonably speculate that al-Bagdádi got their names mixed up when writing his travelogue, perhaps years after visiting Brazil. In that case, Salomão would have been the younger man who was open to the imam's preaching, and José the older man who refused to change his way of practicing Islam. José could well be Rufino—Rufino *José* Maria . . .

The fact that the Muslim presence was firmly established in nineteenth-century Recife came to light about a decade after al-Bagdádi's visit in a series of reports published in the *Diário de Pernambuco* newspaper. They involved a dispute over which groups truly represented Recife's Muslims in dealings with the provincial police. At least, that is what the episode seemed to be about at first glance. As we will see, the fact is that, unlike other African religions, Islam was contended for because it had become a religion that was, if not respected, at least openly tolerated by the political potentates of Pernambuco. The same cannot be said of other African forms of worship.[7]

Agostinho and Rufino, ironically dubbed Divino Mestre I and Divino Mestre II by the *Diário de Pernambuco*, were not the only black men active in the field of religion to become news fodder for that paper. The devotees of Nossa Senhora do Rosário dos Pretos (Our Lady of the Rosary of Black People), were frequently portrayed in its pages, particularly due to the coronation of the Congo King and rulers of other African nations, a festival that was held annually, usually in October or November. The ceremony included a procession through the streets of Santo Antônio parish. Not infrequently, the revels got out of hand, and quarrels and violence ensued.

In an exceptional year, 1851, the *Diário de Pernambuco* reported that the Africans who formed the procession that left the church of Rosário in São Pedro parish, where Rufino lived, "frolicked according to the practices of their nations and processed without any disorderly conduct whatsoever." In 1856, the "little blacks from Rosário [church]" were dispersed by the police "because they went from *maracatu* to bacchanalia, which always leads to disturbances" the newspaper foretold.

There were several reports in 1872. One announced that Nação Velha de Cabinda (Old Nation of Cabinda), a *maracatu* group, would parade the following day along with its queen, leaving from the church of Rosário. Another reported a dispute among members of the Rosário confraternity of Recife about how the body of an important member, D. Antonio de Oliveira Guimarães, a former Congo King, should be conveyed to the cemetery—whether it should be carried or transported in a funeral car. With some assistance from the police, the second proposal won out, according to the wishes of the governor-general of the African nation, Joaquim Tomás de Aquino, the Duke of Congo, who published two notices in the newspaper rebuking his subjects' dissidence.[8]

Reports about Afro-Brazilian religions, called Xangô in Pernambuco, and isolated cases of African shamanism also abounded in the pages of the *Diário*. An interesting episode occurred in 1856 during a devastating cholera epidemic that scourged the province, taking over 37,000 lives in just ten months.[9] Amid the calamity and suspicions about the doctors' medical skills, reports emerged of a slave from the Guararapes plantation who was said to have invented an effective remedy, tested on partners and later lauded by his master and other white people. Given under the supervision of a member of the provincial Hygiene Commission to a patient in a Recife hospital, the medicine was also said to have worked. However, the slave owner did not agree to the request to allow the healer to continue working miracles at the hospital.

While the epidemic spread, another black man, Manuel, supposedly a disciple of the healer from Guararapes, came onto the scene. His cures were vouched for by two commanders and a high-ranking officer in the Imperial army. According to the president of the province, it was reported that "the black man had worked instant cures and that the people applauded him." However, when his medicine was tested on some cholera victims, it failed to cure them. The shaman was arrested for quackery.[10]

We do not know if Rufino engaged in alternative healing practices like these to combat the epidemic. Muslims would only become news again in the *Diário de Pernambuco* ten years later.

It all began in another religious sphere, when the police launched an operation against followers of Xangô in Recife in early July 1877. Eager to make a good showing, the new deputy chief constable of the first district of São José parish, "made an abundant harvest of witches and sorceresses who, abusing the credulity of the gaggle of boors who frequented them, made them pay steep prices for their charms, divination, cures, etc. . . . etc. . . . ," according to the newspaper's account. Escorted by the police, the prisoners were paraded through the city streets, headed by a female version of the "Divino Mestre"—whom the newspaper ironically dubbed the "Divina Mestra" —wearing ritual apparel and forced to carry religious objects confiscated by the police. She was followed by other individuals who carried baskets full of plants and sacrificial animals on their heads. The group was jeered everywhere it went, resulting in scenes of public humiliation. The prisoners joined a Xangô priest who had been arrested the day before. In the next few days the police made further arrests, and more objects were confiscated and burned in the police department's courtyard by the same deputy chief constable. On day three, the police department was so full of prisoners that the "sorcerers"—as the *Diário* labeled them—nearly escaped, taking advantage of the lack of guards, but were prevented from fleeing by a crowd of curiosity seekers that had gathered in the door of the police department.[11] Clearly Pernambuco's tolerance of African religions was not that exemplary.

A more diplomatic response would come a month later. On August 3, 1877, a group of Africans wrote and published a notice in the *Diário de Pernambuco* stating that, having obtained permission from the chief constable of the capital "to engage in the practices of their religion" invited "their countrymen" to attend a religious gathering on the 19th, a Sunday. Attached to that invitation was a copy of the letter sent to the chief constable in which nine "free Africans" asked permission to freely practice the "acts of their religion, which is the Mahommedan [faith], with the ways and customs of their native land." This, they said, was in accordance with the Constitution, which permitted the practice of any religion in places that were not outwardly like a church. Its nine signatories were Roberto Henrique, Silvestre Machado, Frederico Inácio de Oliveira, Joaquim Vieira da Silva, Gregório Pereira da Cunha, Cassiano Antônio Vieira, Rufino Inácio de Oliveira, Pedro Salustiano Meuron, and Jacinto Afonso da Costa.[12]

One week after that notice appeared in the *Diário*, the newspaper published a "protest" from another group of Africans who claimed that they were the only true followers of the Islamic faith in the city and accused the first group of not being Muslims at all. They explained to the readers, including the province's police authorities, that Africa was a more complex place, anthropologically speaking, than they had thought:

> The African population that resides in this Province, as well as the entire Empire [Brazil], is made up of individuals from different parts of Africa that are far removed, by hundreds of kilometres, from each other, and have a variety of customs and religions; that which follows Mohammedanism here, to which we belong, is a small population but distinct from each other, and noting the need to maintain our faith, which also brings us together, because we understand that without a religion, of whatever kind, there can be no social harmony, and based on art. 5 of the constitution of the Empire, we requested permission from the Chief of Police to practice our religion on December 1873.[13]

They included a transcript of the petition they had sent four years earlier, accompanied by a letter of authorization from the chief of police. Then they accused the "supposed followers of Mohammedanism" of being "false," because if they truly were Muslims, they would not have asked permission to practice their religion when authorization had already been issued four years earlier. The letter of protest was signed by Sabino Antônio da Costa, Jovino Lopes Ferreira, Guilherme Manoel Pedro do Bom-Fim, Pedro Joaquim Teixeira, Antônio José Vieira, Sabino Patrício, José Victor de Oliveira, Daniel Rodrigues, José de Oliveira, João Estanislau, Bento Moncor, and Luís Husque.

The following day, the newspaper published the rejoinder of the group accused of fraud, who argued that they never said they were the "only Muslims residing in that city." Their aim was simply to prevent further police repression conducted "on the pretext that they were given to necromancy." They observed that all "Mohammedans" did not belong the same sect, whether in Africa or Pernambuco, as claimed by "the Malês, in whose name the protest was made." The Malês, they wrote, accused them of being "Keferifes," that is, *kaferi*, the Yoruba term for *kafir* (pl. *kafirai*), the Arabic word for unbeliever, pagan, or infidel. It made no difference if they were classified as such. They were, in fact, Muslims, although they belonged to a sect that was closer to Catholic doctrine, because they did not practice polygamy, as the Malês did, or promise "a paradise full of sensual delights." They concluded by stating that they had demonstrated "the different sects that exist," and said that they wanted to "refrain from continuing the controversy in the press."[14]

Let us make the argument very clear. One group of Africans claims to be Muslim and another protests, saying that that claim is false. The former group says it is closer to the tenets of Catholicism because its members do not practice polygamy or promise its male followers "sensual delights" in the afterlife, alluding to certain Islamic traditions that promise the famous seventy-two virgins to faithful Muslims. Therefore, they use the strategy of suggesting a closer relationship between their group and the hegemonic Catholic faith to be viewed in a good light by whites, particularly the authorities. Their adversaries are said to be Malês, in other words, Islamized Nagôs like Rufino, who did not want to let the argument rest.

The Malês returned to the fray with a heavy doctrinal assault. By demonstrating their knowledge of the religion, they intended to establish their authority to speak on behalf of Recife's Muslim community. In their analysis, their adversaries had admitted in their most recent note that they had taken on the identity of Muslims to evade police repression against "sorcery." Since they had confirmed that "they cannot be confused with any of us from the religious standpoint," the Malês said they were relieved to hear it. Furthermore, the Malês were proud that the others had spoken "the real truth, because they must be aware that there is a great ocean between us that divides us in that regard," that is, with regard to their faith. And they go on to indicate their opposition's ignorance of the doctrine of the Qur'ān and Sunnah. Furthermore, they explained, polygamy existed in Africa and was protected both by "polytheistic" religions and Islam. Only Christianity advocated monogamy. Therefore, they agreed on that point. By that, they were saying that, being "polytheists," the Africans they were confronting were also polygamous, and therefore their defense of Christian monogamy was pure hypocrisy.

The Malês took the opportunity to instruct the *Diário*'s readers about Islam. They taught them that it was mainly divided between Sunnis and Shias, claiming to observe the "main dogmas that unite them" as well as abstaining from alcohol, fasting during Ramadan, and the "ban on idolatry." And, apparently familiar with their adversaries' habits, they asked: "Well now, if you make libations with alcoholic beverages, if you tend to your images which you worship and revere, how can you want to be Mahommedans, when that religion condemns your beliefs and ceremonies?" Since they were "keferifes," they should ask permission to practice their pagan beliefs, because the Malês had the "pure and unwavering faith that each must have in the dogmas of their religion, whatever it may be." These words echo Rufino's when he said that everyone had their own religion and the best of them would only be known at the end of time. Despite the fierce dispute, at no time did the Malês justify the police raid that had taken place a few weeks earlier. Reading between the lines, since they had achieved freedom of worship, Africans who followed other religions from Africa should have the same right—in this case, followers of Xangô.[15]

So far, the messages published in the *Diário* had been signed. Following this one, two more were published in which the authors used pseudonyms. In the first—Abdalá Limamo—*lemọmo* being the Yoruba term for imam—addressed "The Malês of Aladino," and below that name, the anonymous author wrote "Allah Bysmilla" (In the Name of Allah), an expression used by devout Muslims to begin any written text, or preceding any action taken. The author ironically dubbed the Malês "servants of Aladdin," a reference to the character from *One Thousand and One Nights*. Then, he recommended that the chief of police suspend the religious permit he had issued, since "the worship of Muhammad, as they practice it . . . should not be tolerated because it is offensive to public morals . . . in the shadow of which they corrupt the customs of their children, who belong to Brazilian society." Here, Abdalá Limamo was employing the familiar political strategy of distinguishing between blacks born in Africa and their Creole children, who should be raised as Catholics because they were born in Brazil.[16]

The following day, a new message addressed "To A. Limamo of the *Diário* of the 6th of this month," also written by an anonymous writer who signed himself "The True One," one of the names of Muhammad. The author challenged Limamo to cast off "the mask of anonymity"—although he himself had not—and show the public what was corrupt and immoral about the Malês' behavior, including the way they raised their children. He accused Limamo of "vile calumny and empty lies of crass ignorance."[17]

We believe that those two anonymous letters were written by a mischievous reader of the *Diário*—perhaps even its editor—who had decided to have fun with the highly serious dispute between Africans. This is because it makes no sense for the ensuing discussion to be carried out anonymously. It is more likely that both missives were written by the same person. Two clues stand out: in the letter signed Abdalá Limamo—the author writes that the chief of police should cancel the Malês' permit because it was allegedly obtained "*ob e subrep[ti]ciamente*" (falsely and surreptitiously)—legal jargon that we do not find in the signed missives. In the second anonymous letter, the evidence lies in the fact that, since the Malês had demonstrated thorough knowledge of Islamic doctrine, none of them would use a name that was only permitted for the Prophet, which would have been a grievous sin.

The true protagonists would only take up the dispute again in the pages of the *Diário de Pernambuco* a few months later, in mid-December. In the streets, however, it probably never abated, and this may explain the even more belligerent tone of the following letters published in that newspaper. The first—dated December 17 and signed by just three of the Malês who had joined in the verbal affray, Jovino Ferreira, Sabino da Costa, and Antônio Vieira—elaborately thanked the chief of police on behalf of the "sectarians of the Mohammedan religion" for the permit granted in 1873, and declared themselves fervent followers "of the precept of the law" in Brazil. Then, they suggested that the authorities cancel the religious permit granted to the "false Muslims," recalling that they were, in fact, the same

> ... individuals in whose homes were seized by the then-chief constable of the first district of the parish of S. José, the Illustrious Mr Netto, an extraordinary quantity of idols, temples [presumably meaning altars] and other objects destined for the practice of fetishism, and all the more so as these individuals, those found in the temples, were imprisoned in the police station, and his worthy predecessor sent them to jail and burned in the inner courtyard of the office, idols, temples, animals in brine, skulls, everything from that vile cult, which they themselves carried![18]

The authors of this letter had clearly changed their position. Previously, they recognized their adversaries' religion as legitimate and, despite being pagan, deserving of legal protection. But now they practically justified—if not encouraged—its repression.

Two days later, the counterattack came, also signed by three Africans—Roberto Henriques, Frederico Oliveira, and Joaquim Vieira da Silva, all of whom had been present since the beginning of the dispute—denying that they were the fetishists described in the newspaper. They explained:

> None of the events specified ... has anything to do with the undersigned, who obtained a permit from the police of this city to engage in religious practices with African customs and traditions without offending the public morals or the state religion, given the unlawful action taken, under the pretext of fetishism, against nearly all Africans in the parish of S. José.[19]

In this letter—the last published in the *Diário* on this matter—the public dispute ended with the words of those who had begun it. The writers had been unjustly arrested because the police had acted unlawfully in August. This criticism of the abuse of police powers was courageous and perhaps made by people who somehow felt safe to do so, not only because they had managed to obtain a permit allowing them freedom of worship but possibly because the recent changes in the highest ranks of the police in that province signaled a return to more tolerant times. They felt so confident that they did not even bother to call themselves Muslims, merely stating that they engaged in "religious practices with African customs and traditions." They therefore denied being "fetishists" and took the opportunity to once again attack the polygamy of the Malês, the main accusation levied in this holy war of words. And they asked the chief of police to be on the lookout for that "abuse" practiced by "those Muslims," therefore repaying the Malês in the same coin.

This polemic makes it clear that the Malês were thoroughly familiar with the doctrine and history of their religion. They wrote of the Qur'ān and Sunnah, of Sunnis and Shiites, as well as mentioning names that had come to represent those two main branches of Islam—the caliphs Omar (reigned from 634 to 644) and Ali (656 to 661), respectively. Those notices which appeared in the Pernambuco press are therefore a rare source of information about Afro-Islam in nineteenth-century Brazil in which that level of Islamic education is clearly established, because not even in the documents found during the Bahia revolt is that aspect of the Malê intellectual experience so clearly expressed. We have seen something like it in this book, although not in such detail, when presenting and discussing the statements Rufino made during his interrogation in 1853. However, unlike Rufino, in 1877 the Malês failed to mention that some members of their community also engaged in divining, propitiatory offerings, healing, and other practices that brought them somewhat closer to those they called "keferifes." It is understandable that they did not touch on that subject because, in the pages of that newspaper, they were making an effort to explain the differences between the two groups and not their similarities. Malês and pagans, however, knew each other, keeping their distance but possibly, on the margins of their faiths, the less orthodox followers might have exchanged ritual knowledge and favors, just as their clients must have done.

A Signature in the Dispute between the Malês and the Xangô Community in 1877

Even if the Malês had not established from the beginning that their opponents were not actually Muslims, this was confirmed by the signature of a well-known figure from the Candomblé of Bahia. Joaquim Vieira da Silva is now invoked in more-or-less private rituals at the Ilê Iya Nassô *terreiro*, also known as Engenho Velho and Casa Branca, which is viewed as the birthplace of the main Candomblé temples that follow the Nagô tradition in Bahia. Joaquim was enslaved by a slave trader, for whom he worked as a sailor. He probably crewed slave ships during the final years of the period when the trade was practiced illegally. He was freed upon his master's death in 1866 and settled in Recife in 1873, where, alongside the famous Babalawo Bamboxê Obiticô, who also lived in Bahia, he probably helped –found Obá Ogunté– (the future Sítio de Pai Adão temple) in 1875.[20] His leading role in the Xangô community of Recife is confirmed by his participation in the struggle for religious freedom in that city in 1877, which sparked the dispute with the Malês. All indications are that Joaquim returned to Bahia in the mid-1890s and died there in 1902. His story is part of a connection between Pernambuco and Bahia that involved other important figures from the Bahian Candomblé of that time, all of whom were linked to Casa Branca. The connection has a clear religious aspect and was not limited to Brazil, because it extended to Africa, particularly Onim, which frequently welcomed Africans and their children who lived in Recife and Salvador. The visitors were not just seeking ritual knowledge but went to that city to study and trade, and sometimes settled down there. Incidentally, the same newspaper that published the religious dispute between Africans in Pernambuco in 1877 also regularly announced the departure of ships to that African port, whether directly from Bahia or from Bahia with a stop in Recife.[21]

Unfortunately, we do not know if Rufino was involved in this dispute in some way or another, even as the *éminence grise* behind a disciple or successor in the Muslim leadership in Recife. We can well imagine that the knowledge the Malês displayed in the pages of the *Diário de Pernambuco* may have been passed on to them by Rufino, who in turn is believed to have learned it (or bolstered his prior knowledge of it) during his sojourns in Sierra Leone. Of course, he also visited other African communities in Brazil—in Bahia, Porto Alegre, possibly Rio Grande, and Rio de Janeiro—where there was a large Muslim presence. At the same time, we must not dismiss the possibility that al-Bagdádi's teachings in Recife, which went on for several months, were also present in the African controversy that took place nearly ten years later. In any case, 1877 enters the calendar of Muslim history in Brazil as the year in which the Malês went public to showcase their doctrine and declare themselves true Muslims, in contrast with other Africans whom they accused of being untrue followers of their faith.

In the second half of the 1860s, al-Bagdádi observed that Muslims and their religion were more tolerant in Pernambuco than in Rio de Janeiro and Bahia. The articles from the pages of the *Diário de Pernambuco* we have just discussed confirm that impression. Even before the imam's visit, the results of the investigation to which Rufino was subjected in 1853 also point in that direction. Greater freedom of religious expression in Recife may have been a factor that Rufino took into consideration when choosing to live there, instead of settling down in other familiar places like Salvador, Porto Alegre, and Rio de Janeiro, where the Muslim communities were larger and stronger but suffered more oppression. In all those cities, particularly Salvador, Rufino's religion was long viewed as a source of social subversion and endured unrelenting persecution. Although they occasionally faced mass slave rebellions, the seigneurial classes of Pernambuco had much bigger problems— revolts staged by the free population in an intense cycle of uprisings that began with the movement of 1817 and ended with the Ronco do Marimbondo in 1852.

However, the Pernambuco authorities' tolerance toward the Malês did not extend to other African religious expressions. As the episode of 1877 illustrates, so-called pagan religions did not receive the same treatment given to Islam. Unlike that faith, which came to be considered a religion whose followers were protected by the Constitution, the others were categorized as witchcraft, superstition, and even criminal activity. In 1877 they were described with the demeaning term *"fetichismo"* (fetishism). Soon, that term would be enshrined in the first evolutionist-oriented anthropological studies of those religious communities conducted in Brazil.

Unlike Islamic monotheism, pagan polytheism was not officially tolerated in 1877 Recife, even though—as we have seen with Rufino—Muslims offered their clients ritual services that were very similar to those provided by the "fetishists." At times they were even similar in form and promised results. However, the success of a folk religion depends on more important things than the tolerance of the high and mighty. Ironically, African Islam waned and disappeared in Pernambuco, whereas Xangô has survived and flourished.

Epilogue

Through his experience of living in different parts of Brazil and Africa, Rufino must have developed a cosmopolitan view of the world that would have been difficult to achieve for most Africans—even less so for his Brazilian contemporaries. First as a captive of the slave trade, then as a cook aboard a slave ship, Rufino crossed the Atlantic in the hold and on deck. He met people from the world over who circulated among the mercantile connections between Brazil, Africa, and Europe—suffice it to recall the multinational makeup of the *Ermelinda*'s crew and, even more so, the varied origins of Sierra Leone's inhabitants. Rufino spoke Yoruba, Portuguese, and perhaps some Arabic (at least enough to communicate with God), as well as a pidgin typical of African slave ports and the Krio patois, a language that was still developing in Sierra Leone in his time. He was therefore multilingual and cosmopolitan, a figure who moved about in a varied range of cultures in a world that was both united and divided—in many senses—by the Atlantic ocean.[1]

Rufino carried out his activities competently—a veritable entrepreneur, he was modestly successful in business, to the point of becoming a small investor in the transatlantic trade. He might have done even better, had he so desired, or if the *Ermelinda* had not been captured. It was an impressive career for someone who arrived in Brazil as a slave twenty years before crewing a slave ship. It is not just impressive because he amassed assets, since other African freedpersons, also involved with the slave trade, are known to have prospered even more than he did in Brazil.[2] By the time of his interrogation, Rufino was the impecunious resident of a basement room in a Recife townhouse in Rua da Senzala Velha. The other African suspects detained during the investigation that led to his arrest were also humble folk. According to the deputy chief constable who searched their homes in 1853, they made a living from "common trade in trays of vegetables and produce from this country."[3] According to Rufino, leading the modest, quiet life of a Malê healer, diviner, and *alufá* was his own choice. Repeating his words, "some ask God for wealth, but he had only asked for wisdom." If we are to believe

The Story of Rufino. João José Reis, Flávio dos Santos Gomes, and Marcus J. M. de Carvalho, Translated by H. Sabrina Gledhill, Oxford University Press (2020) © Oxford University Press.
DOI: 10.1093/oso/9780190224363.001.0001

him, Rufino had tired of serving Caesar and decided to serve God instead. This apparently did not include getting rich or revolutionizing Brazil's Christian, slaveholding world.

Even if he had once been a militant Muslim like the Malê rebels of 1835, Rufino had ceased to be so in 1853. By then, he practiced an "accommodated" form of Islam, an expression Bradford Martin uses to describe a West African branch of the religion that did not emphasize proselytizing or spreading the faith by force; instead, its ministers devoted themselves to dealing with the occasional ills that plagued their clientele and obtaining the benefits those clients sought, no matter what faith they professed.[4] In fact, "accommodation" may be an inappropriate term to apply to these followers of Allah because, very much to the contrary, people like Rufino—and there were not a few among the Malês after 1835— refused to accommodate themselves to a rigid dogma, an iron-clad orthodoxy, on one hand, or to the hegemonic culture around them on the other. Although he was not interested in teaching the doctrine outside the Muslim hosts, there is no doubt that he frequently engaged in dialogue aimed at conversion and even debates like the one on which he embarked with his Catholic interrogators in 1853, or in controversies like the one that his fellow Malês sparked in 1877 with Africans they viewed as "fetishists." Rufino's relations with non-Muslims were similar to those of contemporary priests of Candomblé or Xangô. One of them may have been the *alufá*'s neighbor in Recife, an African freedman found in possession of "a wooden doll without a real shape or form and a calabash with a hole in it," according to a Recife police officer who searched his house in 1853. Using their own rituals and symbols, Rufino and the Xangô priests of Recife— like those of other Afro-Brazilian religions—engaged in many similar activities despite the somewhat purist dispute that the Malês engaged in later on, in 1877.[5]

However, this does not mean that Rufino was not a devout Muslim. His tenacity in maintaining and defending his faith is particularly noteworthy, but that is not all: he was also tenacious in his efforts to improve his knowledge of it, not only to gain expertise in a varied range of services he provided but with the admitted aim of becoming an *alufá*, specifically a religious counselor for Muslims, a teacher, guardian, and preacher of the word of Allah. This aspect of his personality becomes clearly apparent in the course of the interrogation conducted in 1853. Moreover, he was following in the footsteps of his father, also an *alufá*, who may have chosen him to inherit his post. He was therefore trying to return to his old life, from the point where it was interrupted in Africa.

If he was not a Malê jihadist, Rufino represented a different sort of threat—a sort of cultural and even psychological affront to the world of Brazilian whites, because he was a black man who took pride in being different, a Muslim with the powers of healing, divining, making people fall in and out of love, and casting and removing spells, which made him an eminent person among the

Africans of Recife. An African freedman and a Muslim could not easily be integrated into a Catholic slavocracy, particularly if he was as articulate, multilingual, well-traveled, and charismatic as Rufino. Even more important, he was an African who could read and write, thereby mastering a fundamental symbol of civilization for those times, even if his writing was not in a Western language. Despite his detractors, through the skills practiced in a highly competitive religious market Rufino could influence the lives of those who sought him out—including whites.

Even so, it is surprising that Rufino decided to live in a world that was dominated by white Christians who mistrusted, derided, and frequently obstructed the practice of his faith. He could have stayed in Sierra Leone or settled down in some other part of the West African coast where the presence of both Muslims and Yorubas was significant and better tolerated, even the norm. Rufino must have concluded that returning to Africa was not without its risks, including the risk of re-enslavement, which he well knew as a former slave and slave trader.[6] He chose to live in Brazil, where the risk of returning to bondage was real but apparently lower, particularly in the cities, and especially for an older black man with the sort of social connections he had established. Furthermore, despite everything that Rufino had retained from his past, he had changed considerably, even remaking that past. He had put down roots in the country where he was once enslaved, which he had traveled from north to south, where he had fathered a child, had disciples among other exiled Africans, and clients among them and citizens of Brazil. He had not become a Brazilian, but he was no longer an Ọ̀yọ́ man—he was a Nagô. He was no longer an Ìmàle—he was a Malê. In the language of the time, people like Rufino, born in Africa and experienced in the worlds of Atlantic slavery, were called *ladinos* in Brazil and elsewhere in the slave societies of Hispanic America. In this sense, Rufino was an "Atlantic *ladino*," who, nevertheless, had decided to cast anchor once and for all and stay on terra firma in Brazil. The choices he made suggest that, when viewed from the individual angle—but which also pertains to groups—questions posed by historians and anthropologists regarding cultural formation, ethnic identity, and creolization in the New World, Brazil in particular, become much more complex and hard to assign to all-encompassing models.

There are well-known narratives by and about figures like Rufino, including other Muslims. The study of those men—most are men—whose lives were linked to the Atlantic, who crossed it two or more times and visited or lived in different ports on one shore or the other, is now part of a growing literature.[7] Despite being little studied in Brazil so far, small and middling transatlantic traders—also Africans—were not unusual aboard slave ships and other vessels, according to the passports issued for voyages to Africa by the Brazilian port authorities. Some, unlike Rufino, ended up settling down on the other side of the ocean when going back and forth became harder to do, and was even banned (a prohibition that was often flouted) after the 1835 rebellion.[8]

Rufino José Maria enables us to observe the broad range of possibilities that were open to and pursued by Africans enslaved in Brazil, at least some of them. They included the possibility that, once they had obtained their manumission, they could work in the slave trade to fuel the machine of Atlantic slavery that had once victimized them. Although the transatlantic trade in human beings was primarily a business plied by white Brazilian and Portuguese men (and at different times also by Britons, Americans, Jamaicans, Spaniards, Cubans, and Frenchmen, among others), Creole and African blacks of various backgrounds were also involved on both sides of the Atlantic. Similarly, if whites did the most enslaving, Africans and their descendants owned slaves as well, not just in Africa but in the New World—it was widespread in Brazil. For those who are not accustomed to the history of slavery and the slave trade, this aspect is not just more surprising but harder to accept from the moral and ethical standpoint—even painful.

One should not think, however, that a career like Rufino's was within the grasp of most African freedpersons or would even interest them. It was more common for former slaves, debilitated by their enslavement, to live out their freedom in a modest or impoverished fashion in the cities or countryside of the Brazil of that time. Rufino and other freedpersons—some of whom were much better off than he was—therefore represented a small portion of the more than three million Africans (a conservative estimate) believed to have disembarked in Brazil as slaves. The vast majority of those Africans died while enslaved in Brazil, without ever enjoying freedom again. Therefore, Rufino's story was in no way typical. The reason for telling it arises from the fact that history is not just narrated on the basis of the norm but can often be better assimilated when combined and contrasted with the exception. This was, in fact, what we sought to do here: our protagonist has served as a guide to a much larger history that goes beyond his personal experience. He regularly escapes our sights, giving way to the colossal drama of slavery in the Atlantic world in which he played a small but interesting, and sometimes nefarious, part.

ACKNOWLEDGMENTS

The authors would like to recognize the assistance of the following colleagues, students, and friends who provided comments and data and who gathered, suggested, or sent bibliographical references and sources to guide us through the archives: Alberto da Costa e Silva, Almir El-Kareh, André Luis Freire Lima Filho, Andrew Apter, Beatriz Mamigoniam, Bruno Câmara, Carlos Eugênio Líbano Soares, Carlos Francisco da Silva Júnior, Claudia Trindade, Dale Graden, Eduardo Cavalcante, Elaine Falheiros, Gabriela dos Reis Sampaio, Hendrik Kraay, Hildo Leal da Rosa, J. Lorand Matory, Jônatas Caratti, José Luis Mota Menezes, Jovani Scherer, Ligia Bellini, Lisa Earl Castillo, Lucia Miler, Luís Nicolau Parés, Luiz Felipe de Alencastro, Marcia Naomi Kuniochi, Maria Celeste Gomes da Silva, Neuracy de Azevedo Moreira, Nikolay Dobronravin, Ola Fadahunsi, Paul Lovejoy, Paulo César Oliveira de Jesus, Paulo de Moraes Farias, Paulo Roberto Staudt Moreira, Renata Oliveira, Renato da Silveira, Richard Graham, Roquinaldo Amaral Ferreira, Sandra Graham, Sátiro Nunes, Silvana Jeha, Silvia Hunold Lara, Tácito Galvão, Toyin Falola, Urano Andrade, Valéria Costa, Vanessa Rolim Bosi, and Venétia Durando Rios. Without their help, this book would not have been possible.

Mariângela Nogueira read the first draft of this book and made detailed critical comments. A later draft was read by Lilia Schwarcz, who gave us numerous suggestions on editing and content. A few more colleagues and friends perused the final draft before it went to press, in time to include many of their suggestions. They were Roquinaldo Ferreira, who pointed out errors in the African section of the book, as well as furnishing data and documents and recommending bibliographical sources; Paulo Fernando de Moraes Farias and Nikolay Dobronravin, our main consultants on Afro-Muslim matters; and Wlamyra Albuquerque, who observed some slips and inaccuracies of language.

Parts of this book were presented at the colloquium "L'éxpérience coloniale: dynamiques des échanges dans les espaces atlantiques à l'époque de l'esclavage" in Nantes (June 20 to 22, 2005) and at meetings of the Slavery and Invention of Freedom research group of the Universidade Federal da Bahia Graduate Program in History. The matters discussed here have also been presented in lectures at the universities of Michigan (Ann Arbor), Tulane (New Orleans), Texas (Austin), the Universidade Federal do Rio Grande do Sul, and the Clemente Mariani Foundation (Salvador). The people who attended those events made comments that were very useful to improving this book.

We would like to extend our special thanks to the staff members and directors of all the archives, libraries, museums, and other institutions where we conducted research: the Arquivo Nacional, Arquivo Histórico do Itamaraty, and Biblioteca Nacional, all three in Rio de Janeiro; the Arquivo Histórico do Rio Grande do Sul and Arquivo Público do Estado do Rio Grande do Sul, in Porto Alegre; the Arquivo Público Estadual Jordão Emerenciano (Recife) in Recife; the Arquivo Público do Estado da Bahia, Arquivo da Santa Casa de Misericórdia, Museu da Misericórdia, Arquivo da Cúria Metropolitana de Salvador (now in the care of the Laboratório Eugênio Veiga, of the Universidade Católica de Salvador), Arquivo Histórico Municipal de Salvador in Salvador Bahia; the National Archives of Great Britain in London; and the libraries of the universities of Stanford, Texas (Austin), and Duke, in the United States, and the École d'Hautes Études en Sciences Sociales in France. João Reis spent a year at the National Humanities Center (USA), which enabled him to conduct a significant portion of the research (particularly on the British Parliamentary Papers) and produce the first draft of the manuscript. All three authors would like to thank the Brazilian Research Council (CNPq) for its support for the research of this book. We are also grateful to Marta Garcia and her team, particularly Lucila Lombardi and Ana Laura Souza, for their painstaking work in preparing the Brazilian edition for publication. For the present edition, we thank the two anonymous readers for their helpful comments, Sabrina Gledhill for her competent translation, Susan Ferber for her assistance as an editor, and Marcus Rediker for recommending the Oxford University Press as a publisher for *The Story of Rufino*. A 2014 grant from the Brazilian National Library made possible the translation of this book.

NOTES

Preface

1. "Auto de perguntas feitas ao preto forro Rufino José Maria," Arquivo Nacional (AN hereafter), IJ1, 326, *Pernambuco, Ofícios do Presidente da Província ao Ministro da Justiça (1853-1854)*.
2. *Jornal do Commercio*, Rio de Janeiro, September 25, 1853. We would like to thank Hendrik Kraay for providing this source. This report was also published in the Rio Grande do Sul newspaper *O Riograndense*, October 19, 1853. Our thanks to Marcia Naomi Kuniochi for that reference. Unlike the article in *Jornal do Commercio*, highly negative reports on Rufino were published in another Rio newspaper, *Correio Mercantil*, on September 21 and 28, 1853. This source may have been used for the first time by Alberto da Costa e Silva, "Buying and Selling Korans in Nineteenth-Century Rio de Janeiro," *Slavery & Abolition*, 22, no. 1 (2001): 85-86. A somewhat revised translation of that article was published as a chapter of a book by the same author, *Um rio chamado Atlântico: a África no Brasil e o Brasil na África* (Rio de Janeiro: Nova Fronteira, 2003), 177-186.
3. For a reflection on the construction of biographies of individuals like Rufino, see Lara Putnam, "To Study the Fragments/Whole: Microhistory and the Atlantic World," *Journal of Social History*, 39, no. 3 (2006): 615-630

Chapter 1

1. On the decline and fall of Òyọ́, see Robin Law, *The Òyọ́ Empire, c. 1600-c.1836: A West African Imperialism in the Era of the Atlantic Slave Trade* (Oxford: Clarendon Press, 1977); J. F. Ade Ajayi, "The Aftermath of the Fall of Òyọ́," in J.F. Ade Ajayi and Michael Crowder (eds.), *History of West Africa* (London: Longman, 1974), vol. 2, 129-166. On *jihad* in the Hausa nation, see Murray Last, *The Sokoto Caliphate* (New York: Humanities Press, 1967); and Mervyn Hiskett, *The Sword of the Truth: The Life and Times of the Shehu Usuman dan Fodio* (New York: Oxford University Press, 1973), among many other titles. Regarding the slave trade and slavery among the Yoruba, in addition to the abovementioned work by Law, see Peter Morton-Williams, "The Òyọ́ Yoruba and the Atlantic Trade, 1670-1830," *Journal of the Historical Society of Nigeria*, 3, no. 1 (1964): 25-45; and E. Adeniyi Oroge, "The Institution of Slavery in Yorubaland with Particular Reference to the Nineteenth Century," PhD dissertation, Centre of West African Studies, University of Birmingham, 1971.
2. *Jornal do Commercio*, September 25, 1853. The term *alufá* (from the Yoruba *àlùfáà*) is derived from *alfa*, which is more commonly used in West Africa, in addition to the term *marabout*. The same as *mu'alim* in Arabic.
3. We would like to thank Luís Nicolau Parés, Ola Fadahunsi, Andrew Apter, and J. Lorand Matory for their suggestions about the meanings of these two Yoruba names.

4. João José Reis, *Rebelião escrava no Brasil: a história do levante dos malês em 1835* (São Paulo: Companhia das Letras, 2003), 315–319.
5. *Correio Mercantil*, September 21, 1853.
6. On the last two paragraphs, see Hakeem Olumide Danmole, "The Frontier Emirate: A History of Islam in Ilorin," PhD dissertation, University of Birmingham, 1980, chaps. 1 and 2; Law, *The Òyó Empire*, chap. 12; Patrick J. Ryan, "Imale: Yoruba Participation in the Muslim Tradition," PhD dissertation, Harvard University, 1978, 112–117.
7. *Jornal do Commercio*, September 25, 1853.
8. Robin Law, "The Chronology of the Yoruba Wars of the Early Nineteenth Century: A Reconsideration," *Journal of the Historical Society of Nigeria*, 5, no. 2 (1970): 218. Regarding the slave trade from the interior to the coast, see Mahdi Adamu, "The Delivery of Slaves from the Central Sudan to the Bight of Benin," in Henry A. Gemery and Jan S. Hogendorn (eds.), *The Uncommon Market* (New York: Academic Press, 1979), 163–180. The source for the length of time it took to walk from Òyó to the coast is Robin Law, personal correspondence, September 6, 2008. On the rise of Lagos during that period, see Kristin Mann, *Slavery and the Birth of an African City: Lagos, 1760–1900* (Bloomington and Indianapolis: Indiana University Press, 2007), chap. 1.

Chapter 2

1. *Jornal do Commercio*, September 25, 1853.
2. On the war for independence in Bahia, see Braz do Amaral, *História da independência na Bahia* (Salvador: Progresso, 1957) and Luís Henrique Dias Tavares, *Independência do Brasil na Bahia* (Salvador: Edufba, 2005).
3. João José Reis, "O jogo duro do Dois de Julho: o 'Partido Negro' na Independência da Bahia," in João Reis e Eduardo Silva, ed., *Negociação e conflito: a resistência negra no Brasil escravista* (São Paulo: Companhia das Letras, 1989), 79–98; Hendrik Kraay, "Em outra coisa não falavam os pardos, cabras, e crioulos': o 'recrutamento' de escravos na guerra da independência na Bahia," *Revista Brasileira de História*, 22, no. 43 (2002): 109–128.
4. João Gomes was identified as *pardo* on his daughter's death certificate in 1812. Arquivo da Cúria Metropolitana de Salvador (ACMS), *Livro de registro de óbitos da freguesia do Passo, 1797–1844*, fls. 118v–119.
5. Postmortem inventory for Captain Vicente Ferreira de Andrade, Arquivo Público do Estado da Bahia (APEB hereafter), *Inventários*, 04/1575/2044/05, fls. 17 (on the price of a chicken) and 29 (receipt); "Termo por que conferio o partido de Boticário desta Santa Casa a João Gomes da Silva," September 1, 1816, Arquivo da Santa Casa de Misericórdia da Bahia (ASCM hereafter), *Livro de acórdão (1791–1834)*, no. 16, fl. 125v. Regarding the Santa Casa, see A. J. R. Russell-Wood, *Fidalgos and Philanthropists: the Santa Casa da Misericórdia of Bahia, 1550–1755* (London: Macmillan, 1968).
6. The prices of slaves in Bahia in Katia M. de Queirós Mattoso, *Être esclave au Brésil, xvie-xixe siècle* (Paris: Hachette, 1979), 109.
7. Document registering João Gomes da Silva's membership in the Santa Casa confraternity, October 30, 1797, ASCM, *Livro 6º de termos de irmãos, 1797–1834*, est. A, no. 6, fl. 6v; "Registro do Requerimento de João Gomes da Silva," com despacho de 7 de fevereiro de 1825, ASCM, *Livro de registro de requerimentos de partes e informações da mesa*, no. 118, fl. 39. Regarding the Periquitos Revolt, see Luís Henrique Dias Tavares, *Da sedição de 1798 à revolta de 1824 na Bahia* (Salvador: Edufba/São Paulo: Editora da Unesp, 2003), 187–252; and João José Reis and Hendrik Kraay, "'The Tyrant is Dead!': The Revolt of the Periquitos, Bahia, 1824," *The Hispanic American Historical Review*, 89, no. 3 (2009): 399–434.
8. Minutes of Santa Casa board meetings, July 19 and 26, August 9 and September 2, 1829, ASCM, *Livro de acórdão (1791–1834)*, no. 16, fls. 176, 177v–178, 179–179v, 181; ASCM, *Livro 5º de termos do capelão e demais serventuários, 1765–1831*, no. 38, fls. 319v–320; and the board of the Santa Casa to João Gomes da Silva, August 8, 1830, ASCM, *Livro 6º do copiador*, no. 56, fls. 202–202v. Regarding João Gomes's numerous attempts to regain his post as apothecary to the Santa Casa, see ASCM, *Livro de despachos 3º e 4º*, dispatches of August 28 and September 4, 1831, August 5, 1832, August 7, 1835, and August 13, 1836.

9. Archives and Library of the Memorial da Medicina Brasileira, Universidade Federal da Bahia (AMM hereafter), *Livro de Actas do Collegio Medico-Cirurgico da Cidade da Bahia (1816–1855)*, fls. 5v–6.
10. Lycurgo de Castro Santos Filho, *História geral da medicina brasileira* (São Paulo: Hucitec/Edusp, 1991), vol. 2, 365.
11. ACMS, *Livro de óbitos da freguesia de Santo Antônio Além do Carmo, 1806–1819*, fl. 33; ACMS, *Livro de óbitos da freguesia de Santíssimo Sacramento da Rua do Passo, 1797–1844*, fls. 140v, and 146v; and ACMS, *Livro de registro de batismos da freguesia da Sé, 1829-1861*, fls. 54v, 72v, and 91.
12. Johann Baptist von Spix and Karl Friedrich von Martius, *Viagem pelo Brasil, 1817–1820* (Belo Horizonte: Itatiaia; São Paulo: Edusp, 1981), vol. 2, 141.
13. L. F. Tollenare, *Notas dominicais* (Salvador: Progresso, 1956), 302.
14. Zephyr Frank, *Dutra's World: Wealth and Family in Nineteenth-Century Rio de Janeiro* (Albuquerque: University of New Mexico Press, 2004), 47.
15. Data bank of postmortem inventories from the APEB.
16. See Santos Filho, *História geral da medicina*, vol. 1, 329, 330, 333, vol. 2, 366, 369; Spix and Martius, *Viagem pelo Brasil*, vol. 2, 143–144, 157; Betânia Gonçalves Figueiredo, *A arte de curar: cirurgiões, médicos, boticários e curandeiros no século XIX em Minas Gerais* (Belo Horizonte: Argumentum, 2008), 149–169; and Vera Regina Beltrão Marques, *Natureza em boiões: medicinas e boticários no Brasil setecentista* (Campinas: Editora da Unicamp, 1999), 206–215. See also reproductions of laboratories in the illustrations in Marques's book.
17. Santos Filho, *História geral da medicina*, vol. 2, 368; Spix and Martius, *Viagem pelo Brasil*, vol. 2, 152. Regarding the sale of lottery tickets, see receipt issued on August 18, 1827 in ACSM, *Correspondência avulsa*, 01-B; document dated July 27, 1829, in ASCM, *Livro 3° de registro*, no. 87; and ASCM, *Livro contendo as listas e planos das loterias, 1820–1840*, no. 198.
18. Manumission of Matilde, Mina, December 4, 1808, APEB, *Livro de Notas do Tabelião* (*LNT* hereafter), 188, fls. 120v–121; "Escritura de compra, venda, paga e quitação que fazem João Mendes Barreto e sua Mulher Constancia Roza do Amaral por seu procurador João Gomes da Silva" etc., November 27, 1819, APEB, *LNT*, 201, fls. 106v–107; "Escritura de compra, venda, paga e quitação que fazem José Carvalho Moreira e sua mulher Ormina Maria do Sacramento" etc., July 4, 1828, APEN, *LNT*, 223, fl. 80; manumission of Francisca, Jeje, October 18, 1824, APEB, *LNT*, 214, fl. 10v; and manumission of Antonio, APEB, *LNT*, 210, fl. 15.
19. ACMS, *Livro de registro de casamentos da freguesia da Rua do Passo, 1802–1888*, fl. 15; ACMS, *Livro de registro de batismo da freguesia da Sé, 1816–1829*, fl. 290, 293v, 352v-3.
20. ACMS, *Livro de registro de óbitos da freguesia do Passo, 1797–1844*, fls. 118v–119, 140v; ACMS, *Livro de registro de óbitos da freguesia da Sé, 1831–1840*, fls. 330v, 344v; Membership records of the brothers Bernardino Gomes da Silva, João da Silva Gomes Filho and Manoel Gomes da Silva, July 16, 1828, ASCM, *Livro 6° de termos de irmãos, 1797–1834*, est. A, no. 6, fls. 334v, 335–335v.
21. David Eltis, *Economic Growth and the Ending of the Transatlantic Slave Trade* (New York/Oxford: Oxford University Press, 1987), 243–244 (the data shown here has been periodically updated in several of that author's publications); Id., "The Diaspora of Yoruba-Speakers, 1650–1865: Dimensions and Implications," in Toyin Falola and Matt Childs (eds.), *The Yoruba Diaspora in the Atlantic World* (Bloomington: Indiana University Press, 2004), 30–31; Reis, *Rebelião escrava no Brasil*, p. 327. On the Bahian slave trade from the Yoruba-speaking region and its neighbors, see, among other titles, Pierre Verger, *Flux et reflux de la traite des nègres entre le golfe de Benin et Bahia de Todos os Santos* (Paris: Mouton, 1968); Robin Law and Kristin Mann, "West Africa in the Atlantic Community: The Case of the Slave Coast," *The William and Mary Quarterly*, 56, no. 2 (1999): 307–334; Alberto da Costa e Silva, *Francisco Félix de Souza, mercador de escravos* (Rio de Janeiro: Nova Fronteira, 2004). On the 1817 prohibition of the slave trade above the Equator line, see Leslie Bethell, *The Abolition of the Brazilian Slave Trade: Britain, Brazil and the Slave Question, 1807–1869* (Cambridge: Cambridge University Press, 1970), chap. 1, esp. 18–20.
22. On urban slavery in Bahia, see, among other titles, Maria José da Silva Andrade, *A mão-de-obra escrava em Salvador de 1811 a 1860* (São Paulo: Corrupio, 1988); Kátia M. de Queirós Mattoso, *Da revolução dos alfaiates à riqueza dos baianos no século xix* (Salvador: Corrupio, 2004), esp.

135–160; Maria Inês Côrtes de Oliveira, *O liberto: seu mundo e os outros* (Salvador: Corrupio, 1988); Reis, *Rebelião escrava no Brasil*, chap. 11; Mieko Nishida, *Ethnicity, Gender, and Race in Salvador, Brazil, 1808–1888* (Bloomington: Indiana University Press, 2003); and Dale Graden, *From Slavery to Freedom in Brazil: Bahia, 1835–1900* (Albuquerque: University of New Mexico Press, 2006); Wilson Mattos, *Negros contra a ordem: astúcias, resistências e liberdades possíveis (Salvador, 1850–1888)* (Salvador: EDUFBA/EDUNEB, 2008).
23. Regarding these rebellions, see Reis, *Rebelião escrava no Brasil*, chap. 4.
24. "And the event can be used to produce a date," writes Toyin Falola, *A Mouth Sweeter than Salt: An African Memoir* (Ann Arbor: University of Michigan Press, 2004), 8.
25. Regarding Rio de Janeiro, the epicenter of the crisis, see Gladys Sabina Ribeiro, *A liberdade em construção: identidade nacional e conflitos antilusitanos no Primeiro Reinado* (Rio de Janeiro: Relume Dumará, 2002).

Chapter 3

1. Hendrik Kraay, *Race, State, and Armed Forces in Independence Era Brazil: Bahia, 1790's–1840's* (Stanford: Stanford University Press, 2001), 171.
2. Nicolao Dreys, *Noticia descriptiva da Província do Rio Grande de São Pedro do Sul* (Porto Alegre: Livraria Americana, 1927 [1839]), 191.
3. Attached to the chief or police's letter to the president of the province, August 11 and September 1, 1835, Arquivo Histórico do Rio Grande do Sul (AHRGS hereafter), *Polícia. Secretaria da Polícia, correspondência expedida*, maço 61.
4. Luís Edmundo, *O Rio de Janeiro no tempo dos vice-reis, 1763–1808* (Brasília: Senado Federal, 2000), 471; and Artur de Magalhães Basto, "O Pôrto contra Junot," *Revista de Estudos Históricos* (Oporto) 1, no. 4 (1924): 121–147.
5. Francisco de Morais, "Estudantes brasileiros na Universidade de Coimbra," *Anais da Biblioteca Nacional do Rio de Janeiro*, 62 (1940): 237; *Anais do Arquivo Histórico do Rio Grande do Sul* 11 (1995): 557, 597–598, 609, 612, 615; no. 8: 159–167; Adriano Comissoli, "O juiz de dentro: magistratura e ascensão social no extremo sul do Brasil 1808–1831," *Redos: Revista do Corpo Discente do Programa de Pós-Graduação em História da UFRGS*, 2, no. 4 (2009): 24–34; and Márcia Eckert Miranda, "A estalagem e o Império: crise do Antigo Regime, fiscalidade e fronteira na província de São Pedro (1808–1831)," PhD dissertation, Unicamp, 2007, 165. The correspondence of Police Chief Peçanha can be found in the AHRGS, *Secretaria de Polícia. Correspondência expedida*, maços 59, 60, and 61.
6. Document regarding the inauguration to "an ordinary place as Magistrate" by proxy for José Maria Peçanha, September 23, 1824, APEB, *Termos de posse e juramento de cargos da Relação da Bahia, 1653–1889*, livro 124, fl. 113. See also the website of Brazil's Supreme Court, the Supremo Tribunal Federal, with biographies of its ministers: <http://www.stf.jus.br/portal/ministro/verMinistro.asp?periodo=stj&id=268>, accessed January 16, 2010.
7. Arquivo Histórico da Cúria Metropolitana de Porto Alegre, *Livro de óbitos da Catedral*, no. 3, fls. 89, 138v, and 185; id., *Livro de registro de escravos da igreja de Nossa Senhora Mãe de Deus*, no. 3, records for October 4, 1830.
8. Police Chief José Maria Peçanha's letter is in the AHRGS, *Secretaria de Polícia. Correspondência expedida*, maços 59, 60, and 61.
9. Dreys, *Noticia descriptiva*, 193.
10. Mário José Maestri Filho, *O escravo no Rio Grande do Sul: a charqueada e a gênese do escravismo gaúcho* (Porto Alegre: EST/EPUCRS, 1984), 75 et seq.; id., *Deus é grande, o mato é maior! Trabalho e resistência escrava no Rio Grande do Sul* (Passo Fundo: UPF Editora, 2002), 89, 158–159; and Valéria Zanetti, *Calabouço urbano: escravos e libertos em Porto Alegre (1840–1860)* (Passo Fundo: UPF Editora, 2002), 60.
11. Arséne Isabelle, *Viagem ao Rio da Prata e ao Rio Grande do Sul* (Rio de Janeiro: Livraria Editora Zelio Valverde, 1949 [1835]), 271, 274, 275, 282; Auguste de Saint-Hilaire, *Viagem ao Rio Grande do Sul* (Porto Alegre: Erus, 1987), 46; and Maestri Filho, *O sobrado e o cativo. A arquitetura urbana erudita no Brasil escravista: o caso gaúcho* (Passo Fundo: UPF Editora, 2001), 75. Other works on slavery in Porto Alegre in the first half of the nineteenth century include Zanetti, *Calabouço urbano*, chap. 2; Maestri, *O escravo no Rio Grande do Sul: trabalho, resistência, sociedade*, 88–114; Moreira, *Os cativos e os homens de bem*.

12. See announcements and advertisements in *O Mensageiro*, November 10, 17, and 24, and December 8, 11, 18, and 22, 1835; and January 15 and 19, 1836. Facsimiles of several issues of this newspaper have been published by the Museu e Archivo Histórico do Rio Grande do Sul, *Documentos interessantes para o estudo da grande Revolução de 1835-1845* (Porto Alegre: Museu e AHRGS, 1930), vol. 2.
13. Zanetti, *Calabouço urbano*, 85.
14. Justice of the peace of the Central district to the chief of police, October 28, 1833 and July 9, 1834, AHRGS, *Polícia. Secretaria da Polícia, correspondência expedida*, maço 59; Peçanha to the president of the province, April 27, 1835, id., maço 61.
15. Ferreira Gomes to the president of the province, October 29, 1835, AHRGS, *Polícia. Secretaria da Polícia, correspondência expedida*, maço 6; Peçanha to the president of the province, October 8, 1833, and March 1 and June 25, 1834, AHRGS, *Polícia. Secretaria da Polícia, correspondência expedida*, maço 59; *O Mensageiro*, November 9 and 11, and December 29, 1835.
16. Peçanha to the president of the province, June 21, 1835, AHRGS, *Polícia. Secretaria da Polícia, correspondência expedida*, maço 61.
17. Peçanha to the president of the province, November 25, 1833, AHRGS, *Polícia. Secretaria da Polícia, correspondência expedida*, maço 59.
18. Peçanha to the president of the province, July 29, 1834, AHRGS, *Polícia. Secretaria da Polícia, correspondência expedida*, maço 59; Peçanha to the president of the province, March 1 and August 11, 1835, id., maço 59, maço 61.
19. Isabelle, *Viagem*, 275, 282-283.
20. Map of prisoners in the Porto Alegre jail, February 28, 1834, AHRGS, *Polícia. Secretaria da Polícia, correspondência expedida*, maço 59; Map of prisoners in the Porto Alegre jail, June 1834, id., maço 60; Peçanha to the president of the province Braga, April 27, 1835, id., maço 61; justice of the peace of Rosário parish to the chief of police, November 16, 1834, id., maço 60. See also Solimar Oliveira Lima, *Triste Pampa: resistência e punição de escravos em fontes judiciárias* (Porto Alegre: IEL/Edipucrs, 1997), esp. chap. 7, and 135, 161-168, 195-198. Public punishments of slaves ended in 1847. See Zanetti, *Calabouço urbano*, 150.
21. Robin Law, "Ethnicities of Enslaved Africans in the Diaspora: On the Meanings of 'Mina' (Again)," *History in Africa*, 32 (2005): 247-267; Maestri, *Deus é grande*, 172, 174, 175, and 178; and Lima, *Triste Pampa*, 38-39.
22. Regarding Porto Alegre, see Paulo Roberto Staudt Moreira and Tatiani de Souza Tassoni, *Que com seu trabalho nos sustenta: as cartas de alforria de Porto Alegre (1748-1888)* (Porto Alegre: EST Edições, 2007), 17-20; Paulo Roberto Staudt Moreira, *Os cativos e os homens de bem: experiências negras no espaço urbano* (Porto Alegre: EST Edições, 2003), 339-356; id., *Faces da liberdade, máscaras do cativeiro: experiências de liberdade e escravidão, percebidas através das cartas de alforria—Porto Alegre (1858-1888)* (Porto Alegre: Edipucs, 1996), 90-91; and Gabriel Aladrén, *Liberdades negras nas paragens do sul: alforria e inserção social de libertos em Porto Alegre, 1800-1835* (Rio de Janeiro: FGV Editora, 2009), 68. Regarding the city of Rio Grande, see Jovani de Souza Scherer, "Experiências de busca de liberdade: alforrias e comunidade africana em Rio Grande, século xix," Master's Thesis, Universidade do Vale dos Sinos, 2008, 140.
23. Scherer, "Experiências de busca de liberdade," 11-12.
24. Personal communication from Paulo Fernando de Moraes Farias of the University of Birmingham, UK, March 2 and 3, 2010. Regarding the Hausa pronunciation of Allah, see also Nikolay Dobronravin, "Literacy Among Muslims in Nineteenth-Century Trinidad and Brazil," in Behnaz A. Mirzai, Ismael M. Montana and Paul Lovejoy (eds.), *Slavery, Islam, and Diaspora* (Trenton: Africa World Press, 2009), 225.
25. President of the Province of Rio Grande Sul Francisco Álvares Machado to the Justice Minister, January 15, 1841, and annexes, AN, *GIFI—Ministério da Justiça—3ª seção—maço 5C 478*. Paulo Roberto Staudt Moreira kindly provided a copy of that investigation report.
26. Letter from Henrique de Beaupaire-Rohan to the secretary of the Brazilian Historical and Geographic Institute, April 22, 1855, Instituto Histórico e Geográfico Brasileiro (IHGB hereafter), lata 310, doc. 47. The contents of the Malê book from Rio Grande do Sul were identified by Nikolay Dobronravin, from the University of St. Petersburg, Russia. See Dobronravin, "Escritos multilingües em caracteres árabes: novas fontes de Trinidad e Brasil no século xix," *Afro-Ásia*, 31 (2004): 321-322, and for a more detailed analysis, id., "Versos

árabes nos escritos dos muçulmanos negros no Brasil oitocentista" (unpublished article, 2006). We would also like to thank Dobronravin for identifying the lines from these verses in the originals reproduced in Figure 3.3.

Chapter 4

1. Arquivo Público do Estado do Rio Grande do Sul (APERGS), *Livro de notas do primeiro tabelionato*, no. 10, fls. 212–213.
2. Source: www.dji.com.br/dicionario/alvara.htm. Accessed December 17, 2012.
3. The source of this data is APERGS, *Livro de notas do primeiro tabelionato*, no. 10. For Porto Alegre from 1748 to 1888, Moreira and Tassoni, *Que com seu trabalho nos sustenta*, counted 10,055 manumissions, 56 percent of which were for women, a result that is close to the 59 percent (of 662 cases) found for 1800–1835 by Aladrén, *Liberdades negras*, p. 44.
4. Zanetti, *Calabouço urbano*, p. 80.
5. *O mensageiro*, no. 28, Porto Alegre, February 12, 1836; *O americano*, Porto Alegre, October 29, 1842; and Requerimento do sargento Alexandre de Barros, Rio de Janeiro, November 27, 1833, Arquivo Histórico do Exército (RJ), *Requerimentos*, maço 5969.
6. Daniela Vallandro de Carvalho, "Experiências negras de recrutamento, guerra e escravidão: Rio Grande de São Pedro, c. 1835–1850," PhD dissertation, Universidade Federal do Rio de Janeiro, 2013, 40.
7. Peçanha to the president of the province, 1st, 7, 21 (first quotation), 24, 23, 25 (several reports, second quote is from one of them) and October 28, 1834, AHRGS, *Polícia. Secretaria da Polícia, correspondência expedida*, maço 60.
8. Margareth M. Bakos, "A escravidão negra e os Farroupilhas," in Sandra J. Pesavento, ed., *A Revolução Farroupilha*, 2nd ed. (Porto Alegre: Mercado Aberto, 1997), 90 ff.; Spencer Leitman, "The Black Ragamuffins: Racial Hypocrisy in Nineteenth-Century Southern Brazil," *The Americas*, 33, no. 3 (1977): 504–514; and Maestri Filho, *O sobrado e o cativo*, 198–199. See especially Carvalho, "Experiências negras de recrutamento, guerra e escravidão."
9. Ferreira Gomes to the president of the province, December 9, 1835, AHRGS, *Polícia. Secretaria da Polícia, correspondência expedida*, maço 61; and *O Mensageiro*, January 12, 1836.
10. *O Mensageiro*, December 11, 22, and 25, 1835. This newspaper published several minutes of meetings of the Rio Grande do Sul Legislative Assembly in 1835 and 1836. Peçanha to President of the Province Marciano Pereira Ribeiro, September 30, 1835, AHRGS, *Polícia. Secretaria da Polícia*, maço 61; record of President Antonio Braga's reply to Peçanha's request of leave, December 12, 1835, AHRGS, *Correspondência de governantes*, maço A8, 05; and letter from Ladislau do Amaral Brandão to Domingos José de Almeida, Alegrete, March 19, 1840, *Anais do Arquivo Histórico do Rio Grande do Sul*, vol. 5 (1981): 221.

Chapter 5

1. Euzébio de Queiroz to the Minister of Justice, Rio de Janeiro, January 15, 1839; letter from Manoel Joaquim de Souza Medeiros to whom it may concern, December 29, 1838, AN, IJ6, 191, *Série Justiça. Polícia da Corte*. We would like to thank Carlos Eugênio Líbano Soares for first calling our attention to this document.
2. Maurício Goulart, *A escravidão africana no Brasil (das origens à extinção do tráfico)* (São Paulo: Ômega, 1975), 272; Mary Karasch, *A vida dos escravos no Rio de Janeiro, 1808–1850* (São Paulo: Companhia das Letras, 2000), 512–514, n. 2; David Eltis, Stephen Behrendt and David Richardson, "Patterns in the Transatlantic Slave Trade, 1662–1867: New Indications of African Origins of Slaves Arriving in the Americas," in Maria Diedrich, Henry Louis Gates, and Carl Pedersen, (eds.), *Black Imagination and the Middle Passage* (New York: Oxford University Press, 1999), 21–32; David Eltis, *The Rise of African Slavery in the Americas* (Cambridge: Cambridge University Press, 2000), 224–257; Manolo Florentino, *Em costas negras: uma história do tráfico de escravos entre a África e o Rio de Janeiro* (São Paulo: Companhia das Letras, 1997), 44–60 suggests 470,000; Herbert Klein, *The Middle Passage: Comparative Studies in the Atlantic Slave Trade* (Princeton: Princeton University Press, 1978), 181–212 and 73–93. The figure 609,334

for slaves imported into Rio de Janeiro in 1811–1830 comes from the TSTD databank http://www.slavevoyages.org/voyage/search, consulted in November 5, 2017.
3. Karasch, *A vida dos escravos*, 41–42, 112; and Sidney Chalhoub, *Visões da liberdade: uma história das últimas décadas da escravidão na Corte* (São Paulo: Companhia das Letras, 1990), 186–187.
4. Florentino, *Em costas negras*, 79–80.
5. Karasch, *A vida dos escravos*, 35 ff.
6. Luís Carlos Soares, *O "Povo de Cam" na capital do Brasil: a escravidão urbana no Rio de Janeiro do século xix* (Rio de Janeiro: Faperj/7Letras, 2007), 402–403.
7. AN, *Polícia/Suprimentos de despesas com escravos fugidos, 1826*, Códice 359; AN, *Lançamentos de escravos fugidos,1823–1831*, Códice 360; AN, *Devassa da Polícia sobre vários delitos, 1809–1815*, Códice 401; AN, *Relação de presos feitos pela Polícia,1813–1826*, Códice 403; and AN, *Lançamento dos presos remetidos pelos Comissários de Polícia de várias localidades,1827–1830*, Códice 404.
8. Leila Algranti, *O feitor ausente: estudos de escravidão urbana no Rio de Janeiro, 1808–1821* (Rio de Janeiro: Vozes, 1988), 211; Thomas Holloway, *Polícia no Rio de Janeiro: repressão e resistência numa cidade do século XIX* (Rio de Janeiro: Fundação Getúlio Vargas, 1998), 268.
9. Soares, *O "Povo de Cam,"* chap. 5 and p. 419; Karasch, *Vida dos escravos*, chap. 7; Carlos Eugênio Líbano Soares and Flávio dos Santos Gomes, "'Dizem as quitandeiras...': ocupações étnicas em uma cidade escravista: Rio de Janeiro, século xix," *Acervo*, 15, no. 2 (2002): 3–16; id., "Negras minas no Rio de Janeiro: gênero, nação e trabalho urbano no século xix"; and Juliana Barreto Farias, "Ardis da liberdade: trabalho urbano, alforrias e identidades," both in Mariza de Carvalho Soares, ed., *Rotas atlânticas da diáspora africana: da Baía do Benim ao Rio de Janeiro* (Niterói: EDUFF, 2007), 191–224 (first half of the 1800s) and 225–256 (second half of the 1800s), respectively: Juliana Barreto Farias, Carlos Eugênio L. Soares and Flávio dos Santos Gomes, *No labirinto das nações: africanos e identidades no Rio de Janeiro, século xix* (Rio de Janeiro: Arquivo Nacional, 2005), chap. 5.
10. See Silvia Escorel, *Vestir poder e poder vestir: o tecido social e a trama cultural nas imagens do traje negro (Rio de Janeiro—século xviii)*, MA thesis, Universidade Federal do Rio de Janeiro, 2000; and Sílvia Hunold Lara, "The Signs of Color: Women's Dress and Racial Relations in Salvador and Rio de Janeiro, ca. 1750–1815," *Colonial Latin American Review*, 6, no. 2 (1997): 205–224.
11. Charles Expilly, *Mulheres e costumes do Brasil*, 2nd ed. (São Paulo: Editora Nacional, Brasília, 1977), 96.
12. Calculations based on samples of 3,800 slave women listed in probate records between 1825 and 1850. On this subject, see also Carlos Eugênio Líbano Soares and Flávio dos Santos Gomes, "Negras minas no Rio de Janeiro: gênero, nação e trabalho urbano no século xix," in Soares, ed., *Rotas atlânticas*, 208–213.
13. Manolo Florentino, "Alforria e etnicidade no Rio de Janeiro oitocentista: notas de pesquisa," *Topoi*, 5 (2002): 25–40.
14. Sheila de Castro Faria, "Damas mercadoras:—as pretas minas no Rio de Janeiro (século xviii a 1850)," in Soares, ed., *Rotas atlânticas*, 110.
15. Chalhoub, *Visões da liberdade*, 186–187.
16. Regarding housing for slaves and Africans in Rio de Janeiro in the nineteenth century, see Carlos Eugênio Líbano Soares, *Zungu: rumor de muitas vozes* (Rio de Janeiro: Aperj, 1998); Juliana Barreto Farias et al., *Cidades Negras. Africanos, crioulos e espaços urbanos no Brasil escravista do século xix* (São Paulo: Alameda, 2006), 86–96; and Ynaê Lopes dos Santos, "Além da senzala: arranjos escravos de moradia no Rio de Janeiro (1808–1850)," MA thesis, Universidade de São Paulo, 2006.
17. Holloway, *A polícia no Rio de Janeiro*, 122–156; Algranti, *O feitor ausente*, 209–210; and Flávio dos Santos Gomes, *Experiências atlânticas: ensaios e pesquisas sobre a escravidão e o pós-emancipação no Brasil* (Passo Fundo: UPF Editora, 2003), 45–53.
18. Marco Morel, *O período das regências (1831–1840)* (Rio de Janeiro: Jorge Zahar, 2003), 29.
19. Marco Morel and Mariana Monteiro Barros, *Palavra, imagem e poder: o surgimento da imprensa no Brasil do século xix* (Rio de Janeiro: DP&A, 2003), 21.
20. *Pão d'Assucar*, February 13, 1835, 1–2, and March 6, 1835, 1–2.
21. *Pão d'Assucar*, May 2, 1835, 3–4. See also the April 7, 1835 issue, 1–2.

22. Marcelo Basile, "Projetos de Brasil e a construção nacional na imprensa fluminense (1831–1835)," in Marco Morel, Lucia Maria Bastos P. Neves and Tania Maria Bessone da C. Ferreira (eds.), *História e imprensa: representações culturais e práticas de poder* (Rio de Janeiro: DP&A/Faperj, 2006), 60–93; and Morel and Barros, *Palavra, imagem e poder*, 21–33.
23. See Tâmis Peixoto Parron, "Política do tráfico negreiro: o Parlamento imperial e a reabertura do comércio de escravos na década de 1830," *Estudos Afro-Asiáticos*, 29, no. 1, 2, and 3 (2007): 91–121; and id., *A política da escravidão no Império do Brasil, 1826–1865* (Rio de Janeiro: Civilização Brasileira, 2011).
24. Bethell, *The Abolition*, 391.
25. Robert E. Conrad, *Tumbeiros: o tráfico escravista para o Brasil* (São Paulo: Brasiliense, 1985), 213.
26. Ofícios da Polícia, February 2, 1836, AN, IJ⁶ maço 172.
27. *Diário do Rio de Janeiro*, February 17, 1835, 3.
28. *Jornal do Commercio*, June 3, 1855; January 13, 1837; and October 19, 1830.
29. Arquivo Histórico do Itamaraty (AHI hereafter), Consulado, Londres, *Ofícios de 1833–1839*, Estante 254, prateleira 3, maço 5.
30. Euzébio de Queiroz to the Minister of Justice, Antonio Paulino Limpo de Abreu, February 23, 1836, AN, IJ⁶ *Ofícios de Polícia da Corte*, maço 172.

Chapter 6

1. Carlos Eugênio L. Soares and Flávio dos Santos Gomes, "'Com o pé sobre um vulcão': africanos minas, identidades e a repressão antiafricana no Rio de Janeiro (1830–1840)," *Estudos Afro-Asiáticos*, 23, no. 2 (2001): 335–377.
2. Euzébio de Queiroz to the Minister of Justice Antonio Paulino Limpo de Abreu, December 18 and 22, 1835, AN, *Ofícios da Polícia da Corte*, Códice 334.
3. Euzébio de Queiroz to the Minister of Justice Justiça Antonio Paulino Limpo de Abreu, January 30, 1836, AN, IJ6, *Ofícios da Polícia da Corte*, maço 172.
4. Euzébio de Queiroz to the Minister of Justice Antonio Paulino Limpo de Abreu, January 26, 1836, AN, IJ6, *Ofícios de Polícia da Corte*, maço 172; and Euzébio de Queiroz to Minister of Justice Antonio Paulino Limpo de Abreu, January 7 and 27, 1836, AN, *Registro dos Ofícios do Chefe de Polícia*, Códice 334.
5. Euzébio de Queiroz to the Minister of Justice Manoel Alves Branco, December 11, 1835, AN, *Registro dos Ofícios do Chefe de Polícia*, Códice 334; and Letter from the President of Rio de Janeiro Province to the Minister of Justice, December 18, 1835, AN, IJ1, *Ofícios de Presidentes de Província (rj)*, maço 859.
6. Letter from the President of the Province to the Minister of Justice, March 18, 1835, AN, IJ1, *Ofícios de Presidentes de Província (RJ)*, maço 859; and Letter from the President of the Province to the Minister of War, December 10, 1835, AN, IG1, *Ofícios do Ministério da Guerra*, maço 139; Letter from the Minister of Justice to the President of the Province, March 6, 1835, APERJ, Coleção 2; Imperial Government Order sent to the Commander General of the Permanent National Guard, March 18, 1835, id., Coleção 216; and Letter from the Municipal Judge of the Town of Magé to the President of the Province (RJ), December 30, 1835, Coleção 166, documento 1.
7. Letter from the Justice Minister to the Chief of Police of Rio de Janeiro, December 11, 1835, AN, Códice 334, fl. 13v; Letter from the President of the Province to the Minister of Justice, December 18, 1835, AN IJ1, *Ofícios de Presidentes de Província (RJ)*, maço 859; and Letter from the President of the Province to the Minister of War, December 10, 1835, AN, IG1, *Ofícios do Ministério da Guerra*, maço 139.
8. Imperial Government Order to the Commander General of the Permanent National Guard, March 18, 1835, APERJ, Coleção 216.
9. Letter from the Municipal Judge of the Town of Magé to the President of the Province (RJ), December 30, 1835, APERJ, Coleção 166, documento 1.
10. "Partes Policiais," May 27, 1835, AN, IJ6, *Ofícios de Polícia da Corte*, maço 170.
11. See, for example, Marina de Mello e Souza, *Reis negros no Brasil escravista: história da festa de coroação de Rei Congo* (Belo Horizonte: Editora UFMG, 2002); Elizabeth W. Kiddy, *Blacks*

of the Rosary: Memory and History in Minas Gerais, Brazil (University Park: The Pennsylvania State University Press, 2005); and id., "Who Is the King of Congo? A New Look at African and Afro-Brazilian Kings in Brazil," in Linda M. Heywood, ed., *Central Africans and Cultural Transformations in the American Diaspora* (Cambridge: Cambridge University Press, 2002), 153–182. On black kings in US territory, see William D. Piersen, *Black Yankees: The Development of an Afro-American Subculture in Eighteenth-Century New England* (Amherst: The University of Massachusetts Press, 1988), chaps. 10 and 11.

12. Letters from the Chief of Police, May 4 and 20 and June 4, 1835, AN, IJ6, *Ofícios de Polícia da Corte*, maço 170.
13. Justice of the Peace of Areias to the Chief of Police, June 20, 1835, AN, IJ6, *Ofícios de Polícia da Corte*, maço 170.
14. Letter from the President of the Province to the Minister of Justice, March 18, 1835, AN, IJ1, *Ofícios de Presidentes de Província*, maço 859.
15. Chalhoub, *Visões de liberdade*, 187.
16. Bulletin to Deputy Chief Constables and Justices of the Peace, March 17, 1835, AN, Códice 334, *Correspondência reservada de polícia*. Also quoted in Carlos Eugênio L. Soares. *A capoeira escrava e outras tradições rebeldes no Rio de Janeiro (1808–1850)*, 2nd ed. (Campinas: Editora da Unicamp, 2004), 361.
17. Letter from the Minister of Justice to the Chief of Police, March 17, 1835, AN, Códice 334, *Correspondência reservada de polícia*, fls. 9, 10 and 10v.
18. Letter to the Chief of Police, March 17, 1835, AN, *Correspondência reservada da polícia, 1833–1846*, Códice 334.
19. *Diário do Rio de Janeiro*, October 1, 1836, p. 1.
20. The Confraternity of Santo Elesbão and Santa Efigênia was created in 1740, and as of 1764, West Africans controlled its administration, holding all posts. See Mariza Soares, *Devotos da Cor. Identidade étnica, religiosidade e escravidão no Rio de Janeiro, século xviii* (Rio de Janeiro: Civilização Brasileira, 2000), 169, 188–194.
21. Euzébio de Queiroz to Minister of Justice Manoel Alves Branco, March 17 and 28, and May 13, 1835, AN, *Correspondência reservada recebida pela polícia*, Códice 334; Letter from Justice of the Peace Jose Correia Vasques da Fonseca to the Minister of Justice, June 6, 1835, AN, GIFI, pacote 5 B, 394.
22. Euzébio de Queiroz to Minister of Justice Manoel Alves Branco, March 28, 1835, AN, *Correspondência reservada recebida pela polícia*, Códice 334.
23. Martha Abreu, *O Império do Divino: festas religiosas e cultura popular no Rio de Janeiro, 1830–1900* (Rio de Janeiro: Nova Fronteira, 1999), 198–216.
24. Euzébio de Queiroz to Minister of Justice Manoel Alves Branco, December 12, 1835, AN, IJ6, *Ofícios de Polícia da Corte*, maço 171.
25. Soares, *A capoeira escrava*, 387–388.
26. Letter from the Chief of Police to the Minister of Justice, March 9, 1836, AN, IJ6, *Ofícios da Polícia da Corte*, maço 172.
27. Letter from the Chief of Police to the Minister of Justice, February 28, 1837, AN, IJ6, *Ofícios da Polícia da Corte*, maço 174.
28. *Coleção das Leis do Império do Brasil de 1835* (Rio de Janeiro: Typographia Nacional, 1864), vol. 1, 75.
29. Letters from the Chief of Police of Rio de Janeiro, March 21 and April 14, 1835, AN, IJ6, pacote 170.
30. Petition from João Ventura Rodrigues, May 2, 1835, AN, GIFI, pacote 5 B 427.
31. *Ofícios da Polícia da Corte*, June 27, 1836, AN, IJ6, maço 172.
32. Letter from the Chief of Police, May 27, 1835, quoted in Soares, *Capoeira escrava*, 358–359.
33. Letters from the Chief of Police, December 4 and 21, 1835, AN, IJ6, pacote 171.
34. *Jornal do Commercio*, February 5, 6, 8, 10, 11, 18, and 25, 1836.
35. *Jornal do Commercio*, February 6, 1836, p. 2.
36. *Pão d'Assucar*, June 16, 1835, pp. 1–2; *Pão d'Assucar*, November 13, 1835, pp. 1–2; *Pão d'Assucar*, August 18, 1835, pp. 2–3. Regarding the impact of the Revolt of the Malês on Rio's press, see Tatiane Silva Tereza, "Notícias da Bahia: a repercussão da revolta dos malês na Corte Imperial do Rio de Janeiro na primeira metade do século xix," MA thesis in

History, UFRJ, 2006, esp. pp. 79–116; and José Antônio Teófilo Cairus, "*Jihad*, cativeiro e redenção: escravidão, resistência e irmandade, Sudão Central e Bahia (1835)," MA thesis, UFRJ, 2002, chap. I.
37. *Aurora fluminense*, February 16, 1835, p. 5.
38. See *Pão d'Assucar*, April 10, 1835, pp. 1–2; June 16, 1835, July 21, 1835, pp. 2–3; November 27, 1835, p. 1; and May 4, 1835, p. 4. This subject has been discussed in Reis, *Rebelião escrava*, chaps. 15 and 16. Regarding free Africans in Brazil, see Beatriz G. Mamigonian, "To be a Liberated African in Brazil: Labour and Citizenship in the Nineteenth Century," PhD dissertation, University of Waterloo, 2002; and the articles collected in "Dossiê – 'Para inglês ver'? Revisitando a Lei de 1831," edited by Beatriz Mamigonian and Keila Grinberg in *Estudos Afro-Asiáticos* 29, no. 1/3 (2007): 87–340.
39. Letter from the Chief of Police to the Minister of Justice, February 27, 1835, IJ6, *Ofícios do Chefe de Polícia da Corte*, maço 170; Letter from the Minister of Justice to the Chief of Police of Rio de Janeiro, November 1, 1835, AN, *Correspondência reservada recebida pela polícia*, Códice 334, fl. 14v.
40. Justice of the Peace of S. José Parish to the Chief of Police, November 1, 1835, AN, *Ofícios da Polícia da Corte*, Códice 334, fl. 14v.
41. Letter from the Chief of Police to the Justice of the Peace of S. José Parish, November 1, 1835, id., fl. 15.
42. Quoted in Soares, *Capoeira escrava*, 420, n. 76.
43. Karasch, *A vida dos escravos*, 64–65, 298–299, 375–376; Reis, *Rebelião escrava*, 491–495; Alberto da Costa e Silva, "Buying and selling Korans in Nineteenth-Century Rio de Janeiro," *Slavery & Abolition*, 22, no. 1 (2001): 83–90; Abdurrahman al-Baghdádi, *Deleite do estrangeiro em tudo o que é espantoso e maravilhoso*, translated and edited by Paulo Farah (Rio de Janeiro: Fundação Biblioteca Nacional; Algiers: Bibliothèque Nationale d'Algérie, 2007), 61–101.

Chapter 7

1. Eltis, *Economic Growth*, 244. See also Luís Henrique Dias Tavares, *Comércio proibido de escravos* (São Paulo: Ática, 1988), 121–122.
2. Isabelle, *Viagem ao Rio da Prata*, 280.
3. See Luiz Geraldo Silva, *A faina, a festa e o rito: uma etnografia histórica sobre as gentes do mar* (Campinas, SP: Papirus, 2001), 188–189; W. Jeffrey Bolster, *Black Jacks: African American Seamen in the Age of Sail* (Cambridge: Harvard University Press, 1997), 81–82, 167–168; Emma Christopher, *Slave Ship Sailors and Their Captive Cargoes, 1730–1807* (Cambridge: Cambridge University Press, 2006), esp. pp. 231–237.
4. Marcus Rediker, *The Slave Ship: A Human History* (New York: Viking, 2007), 60, 229. Regarding the "ship's mode of production," see, by the author, *Between the Devil and the Deep Blue Sea: Merchant Seamen, Pirates, and the Anglo-American Maritime World, 1700–1750* (Cambridge: Cambridge University Press, 1987).
5. Lucy Maffei Hutter, *Navegação nos séculos xvii e xviii. Rumo: Brasil* (São Paulo: Edusp, 2005), 196–197. Regarding shipboard diseases, particularly scurvy in the Luso-Brazilian Atlantic, see also Jaime Rodrigues, *De costa a costa: escravos, marinheiros e intermediários do tráfico negreiro de Angola ao Rio de Janeiro (1780–1860)* (São Paulo: Companhia das Letras, 2005), chap. 5; and id., "Um sepulcro grande, amplo e fundo: saúde alimentar no Atlântico, séculos XVI ao XVIII," *Revista de História*, no. 168 (2013), 325–350.
6. Robert Edgar Conrad, *Children of God's Fire: A Documentary History of Black Slavery in Brazil* (Princeton: Princeton University Press, 1983), 36.
7. Surgeons and physicians were different professions. The first resulted from a shorter period of training associated with bloodletting and was less prestigious than that of apothecary, especially when the professional was a barber-surgeon, an occupation that was disappearing in the nineteenth century and was commonly practiced by blacks. See Betânia Gonçalves Figueiredo, "Barbeiros e cirurgiões: atuação dos práticos ao longo do século xix," *História, Ciências e Saúde—Manguinhos*, 6, no. 2 (1999): 277–291. Regarding the rare presence of "health professionals" aboard slave ships, see Rodrigues, *De costa a costa*, 271–272.

8. Dale Graden, *Disease, Resistance, and Lies: The Demise of the Transatlantic Slave Trade to Brazil and Cuba* (Baton Rouge: Louisiana State University Press, 2014), chap. 1; Tavares, *Comércio proibido*, 84–92; and Gerald Horne, *The Deepest South: The United States, Brazil, and the African Slave Trade* (New York and London: New York University Press, 2007), 56–59.
9. Regarding the tonnage and number of crewmen aboard ships, see Rodrigues, *De costa a costa*, 146–148, 170. We have calculated the capacity of slaves aboard ships on the basis of the Portuguese Crown Charter of November 24, 1813, which determined "the ratio of five blacks to every two tons." See *Colleção das Leis do Brazil de 1813* (Rio de Janeiro: Imprensa Nacional, 1890), 49–50. Verger, *Flux et reflux*, 662–663, suggests that these proportions were rarely achieved, reaching about 53 percent of that figure. Other authors suggest much larger ones. For the Rio slave trade, for example, it was 97.6 percent between 1795 and 1817, according to Herbert Klein, *The Middle Passage: Comparative Studies in the Atlantic Slave Trade* (Princeton: Princeton University Press, 1978), 30. See also The Transatlantic Slave Trade Database, <www.slavevoyages.org/tast/index.faces> (henceforth TSTD), which suggests ratios that often exceeded four captives per ton. We will use the notation TSTD # followed by the number of the specific voyage shown in the database.
10. Keep in mind, however, that since 1817–1818, the slave trade from ports above the Equator line, which included the Bight of Benin (Slave Coast), had been forbidden.
11. David Eltis and David Richardson, *Atlas of the Transatlantic Slave Trade* (New Haven: Yale University Press, 2010), 185, 186 (quote), 187.
12. The Melville quotation is cited in Hugh Thomas, *The Slave Trade: The Story of the Atlantic Slave Trade, 1440–1870* (New York: Simon & Shuster, 1997), 709.
13. Conrad, *Children of God's Fire*, 33, 38.
14. Kenneth F. Kipple and Brian T. Higgins, "Mortality Caused by Dehydration During the Middle Passage," in Joseph E. Inikori and Stanley L. Engerman (eds.), *The Atlantic Slave Trade: Effects on Economies, Societies and Peoples in Africa, the Americas, and Europe* (Durham: Duke University Press, 1992), 321–337 (the quotation is from p. 323). The crews of merchant and military vessels often had to endure water and food rationing and other hardships when sailing in the tropics, although their suffering was not as cruel as that of the captives in the holds of the slave ships. See Hutter, *Navegação nos séculos xvii e xviii*, chap. 3.
15. Robert Walsh, *Notices of Brazil (1828 and 1829)* (London: Frederick Westley and A. H. Davis, 1830), vol. 2, 479–486.
16. TSTD, voyages # 619, 851, and 1010.
17. James Henry Matson, *Remarks on the Slave Trade and the African Squadron*, 4th ed. (London: James Ridgeway, 1848), vol. 1, 17.
18. These figures were kindly provided by David Eltis. Regarding the slave trade between Brazil and Angola during different periods, see Joseph Miller, *Way of Death: Merchant Capitalism and the Angolan Slave Trade, 1730–1830* (Madison: Wisconsin University Press, 1988); Manolo Florentino, *Em costas negras: uma história do tráfico de escravos entre a África e o Rio de Janeiro* (São Paulo: Companhia das Letras, 1997); Luiz Felipe de Alencastro, *O trato dos viventes: formação do Brasil no Atlântico Sul* (São Paulo: Companhia das Letras, 2000); id., "La dérive des continents: l'indépendance du Brésil (1822), le Portugal et l'Afrique," paper presented during the colloqium "L'éxpérience coloniale: dynamiques des échanges dans les espaces atlantiques à l'époque de l'esclavage," Nantes, June 20–22, 2005; id., "Le versant brésilien de l'Atlantique-Sud: 1550–1850," in *Annales: Histoire, Sciences Sociales*, 61, no. 2 (2006): 339–382; Roquinaldo Amaral Ferreira, "Dos Sertões ao Atlântico: tráfico ilegal de escravos e comércio lícito em Angola, 1830–1860," MA thesis, UFRJ, 1996; and Rodrigues, *De costa a costa*.
19. Matson, *Remarks on the Slave Trade*, 22–24.
20. Miller, *Way of Death*, chap. 4, 388–389; and id., "The Significance of Drought, Disease, and Famine in Agriculturally Marginal Zones of West-Central Africa," *The Journal of African History*, vol. 23, no. 1 (1982): 17–61 (28–29 on the selling of children in times of famine, though the author is cautious not to generalize). Methods of enslavement, and the production of captives for the transatlantic slave trade while it lasted, included, besides wars, raids, kidnapping, indebtedness, legal punishment, gifts, and payment of tribute. See Roquinaldo Ferreira, *Cross-Cultural Exchange in the Atlantic World: Angola and Brazil during the Era of the Slave Trade*

(Cambridge: Cambridge University Press, 2012); and Mariana P. Candido, *An African Slaving Port and the Atlantic World: Benguela and Its Hinterland* (Cambridge: Cambridge University Press, 2013), chap. 4.

21. Eltis and Richardson, *Atlas*, 159, 166.
22. The data in this paragraph was kindly provided by Roquinaldo Ferreira. See also Joaquim Baptista Moreira to the Minister of Foreign Affairs, April 30, 1840; July 20, 1840; October 26, 1840; January 9, 1841, and November 30, 1841, Arquivo Nacional da Torre do Tombo, Lisbon (ANTT), *Coleção do Ministério dos Negócios Estrangeiros, Pernambuco*, caixa 2; Joaquim Baptista Moreira to the Minister of Foreign Affairs, February 10, 1842, ANTT, *Coleção do Ministério dos Negócios Estrangeiros, Pernambuco*, caixa 3. These documents confirm that Joaquim Ribeiro de Brito lived in Luanda and was in fact the owner of the *São José*. See also TSTD # 157, 2141, 3715, 40548, 40609, 47129, 47159, 48697, and 48751.
23. Based on data from the TSTD, we have calculated that the average mortality rate during the crossing was 8.9 percent between 1815 and 1848. Mortality rates for the era of illegal trade "increased substantially" (Eltis and Davidson, *Atlas*, 184–187), but only two of Brito's presumably successful voyages fell in years of prohibition, 1832 and 1840, and the estimated mortality rates were way below the average for this epoch, both around 9 percent. See also Herbert S. Klein and Stanley Engerman, "Long-Term Trends in African Mortality in the Transatlantic Slave Trade," in *Slavery & Abolition*, 18, no. 1 (1997): 36–48, who calculate a mortality rate of 9.1 percent for the Luso-Brazilian slave trade and 7.1 percent for the transatlantic trade from West Central Africa, including Angola, between 1821 and 1867 (pp. 43–44). In a more recent paper by Klein and Engerman, there is a slight change in those rates, which drop to 8.8 and 6.9 percent, respectively, between 1821 and 1864. See Herbert S. Klein, Stanley L. Engerman, Robin Haines, and Ralph Shilomowitz, "Transoceanic Mortality: The Slave Trade in Comparative Perspective," *William and Mary Quarterly*, Third Series, 58, no. 1 (2001): 93–118, Appendix, tables V and VI (a).
24. TSTD # 157, 2141, 3715, 40548, 40609, 47129, 47159, 48697, and 48751; letter from Governor José Oliveira Barboza to the *ouvidor-geral* (senior judge) of Angola, Euzébio de Queiroz Coutinho da Silva, August 26, 1814, and the attachment "Copy of the request mentioned in the above letter," Arquivo Histórico Nacional de Angola, Códice 154, fls. 154–157. We would like to thank Roquinaldo Ferreira for sharing this source with us. Also regarding Brito's activities, see Florentino, *Em costas negras*, 112.
25. Marcus J. M. de Carvalho, *Liberdade: rotinas e rupturas do escravismo, Recife, 1822-1850* (Recife: Editora da UFPE, 1998), 122 and 125. See also TSTD #1934, 2005, 2193, and 5032; House of Commons Parliamentary Papers (HCPP), Class B, *Correspondence with Foreign Powers Relating to the Slave Trade, 1842*, 437–340; Consul Cowper to Lord Aberdeen, August 4, 1843, op. cit., 364 (regarding Azevedo).
26. "Auto de perguntas feitas ao preto forro Rufino José Maria." ANTT, *Coleção do Ministério dos Negócios Estrangeiros, Pernambuco*, caixa 1, August 26, 1837, April 20, 1838; caixa 2, March 6, 1839, April 3, 1839, April 30, 1840, July 20, 1840, October 26, 1840, January 9, 1841, November 30, 1841. Regarding the beaches used to offload slaves in secret and other tactics for flouting the law, see Carvalho, *Liberdade*, 102–104.
27. TSTD # 2141.
28. Calculations based on data from the TSTD, in addition to data presented by Carvalho, *Liberdade*, 135, and Daniel Barros Domingues and David Eltis, "The Slave Trade to Pernambuco, 1561–1851," in David Eltis and David Richardson (eds.), *Extending the Frontiers: Essays on the New Transatlantic Slave Trade Database* (New Haven and London: Yale University Press, 2008), 95–129, esp. 105.
29. Mr. Goring to Viscount Palmerston, July 26, 1841, in HCPP, Class B, *Correspondence with Foreign Powers Relating to the Slave Trade, 1841*, 752–755. Regarding the bribery of officials by slave traders during the illegal period, see, for example, Conrad, *Tumbeiros*, 123–130.
30. Cowper to Lord Aberdeen, July 6, 1842, in HCPP, Class B, *Correspondence with Foreign Powers Relating to the Slave Trade, 1842*, 439. Regarding anti-British campaign due to pressure against the slave trade, see Paulo César Oliveira de Jesus, "O fim do tráfico de escravos na imprensa baiana, 1811–1850," MA thesis, Universidade Federal da Bahia, 2004; and Jaime Rodrigues, O infame comércio: propostas e experiências no final do tráfico africano

de escravos para o Brasil (1800–1850) (Campinas: Editora da UNICAMP/CECULT, 2000), esp. chap. 3.
31. Ferreira, "Dos Sertões ao Atlântico," chap. 1. Regarding the capture of the *Destemida*, see Rodrigues, *De costa a costa*, 179–180; and Ana Flávia Cicchelli Pires, "O caso da escuna *Destemida*: repressão ao tráfico na rota da Costa da Mina—1830–1831," in, *Rotas atlânticas*, edited by Carvalho, 157–189. Regarding the slavers' subterfuges, see also Verger, *Flux et reflux*, 418–424.
32. Lamb, *cordeiro* in the original, is an ironic reference to Angelo Francisco Carneiro (*carneiro* also translates as lamb), a powerful slave trader.
33. *Diário de Pernambuco*, no. 84, April 17, 1837.

Chapter 8

1. Data provided by Roquinaldo Ferreira, calculated on the basis of the TSTD. See also Ferreira, "The Suppression of the Slave Trade and Slave Departures from Angola, 1830s–1860s," in David Eltis and David Richardson (eds.), *Extending the Frontiers*, 313–334, and 322 for the quotation.
2. Regarding the population of Luanda in Rufino's day, we lack consistent estimates because censuses were not conducted between 1833 and 1844, according to José C. Curto and Raymond R. Gervais, "A história da população de Luanda no período final do tráfico transatlântico de escravos, 1781–1844," *Africana Studia*, 5 (2002): 83. Our suggested estimate is based on Table III in that article. Regarding the slave trade and traders in Benguela, see Mariana Pinho Candido, "Enslaving Frontiers: Slavery, Trade and Identity in Benguela, 1780–1850," PhD dissertation, York University, Canada, 2006; and Roquinaldo Ferreira, "Biografia, mobilidade e cultura atlântica: a microescala do tráfico de escravos em Benguela, séculos XVIII–XIX," *Tempo*, 20 (2006): 33–59.
3. For the description of Luanda thus far, see Georg Tams, *Visita às possessões portuguezas na costa occidental d'Africa* (Porto: Typographia da revista, 1850), vol. 1, chap. VI (quotations on pp. 191, 226, 227), as well as 249–550, and vol. 2, chap. VII; C. Herbert Gilliland, *Voyage to a Thousand Cares: Master's Mate Lawrence with the African Squadron, 1844–1846* (Annapolis: Naval Institute Press, 2004), 148–152; Joaquim José de Carvalho e Menezes, *Demonstração geographica e política do Territorio Portuguez na Guine Inferior, que abrange o Reino de Angola, Benguella, e suas Dependências etc.* (Rio de Janeiro: Typ. Classica de F. A. de Almeida, 1848), 17, 26. On Tams's observations about the slave trade and his defense of the "legitimate trade" in orchella weeds, see Maria Cristina Cortez Wissenbach, "As feitorias de urzela e o tráfico de escravos: Georg Tams, José Ribeiro dos Santos e os negócios da África Centro-Ocidental na década de 1840," *Afro-Ásia*, 43 (2011): 43–90.
4. Tams, *Visita às possessões portuguezas*, vol. 1, 227. For an excellent discussion of Luanda in Rufino's time, see also Anne Stamm, "La société créole à Saint-Paul de Loanda dans les années 1838–1848," *Revue française d'histoire d'Outre-mer*, LIX, no. 217 (1972): 578–610; and Jill Dias, "Angola," in *Nova História da expansão portuguesa*, edited by Joel Serrão and A. H. de Oliveira Marques, vol. X: *O império africano, 1825–1890*, Part 2, edited by Valentim Alexandre and Jill Dias (Lisbon: Estampa, 1998), 349–367. Specifically regarding slave traders, see José Capela, *As burguesias portuguesas e a abolição do tráfico da escravatura, 1810–1842* (Porto: Afrontamento, 1979), 86–117. These authors make extensive use of Tams's narrative. See also the detailed study by João Pedro Marques, *Os sons do silêncio: o Portugal de Oitocentos e a abolição do tráfico de escravos* (Lisbon: Imprensa de Ciências Sociais, 1999), chap. 5; Roquinaldo Ferreira, "Abolicionismo e fim do tráfico de escravos em Angola, séc. XIX," *Cadernos do CHDD*, special issue (2005): 171–173; and id., "The Suppression of the Slave Trade," esp. 322–323. These last two references focus on the governors' of Luanda's involvement with or tolerance of the slave trade.
5. Dias, "Angola," 354.
6. Gilliland, Voyage to a Thousand Cares, 150.
7. Tams, Visita às possessões portuguezas, vol. 1, 207–208. On Debret, see Valéria Lima, *J.-B. Debret, historiador e pintor: a viagem pitoresca e histórica ao Brasil (1816–1839)* (Campinas: Editora UNICAMP/CECULT, 2007). Regarding escapes and other forms of

slave rebellion in Angola, including Luanda, see Roquinaldo Ferreira, "Escravidão e revoltas de escravos em Angola (1830-1860)," Afro-Ásia, 21/22 (1998-1999): 9-44, but most of the evidence is for the period between the mid-1840s and the following decade. See also José C. Curto, "Resistência à escravidão na África: o caso dos escravos fugitivos recapturados em Angola, 1846-1876," Afro-Ásia, 33 (2005): 67-86.
8. Stamm, "La société créole," 582.
9. Tams, Visita às possessões portuguezas, quotations from vol. 1, 192-193, 212. Regarding Carpo's rise and fall, see Stamm, "La société créole," 597-599; Jacopo Corrado, "The Rise of a New Consciousness: Early Euro-African Voices of Dissent in Colonial Angola," e-Journal of Portuguese History, 5, no. 2 (2007), <http://www.ejph/v5n2/v5n2a03>; and particularly, these most informative articles by Carlos Pacheco, "Arsénio Pompílio Pompeu de Carpo: uma vida de luta contra as prepotências do poder colonial em Angola," Revista internacional de estudos africanos, 16/17 (1992-4): 49-102; and João Pedro Marques, "Arsénio Pompílio Pompeu de Carpo, um percurso negreiro no século XIX," Análise Social, 36, no. 160 (2001): 609-638.
10. Ferreira, "Dos Sertões ao Atlântico," 215-218, 278.
11. Tams, Visita às possessões portuguezas, vol. 1, 217.
12. Tams, Visita às possessões portuguezas, vol. 1, 195-200.
13. Menezes, Demonstração geographica e política, 203-205 (notes); and regarding the predominance of Kimbundu, see Dias, "Angola," 350; and Roquinaldo Ferreira, "'Ilhas crioulas': o significado plural da mestiçagem cultural na África atlântica," Revista de História, 155 (2006): 29 (quoting the governor). And also, Ferreira, Cross-Cultural Exchange, 139-143.
14. Dias, "Angola," 367-368.

Chapter 9

1. "The Slave Trade in Brazil," The North Star, Rochester, NY, October 5, 1849.
2. "Certificado de Matrícula da Barca Brasileira Ermelinda," June 11, 1841, AHI, Comissão Mista, lata 13, maço 3; Arquivo Público Estadual Jordão Emerenciano (hereafter APEJE), Registro de Passaportes, vol. 228, registro no. 38, October 9, 1838. Regarding wood from Alagoas, see José Mendonça de Mattos Moreira, "As matas das Alagoas: providências acerca delas e sua descrição," in Luís Sávio de Almeida, ed., Mata e Palmares nas Alagoas (Arapiraca: Edual, 2004), 21-39. According to Dirceu Lindoso, when royal protection of the forests ended, large rural landowners invaded them. That caused a chain reaction among the "forest folk," who fought for their rights in the Cabanada rebellion (1832-1836). Dirceu Lindoso, A utopia armada: rebeliões de pobres nas matas do tombo real (Rio de Janeiro: Paz e Terra, 1983).
3. See the highly baroque Senos Fonseca, "Filinto Elisio (1734-1819)," <http://senosfonseca.com/media/figuras/figuras.filinto_elisio.pdf>.
4. £1.00 = 7.83 mil-réis in 1841 current exchange rate. For exchange rates used here see Heitor Pinto Moura Filho, "Taxas cambiais do mil-réis (1795-1913)," Cadernos de História, vol. 11, no. 15 (2010): 32, also available at <https://mpra.ub.uni-muenchen.de/5210/1/MPRA_paper_5210.pdf>.
5. M. L. Melville and James Hook to Aberdeen, September 23, 1845, no. 62, HCPP, 1845, Correspondence with British Commissioners Relative to the Slave Trade, etc [Class A], vol. 29, 291.
6. Ação de Justificação, Justificante Antonio Carneiro Lisboa por seu procurador, Primeira Vara, Juízo Cível do Recife, The National Archives of Great Britain (hereafter NAGB), Foreign Office (FO), 315, 50, 61, fl. 5.
7. Diário de Pernambuco, June 28, 1836. Unlike the British slave trade, which took textiles from England to Africa, then slaves to the British Caribbean and mainland, and finally American products to England, the Luso-Brazilian slave trade was usually bilateral, from Brazilian to African ports and back. See Verger, Flux et reflux; and Alencastro, O trato dos viventes.
8. "Number and Names of Vessels which have arrived from the coast of Africa, within the Province of Pernambuco, during the year 1840," August 4, 1843, in HCPP, 1844, Correspondence with Foreign Powers, etc, [Class B and C] 1st Enclosure in no. 307, vol. 26, 372; Joaquim Baptista Moreira to the Secretary of State for Foreign Affairs, July 20, 1840, September 28, 1840, and January 9, 1841, ANTT, Coleção do Ministério dos Negócios Estrangeiros, Pernambuco, caixa 2.

9. After Pedro I was forced to abdicate the throne in 1831, there were demonstrations, mutinies, and protests by Portuguese who felt threatened by the new, profoundly nativist atmosphere. The Abrilada was an uprising of Portuguese army and militia officers with the backing of merchants, civil servants, and artisans, which spread from Recife into the interior, sparking the Cabanada rebellion in Pernambuco and Alagoas (1832–1835). José Francisco de Azevedo Lisboa was arrested by the provincial government and charged with taking part in the Abrilada uprising. The Portuguese consul Joaquim Baptista Moreira wrote letters in which he vehemently defended him and demanded his immediate release. "Correspondência Oficial," April 23, 1832, in *Diário de Pernambuco*, May 5, 1832; Joaquim Baptista Moreira to the President of the Province of Pernambuco, May 28 and June 20, 1832, APEJE, *Documentos Consulares*, vol. 2, fls. 289 and 301.
10. Carvalho, "O galego atrevido," 211.
11. "Certificado de Matrícula da Barca Brasileira Ermelinda," June 11, 1841, AHI, *Comissão Mista*, lata 13, maço 3; "Statement of the case," NAGB, HCA 36-6-2. But, see especially the set of documents listed as NAGB, FO, 315, 50, 61. Regarding the technical details that differentiate a barca from a brigue, particularly the number of masts, see Humberto Leitão and José Vicente Lopes, *Dicionário da linguagem de marinha antiga e actual*, 2nd ed. (Lisbon: Centro de Estudos Históricos Ultramarinos, 1974), 55, 82–83, *armação, barca, brigue*, and *vela* entries.
12. "Statement of the case," NAGB, HCA 36-6-2; and STVD # 2148. To calculate the space available aboard the ship, we used Leitão and Lopes, *Dicionário*, 511, *tonelagem* entry.
13. The nautical terms in Portuguese can be found in conventional dictionaries. For more specialized information, see Leitão and Lopes, *Dicionário*. Regarding ship repairs in colonial Brazil, see Hutter, *Navegação nos séculos xvii e xviii*, chap. 5. (Translator's note: for the nautical terms in English, see John Fincham, *An Introductory Outline of the Practice of Ship-building, &c. &c* (Philadelphia: W. Woodward,1825).)
14. "Conta do custeio e mais despesas etc.," July 1, 1841, AHI, *Comissão Mista*, lata 13, maço 3, doc. 28. Regarding the price of slaves in Pernambuco, see Flávio Rabelo Versiani and José Raimundo Oliveira Vergolino, "Preços de escravos em Pernambuco no século xix," *Textos para Discussão*, Department of Economics, Universidade de Brasília (October 2002), no. 252, 15.
15. Statement from Captain Coutinho, Sierra Leone, December 27, 1841, NAGB, FO, 84, 391, fl. 186v. Regarding class tensions aboard ships and in ports on the Brazilian Atlantic, see José Carlos Barreiro, *Imaginário e viajantes no Brasil do século xix: cultura e cotidiano, tradição e resistência* (São Paulo: Editora UNESP, 2002), 179 et seq.
16. See the Qur'ān, surahs "The Dinner Table" (5: 3); "The Cow" (2: 173); "The Cattle" (6: 175); "The Bee" (16: 115).
17. Copy of the receipt issued by Francisco Lisboa on June 21, 1841, AHI, *Comissão Mista*, lata 13, maço 3, doc. 18.
18. Regarding slave ship crews, see Rodrigues, *De costa a costa*, chap. 5. Regarding the large number of slaves on coastal shipping vessels, see Silva, *A faina*, 181–197.
19. David Richardson, "Shipboard Revolts, African Authority, and the Slave Trade," in Sylviane A. Diouf, ed., *Fighting the Slave Trade: West African Strategies* (Athens: Ohio University Press, 2003), 199–218, and Rodrigues, *De costa a costa*, 245–251, regarding rebellions; Rediker, *The Slave Ship*, which compares slave ships to prisons throughout the book. He explains that the cannons could be loaded with musket balls (p. 234), but they could also be packed with rock salt, for example, to be used against rebellious captives without doing as much damage to the ship as a cannon ball. The expression "prison-ship" was used in Rufino's day by F. Harrison Rankin, *The White Man's Grave: A Visit to Sierra Leone in 1834* (London: Richard Bentley, 1836), vol. II, 119, for example, and was often used by opponents of the slave trade at the time.
20. Regarding the muskets aboard the *Ermelinda*, see "Inventory of the Barque 'Ermelinda' made by the Marshall . . .," December 29, 1841, NAGB, 315, 50, 61, doc. 111/2. Regarding the *Veloz*, see H. W. Macaulay and Walter W. Lewis to Lord Palmerston, January 24, 1838, and attachments, HCPP, 1839, *Correspondence with British Commissioners and Foreign Powers, Class A and Class B, Number 24*, vol. 16, 15–67. Regarding the schooner *Dona Bárbara*, see AHI, *Comissão Mista*, lata 3, maço 5, pasta 1. About the 1829 rebellion, see Consul John Parkinson to Lord Aberdeen, Recife, February 13, 1830 (and attachment no. 64), in HCPP, 1830, *Correspondence with British Commissioners and Foreign Powers*, Class B, vol. 12, 118.

21. "Registro do Testamento com que faleceu Duarte José Martins da Costa," *Livro de testamento, 1853–54*, Memorial de Justiça de Pernambuco (MJPE), mapoteca 13, gaveta E, fl. 123. We would like to thank Valéria Costa for providing us with a copy of this document.
22. Regarding the multinational crews of Brazilian slave ships, see Rodrigues, *De costa a costa*, 186–187. The same was true in the North Atlantic in the previous century. See Christopher, *Slave Ship Sailors*, chap. 2; and Rediker, *The Slave Ship*, 229–230.
23. Sigismund Wilhel Koelle, *Polytglotta Africana*, Graz: Akademische Druck—U. Verlagsanstalt, 1963 [1854], 15.
24. AHI, *Comissão mista*, lata 23, maço 4, pasta 1, fls. 33ff.
25. See also Rodrigues, *De costa a costa*, 192–193.
26. Narciso is a character in João José Reis, "Slaves Who Owned Slaves in Nineteenth-Century Bahia, Brazil" (unpublished paper, 2014). For Narciso's voyages, see STVD # 7334 (1812); # 47178 (1812); # 7356 (1813); # 7396 (1815); # 9 (1817); # 48667 (1818); # 48826 (1819); and # 574 (1825).
27. Ibid., 186–187.
28. "Termo pelo qual se obriga Bastos, Oliveira e Lopes, por dona Anna Francisca Ferreira Ubertali, consignatária do bergatim brasileiro Flor de Luanda, etc." October 12, 1839, AHNA, cod. 2563. fl. 179v; "Termo que se obriga José da Silva Rego a apresentar nesta secretaria, no prazo de cento e vinte dias, sete marinheiros seus escravos etc." February 24, 1839, AHNA, cod. 2563, fls. 145v-6; and Letter from Governor Manuel Eleuterio Malheiro to the Minister of the Navy and Overseas Colonies, May 30, 1840, AHNA, cod. 15. fls. 7-7v. Roquinaldo Ferreira provided copies of these documents, for which we thank him.
29. "Lista da Equipagem da Barca Brasileira Hermelinda, que segue viagem para Angola etc." Recife, June 1841, AHI, *Comissão Mista*, lata 13, maço 3.
30. Seaman Gabriel Antonio was apparently illiterate because he signed his name with an "x" twice, among the signatures of the other crew and passengers aboard the ship in the document "Sentença cível de ratificação ao protesto e sinistro feito na Barca Brasileira que a seu favor alcançou o Supplicante Joaquim Antonio de Carvalho Coutinho, Capitão da mesma Barca etc." Bahia, July 19, 1841, AHI, *Comissão Mista*, lata 13, maço 3, doc. 29. It also states that he was unmarried.
31. Carvalho, *Liberdade*, 118; and Marcus J. M. Carvalho, "O 'galego atrevido' e 'malcriado', a 'mulher honesta' e o seu marido, ou política provincial, violência doméstica e Justiça no Brasil escravista," in Rachel Sohiet, Maria Fernanda Bicalho, and Maria de Fátima Gouveia (eds.), *Ensaios de História Cultural, História Política e ensino de História* (Rio de Janeiro: FAPERJ/Mauad, 2005), 201–234.
32. TSTD # 1176, 1181, 1926, 1931, 2058, 3418, 3593, 4607, 48699, and 48700; and Carvalho, "O galego atrevido e malcriado," 212 (the quote from the Portuguese consul).
33. Copy (translated from the original English) of a letter from Gabriel Antonio to Manoel Constantino, Recife, July 4, 1841, attachment to Michael L. Melville and W. Ferguson to Captain Foote, January 28,1842, NAGB, FO, 84, 391, fls. 204-4v. The same document in NAGB, FO, 315, 50, 61 attachment 10, and published in HCPP, 1843 (382), Class A, *Correspondence with the British Commission Relating to the Slave Trade, 1842*, 83. Regarding Manoel Constantino, see Ferreira, "Dos Sertões ao Atlântico," 25–32.

Chapter 10

1. Silva, *Francisco Felix de Souza*, 145.
2. Arquivo Histórico Ultramarino (AHU), *Conselho Ultramarino*, 015, caixa 290 (Projeto Resgate, doc. 20009).
3. H. W. Macaulay and Walter W. Lewis to Lord Palmerston, January 24, 1838 and enclosures, HCPP, 1839, *Correspondence with British Commissioners and Foreign Powers, Class A and Class B, Number 24*, vol. 16, 15–67.
4. João Pedro Marques, "Tráfico e supressão no século XIX: o caso do brigue Veloz," *Africana Studia*, 5 (2002): 155.
5. See the statement by crewmember Francisco José, given on January 24, 1838, in HCPP, 1839, *Correspondence with British*, enclosure 2, no. 24, vol. 16, 20.

6. "Report of the Case of the Portuguese Brig Camões, Antonio Gomes da Silva, Master," January 24, 1838, enclosure 1, no. 24, id., 16–18; H. W. Macaulay to Lord Palmerston, May 30, 1838, id., 43–45.
7. Regarding the court hearing on the *Camões* and *Veloz*, see Marques, "Tráfico e supressão no século XIX," 175–176.
8. Idem, 19. The lack of experience of the British in taking care of the captives aboard captured slave ships was recounted in horrifying detail by an eyewitness to one of those voyages in 1843. Of the 447 people rescued on the coast of Mozambique (Quilimane), 163 (36.5 percent) died on the way to Cape Town. See Pascoe Grenfell Hill, *Cinquenta dias a bordo de um navio negreiro* (Rio de Janeiro: José Olympio, 2008). See also Thomas, *The Slave Trade*, chap. 33. The high mortality rates aboard the slave ships taken to Sierra Leone by the British are addressed in an article by David Northrup, "African Mortality in the Suppression of the Slave Trade: The Case of the Bight of Biafra," *Journal of Interdisciplinary History*, 9, no. 1 (1978): 47–64, which discusses various aspects of the matter (winds and tides, length of voyage, type of vessel, etc.) and compares the proportionally smaller mortality rate on transatlantic voyages. Finally, for the quotation in this paragraph, see Simon Schama, *Rough Crossings: Britain, the Slaves and the American Revolution* (New York: Harper Collins, 2006), 169.
9. Marques, "Tráfico e supressão no século XIX," 155.
10. Statement by George Sayer Boys, in "Report of the Case of the Portuguese Brig Camões, Antonio Gomes da Silva, Master," 21.
11. Idem, *passim*, 15–67. The contract is in enclosure 4, no. 32, 49–50.
12. Marques rightly emphasizes this aspect in "Tráfico e supressão no século XIX," 157 and 177, for example, although we disagree that the company was formed "by people without experience in the business," even considering that the slave traders involved had embarked on such a business venture during the illegal period. In any event, the author seems to be unaware of Azevedinho's importance in Pernambuco's slave trading community, because he merely refers to him as "a certain José Francisco de Azevedo Lisboa" (p. 158).
13. Azevedinho's detailed instructions can be found in HCPP, 1839, *Correspondence with British Commissioners and Foreign Powers, Class A and Class B, Number 24*, vol. 16, 51–52. See also Marques, "Tráfico e supressão no século XIX," 158, 160, 162.
14. Marques, "Tráfico e supressão no século XIX," 170.
15. HCPP, 1839, *Correspondence with British Commissioners and Foreign Powers, Class A and Class B, Number 24*, vol. 16, 51–52; and Marques, "Tráfico e supressão no século XIX," 165–168.
16. HCPP, 1839, Ibid.; and Marques, "Tráfico e supressão no século XIX," 165.
17. Different types of optical telegraphs were then in use by the military and navy of several nations. They were much simpler devices than the electromagnetic telegraph that came later in the nineteenth century. This earlier technology, the most advanced at the time, was not unknown to slave traders. One of the slave ships that operated in Pernambuco in the 1820s was the *Conceição Telégrafo*. The owner of that vessel was Manoel Alves Guerra, one of the two consultants of Azevedinho in the firm. TSTD # 47011, 47018 and 47019, 49793.
18. João Baptista Cézar to Francisco de Azevedo Lisboa, August 4, 1837, in "Report from the Principal Agent in Benin and Proceedings of the Company's Factories established in that river," 58–61.
19. Id., 59–60; and Cowper to Lord Aberdeen, January 14, 1842, enclosure 1, NAGB, FO, 84, 411, fls. 282v and 283.
20. Statement by Antonio Gomes da Silva, id., 20.
21. Coimbra to João Baptista Cézar, June 25, 1837, id., 63.
22. Joaquim Pedro to Joaquim Gomes Coimbra, July 3, 1837, id., 65.
23. José Francisco de Azevedo Lisboa to João Baptista Cézar, April 29, 1837, HCPP, 1839, *Correspondence with British Commissioners and Foreign Powers, Class A and Class B*, vol. 16, 56. Corroborating David Eltis, Marques recalls that at that juncture it was not uncommon for traders to fit out their ships for the slave trade or even build them on the coast of Africa. "Tráfico e supressão no século XIX," 165–166.
24. Azevedo Lisboa to João Baptista Cézar, April 29, 1837, 56.
25. João Baptista Cezar to José Francisco de Azevedo Lisboa, Benim, September 16, 1837, NAGB, FO 315/69.

26. João Baptista Cézar to Francisco de Azevedo Lisboa, August 4, 1837, id., 58.
27. Regarding the health problems encountered by workers at the trading post, see Marques, "Tráfico e supressão no século XIX," 172–173.
28. João Baptista Cézar to Francisco de Azevedo Lisboa, August 4, 1837, id., 58.
29. Delgado and Joaquim Gomes Coimbra to João Baptista Cézar, June 30, 1837, id,, 64.
30. E. J. Alagoa, "Long-distance Trade and States in the Niger Delta," *The Journal of African History*, 11, no. 3 (1970), 319–329; and Alberto da Costa e Silva, *A manilha e o libambo: a África e a escravidão de 1500 a 1700* (Rio de Janeiro: Nova Fronteira, 2002), chap. 9, esp. 311–316, 324–326.
31. João Baptista Cézar to Francisco de Azevedo Lisboa, September 16, 1837, HCPP, 1839, *Correspondence with British*, vol. 16, 61.
32. Marques, "Tráfico e supressão no século XIX," 162, 176.
33. "Mapa das Embarcações entradas no Porto do Recife, 1º semestre de 1837," in Joaquim Baptista Moreira para o secretário de Estado dos Negócios Estrangeiros, July 9, 1837, ANTT, *Coleção do Ministério dos Negócios Estrangeiros, Pernambuco*, caixa 1.
34. João Baptista Cézar to José Francisco de Azevedo Lisboa, August 4, 1837, HCPP, 1839, *Correspondence with British*, vol. 16, 60.
35. "List of the Vessels under the Portuguese Flag, now in the Port of Pernambuco, etc." December 31, 1839, HCPP, *Correspondence with Foreign Powers Relative to the Slave Trade Class B, C and D*, enclosure 3, no. 124, vol. 19, 135. Regadas is listed among other merchants and shipowners who moved to Brazil in the mid-1830s, according to Carlos Pacheco, "Arsénio Pompílio Pompeu de Carpo: uma vida de luta contra as prepotências do poder colonial em Angola," *Revista Internacional de Estudos Africanos*, 16/17 (1992–1994), 74.
36. "List of those Vessels under the Portuguese Flag which have sailed from Pernambuco for the Coast of Africa, etc.," December 31, 1839, enclosure 1, no. 124, id., 133.
37. "List of the Vessels under the Portuguese Flag which have arrived from the Coast of Africa, etc." July 31, 1840, HCPP, 1840, *Correspondence with British*, enclosure 2, no. 197, vol. 20, 216.
38. Joaquim Baptista Moreira para o secretário de Estado dos Negócios Estrangeiros, January 5, 1839, ANTT, *Coleção do Ministério dos Negócios Estrangeiros, Pernambuco*, caixa 2.
39. "List of those Vessels under the Portuguese Flag which have arrived in the Port of Pernambuco from the Coast of Africa, etc.," December 31, 1839, enclosure 2, vol. 19, 134.
40. Copy (translated into English) of the letter from Gabriel Antonio to Manoel Constantino, Recife, July 4, 1841; regarding Manoel Constantino, see Ferreira, "Dos Sertões ao Atlântico," 25–32.
41. HCPP, Class B, *Correspondence with Foreign Powers Relating to the Slave Trade, 1842*, 437, and 439.
42. AHI, *Comissões Mistas*, lata 2, maço 1, pasta 1.
43. Ibid.
44. *Diário de Pernambuco*, September 19, 1843.
45. "List of Departure of Vessels suspected of being employed in Slave Trade from Pernambuco, etc." January 1, 1844, HCPP, 1845. *Correspondence with Foreign Powers Relative to the Slave Trade Class B and C*, enclosure 2, no. 265, vol. 28, 412.
46. *Diário de Pernambuco*, April 20, 1844.
47. Last Will and Testament of José Francisco de Azevedo Lisboa, Instituto Arqueológico, Histórico e Geográfico de Pernambuco (IAHGP), not catalogued. The document is in an extremely poor state of conservation. We would like to thank Tácito Galvão for allowing us access to it.
48. Marriage certificate for Antonio Bernardo Ferreira and Antonia Rita deAzevedo Lisboa, the widow of José Francisco de Azevedo Lisboa, Recife, January 27, 1849 (Appellant: Antonio Bernardo Ferreira. Appellee: Joaquim Ribeiro de Brito), IAHGP, *Tribunal da Relação, ano: 1848, Juízo do Cível da Cidade do Recife (1848–52)*, caixa 5, fl. 15.

Chapter 11

1. Stamm, "La société créole," 587.
2. "Conta do costeio e mais despeza etc." and "Sentença cível de ratificação ao (. . .) protesto e sinistro feito na Barca Brasileira que a seu favor alcançou o Supplicante Joaquim Antonio

de Carvalho Coutinho, Capitão da mesma Barca, etc.," Bahia, July 19, 1841, AHI, *Comissão Mista*, lata 13, maço 3, docs. 28 and 29; HCCP, 1843 (482), Class A, *Correspondence with the British Commission Relating to the Slave Trade, 1842*, p. 80.
3. Stephanie E. Smallwood, *Saltwater Slavery: A Middle Passage from Africa to American Diaspora* (Cambridge, MA; London: Harvard University Press, 2007), 65.
4. Wise is quoted by Matson, *Remarks on the Slave Trade*, vol. 1, p. 65. Regarding Wise's diplomatic activities in Rio de Janeiro, particularly regarding the slave trade, see Horne, *The Deepest South*, chap. 4; and Graden, *Disease, Resistance, and Lies*, chap. 1. Regarding British interests in the illegal slave trade, see Conrad, *Tumbeiros*, 139–147; Tavares, *Comércio proibido*, 58–59, 129–134; and Eltis, *Economic Growth*, 83–84, 155–157. Marika Sherwood gives an overview of the advantages several British interest groups and individuals derived from the continuation of the slave trade outside British dominions in *After Abolition: Britain and the Slave Trade since 1807* (London and New York: I. B. Tauris, 2007).
5. José Curto calculates that between 1710 and 1830, Brazilian spirits purchased 25 percent of the slaves exported from Angola to Brazil. Curto, cited by Luiz Felipe de Alencastro, "The Economic Network of Portugal's Atlantic World," in Francisco Bethencour and D. Ramada Curto (eds.), *Portuguese Oceanic Expansion,1400–1800*, ed. (Cambridge: Cambridge University Press, 2007), 121. For an in-depth study of the role of jeribita in the slave trade with Angola, see José C. Curto, *Álcool e escravos: o comércio luso-brasileiro do álcool em Mpinda, Luanda e Benguela durante o tráfico atlântico de escravos (c. 1480–1830) e o seu impacto nas sociedades da África Central Ocidental* (Lisbon: Vulgata, 2002). Also regarding the subjects covered in this paragraph, see Roquinaldo Amaral Ferreira, "Fazendas em troca de escravos: circuitos de créditos nos Sertões de Angola, 1830–1860," *Estudos Afro-Asiáticos*, 32 (1997): 76–96; id., "Dos Sertões ao Atlântico," 202–203; id., "Dinâmica do comércio intracolonial: jeribitas, panos asiáticos e guerra no tráfico angolano de escravos (século xviii)," in João Fragoso, Maria Fernanda Bicalho, and Maria de Fátima Gouvêa (eds.), *O Antigo Regime nos trópicos: a dinâmica imperial portuguesa — séculos xvi–-xviii* (Rio de Janeiro: Civilização Brasileira, 2001), pp. 349–350; and Alencastro, *O trato dos viventes*, p 322 and 324.
6. Tams, *Visita às possessões portuguezas*, vol. 2: 22. See also Miller, *Way of Death*, 76, who mentions "guloseimas portuguesas" ("Portuguese sweetmeats") consumed in Luanda by "nostalgic emigrants living in the city." Regarding the contents of the *Ermelind's* cargo, see NAGB, FO, 84/391, fls. 173v-4, 177, 179, 180–181v; Carvalho, *Liberdade*,122–123; and particularly "Resumo de todo carregamento que do Porto de Pernambuco condusio para o de Loanda a Barca Brasileira Ermelinda, etc.," Pernambuco, July 1, 1846, AHI, *Comissão Mista Brasil-Grã-Bretanha. Embarcações. Ermelinda, 1841-46*, lata 13, maço 3. The latter document contains a detailed cargo manifest.
7. Regarding slaves in Luanda being worth about seven times less than those purchased in Brazil, see "Apontamentos sobre Angola em 27 de maio de 1841," AHU, *Papéis de Sá da Bandeira*, maço 827. Roquinaldo Ferreira provided us with this source. Prices of slaves and manumissions in Rio came from Flávio Gomes's database. Florentino, "Alforria e etnicidade no Rio de Janeiro," 16, observes that in Rio, the prices of slaves and manumissions fluctuated at about the same level at the time. For the prices of manumission in Bahia, see Kátia M. de Queirós Mattoso, Herbert S. Klein, and Stanley L. Engerman, "Notas sobre as tendências e padrões dos preços de alforrias na Bahia, 1819–1888," in João José Reis, ed., *Escravidão e invenção da liberdade: estudos sobre o negro no Brasil* (São Paulo: Brasiliense, 1988), 60–72.
8. In the crew`s list the cabin boy was registered as Duarte Martins da Costa; in the shippers´ list he was registered as Duarte José Martins Pereira; in his 1854 will and testament his name was Duarte José Martins da Costa. None of these records matches this shipper's brand. The changes in names reflect the legal instability of freedpersons in imperial Brazil. Regarding the appointment/naming of slaves and freedpersons, see Jean Hébrard, "Esclavage et dénomination: imposition et appropriation d'un nom chez les esclaves de la Bahia au xixe siècle," *Cahiers du Brésil Contemporain*, 53–54 (2003): 31–92.
9. AHI, *Comissão Mista*, lata 31, maço 2, pasta 1, doc. 4.
10. On Africans involved in the slave trade, see Verger, *Os libertos*; Jaime Rodrigues, *Em mar e em terra: história e cultura de trabalhadores escravos e livres* (São Paulo: Alameda, 2016), chap. 3;

Luís Nicolau Parés, "Milicianos, barbeiros e traficantes numa irmandade católica de africanos minas e jejes (Bahia, 1770–1830)," *Tempo*, 20 (2014), http://www.historia.uff.br/tempo.
11. AHI, *Comissão Mista*, lata 31, maço 2, pasta 1, doc. 4.
12. Regarding the shipment of cloth for Joaquim Ribeiro de Brito, see the copy of an untitled, incomplete document dated June 20, 1841, vouched for by Angelo Carneiro on May 28, 1846, AHI, *Comissão Mista*, lata 64, maço 3, pasta 1.
13. See, for Rio, Florentino, *Em costas negras*. Regarding the second half of the eighteenth century, covering several parts of the South Atlantic but with particular emphasis on the links between slave-trading families and the Port of Benguela, see Estevam Costa Thompson, "Negreiros nos mares do Sul: famílias traficantes nas rotas entre Angola e Brasil em fins do século xviii," MA thesis, Universidade de Brasília, 2006.
14. "Resumo de todo carregamento que do Porto de Pernambuco condusio para o de Loanda a Barca Brasileira Ermelinda etc.," op. cit. The Carneiro family seems to have been involved in the slave trade since at least 1813, when the name Antonio Joaquim José Carneiro appears as the captain of a slaver, the bergantim *Vigilante Africano*. See TSTD # 48594.
15. TSTD # 40525, 40559, 47085, 47098, 47115, 48902, 49885, and 49886. Regarding Carneiro's transaction with Brito, see "Receita da siza dos predios desta cidade entre 1808 e 1833," Biblioteca Municipal de Luanda, Códice 37, fl. 111. We thank Roquinaldo Ferreira for providing that document. As in the case of commander Angelo Carneiro, Manolo Florentino has observed that not only were there family networks of slave traders in Rio de Janeiro, but they had privileged relations with the government, from which they obtained official posts and all kinds of commendations and titles. See Florentino, "Slave Trading and Slave Traders in Rio de Janeiro, 1790–1830," in José C. Curto and Paul Lovejoy (eds.) *Enslaving Connections: Changing Cultures of Africa and Brazil during the Era of Slavery* (Amherst, Humanity Books, 2004), 73–75. See also Conrad, *Tumbeiros*, 120–122.
16. HCCP, Class B, *Correspondence with Foreign Powers Relating to the Slave Trade, 1842*, pp. 437–438; id., 1844, p. 754; and Cowper to Lord Aberdeen, August 3, 1842, NAGB, FO, 84–411, fl. 304.
17. José Capela quoted by Aline Emanuelle de Biase Albuquerque, "De 'Angelo dos Retalhos' a Visconde de Loures: a trajetória de um traficante de escravos (1818–1858)," MA thesis, Universidade Federal de Pernambuco, 2016, p. 10. Albuquerque's work is the most complete to date about Angelo Carneiro.
18. ANTT, *Coleção do Ministério dos Negócios Estrangeiros, Pernambuco*, caixa 2 and 3; and letter from Joaquim Batista Moreira to the Foreign Minister, November 8, 1848, *Coleção do Ministério dos Negócios Estrangeiros, Pernambuco*, caixa 3; and *Nobreza de Portugal*, edited and compiled by Afonso Eduardo Martins Zúquete (Lisbon: Editorial Enciclopedia, 1960), vol. 2: 699–700.
19. For Angola in the seventeenth and eighteenth centuries, emphasizing the little-known military use of horses, see Roquinaldo Amaral Ferreira, "Transforming Atlantic Slaving: Trade, Warfare and Territorial Control in Angola, 1650–1800," PhD dissertation, University of California, Los Angeles, 2003, chap. 5 (pp. 185–186, 204 on the preference for horses from Pernambuco). Regarding the presence of horses during the early days of the slave trade in West Africa, see Ivana Elbl, "The Horse in Fifteenth-Century Senegambia," *International Journal of African Historical Studies*, vol. 28, no. 1 (1991): 85–109; and Alencastro, *O trato dos viventes*, 49–50, and regarding Angola p. 97, 248. Regarding the use of horses in Luanda at Rufino's time, see Tams, *Visita às possessões portuguezas*, vol. 1: 211–212.
20. João Pedro Marques, "Arsénio Pompílio Pompeu de Carpo, um percurso negreiro no século xix," *Análise Social*, vol. 36, no. 160 (2001): 615; Pacheco, "Arsénio Pompílio Pompeu de Carpo" 67–71; and *Diário de Pernambuco*, May 9, 1829.
21. Tams, *Visita às possessões portuguezas*, vol. 1: 212.
22. Dias, "Angola," 354.
23. Marques, "Arsénio Pompílio," p. 612.
24. Copy of an untitled, incomplete document dated June 20, 1841, and vouched for by Angelo Carneiro on May 28, 1846, AHI, *Comissão Mista*, lata 64, maço 3, pasta 1; Tams, *Visita às possessões portuguezas*, vol. 2, pp. 24–25, 109–110; and Stamm, "La société créole," p. 597.

25. Amounts calculated on the basis of "Resumo de todo carregamento que do Porto de Pernambuco condusio para o de Loanda a Barca Brasileira Ermelinda, etc."

Chapter 12

1. "Sentença cível de ratificação ao (?) protesto e sinistro feito na Barca Brasileira que a seu favor alcançou o Supplicante Joaquim Antonio de Carvalho Coutinho, Capitão da mesma Barca, etc." July 19, 1841, op. cit.
2. Ibid.
3. Like other sailors, Rufino also received 5,400 réis for the 27 days he spent aboard in Recife and Salvador, being a daily wage of 200 réis.
4. "Conta, Despeza feita com o Protesto, Justificação, Vistoria, Julgação, e Sentença da Barca Nacional Ermelinda, etc." Recife, July 7, 1846, AHI, *Comissão Mista*, lata 13, maço 3.
5. BN, *Correio Mercantil*, Salvador (dates illegible), several issues June and July, 1841.
6. HCPP, 1842 (551) (551-ii), *Select Committee on West Coast of Africa, Report, Minutes of Evidence, Appendix, Index*, 268–269.
7. Matson, *Remarks on the Slave Trade*, 22, 95.
8. Tams, *Visita às possessões portuguezas*, vol. 1, 194–195; José Eduardo Agualusa, *Nação crioula* (Lisbon: TV Guia Editora, 1997), 14.
9. See Marques, "Arsénio Pompílio," 23–26.
10. Johnson U. J. Asiegbu, *Slavery and the Politics of Liberation, 1787–1861: A Study of Liberated African Emigration and British Anti-slavery Policy* (New York: African Publishing Corporation, 1969), 119–120.
11. TSTD # 3150.
12. Tams, *Visita às possessões portuguezas*, vol. 1, 250–251; Rediker, *The Slave Ship*, 274.
13. TSTD # 3149.
14. Tams, *Visita às possessões portuguezas*, vol. 2, 109–110.
15. Ibid., 103–104. Matson staunchly defended the effectiveness of those launches in combating the slave trade, although they had their detractors. See *Remarks on the Slave Trade*, 33.

Chapter 13

1. Capela, *As burguesias portuguesas*, 97. On Angolan secessionist feelings, see Roquinaldo Ferreira, *Cross-Cultural Exchange in the Atlantic World: Angola and Brazil during the Era of the Slave Trade* (Cambridge: Cambridge University Press, 2012), ch. 6; and Mariana P. Candido, *An African Slaving Port and the Atlantic World: Benguela and its Hinterland* (Cambridge: Cambridge University Press, 2013), 110–111, specifically on Benguela.
2. Marquês de Sá da Bandeira, *O tráfico da escravatura e o Bill de Lord Palmerston* (Lisbon: Ulmeiro, 1997 [1840]), 25. Regarding the Portuguese slave trade during that period, see also Tavares, *O comércio proibido*, chap. iv, and Capela, *As burguesias portuguesas*. For a detailed background of the diplomacy that led to the Equipment Act, see Leslie Bethell, "Britain, Portugal and the Suppression of the Brazilian Slave Trade: The Origins of Lord Palmerston's Act of 1839," *English Historical Review*, 80 (1965): 761–784; id., *The Abolition*, chap. 6; and the most recent and complete study by Marques, *Os sons do silêncio*, chaps. 4 and 5, which also contains a broader discussion of the slave trade in Portuguese Africa in the 1840s. Regarding the movement in 1823 in Benguela and fears in Lisbon of Angolan separatism in the 1830s and 1840s, see Dias, "Angola," 368–369, 376–378, in addition to Marques, cited above.
3. J. Gallagher, "Fowell Buxton and the New African Policy, 1838–1842," *Cambridge Historical Journal*, vol. 10, no. 1 (1950): 54.
4. Quoted by Eltis, *Economic Growth*, 85.
5. Robin Law, "Abolition and Imperialism: International Law and the Suppression of the Slave Trade," in Derek R. Peterson, ed., *Abolitionism and Imperialism in Britain, Africa, and the Atlantic* (Athens: Ohio University Press, 2010), 160.
6. Regarding reactions in Portugal to the British policy of suppressing the slave trade, see Marques, *Os sons do silêncio*, esp. 250–296; and in Brazil, see Jaime Rodrigues, *O infame comércio: propostas e experiências no final do tráfico de africanos para o Brasil (1800–1850)* (Campinas: Editora da Unicamp/Cecult, 2000), 101–107.

7. Matson, *Remarks on the Slave Trade*, 54 (quotation), 55.
8. http://www.pdavis.nl/Legis_11.htm, accessed May 24, 2016.
9. HCPP, 1847–1848 (116), *Abstract Return of Number of Slaves Captured, 1810–46*, 1. Different numbers appear in Matson, *Remarks on the Slave Trade*, 8: in 1839, 5,566 slaves were said to have been seized, and 3,616 in 1840. See also Eltis, *Economic Growth*, chap. 6 and p. 244.
10. Sherwood, *After Abolition*, 117–120; HCPP, 1847 (653), *Return of Appropriation of Sums Received as Proceeds of Vessels Condemned for Violation of Laws prohibiting the Slave Trade; sums paid to captors since 1807*; Rankin, *The White Man's Grave*, vol. II, 106.
11. "Abstract of the proceedings in the British and Brazilian Court of Mixed Commission at Sierra Leone, for the repression of the slave trade during the year of 1841," in Melville to Aberdeen, December 31, 1841, NAGB, FO, 84, 346, fls. 162–170v, 223; HCPP, *Class A*, 1842 [402], *Correspondence with British Coms. At Sierra Leone, Havana, Rio de Janeiro and Surinam on Slave Trade: 1841*, 129–130. Francisco José da Silva is included in the list of slave traders compiled by Florentino, *Em costas negras*, 256.
12. "Abstract of the proceedings in the British and Brazilian Court of Mixed Commission at Sierra Leone, for the repression of the slave trade during the year of 1841," in Melville to Aberdeen, December 31, 1841, fls. 173v–174.
13. TSTD # 1769.
14. "Abstract of the proceedings in the British and Brazilian Court of Mixed Commission at Sierra Leone, for the repression of the slave trade during the year of 1841," fls. 171–174v, 223.
15. Regarding the Cabindas in Rio de Janeiro, see Flávio dos Santos Gomes, Carlos Eugênio Líbano Soares, and Juliana Barreto Farias, "Primeiras reflexões sobre travessias e retornos: cabindas, redes do tráfico e diásporas num Rio de Janeiro atlântico," *Textos de História*, 12, no. 1/2 (2004): 65–105.
16. "Abstract of the proceedings in the British and Brazilian Court of Mixed Commission at Sierra Leone, for the repression of the slave trade during the year of 1841," op. cit., fls. 175–179v, 223.
17. Florentino, *Em costas negras*, 237, 256.
18. See voyages in the TSTD, in which José Bernardino de Sá is shown as the owner of the ship. The voyage of the *Espardate* is listed in the TSTD under # 1999.
19. "Abstract of the proceedings in the British and Brazilian Court of Mixed Commission at Sierra Leone, for the repression of the slave trade during the year of 1841," op. cit., fls. 180–183v, 223.
20. TSTD # 2153. On the powerful Brazilian slave trader based in Ouidah, see Silva, *Francisco Félix de Souza*, and Robin Law, "A carreira de Francisco Félix de Souza na África Ocidental (1800–1849)," *Topoi*, no. 2 (2001): 9–40.
21. "Abstract of the proceedings in the British and Brazilian Court of Mixed Commission at Sierra Leone, for the repression of the slave trade during the year of 1841," op. cit., fls. 184–186v, 223.
22. Ibid., fls. 186v–190, 223.
23. Ibid., 190v–192, 223.
24. Ibid., fls. 192–199, 223.
25. Ibid., fls. 199–203v, 223.
26. Regarding the medical situation in Benguela at the time, see Tams, *Visita às possessões portuguezas*, 145–148.
27. "Abstract of the proceedings in the British and Brazilian Court of Mixed Commission at Sierra Leone, for the repression of the slave trade during the year of 1841," op. cit.
28. NAGB, FO, 84, 346, fl. 227v; HCPP, 1847–1848 (231), *Return of Vessels Captured Under Suspicion of Being Engaged in the Slave Trade, 1832-47*, 1.
29. Letter from Manoel Joaquim Ricardo to Joaquim Antonio da Silva, Bahia, April 24, 1841, NAGB, FO, 315, 50, doc. 48. This document was kindly provided by Lisa Earl Castillo.

Chapter 14

1. Regarding the fact that crewmen from seized ships returned to the slave trade, see Michael Melville and James Hook to Aberdeen, Sierra Leone, December 31, 1831, NABG, FO 84, 393, fls. 181v-2.
2. About St. Helena, see Daniel A. Yon, "Making Place, Making Race: St. Helena and the South Atlantic World," in Boubacar Barry, Elisée Soumoni, and Livio Sansone (eds.), *Africa, Brazil*

and the Construction of Trans-Atlantic Black Identities (Trenton: Africa World Press, 2008), 114–126.
3. James Prior, *Voyage along the Eastern Coast of Africa to Mosambique, Johanna, and Quiloa, to St. Helena, to Rio de Janeiro, Bahia, and Pernambuco in Brazil, in the Nisus Frigate* (London: Richard Phillips and Co., 1819), 83. Another work on St. Helena from that period is W. Innes Pocock, *Five Views of the Island of St. Helena* (London: S. and J. Fuller, 1815).
4. Yon, "Making Place, Making Race," 119.
5. NAGB, FO, 315/17, fls. 550–553, 573–575; NAGB, FO, 84/392, fl. 39v; Report from José Mauricio Fernandes Pereira de Barros to Foreign Minister Antonio Coelho de Sá Albuquerque, September 2, 1867, AHI, *Comissão Mista*, lata 64, maço 3, pasta 1, fl. 69.
6. The TSTD estimates that between 1821 and 1823, 12,295 slaves embarked in Molembo and disembarked in Bahia, but just 7,365 embarked in ports on the Bight of Benin and disembarked in Bahia. However, it is a well-known fact that most Africans who entered Bahia at the time came from the latter African region. On this subject, see Verger, *Flux et reflux*, passim, and 403–405 specifically regarding the fiction that Molembo was the destination of Bahian slave traders after 1817; and Alexandre Ribeiro Vieira, "The Transatlantic Slave Trade to Bahia,1582–1851," in Eltis and Davidson (eds.), *Extending the Frontiers*, 139 and 141 (Table 4.4). Eight of the ten ships captured by the British between 1822 and 1824 in the zone where the slave trade was banned stated that their destination was the legitimate port of Molembo. See Pires, "O caso da escuna *Destemida*," 169.
7. AHI, lata 28, maço 5, pasta 1, fls. 19 and 19v.
8. AHI, *Comissão Mista*, lata 30, maço 1, pasta 1, fls. 8 and 8v.
9. See data in Eltis, "The Diaspora of Yoruba Speakers," 24.
10. AHI, *Comissão Mista*, lata 24, maço 2.
11. Regarding the conception, preparations for, and first two decades of the Sierra Leone colony—and the basis for the next four paragraphs—we consulted J. J. Crooks, *A History of the Colony of Sierra Leone, Western Africa* (London: Frank Cass, 1972 [1903]), chaps. 1–6; Christopher Fyfe, *A History of Sierra Leone* (London: Oxford University Press, 1962), chaps. 1–4; Gibril R. Cole, *The Krio of West Africa: Islam, Culture, Creolization and Colonialism in Nineteenth-Century* (Athens: Ohio University Press, 2013), chap. 1; Schama, *Rough Crossings*; Stephen J. Braidwood, *Black Poor and White Philanthropists: London's Black and the Foundation of the Sierra Leone Settlement* (Liverpool: Liverpool University Press, 1994); Cassandra Pybus, *Epic Journeys of Freedom: Runaway Slaves of the American Revolution and their Global Quest for Liberty* (Boston: Beacon Press, 2006), esp. chaps. 5 and 9; Mavis Campbell, *The Maroons of Jamaica, 1655–1796: A History of Resistance, Collaboration and Betrayal* (Trenton, NJ: Africa World Press, 1990), chap. 7; and James Lockett, "The Deportation of the Maroons of Trelawny Town to Nova Scotia, then Back to Africa," *Journal of Black Studies*, vol. 30, no. 1 (1999): 5–14.
12. Quoted in Schama, *Rough Crossings*, 210–211.
13. Gallagher, "Fowell Buxton and the New African Policy," 37.
14. Regarding the Mixed Commissions, see Leslie Bethell, "The Mixed Commissions for the Suppression of the Transatlantic Slave Trade in the Nineteenth Century," *Journal of African History*, vol. 7, no. 1 (1966): 79–93; and id., *The Abolition*, chap. 5.
15. NAGB, FO, 84, 346, fls. 227, 240.
16. Robert Clarke, *Sierra Leone. A description of the Manners and Customs of the Liberated Africans; with observations upon the Natural History of the Colony, and a Notice of the Native Tribes, &c. &c.* (London: James Risdway; Holborn, Johnson & Co., 1843), 84–85. See also Rankin, *The White Man's Grave*, vol. ii, 119–125.
17. Regarding the people apprenticed to the Jolofs and Mandigos, see Rankin, *The White Man's Grave*, vol. ii, 105.
18. Letter from João Altavilla to Minister Thomaz Antônio de Vila Nova Portugal, June 27, 1820, AHI, *Correspondência para a Comissão Mista em Serra Leoa*, lata 57, maço 2, pasta 1; Rosanne Marion Aderley, *"New Negroes from Africa": Slave Trade Abolitionism and Free African Settlement in the Nineteenth-Century Caribbean* (Bloomington: Indiana University Press, 2006); and Beatriz Mamigonian, "In the Name of Freedom: Slave Trade Abolition, the Law, and the Brazilian Branch of the African Emigration Scheme (Brazil-British West Indies, 1830s–1850s)," *Slavery & Abolition*, vol. 30, no 1 (2009): 41–66.

19. James Holman, *Travels in Madeira, Sierra Leone, Teneriffe, St. Jago, Cape Coast, Fernando Po, Princes Island etc., etc.*, 2nd ed. (London: George Routledge, 1840), 106; and Clarke, *Sierra Leone*, 23, 59–60.
20. Several European travelers who visited Sierra Leone during that period mentioned the presence of the Kru in that colony and other sea ports in the region. See, for example, J. F. Napier Hewett, *European Settlements in the West Coast of Africa; with Remarks on the Slave-Trade and the Supply of Cotton* (New York: Negro Universities Press, 1969 [1862]), 111–113. Regarding the Mandinka in Sierra Leone, see David E. Skinner, "Mande Settlement and the Development of Islamic Institutions in Sierra Leone," *The International Journal of African Historical Studies*, vol. 11, no. 1 (1978): 32–62.
21. Koelle, *Polytglotta Africana*, III.
22. Elizabeth Helen Melville [A Lady], *A Residence at Sierra Leone, Described from a Journal Kept on the Spot, and from Letters Written to Friends* (London: John Murray, 1849), 256–259. As we will see further on, the Aku was an umbrella Yoruba-speaking ethnonym that included the very large Ọyọ́ group (Melville's "Eyoes"), and therefore Aku and Ọyọ́ were not synonymous.
23. Ibid., 22.
24. Clarke, *Sierra Leone*, 33–35, 38.
25. Hewett, *European Settlements on the West Coast of Africa*, 110–111.
26. Melville, *A Residence at Sierra Leone*, 13. See also, regarding British residents of the colony and ethnic divisions, the highly racist observations of Richard F. Burton, *Wanderings in West Africa* (New York: Dover, 1991 [1862]), vol. 1, 214–215 and 219–220, respectively.
27. Holman, *Travels*, chaps. 4 and 5; Hewett, *European Settlements*, 113. See also the references in the following note.
28. Melville, *A Residence at Sierra Leone*, 21–22, 191–192, 277; Clarke, *Sierra Leone*, 38, 40, 49, and chap. VI; Holman, *Travels*, 119–120; Hewett, *European Settlements*, 110–113.

Chapter 15

1. Strictly speaking, during that period the term *Yoruba* referred to natives of Ọyọ́—in fact, it was derived from another word coined by the Hausas, *Yarriba*, later adopted in Sierra Leone by Christian missionaries, who extended it to all groups which spoke the language that came to be known as Yoruba in its various regional dialects. In fact, it was those missionaries who promoted the idea of a single Yorubaland that included sons and daughters of Egba, Egbado, Ife, Ilesha, Ijebu, Ibadan, Ketu, Ondo and so on, as well as Ọyọ́, among the other kingdoms and cities that spoke a common language. See J. D. Y Peel, "The Cultural Work of Yoruba Ethnogenesis," in E. Tonkin, E. M. McDonald, and M. Chapman (eds.), *History and Ethnicity* (London and New York: Routledge & Kegan Paul, 1989), 198–215.
2. In the context of the slave trade, a "palaver" sealed the sale of slaves between buyer and seller. Clarke, *Sierra Leone*, pp. 53–57, 78; Hewett, *European Settlements*, p. 163. Regarding the 1848 census, see Philip Curtin, *The Atlantic Slave Trade: A Census* (Madison: The University of Wisconsin Press, 1969), 244.
3. Clarke, *Sierra Leone*, 150, 152 (quotes).
4. Thomas Bowen, *Adventures and Missionary Labours in Several Countries in the Interior of Africa from 1849 to 1856* (London: Frank Cass, 1978 [1857]), 210.
5. Koelle, *Polyglota Africana*, 5–6.
6. Melville, *A Residence at Sierra Leone*, 257; Clarke, *Sierra Leone*, 29, 40; Hewett, *European Settlements*, 114–115. Always seeking a critical angle for viewing Africans, Burton, in *Wanderings in West Africa*, vol. 1, 219, noted the existence of intimidating Aku secret societies whose adversaries called their activities the "Aku tyranny" or "Aku inquisition."
7. Samuel Ajayi Crowther, "The Narrative of Samuel Ajayi Crowther," introduction by J. F. Ade Ajayi, in Philip Curtin, ed., *Africa Remembered* (Madison: The University of Wisconsin Press, 1967), 289–316.
8. "Farobê" is mentioned in the report in *Jornal do Commercio*, September 25, 1853. Rufino's words are from "Auto de perguntas feitas ao preto forro Rufino José Maria," op. cit.
9. Fourah seems to be derived from *fúrá*, a Hausa word incorporated into the Yoruba language, and means "balls of cooked flour for cooking in milk," according to R. C. Abraham, *Dictionary*

of Modern Yoruba (London: University of London Press, 1958), 227. In Sierra Leone, it meant balls of sweetened rice flour, a common dish among Islamized Akus. See Jack Barry, *A Dictionary of Sierra Leone Krio* (1966), 25, available online: ERIC—Education Resources Information Center, item no. ed012454. In Brazil, *furá* or *efurá* is a drink made from corn or rice and honey, among other ingredients, which has ritual functions in Afro-Brazilian religions. See Sergio Ferretti, *Querebentan de Zomadonu: etnografia da Casa das Minas* (São Luis: Edufma, 1985), 291; and Yeda Pessoa de Castro, *Falares africanos na Bahia*, 2nd ed. (Rio de Janeiro: Topbooks/ABL, 2005), 226, 238.

10. Cole, *The Krio of West Africa*, 92.
11. For Muslim religious leadership and Muslim education in Sierra Leone, see Cole, *The Krio of West Africa*, chaps. 2 and 4; id., "Liberated Slaves and Islam in Nineteenth-Century West Africa," in Toyin Falola and Matt Childs (eds.), *The Yoruba Diaspora in the Atlantic World* (Bloomington: Indiana University Press, 2005), 383–403; David E. Skinner, "Islam and Education in the Colony and Hinterland of Sierra Leone (1750–1914)," *Canadian Journal of African Studies/Revue Canadienne des Études Africaines*, vol. 10, no. 3 (1976): 514–515; and Barbara E. Harrell-Bond, Allen M. Howard, and David E. Skinner, *Community Leadership and the Transformation of Freetown (1801–1976)* (The Hague: Mouton, 1978), 107–109 (quote on p. 107). Regarding the Mandingo (Malinke) influence on the spread of Islam in the region, see Skinner, "Mande Settlement."
12. We would like to thank Paulo Farias for explaining the meaning of Imam Ratibou.
13. AHI, *Comissão Mista*, lata 15, maço 1, pasta 1, letter dated April 7, 1822.
14. Holman, *Travels*, 82–83; Skinner, "Mande Settlements," 58.
15. Cole, *The Krio of West Africa*, 94–101; id., "Liberated Slaves and Islam"; and Skinner, "Islam and Education," 512–513.
16. Gallagher, "Fowell Buxton and the New African policy," 52; "An Act for granting additional duties of Customs," March 29, 1841, NAGB, FO, 84, 347; Skinner, "Mande Settlement," 39–41. Regarding Muslim involvement in the slave trade and legitimate commerce in the Sierra Leone region, see contemporary reports from Rankin, *The White Man's Grave*, vol. I, 122–126, 139–140; Holman, *Travels*, 74–75 and 119–122; Clarke, *Sierra Leone*, 29–30; Hewett, *European Settlements*, 154 and 171–173; and Burton, *Wanderings in West Africa*, vol. 1, 232.
17. *Jornal do Commercio*, September 25, 1853.
18. Harrell-Bond, Howard, and Skinner, *Community Leadership*, 108–109. Regarding Sufism in West Africa, see Bradford Gary Martin, *Muslim Brotherhoods in Nineteenth-Century Africa* (Cambridge: Cambridge University Press, 1976), chap. 1.

Chapter 16

1. Hermenegildo Niterói to Walter Lewis, Sierra Leone, December 20, 1841, HCPP, 1843 (482), Class A, *Correspondence with the British Comission Relating to the Slave Trade, 1842*, 70–73, regarding Niterói's illness and his disputes with the British commissioners.
2. See NAGB, FO, 84/391, fls. 178v, 188v, 257–314. See also "Relatório de José Mauricio Fernandes Pereira de Barros," op. cit., fl. 69v, and "Relatório de Hermenegildo Niterói ao presidente da Província de Pernambuco," Freetown, May 4, 1842, AHI, *Comissão Mista*, lata 13, maço 3, Pasta 1.
3. Cristina Wissenbach, "Cirurgiões e mercadores nas dinâmicas do comércio atlântico de escravos (séculos XVIII e XIX)," in Laura Mello Souza, Júnia Furtado, Maria Fernanda Bicalho (eds.), *O governo dos povos: relações de poder no mundo ibérico na época Moderna* (São Paulo: USP/Alameda, 2009), 291.
4. Olaudah Equiano, *The Life of Olaudah Equiano*, published by Paul Edwards, Essex: Longman, 1987 [1789]), 25, 31. See also Miller, *Way of Death*, 389, 413; and Rediker, *The Slave Ship*, 266–267. Regarding the rescued captives' impression that the British were cannibals, see Rankin, *The White Man's Grave*, vol. II, 104, 120. About Equiano's involvement in the Sierra Leone project, see Vincent Carreta, *Equiano the African: Biography of a Self-Made Man* (Athens: The University of Georgia Press, 2005), chap. 10, in addition to his own words in his autobiography.
5. Among others, Caretta, *Equiano the African*, raises doubts as to whether Equiano was actually born in Africa and crossed the Atlantic in the hold of a slave ship, which is contested by Paul

Lovejoy, "Autobiography and Memory: Gustavus Vassa, alias Olaudah Equiano, the African," *Slavery & Abolition*, 27, no. 3 (2006): 317–347. See also the dossier in "Olaudah Equiano, the South Carolinian? A Forum," *Historically Speaking: The Bulletin of the Historical Society*, 7, no. 3 (2006). <www.bu.edu/historic/hs/jafeb06.html#forum1>. The dispute is still unresolved.

6. About the rebellion aboard the Bahian slave ship, see APEBA, *Insurreições escravas*, maço 2845; and Augustino's statement, Sierra Leone, May 24, 1849, in HCPP, 1850, *Reports from the Select Committee of the House of Lords, etc.*, vol. 6, 163; and Crowther, "The Narrative of Samuel Ajayi Crowther," 313.

7. Saidiya Hartman, *Lose Your Mother: A Journey Along the Atlantic Slave Route* (New York: Farrar, Straus and Giroux, 2007), 114. Along the same lines, see Stephen Palmié, *Wizards & Scientists: Explorations in Afro-Cuban Modernity & Tradition* (Durham: Duke University Press, 2002), 179.

8. William Ferguson and Michael Melville to Aberdeen, Sierra Leone, January 25, 1842, NAGB, FO, 84, 391, fls. 170v–171.

9. Last two paragraphs: "Abstract of the proceedings in the British and Brazilian Court of Mixed Commission established in Sierra Leone [. . .] during the year 1841," NAGB, FO, 84, 393, fl. 138v; and NAGB, FO, 84, 391, fls. 178–187; HCPP, 1843 (382), Class A, *Correspondence with the British Commission Relating to the Slave Trade, 1842*, 80–82.

10. Statements from Rufino and Barbosa, Sierra Leone, December 27, 1841, NAGB, FO, 84, 391, fls. 187–190; HCPP, 1843 (382), Class A, *Correspondence with the British Commission Relating to the Slave Trade, 1842*, 81. The British recorded the cook's name as Rufino Bernardo de Almeida, which was the name listed in the crew roster drawn up in Recife, as we have seen.

11. Affidavit from R. Burstal, Sierra Leone, January 22, 1842, NAGB, FO, 84, 391, fls. 200–201.

12. Ibid, 201–202.

13. See Malek Chebel, *Dictionaire des symboles musulmans* (Paris: Albin Michel, 1995), 96–97; Al Quayrawani, *La Risâla: épitre sur les éléments du dogme et de la loi de l'Islam selon le rite malikite* (Paris: IQRA, 1996), 243; Samuel Moore (compiler), *An Interesting Narrative: Biography of Mahommah G. Baquaqua* (Detroit: Geo E. Pomeroy and Co., Tribune Office, 1854), 46. Confirming the widespread use of the insult, Captain Hewett, *European Settlements*, 158, used the expression "Christian dogs" ironically in the 1850s to say that even they could purchase Muslim amulets in Sierra Leone, while suggesting the peaceful coexistence between people of different faiths in the British colony.

14. Regarding the languages spoken in the slave trade circuit, see Rodrigues, *De costa a costa*, 197–207.

15. For example, there is the case of two Brazilian ships captured in 1843 which, according to commissioner Melville carried "slave-decks, slave-irons, slave-coppers, slave-night-tubs, slave-mess-tins, slave-gratings, slave-provisions; in short, a complete equipment for the Slave Trade." Nevertheless, Niterói refused to condemn them. Melville to Aberdeen, Sierra Leone, June 28, HCPP, 1843, Class A, *Correspondence with the British Commission Relating to the Slave Trade, 1844*, 35–36.

16. See Bethell, *The Abolition*, 193–195, regarding Niterói's and Amaral's appointment and the exceptional nature of this case. The minutes of the trial can be found in NAGB, FO, 315, 17, fls. 550–553. Regarding the disputes between the parties, see the full records of the trial in NAGB, FO, 84, 391, and NAGB, FO, 315, 14, fls. 1–25, among other sources.

17. Last four paragraphs: Ferguson and Melville to Aberdeen, Sierra Leone, January 8, 1842; Niterói to Walter Lewis, December 20, 1841; Melville to Aberdeen, Sierra Leone, January 20, 1842, and the attachments to that letter, particularly the minutes of the commissioners' meeting on December 23, 1841, and the clerk's letter to the British commissioners, dated January 12, 1842, all found in NAGB, FO, 84, 391, fls. 3–21v, 41–48v, 60–64v, 111v–133. See also, Walter Lewis, the British commissary judge, to Niterói, Sierra Leone, December 13, 1841, NAGB, FO, 315, 14, 1–9v, in which the Englishman expounds at length on Niterói's unlawful behavior in being present at Barbosa's interrogation, citing the modus operandi of the Mixed Commissions of several countries and Britain, including Brazil in previous trials. Lord Aberdeen backed his commissioners, not because the treaties were clear on this subject but because there was an established custom that judges should not be present when statements were taken. See HCPP, 1843 (382), Class A, *Correspondence with the British Commission*

Relating to the Slave Trade, 1842, 89–90. Regarding the interpreter's name, see NAGB, FO, 315, 17, fls. 550–553.
18. Walsh, *Notices of Brazil*, vol. 2, 475, 477.
19. Matson, *Remarks on the Slave Trade*, 62. See also Bethell, *The Abolition*, 181.
20. Petition from Robert Dougan to Walter William Lewis, commissary judge, and Michael Melville, commissioner of arbitration, Sierra Leone, January 10, 1842, NAGB, FO, 84, 391, fls. 139–142v; HCPP, 1847 (653), *Return of Appropriation of Sums Received as Proceeds of Vessels Condemned for Violation of Laws Prohibiting the Slave Trade*, 5–7; NAGB, HCA 36-6-2; Sherwood, *After Abolition*, 117, regarding Matson's prize money awarded between 1839 and 1843, and the calculation of its value in 2005.
21. Christopher Leslie Brown, *Moral Capital: Foundations of British Abolitionism* (Chapel Hill: University of North Carolina Press, 2006).
22. See Rodrigues, *O infame comércio*, 101–107. Regarding the Aberdeen Bill and its repercussions, see Bethell, *The Abolition*, chaps. 9 and 10. See also Parron, *A política da escravidão*, ch. 3.

Chapter 17

1. Niterói to the President of the Province of Pernambuco, May 4, 1842, AHI, *Comissão Mista. Minutas de ofícios*, lata 57, maço 3, doc. 19.
2. Records of this episode can be found in two sources: NAGB, FO, 84, 391, fls. 257–314; and HCPP, 1844 (573), Class A, *Correspondence with British Commission in Sierra Leone, Havana, etc., 1843*, 402–410.
3. Regarding the procedures to which captured slave ships were subjected, see Ranking's observations in *The White Man's Grave*, vol. II, 105–156, 118–119. The list of goods removed from the *Ermelinda* can be found in NAGB, 315, 50, 61.
4. Melville to Aberdeen, March 1, 1842, NAGB, FO 84, 391, fls. 269v–271.
5. Statements from Richard Lawrence, February 8, 1842, and John D. Thorpe, February 9, 1842, NAGB, FO 84, 391, fls. 277v–279v, 299v–291v.
6. Statement from James Williams, February 8, 1842, NAGB, FO, 84, 391, fls. 279v–281v. The contents of Williams's note to Thorpe are on fl. 279.
7. Statement from Sam Williams, February 8, 1842, NAGB, FO, 84, 391, fls. 282–284v.
8. Statement from Samuel Boyle, February 10, 1842, NAGB, FO, 84, 391, fls. 296v–298; and HCPP, 1844 (573), Class A, *Correspondence with British Commission in Sierra Leone, Havana, etc., 1843*, 405.
9. Statements from Anthony Mason, February 8, 1842, and Thomas Bucknor and Abraham Cole, February 11, 1842, NAGB, FO, 84, 391, fls. 300–302.
10. Statement from Augustine, February 11, 1842, NAGB, FO, 84, 391, fls. 302–324.
11. Statement from Joseph Reffell, February 11, 1842, NAGB, FO, 84, 391, fls. 305–305v. Regarding the sort of work done by prisoners sentenced to hard labor, see Holman, *Travels*, 110. Regarding Thorpe's firing, see Melville and MacDonald to Aberdeen, July 4, 1842, NAGB, FO, 84, 392, fls. 177–178.
12. Statement from Richard Lawrence, February 8, 1842, NAGB, FO, 84, 392, fl. 278v.

Chapter 18

1. For the most complete study of the mutiny aboard the *Amistad*, see Marcus Rediker, *The Amistad Rebellion: An Atlantic Odyssey of Slavery and Freedom* (New York: Viking, 2012), particularly 217–223 regarding the ship's arrival in Sierra Leone. See also the pioneering work by Howard Jones, *Mutiny on the Amistad* (Oxford: Oxford University Press, 1987). Regarding the ramifications of the Cuban slave trade involved in this episode, see Orlando García Martinez and Michael Zeuske, *La sublevación esclava en la goleta Amistad: Ramón Ferrer y las redes de contrabando en el mundo atlántico* (Havana: Ediciones Unión, 2012). The 1997 film about this event, directed by Steven Spielberg, is analyzed by Natalie Zemon Davis in *Slaves on Screen: Film and Historical Vision* (Cambridge, MA: Harvard University Press, 2000), chap. 4.
2. Regarding Pedro Blanco, see Jose Luciano Franco, *Comercio clandestino de esclavos* (Havana, Cuba: Editorial de Ciencias Sociales, 1980), 236–245; Tavares, *Comércio proibido*, 49–50;

and Thomas, *The Slave Trade*, 687–689. The destruction of the barracoons on the Gallinas River is discussed by Asiegbu, *Slavery and the Politics of Liberation*, chap. 6.

3. The case of the *Galiana*, like that of the *Ermelinda*, is entirely covered by the British records: NAGB, FO, 315, 50, 61 and FO, 84, 391, fls. 69–74, for example. See also, "Return showing the several proceeds of vessels and property condemned, etc." Sierra Leone, December 31, 1842; Michael Melville and James Hook to Aberdeen, Sierra Leone, December 31, 1842, NABG, FO, 84, 393, fls. 166, 169–184 (the later letter gives an optimistic report on the progress the British were making in combating the slave trade, particularly north of the Equator); and Ferguson and Melville to Aberdeen, January 13, 1842, HCPP, 1843 (482), Class A, *Correspondence with the British Commission Relating to the Slave Trade, 1842*, 74–87. It is clear on page 76 of that report that the British were not aware of who Chachá actually was, saying that he called himself "José Telles de Souza, of Ouidah (also known as Char Char)." One of Chachá's sons-in-law, Joaquim Telles de Menezes, was believed to be aboard the *Galiana*, according to Robin Law, *Ouidah: The Social History of a West African 'Port,' 1727–1892* (Athens: Ohio University Press; Oxford: James Currey, 2004), 173.

4. Aureliano de Souza and Oliveira Coutinho to Niterói, April 5, 1842; Coutinho to Amaral, October 5, 1842; and Report from Niterói to the President of the Province of Pernambuco, May 2, 1842, AHI, *Comissão Mista. Minutas de ofícios*, lata 57, maço 3. Those records also contain information about the age of Captain Coutinho in the "Lista da equipagem da Barca Ermelinda, etc." of June 1841, op. cit.

5. Captain John Adams, *Remarks on the Country Extending from Cape Palmas to the River Congo, Including Observations on the Manners and Customs of the Inhabitants* (London: G. and W. B. Whittaker, 1823), v.

6. Rankin, *The White Man's Grave*, vol. ii, chap. 18; Vincent Brown, *The Reaper's Garden: Death and Power in the World of Atlantic Slavery* (Cambridge, MA: Harvard University Press, 2008), 176. Klein, *The Middle Passage*, 70, mentions the extremely high European mortality rate of 483 to 668 per 1,000 in West Africa as a whole, including Sierra Leone. See also Stephen D. Behrendt, "Crew Mortality in the Transatlantic Slave Trade in the Eighteenth Century," *Slavery & Abolition*, 18, no. 1 (1997), 49–71, which calculated average losses of 17.2 percent for the French slave trade and 17.8 percent for the British (Liverpool) in the eighteenth century. See also Rediker, *The Slave Ship*, 244–247.

7. Clarke, *Sierra Leone*, 14–15, 77–78.

8. Gilliland, *Voyage to a Thousand Cares*, 24, 291.

9. Holman, *Travels*, chap. III, esp. 66. See also Crooks, *A History of the Colony of Sierra Leone*, passim; Richard Phillips, "Dystopian Space in Colonial Representation: Sierra Leone as 'The White Man's Grave,'" *Geografiska Annaler*, vol. 86, no. 3/4 (2002): 189–200. Regarding Niterói's and Amaral's state of health, see Walter W. Lewis e Michael L. Melville to Niterói and Amaral, December 20, 1841; G. MacDonald and Melville to Amaral, April 28, 1842, NAGB, FO, 315, 14, fls. 12–14, 57.

10. Report from Niterói to the President of the Province of Pernambuco, May 4, 1842; Report from José Mauricio Fernandes Pereira de Barros, op. cit., fls. 69–70; G. MacDonald and M. Melville to Aberdeen, April 19, 1842, NAGB, FO, 84, 392, fls. 24–47 (quote fls. 25–25v), including attached documents. Copies of those documents can also be found in NAGB, FO, 315, 50, 61. Some of the documents on the dispute whether Senna had the right to represent the owner of the *Ermelinda* in the suit for damages are published in HCPP, 1843 (382), Class A, *Correspondence with the British Commission Relating to the Slave Trade, 1842*, 84–89. Regarding Rufino's expenses, see, AHI, *Comissão Mista*, lata 13, maço 3, doc. 16.

11. G. MacDonald and M. Melville to Aberdeen, April 19, 1842, NAGB, FO, 84, 392, fl. 34.

12. See a copy of the receipt Wilkinson issued to Angelo Carneiro on July 2, 1842 in AHI, *Comissão Mista*, lata 13, maço 3.

13. Report from Niterói to the President of the Province of Pernambuco, May 4, 1842 (quote); MacDonald and Melville to Aberdeen, May 7, 1842, NAGB, FO, 84, 392, fls. 91–93v, all op. cit.

14. "List of crew," drawn up by John Cormack on April 7, 1842. AHI, *Comissão Mista*, lata 13, maço 3.

15. Certificate from Niterói regarding the list of equipment required to send the *Ermelinda* to Pernambuco, May 5, 1842; Report from Niterói to the President of the Province of Pernambuco, May 4, 1842, op. cit.; Report from José Mauricio Fernandes Pereira de Barros, op. cit., fl. 70. See also NAGB, FO, 315/17, fls. 550ff; and FO, 84/391, 195–198, 253, FO, 84/392, fls. 24, 91–92 et seq.
16. Matson, *Remarks on the Slave Trade*, 15–16; and the statement from Captain Henry James Matson, June 21, 1849, HCPP, 1850, *Reports from the Select Committee of the House of Lords etc.*, vol. 6, 202.
17. "Abstract of the Proceedings in the British and Brazilian Court of Mixed Commission Established in Sierra Leone . . . During the Year 1841," December 31, 1842, NAGB, FO, 84, 393, fls. 135-48v; and particularly, NAGB, FO, 315, 50, 61; Letter from the Governing Council of Angola to the Portuguese Minister of the Navy and Overseas Affairs, September 4, 1842, AHNA, cód. A-3-6, no. 15, fls. 157v-8. We would like to thank Roquinaldo Ferreira for passing on to us this document.

Chapter 19

1. Report from José Mauricio Fernandes Pereira de Barros to Foreign Minister Antonio Coelho de Sá Albuquerque, September 2, 1867, op. cit., fl. 70.
2. Cowper to Lord Aberdeen, August 3, 1842, NAGB, FO, 84–411, fl. 304.
3. Ibid.; NAGB, HCA 36-6-2; Accounts of the disembarkation of the *Ermelinda* in Viana Souza to Angelo Carneiro, July 12, 1842, AHI, *Comissão Mista*, lata 13, maço 3.
4. Copy (translated into English) of the power of attorney Antonio Carneiro Lisboa issued to Richard Lawrence and others, Lisbon, August 2, 1842, NAGB, FO, 315, 50, 61.
5. Richard Lawrence to J. C. Weston, clerk of the Mixed Commission, September 3, 4, and 5, 1845, NAGB, FO, 315, 50, 61.
6. . Lawrence to Carneiro, June 12, 1843, AHI, *Comissão Mista*, lata 13, maço 3, doc. 27.
7. Parron, *A política da escravidão*, 206.
8. Letter from Aureliano de Souza e Oliveira Coutinho to Hermenegildo Niterói, April 5 and June 13, 1842; letter from Niterói to Coutinho requesting leave, n.d.; Coutinho to Joaquim Thomaz do Amaral, October 5, 1842, AHI, *Comissão Mista*, lata 64, maço 3, pasta 1. Three years later Amaral would become the Brazilian ambassador (or minister plenipotenciary) in London, in which capacity he served for almos ten years.
9. Coutinho to Niterói, January 27 and October 23, 1843, AHI, *Comissão Mista*, lata 64, maço 3, pasta 1.
10. *Jornal do Commercio*, September 25, 1853.
11. See receipt issued by Rufino (Appendix 4), several receipts issued by Wilkinson and Roberts, and letters from Lawrence to Francisco Lisboa, Sierra Leone, April 27 and May 4 (quote), 1842, AHI, *Comissão Mista*, lata 13, maço 3, docs. 27, 40, 41, 42, 43, and 44.
12. Statement from Henrique José Vieira da Silva, April 7, 1843, AHI, *Comissão Mista*, lata 13, maço 3, doc. 2.
13. "Lista da equipagem do Hiate Brasileiro Santo Antonio Flor do Brasil, que segue viagem para Benguela, Serra Leoa, e Ilhas do Príncipe, e S. Thomé etc.," April 5, 1843, attached to the letter from the Baron of Boa Vista to Joaquim José Rodrigues Torres, April 5, 1843, AN, *Marinha. Presidentes da província de Pernambuco*, maço—XM 332 (we would like to thank Silvana Jeha for this document); and receipts issued by Rufino and the owner of the *Santo Antonio Flor do Brasil* found in the AHI, *Comissão Mista*, lata 13, maço 3.
14. Report from José Mauricio Fernandes Pereira de Barros to Foreign Minister Antonio Coelho de Sá Albuquerque, September 2, 1867, op. cit.
15. Id.; and Rodrigues, *De costa a costa*, 147.

Chapter 20

1. "Auto de perguntas feitas ao preto forro Rufino José Maria," op. cit. Rufino's passport, no. 1224, is dated April 16, 1845, and is valid for one month – the standard period. See APEB,

Polícia. Passaportes, maço 6352. We would like to thank Lisa Earl Castillo for sharing this document, as well as the one mentioned in note 2.
2. Atestado da Mesa do Consulado, December 20, 1845, APEB, *Polícia. Passaportes*, maço 6353.
3. "Auto de Busca dada na casa do preto forro Rufino José Maria, e de achada de diversos objetos," September 3, 1853, AN, IJ[1] 326, *Pernambuco, Ofícios do Presidente da Província ao Ministro da Justiça (1853–1854)*.
4. *Diário de Pernambuco*, January 17, 1846; Almir Chaiban El-Kareh, "A Companhia Brasileira de Paquetes a Vapor e a centralidade do poder monárquico," *História Econômica & História de Empresas*, 2 (2002): 7–27; *O Mensageiro*, December 8, 1835.
5. "Procuração bastante que fazem Joaquim Duarte, e outros abaixo declarados e assinados," May 29, 1846, AHI, *Comissão Mista*, lata 13, maço 3, doc. 24; and Relatório de José Mauricio Fernandes Pereira de Barros ao ministro do Estrangeiro Antonio Coelho de Sá Albuquerque, September 2, 1867, op. cit.
6. "Registro do Testamento com que faleceu Duarte José Martins da Costa," op. cit., fl. 123v.
7. Marcus J. M. de Carvalho, "De portas adentro e de portas afora: trabalho doméstico e escravidão no Recife, 1822–1850," *Afro-Ásia*, 29/39 (2003): 44–45.
8. We would like to thank José Luiz Mota Menezes for this information. See also Francisco Augusto Pereira da Costa, *Anais Pernambucanos* (Recife, Fundarpe, 1983–1985), vol. 6: 49; vol. 2: 163; and José Antonio Gonsalves de Mello, *Gente de Nação* (Recife: Massangana, 1989), 274, 422–423.
9. *Folhinha de Algibeira* (Recife: Typografia M. F. de Faria, 1853).
10. Deputy Chief Constable Francisco Baptista de Almeida to the President of the Province, September 5, 9 and 10, 1853, AN, IJ[1] 326, *Pernambuco, Ofícios do Presidente da Província ao Ministro da Justiça (1853–1854)*.
11. APEJE, *Petições: Senhores e Escravos. Recife*, pasta 45, 2/1, doc. no. 20, September 13, 1852.
12. José Idelfonso de Souza Ramos to the President of the Province, July 27, 1850, APEJE, JM, vol. 9, p. 243. On the free Africans, see Beatriz G. Mamigonian, *Africanos livres: a abolição do tráfico de escravos no Brasil* (São Paulo: Companhia das Letras, 2017).
13. *Jornal do Commercio*, September 25, 1853; *O Echo Pernambucano*, September 9, 1853.
14. *Diário de Pernambuco*, June 21, 1827; and Verger, *Flux et reflux*, 642, 646.
15. *Diário de Pernambuco*, May 16, 1829.
16. See several documents in the ANTT, *Coleção do Ministério dos Negócios Estrangeiros, Pernambuco*, caixa 2 and 3, *passim*.
17. Portuguese Consul in Recife to Portuguese Minister of Foreign Affairs, December 10, 1844, ANTT, *Coleção do Ministério dos Negócios Estrangeiros, Pernambuco*, caixa 3.
18. *Diário de Pernambuco*, March 13, 1844 and March 7, 1848; and Gilberto Freyre, *Os escravos nos anúncios de jornais brasileiros do século XIX*, 2nd ed. (São Paulo: Editora Nacional; Recife: Instituto Joaquim Nabuco de Pesquisas Sociais, 1979), 35, 65, *passim*.
19. Moore, *An Interesting Narrative*; Paul Lovejoy, "Identidade e a miragem da etnicidade: a jornada de Mohammah Gardo Baquaqua para as Américas," *Afro-Ásia*, 27 (2001): 9–39. See also Robin Law and Paul Lovejoy (eds.), *The Biography of Mahommah Gardo Baquaqua: His Passage from Slavery to Freedom in Africa and America* (Princeton: Marcus Wiener, 2001), which includes a long and useful introduction that provides additional information about the life of this fascinating character.

Chapter 21

1. *Jornal do Commercio*, September 25, 1853.
2. Ibid.
3. *Correio Mercantil*, September 21, 1853.
4. "Auto de perguntas feitas ao preto forro Rufino José Maria," op. cit.
5. *Diário de Pernambuco*, September 6 and 9, 1853; and regarding Cipriano José Pinto's merchandise, see APEB, Judiciária. Tribunal da Relação. Execução cível, nos. 22/0768/14 and 12/411/14. For more on that African, see Reis, *Domingos Sodré*, 249–258.
6. Cole, *The Krio*. See also Abraham, *Dictionary of Modern Yoruba*, 363.
7. Skinner, "Islam and Education," 503.

8. Clarke, *Sierra Leone*, 40–14; Hewett, *European Settlements*, 153, 156–158; and Cole, *The Krio*, chap. 5.
9. Skinner, "Mande Settlements," 58.
10. *Jornal do Commercio*, September 25, 1853.
11. Dom Obá II was a veteran of the Paraguay War, born in Bahia to African parents. A popular figure in Rio de Janeiro in the second half of the nineteenth century, he was a devotee of St. Barbara and the African divinity of war and metalwork, Ògún. See Eduardo Silva, *Dom Obá II d'África, o príncipe do povo: vida, tempo e pensamento de um homem livre de cor* (São Paulo: Companhia das Letras, 1997), 165: Dom Obá wrote, "when God wills, cold water heals." A similar expression—"Having faith, cold water is medicine"—was also common at the time. See Figueiredo, *A arte de curar*, 98.
12. Regarding the making and use of amulets and the practice of Islamic divination in Sierra Leone during that period, see Cole, *The Krio*, 96; and Skinner, "Islam and Education," 502, 512. The use of amulets in the Bahia of the Yoruba Muslims is extensively discussed in Reis, *Rebelião escrava*, esp. chaps. 6–8, in the context of the 1835 Malê revolt.
13. "Auto de perguntas feitas ao preto forro Rufino José Maria," op. cit.
14. *Diário de Pernambuco*, September 6, 1853, in José Antônio Gonsalves de Mello (compiler), *Diário de Pernambuco: economia e sociedade no 2o Reinado* (Recife: Editora Universitária/ Editora da UFPE, 1996), 71.
15. *Jornal do Commercio*, September 25, 1853.
16. Rio Police Chief Alexandre Joaquim de Sequeira to the Minister of Justice José Thomas Nabuco de Araújo, October 5, 1853, AN IJ6 216.
17. José Bento da Cunha Figueiredo to the Minister of Justice, October 21, 1853, AN IJ1 326, Pernambuco, Ofícios do Presidente da Província ao Ministro da Justiça (1853–1854).
18. The document is attached to the letter written by the Rio Chief of Police, Alexandre Joaquim de Sequeira, to the Minister of Justice, José Thomas Nabuco de Araújo, October 5, 1853, cited in the previous note. Both were kindly generously provided to us by Dale Graden. The photographic reproduction of the document was published in his book *From Slavery to Freedom in Brazil, Bahia, 1835–1900* (Albuquerque: University of New Mexico Press, 2006), 30–31.
19. Translated and annotated by Professor Paulo F. de Moraes Farias, for which we are deeply grateful.
20. Note by Paulo Farias: That is, except those who are their slaves, whom they could use as they wished.
21. Note by Paulo Farias: see also Q. 4:24, for the last lines.
22. Note by Paulo Farias: "Without pressure" is the best translation I can offer for the word *mahlā* that comes after the name "Hawa" ("Eve"\ "Eva"), which is the first word of line 15, page 1 of the original manuscript. This word does not seem to be one of those whose Arabic spelling is distorted in the manuscript, except for the indication of the accusative (which I presumed).
23. Note by Paulo Farias: An allusion to Q. 3:18 and Q. 4:166.
24. Note by Paulo Farias: It seems to be a mistake made by whoever wrote the text in Arabic (presumably Rufino), who forgot to add the letter *tā marbūṭa* to the end of the word, which would have given it the meaning of dowry (it could also be *al-ṣaduqa*, also with *tā marbūṭa* at the end, as in Q. 4:4, which also means dowry). In the grammatical context of the word in Rufino's sermon, the letter *tā marbūṭa* would be mute, which would have made it easily forgotten.
25. Note by Paulo Farias: *Fulān b. Fulān*, literally "X son of Y."
26. Note by Paulo Farias: It is not easy to translate this sentence word for word, above all if we try to follow the order of the words in the Arabic text.
27. Note by Paulo Farias: Literally, "Lord of the Two Worlds (this world and the next)."
28. See, for example, Abdullah Yusuf Ali's comments in *The Meaning of the Glorious Quran*, Cairo: Dar Al-Kitab Al-Masri Publisher/ Beirut: Dar Al-Kitab Allubnani, [1989?], vol. 1: 187. He is followed by Samir El Hayek in *Os significados do Alcorão Sagrado*, commented and translated by El Hayek, 11th ed. (São Paulo: Marsa M. Editora Jornalística Ltda., 2001), 111. If verse 24 omits the obligation of the slave woman/wife to be a Muslim, in the following verse that condition is required for a Muslim man to marry his slave woman.

29. See Bassir, "Marriage Rites among the Aku (Yoruba) of Freetown," *Africa*, 24: 3 (1954): 251–256.
30. Decree no. 1,144, September 11, 1861, in *Collecção das leis do imperio do Brasil de 1861*, Rio de Janeiro, Typographia Nacional, 1862, pp. 19–21.
31. *Correio Mercantil*, September 21, 1853; and "Auto de perguntas feitas ao preto forro Rufino José Maria," op. cit.
32. *Jornal do Commercio*, September 25, 1853. Conversion to Islam as a strategy for material improvement among the Hausas, for example, is discussed by Murray Last, "Some Economic Aspects of Conversion in Hausaland," in N. Levtzion, ed., *Conversion to Islam* (New York: Holmes & Meier, 1979), 236–246.
33. Nasr, *Tradução do Sentido do Nobre Alcorão*, 134.

Chapter 22

1. *Correio Mercantil*, September 21, 1853.
2. http://www.jornaldepoesia.jor.br/calve158.html. See also Maria Luiza Ferreira de Oliveira, "As guerras nas matas de Jacuípe," *Clio*, 33, no. 2 (2015): 100–138.
3. Victor de Oliveira to the Minister of Justice, January 18, 1852, APEJE, *Registro de Ofícios. Correspondência do Presidente da Província com o Ministro da Justiça*, vol. 4 (RO 4/4). Regarding the Ronco do Marimbondo, or Ronco da Abelha (Roar of the Bee), see Guillermo Palácios, "Revolta camponesa no Brasil escravista: a 'Guerra dos Marimbondos' (Pernambuco 1851–1852)"; Hebe Maria Mattos, "Identidade camponesa, racialização e cidadania no Brasil monárquico: o caso da Guerra dos Marimbondos em Pernambuco a partir da leitura de Guillermo Palácios"; and Maria Luiza Ferreira de Oliveira, "Sobreviver à pressão escapando ao controle: embates em torno da 'lei do cativeiro' (a Guerra dos Marimbondos em Pernambuco, 1851–1852)," all published in the *Almanak Braziliense*, 3 (2006), <www.almanak.usp.br>. See also Hamilton Monteiro, *Crise agrária e luta de classes* (Brasília: Horizonte, 1980); Silva, *A faina*, 218–227; Fábio Faria Mendes, "A economia moral do recrutamento militar no Império brasileiro," *Revista Brasileira de Ciências Sociais*, 13, no 38 (1998): 81–96; Botelho Tarcísio Rodrigues, "População e nação no Brasil do século XIX," PhD dissertation, Universidade de São Paulo, 1998, 38–40; and Renata Franco Saavedra, "População, recenseamento e conflito no Brasil imperial: o caso da Guerra dos Marimbondos," MA thesis, UNIRIO, 2011. Regarding the enslavement of free and freed black individuals in imperial Brazil, see Sidney Chalhoub, "The Politics of Silence: Race and Citizenship in Nineteenth-Century Brazil," *Slavery & Abolition*, 27, no. 1 (2006): 73–87, and, by the same author, *A força da escravidão: ilegalidade e costume no Brasil oitocentista* (São Paulo: Companhia das Letras, 2012).
4. Victor de Oliveira to the Minister of Justice, January 18, 1852, op. cit.; and *Relatorio que a Assembléa Legislativa Provincial de Pernambuco apresentou na sessão ordinaria do 1° de março de 1852 o excellentissimo presidente da mesma provincia, o dr. Victor de Oliveira* (Pernambuco: Typ. de M. F. de Faria, 1852).
5. President of the Province of Pernambuco to the Minister of Justice, April 22 and May 21, 1853, AN, IJ1 326, *Pernambuco, Ofícios do Presidente da Província ao Ministro da Justiça (1853–1854)*.
6. Amaro Quintas, *O sentido social da Revolução Praieira* (Recife: Editora da UFPE, 1977); Mário Márcio de Almeida, *Um homem contra o Império: Antônio Borges da Fonseca* (João Pessoa: União, 1994), 269–270; Vamireh Chacon, "Introdução," in *Autos do inquérito da Insurreição Praieira* [1849] (Brasília: Senado Federal, 1979), lxiii; *O Tribuno*, September 10, 1847; Almeida, *Um homem contra o Império*, 143. Regarding Borges da Fonseca's political activities in Rio during the reign of Pedro I, see Maria Lúcia de Souza Ricci, *A atuação política de um publicista: Antonio Borges da Fonseca* (Campinas: Pontifícia Universidade Católica, 1995), and Ribeiro, *A liberdade em construção*, 267–268. On the Praieira Rebellion, see Jeffrey C. Mosher, *Political Struggle, Ideology, and State Building: Pernambuco and the Construction of Brazil, 1817–1850*, Lincoln: University of Nebraska Press, 2008.
7. Autos do inquérito, 86.
8. President of the Province of Pernambuco to the Minister of Justice, April 22, 1853, NA, IJj1 326, *Pernambuco, Ofícios do Presidente da Província ao Ministro da Justiça (1853–1854)*.

9. Francisco Antonio Pereira da Silva, Chief Constable of the Second District of Recife, to the President of the Province, Recife, September 1, 1853; President of the Province of Pernambuco to the Minister of Justice, September 2, 1853, AN, IJ1 326, *Pernambuco, Ofícios do Presidente da Província ao Ministro da Justiça (1853-54)*; and João José Reis and Eduardo Silva, *Negociação e conflito: a resistência negra no Brasil escravista* (São Paulo: Companhia das Letras, 1989), 68 and 136, n. 19. Travelers Spix and Martius, *Viagem pelo Brasil*, 141, counted 35 saints' days on which, in addition to Sundays, "slaves are free from working for the masters and can act in their own interests." Obviously not all masters obeyed the Church in this regard.
10. Joaquim Eduardo Pina to the President of the Province of Pernambuco, September 1, 1853, APEJE, JM 11; and President of the Province of Pernambuco to the Minister of Justice, September 2, 1853, AN IJ1 326, *Pernambuco, Ofícios do Presidente da Província ao Ministro da Justiça (1853-1854)*.
11. President of the Province of Pernambuco to the Minister of Justice, September 1, 1853, AN IJ1 326, *Pernambuco, Ofícios do Presidente da Província ao Ministro da Justiça (1853-1854)*.
12. Captain Francisco Antonio de Souza Camizão to the President of the Province, Nazaré, September 24, 1853, AN IJ1 326, *Pernambuco. Ofícios do Presidente da Província ao Ministro da Justiça (1853-1854)*. See also Manoel da Cunha Wanderley to the President of the Province, September 4, 1853, APEJE, *Polícia Civil*, vol. 336.
13. President of the Province of Pernambuco to the Minister of Justice, Recife, September 3, 1853, AN, IJ1 326, *Pernambuco, Ofícios do Presidente da Província ao Ministro da Justiça (1853-1854)*.
14. Captain Francisco Antonio de Souza Camizão to the President of the Province, Nazaré, September 24, 1853, op. cit.; and José Bento da Cunha Figueiredo to the Minister of Justice, September 30, 1853, APEJE, *Registro de Ofícios. Correspondência do Presidente da Província com o Ministro da Justiça*, vol. 4 (RO 4/4). *Maracatu* is a popular Afro-Brazilian street festival characterized by dancing, drumming, and theater performed as a cortege. For the participants, *Maracatu* has a strong religious meaning.
15. President of the Province of Pernambuco to the Minister of Justice, September 13, 1853, APEJE, RO 4/4; and Manoel da Cunha Wanderley to the President of the Province, September 4, 1853, APEJE, *Polícia Civil*, vol. 336. See also Francisco Antonio Pereira da Silva, Chief Constable of the second district of Recife to the President of the Province, September 1, 1853; Manoel Teixeira Peixoto to the Preisdent of the Province, Pau d'Alho, September 1, 1853; and Francisco do Rego Albuquerque to the President of the Province, Pau d'Alho, September 1, 1853, NA IJ1 326, *Pernambuco, Ofícios do Presidente da Província ao Ministro da Justiça (1853-1854)*.
16. President of the Province of Pernambuco to the Minister of Justice, September 30, 1853, AN, IJ1, 326, *Pernambuco, Ofícios do Presidente da Província ao Ministro da Justiça (1853-1854)*.
17. Deputy Chief Constable Francisco Baptista de Almeida to the president of the province, September 5, 9 and 10, 1853, NA, IJ1 326, *Pernambuco, Ofícios do Presidente da Província ao Ministro da Justiça (1853-1854)*.

Chapter 23

1. Unlike Spanish America, where *moreno* meant black, in Brazil it meant—and still means—light-skinned, mixed-race individuals. However, in the context of this particular document, the term is clearly used to signify all persons of African descent.
2. Marcus J. M. de Carvalho, "Que crime é ser cismático? As transgressões de um pastor negro no Recife patriarcal, 1846," *Estudos Afro-Asiáticos*, 36 (2004): 97–122; and id., "'É fácil serem sujeitos de quem já foram senhores': o abc do Divino Mestre," *Afro-Ásia*, 31 (2004): 327–334.
3. Regarding the Sabinada, see Paulo César Souza, *A Sabinada: a revolta separatista da Bahia* (São Paulo: Brasiliense, 1987); Hendrik Kraay, "'As Terrifying as Unexpected': the Bahian Sabinada, 1837–1838," *The Hispanic American Historical Review*, 72, no. 4 (1992): 501–527; Douglas G. Leite, *Sabinos e diversos: emergências políticas e projetos de poder na revolta baiana de 1837* (Salvador: EGBA/Fundação Pedro Calmon, 2007); and Juliana Sezerdello Crespim Lopes, "Identidades políticas e raciais na Sabinada (Bahia, 1837–1838)," MA thesis, Universidade de São Paulo, 2008.

4. "Auto de perguntas feitas ao preto forro Rufino José Maria," op. cit. As we have seen, Rufino left Porto Alegre in December 1835, after obtaining his manumission.
5. *Correio Mercantil*, September 21, 1851.
6. Manoel Clementino Carneiro da Cunha to the President of the Province, September 10 and 13, 1853, AN, IJ1 326, *Pernambuco, Ofícios do Presidente da Província ao Ministro da Justiça (1853-1854)*.
7. *Diário de Pernambuco*, September 10, 1853, apud Gonsalves de Mello (comp.), *Diário de Pernambuco*, 72.
8. *Diário de Pernambuco*, October 4, 1847 and September 16, 1853, apud Gonsalves de Mello (comp.), *Diário de Pernambuco*, 64 and 71.
9. *Diário de Pernambuco*, September 19, 1853, apud Gonsalves de Mello (comp.), *Diário de Pernambuco*, p. 72.
10. *Relatório que à Assembleia Legislativa Provincial de Pernambuco apresentou no dia da abertura da sessão ordinária de 1854 o Exmo. Sr. Conselheiro Dr. José Bento da Cunha e Figueiredo, Presidente da mesma Província* (Pernambuco: Typographia de M. F. de Faria, 1854), 4–5.
11. *Correio Mercantil*, September 21 and 28, 1853. See also Costa e Silva, "Buying and Selling Korans," 86.
12. Regarding the deportation or threat of deportation of African "sorcerers" by the government of Bahia in the nineteenth century, see Reis, *Divining Slavery and Freedom*, 152–166; and regarding the deportation of freedmen suspected of being Muslims after the Revolt of the Malês in 1835, see Reis, *Rebelião escrava*, ch. 15.
13. *O Echo Pernambucano*, September 9, 1853.
14. *Chronica Nacional: Folhinha dos bons costumes para o anno de 1855* (Rio de Janeiro: Eduardo & Henrique Laemmert, 1855), 142–143.

Chapter 24

1. Al-Baghdádi, *Deleite do estrangeiro*. Al-Baghdádi's report has been known to specialists for some time, but was only recently translated into Portuguese by Paulo Farah. In Brazil, this report was first mentioned in Rosemarie Quiring-Zoche, "Luta religiosa ou luta política? O levante dos malês na Bahia segundo uma fonte islâmica," *Afro-Ásia*, 19–20 (2000): 229–238.
2. Al-Baghdádi, *Deleite do estrangeiro*, 114.
3. See Rolf Reichert, *Os documentos árabes do Arquivo Público do Estado da Bahia* (Salvador: Centro de Estudos Afro-Orientais da UFBA, 1970), for example, documents 21 and 29.
4. See, for example, Ryan, *Imale*, 164–176, regarding the Yoruba. These practices have also been observed in northern Africa and, for a long time, by European scholars. See Edward Westermarck, *Pagan Survivals in Mohammedan Civilisations* (London: Macmillan, 1933), esp. chap. 2. The complex Yoruba method of divination through Ifá is, according to some specialists, the result of the influence of Muslim divination methods using the *tessubá*. See, in this regard, Bernard Maupoil, *Contribution à l'étude de l'origine musulmane de la géomancie dans le Bas-Dahomey* (Paris: Imprimerie Protat Frères, 1945).
5. José Bento da Cunha Figueiredo to the Minister of Justice, September 13, 1853, AN, IJ1 326, *Pernambuco, Ofícios do Presidente da Província ao Ministro da Justiça (1853-1854)*.
6. Al-Baghdádi, *Deleite do estrangeiro*, 113–114.
7. See *Diário de Pernambuco*.
8. *Diário de Pernambuco*, October 20 and November 20, 1851, November 11, 1856, February 10, July 24, August 9 and 10, 1872, in Gonsalves de Mello (comp.), *Diário de Pernambuco*, 69–70, 74, 85–88. Regarding the Kings of Congo in Recife during that period, see Marcelo Mac Cord, *O Rosário de Dom Antonio: irmandades negras, alianças e conflitos na história social do Recife, 1848-1872* (Recife: Editora da UFPE/FAPESP, 2005).
9. *Relatorio que à Assemblea Legislativa Provincial de Pernambuco apresentou no dia da abertura da sessão ordinaria de 1857 o exmo. sr. conselheiro Sergio Teixeira de Macedo, presidente da mesma província* (Recife: Typ. de M.F. de Faria, 1857), 57.
10. José Bento da Cunha, President of Pernambuco, to Luiz Pereira do Couto Ferraz, Imperial Minister, March 24, 1856, in *Diário de Pernambuco*, May 7, 1856, apud Gonsalves de Mello (comp.), *Diário de Pernambuco*, 74–81.

11. *Diário de Pernambuco*, July 5, 6, and 7, 1877, *apud* Gonsalves de Mello (comp.), *Diário de Pernambuco*, 91–93.
12. "Ao público," *Diário de Pernambuco*, August 21, 1877, *apud* Gonsalves de Mello (comp.), *Diário de Pernambuco*, 93–94.
13. "Protesto contra os supostos do culto maometano," *Diário de Pernambuco*, August 28, 1877, *apud* Gonsalves de Mello (comp.), *Diário de Pernambuco*, 94–95.
14. "Explicação necessária," *Diário de Pernambuco*, August 29, 1877, *apud* Gonsalves de Mello, *Diário de Pernambuco*, 96–97.
15. "Aos supostos do maometismo," *Diário de Pernambuco*, September 4, 1877, *apud* Gonsalves de Mello (comp.), *Diário de Pernambuco*, 97–99.
16. "Aos malês de Aladino," *Diário de Pernambuco*, September 4, 1877, *apud* Gonsalves de Mello (comp.), *Diário de Pernambuco*, 99–100.
17. "Ao A. Limamo do Diário de 6 do corrente," *Diário de Pernambuco*, September 7, 1877, *apud* Gonsalves de Mello (comp.), *Diário de Pernambuco*, 97–99.
18. "Ao Ilmo. Sr. Dr. Chefe de Polícia interino," *Diário de Pernambuco*, December 18, 1877, *apud* Gonsalves de Mello (comp.), *Diário de Pernambuco*, 101.
19. *Diário de Pernambuco*, December 20, 1877, *apud* Gonsalves de Mello (comp.), *Diário de Pernambuco*, 102.
20. Those two priests also helped found the Ilê Axé Opô Afonjá *terreiros* in Rio de Janeiro and Bahia.
21. The story of Joaquim Vieira da Silva is recounted by Lisa Earl Castillo in "Entre memória, mito e história: viajantes transatlânticos da Casa Branca," in João José Reis and Elciene Azevedo (eds.), *Escravidão e suas sombras* (Salvador: Edufba, 2012), 65–110. Regarding ships that sailed from Recife to Lagos, *Diário de Pernambuco*, January 17 and December 18, 1874, July 25, 1877, January 24, 1878, and April 15, 1880, *apud* Gonsalves de Mello (comp.), *Diário de Pernambuco*, 89, 93, and 103, for example.

Epilogue

1. Cole, *The Krio of West Africa*, 49–51, regarding the Krio language.
2. Meet, for example, three remarkably prosperous freed Africans in Elaine Falheiros, "Luis e Antônio Xavier de Jesus: mobilidade social de africanos na Bahia oitocentista," MA thesis, Universidade Federal da Bahia, 2013; and João José Reis, "De escravo a rico liberto: a trajetória do africano Manoel Joaquim Ricardo na Bahia oitocentista," *Revista de História*, 174 (2016): 15–68. Other examples of a growing literature on African freedpersons in Bahia, prosperous or otherwise, are Oliveira, *O liberto*; Kátia Mattoso, *Testamentos de escravos libertos na Bahia no século XIX: uma fonte para o estudo de mentalidades* (Salvador: Centro de Estudos Baianos, 1979); Pierre Verger, *Os libertos: sete caminhos na liberdade de escravos da Bahia no século XIX* (São Paulo: Corrupio, 1992); Reis, *Divining Slavery and Freedom*; Lisa Earl Castillo and Luis Nicolau Parés, "Marcelina da Silva e seu mundo: novos dados para uma historiografia do candomblé ketu," *Afro-Ásia*, 36 (2007): 111–150; and Parés, "Milicianos, barbeiros e traficantesto, to cite just a few titles.
3. Deputy Chief Constable Francisco Baptista de Almeida to the president of the province, September 5, 1853 AN, IJ1 326, *Pernambuco, Ofícios do Presidente da Província ao Ministro da Justiça (1853–1854)*.
4. Martin, *Muslim Brotherhoods*, 16–17.
5. Regarding ways of operating and socially diverse clienteles like Rufino's, among Candomblé priests in Bahia, see Reis, *Divining Slavery and Freedom;* and Reis, "Candomblé in Nineteenth-Century Bahia: Priests, Followers, Clients," *Slavery & Abolition*, 22 no. 1 (2001): 116–134. For Rio, see the case studied by Gabriela dos Reis Sampaio, *Juca Rosa, um pai de santo na Corte imperial* (Rio de Janeiro: Arquivo Nacional, 2009).
6. Regarding that risk, see Lindsay, "'To Return to the Bosom of their Fatherland,'" 26–27; and Cunha, *Negros, estrangeiros*, 107.
7. See, for a few examples, Carretta, *Equiano the African*; Douglas Grant, *The Fortunate Slave: An Illustration of African Slavery in the Early Eighteenth Century* (London: Oxford University Press, 1968); Terry Alford, *Prince among Slaves: The True Story of an African Prince Sold into*

Slavery in the American South (New York: Oxford University Press, 1977); Paul Lovejoy, "Identidade e a miragem da etnicidade: a jornada de Mohammah Gardo Baquaqua para as Américas." *Afro-Ásia*, 27 (2002): 9–39; James H. Sweet, *Domingos Álvares, African Healing, and the Intellectual History of the Atlantic World* (Chapel Hill: University of North Carolina Press, 2011); Randy J. Sparks, *The Princes of Calabar: An Eighteenth-Century Atlantic Odyssey* (Cambridge, MA: Harvard University Press, 2004); and selected chapters in Lisa A. Lindsay and John Wood Sweet (eds.), *Biography and the Black Atlantic* (Philadelphia: Umiversity of Pennsylvania Press, 2014). Jerome Handler, "Survivors of the Middle Passage: Life Histories of Enslaved Africans in British America," *Slavery & Abolition*, 23, no. 1 (2002): 25–56, discusses the experiences of being captured and put aboard slave ships in Africa and crossing the Atlantic.

8. See, for example, the series "Polícia. Passaportes" in the APEBA, Seção Histórica, and Lisa Earl Castillo's use of those documents in "Entre memória e mito"; also Mônica Lima e Souza, "Entre margens: o retorno a África de libertos no Brasil, 1830–1870," PhD dissertation, Universidade Federal Fluminense, 2008.h

SOURCES AND WORKS CITED

Archives

Arquivo do Memorial da Medicina Brasileira, Universidade Federal da Bahia
Arquivo Histórico do Itamaraty (AHI)
Arquivo Histórico Ultramarinho (AHU)
Arquivo Municipal de Salvador (AMS)
Arquivo Histórico da Cúria Metropolitana de Porto Alegre (AHCMPa)
Arquivo Histórico do Rio Grande do Sul (AHRS)
Arquivo Nacional, Rio de Janeiro (AN)
Arquivo Nacional da Torre do Tombo, Lisbon (ANTT)
Arquivo Público Estadual Jordão Emerenciano, Recife (APEJE)
Arquivo Público do Estado da Bahia (APEB)
Arquivo Público do Estado do Rio Grande do Sul (APERGS)
Arquivo da Cúria Metropolitana de Salvador (ACMS)
Arquivo da Santa Casa de Misericórdia da Bahia (ASCM)
Biblioteca Municipal de Luanda
National Archives of Great Britain, London (NAGB)

Online Sources and Databanks

British Parliamentary Papers online. <http://ucsd.libguides.com/intlgovinfo/ukparliament>
Hemeroteca Digital, Biblioteca Nacional, Rio de Janeiro, Brasil. <http://bndigital.bn.gov.br/hemeroteca-digital/>
The Transatlantic Slave Trade Database <http://www.slavevoyages.ed/voyage/search>
william, Loney R. N.—Victorian Royal Surgeon <www.pdavis.nl/Legis_11.htm>

Newspapers and Magazines

Correio Mercantil (Recife)
Correio Mercantil (Salvador)
Diario de Pernambuco (Recife)
O Echo Pernambucano (Recife)
The Illustrated London News (London)
Jornal do Commercio (Rio de Janeiro)
Le Magasin Pittoresque (Paris)
O Mensageiro (Porto Alegre)

O Noticiador Catholico (Salvador)
O Riograndense (Rio Grande)
O Tribuno (Recife)

Other Printed Sources

Adams, Captain John. *Remarks on the Country Extending from Cape Palmas to the River Congo, Including Observations on the Manners and Customs of the Inhabitants*. London: G. and W. B. Whittaker, 1823.
Affaire de la Vigilante, batiment négrier de Nantes. Paris: Imprimerie de Capelet, 1823.
Ajayi, J. F. Ade. "Samuel Crowther of Ọ̀yọ́." In Philip Curtin (ed.), *Africa Remembered* (Madison: The University of Wisconsin Press, 1967): 289–316.
Al-baghdádi, 'Abdurrahman. *Deleite do estrangeiro em tudo o que é espantoso e maravilhoso*. Translated and annotated by Paulo Farah. Rio de Janeiro: Fundação Biblioteca Nacional; Argel: Bibliothèque Nationale d'Algérie, 2007.
Ali, Abdullah Yusuf. *The Meaning of the Glorious Quran*. Cairo: Dar Al-Kitab Al-Masri Publisher; Beirut: Dar Al-Kitab Allubnani, s/d.
Al Quayrawani. *La Risâla:épitre sur les éléments du dogme et de la loi de l'Islam selon le rite malikite*. Paris: Editions IQRA, 1996.
Almanach para o ano de 1845. Bahia: Typ. de M. A. da S. Serva, 1844.
Autos do inquérito da Insurreição Praieira. Brasília: Senado Federal, 1979 [orig. 1849].
Baquaqua, Mahommah Gardo. *The Biography of Mahommah Gardo Baquaqua: His Passage from Slavery to Freedom in África and America*. Edited and annotated by Robin Law and Paul Lovejoy. Princeton: Marcus Wiener, 2001 [orig. 1854].
Baquaqua, Mahommah Gardo. *An Interesting Narrative: Biography of Mahommah G. Baquaqua*. Compiled by Samuel Moore. Detroit: Tribune Office, 1854.
Burton, Richard. *Wanderings in West Africa*. New York: Dover, 1991 [orig. 1862].
Bowen, Thomas. *Adventures and Missionary Labours in Several Countries in the Interior of Africa from 1849 to 1856*. London: Frank Cass, 1978 [orig. 1857].
Chamberlain, Henry. *Vistas e costumes de cidade e arredores do Rio de Janeiro em 1819–1820*. Rio de Janeiro: Livraria Kosmos Editora/São Paulo: Erich Eichner & Cia. Ltda, 1943.
Chronica Nacional: Folhinha dos bons costumes para o anno de 1855, contendo elementos de éthica, uma colleção de máximas novas, assim como a Chronica Nacional e entre as noticias curiosas e interessantes uma descripção authentica do terremoto de Lisboa de 1755: 16º anno. Rio de Janeiro: Eduardo & Henrique Laemmert, 1855.
Clarke, Robert. *Sierra Leone. A description of the Manners and Customs of the Liberated Africans; with observations upon the Natural History of the Colony, and a Notice of the Native Tribes, &c. &c.* London: James Ridgway; Holborn, Johnson & Co., 1843.
Collecção das leis do Imperio do Brasil de 1861. Rio de Janeiro: Typographia Nacional, 1862.
Colleção das Leis do Brazil de 1813. Rio de Janeiro: Imprensa Nacional, 1890.
Crowther, Samuel Ajayi. "The Narrative of Samuel Ajayi Crowther." Introduced and annotated by J. F. Ade Ajayi. In Philip D. Curtin (ed.), *Africa Remembered: Narratives by West Africans from the Era of the Slave Trade*. Long Grove: Waveland Press, 1967, 289–316.
Drake, Richard. *Revelations of a Slave Smuggler*. New York: Robert M. De Witt, Publisher, 1860.
Dreys, Nicolao. *Noticia descriptiva da Província do Rio Grande de São Pedro do Sul*. Porto Alegre: Livraria Americana, 1927 [orig. 1839].
Equiano, Olaudah. *The Life of Olaudah Equiano*. Edited by Paul Edwards. Essex: Longman, 1989 [1789].
Expilly, Charles. *Mulheres e costumes do Brasil*, 2ª Ed., São Paulo: Editora Nacional, Brasília, 1977.
Folhinha de Algibeira. Recife: Typografia M. F. de Faria, 1853.
Gilliland, C. Herbert. *Voyage to a Thousand Cares: Master's Mate Lawrence with the African Squadron, 1844–1846*. Annapolis: Naval Institute Press, 2004.

Graham, Maria [Lady Maria Callcott]. *Journal of a voyage to Brazil and residence there, during part of the years 1821, 1822, 1823.* London: Longman, Hurst, Rees, Orme, Brown, and Green, 1824.
Gréhan, Amédée. *La France Maritime.* Paris: Postel, 1837.
Hewett, J. F. Napier. *European Settlements in the West Coast of Africa; with Remarks on the Slave-Trade and the Supply of Cotton.* New York: Negro Universities Press, 1969 [orig. 1862].
Hill, Pascoe Grenfell. *Cinquenta dias a bordo de um navio negreiro.* Rio de Janeiro: José Olympio, 2008 [orig. 1848].
Holman, James. *Travels in Madeira, Sierra Leone, Teneriffe.* London: George Routledge, 1840.
Isabelle, Arséne. *Viagem ao Rio da Prata e ao Rio Grande do Sul.* Rio de Janeiro: Livraria Editora Zelio Valverde, 1949 [orig. 1835].
Kidder, Daniel P.; and Fletcher, J. C. *Brazil and the Brazilians: Historical and Descriptive Sketches.* Philadelphia: Childs and Petterson; Boston: Phillips, Sampson & Co., 1857.
Koelle, Sigismund Wilhel. *Polytglotta Africana.* Graz: Akademische Druck—U. Verlagsanstalt, 1963 [orig. 1854].
Livingstone, David and Charles. *Narrative of an Expedition to the Zambesi and its Tributaries; and of the Discovery of the Lakes Shirwa and Nyassa, 1858–1864.* London: John Murray, 1865.
Matson, James Henry. *Remarks on the Slave Trade and the African Squadron.* 4th ed., London: James Ridgeway, 1848.
Mello, José Antônio Gonsalves de (compilador). *Diário de Pernambuco: economia e sociedade no 2º Reinado.* Recife: Editora da Ufpe, 1996.
Melville, Elizabeth Helen, [A Lady]. *A Residence at Sierra Leone, described from a journal kept on the spot, and from letters written to friends.* London: John Murray, 1849.
Menezes, Joaquim José de Carvalho e. *Demonstração Geographica e Política do Territorio Portuguez na Guine Inferior, que abrange o Reino de Angola, Benguella, e suas Dependências, causas da sua decadência e atrasamento, suas conhecidas producções e os meios que se podem applicar para o seu melhoramento e utilidade geral da nação.* Rio de Janeiro: Typ. Classica de F. A. de Almeida, 1848.
Museu e Archivo Histórico do Rio Grande do Sul. *Documentos interessantes para o estudo da grande Revolução de 1835–1845.* Porto Alegre: Museu e Arquivo Histórico do Rio Grande do Sul, 1930.
Pocock, W. Innes. *Five Views of the Island of St. Helena.* London: S. and J. Fuller, 1815.
Prior, James. *Voyage along the Eastern Coast of Africa to Mosambique, Johanna, and Quiloa, to St. Helena, to Rio de Janeiro, Bahia, and Pernambuco in Brazil, in the Nisus Frigate.* London: Richard Phillips and Co., 1819.
Quiller-Couch, Arthur Thomas (ed.). *The Story of the Sea.* London: Cassell and Co., 1895–1896.
Rankin, F. Harrison. *The White Man's Grave: A Visit to Sierra Leone in 1834.* 2 vols. London: Richard Bentley, 1836.
Relatorio que à Assemblea Legislativa Provincial de Pernambuco apresentou no dia da abertura da sessão ordinaria de 1857 o exm. sr. conselheiro Sergio Teixeira de Macedo, presidente da mesma província. Recife: Typ. de M. F. de Faria, 1857.
Rugendas, Johann Moritz. *Malerische Reise in Brasilien.* Paris: Engelmann & Cie., 1835.
Sá da Bandeira, Marquês de. *O tráfico da escravatura e o Bill de Lord Palmerston.* Lisbon: Ulmeiro, 1997 [orig. 1840].
Saint-Hilaire, Auguste de. *Viagem ao Rio Grande do Sul.* Porto Alegre: Erus, 1987.
Société de la Morale Chrétienne. *Faits relatifs a la traite des noirs.* Paris: Imprimerie de Chapelet, 1826.
Spix, Johan Baptist von; and Martius, Karl Frederich von. *Viagem pelo Brasil, 1817–1820.* Belo Horizonte: Itatiaia; São Paulo: EDUSP, 1981 [orig. 1823–1831].
Tams, George. *Visita às possessões portuguezas na costa occidental d'Africa.* Oporto: Typographia da Revista, 1850.
Tollenare, L. F. *Notas dominicais.* Salvador: Progresso, 1956.
Tucker Sarah. *Abeokuta; or, sunrise within the tropics: an outline of the origin and progress of the Yoruba mission.* London: James Nisbet and Co., 1853.

Walsh, Robert. *Notices of Brazil (1828 and 1829)*. 2 vols. London: Frederick Westley and A. H. Davis, 1830.
Wendroth, Herman Rudolf. *O Rio Grande do Sul em 1852: aquarelas*. Porto Alegre: Governo do Rio Grande do Sul, 1983.

Works Cited

Abraham, R. C. *Dictionary of Modern Yoruba*. London: University of London Press, 1958.
Abreu, Martha. *O Império do Divino: festas religiosas e cultura popular no Rio de Janeiro, 1830–1900*. Rio de Janeiro: Nova Fronteira, 1999.
Adamu, Mahdi. "The Delivery of Slaves from the Central Sudan to the Bight of Benin." In Henry A. Gemery and Jan S. Hogendorn (eds.), *The Uncommon Market*. New York: Academic Press, 1979: 163–180.
Aderley, Rosanne Marion. *"New Negroes from Africa": Slave Trade Abolitionism and Free African Settlement in the Nineteenth-Century Caribbean*. Bloomington: Indiana University Press, 2006.
Agualusa, José Eduardo. *Nação crioula*. Lisbon: TV Guia, 1997.
Ajayi, J. F. Ade. "The Aftermath of the Fall of Òyó." In J. F. Ade Ajayi and M. Crowder (eds.), *History of West Africa*. London: Longman, 1974: ii, 129–166.
Akinjogbin, I. A. "Wars in Yorubaland, 1793–1893: An Analytical Categorisation." In Adeagbo Akinjogbin (ed.), *War and Peace in Yorubaland, 1793–1893*. Ibadan: Heineman Nigeria, 1998: 33–52.
Alagoa, E. J. "Long-Distance Trade and States in the Niger Delta." *The Journal of African History*, 11, no. 3 (1970): 319–329.
Aladrén, Gabriel. *Liberdades negras nas paragens do sul: alforria e inserção social de libertos em Porto Alegre, 1800–1835*. Rio de Janeiro: Editora FGV, 2009.
Albuquerque, Aline Emanuelle de Biase. "De 'Angelo dos Retalhos' a Visconde de Loures: a trajetória de um traficante de escravos (1818-1858)", MA thesis, Universidade Federal de Pernambuco, 2016.
Alencastro, Luiz Felipe de. *O trato dos viventes: formação do Brasil no Atlântico Sul*. São Paulo: Companhia das Letras, 2000.
Alencastro, Luiz Felipe de. "La dérive des continents: l'indépendance du Brésil (1822), le Portugal et l'Afrique." Paper presented to the conference "L'éxpérience coloniale: dynamiques des échanges dans les espaces atlantiques à l'époque de l'esclavage." Nantes, June 20–22, 2005.
Alencastro, Luiz Felipe de. "Le versant brésilien de l'Atlantique-Sud: 1500–1850." *Annales: Histoire, Sciences Sociales* 2 [61ᵉ année] (2006): 339–382.
Alencastro, Luiz Felipe de. "The Economic Network of Portugal's Atlantic World." In Francisco Bethencour and D. Ramada Curto (eds.), *Portuguese Oceanic Expansion,1400–1800*. Cambridge: Cambridge University Press, 2007: 109–137.
Alford, Terry. *Prince among Slaves: The True Story of an African Prince Sold into Slavery in the American South*. New York: Oxford University Press, 1977.
Algranti, Leila. *O feitor ausente: estudos de escravidão urbana no Rio de Janeiro, 1808–1821*. Rio de Janeiro: Vozes, 1988.
Almeida, Mário Márcio de. *Um homem contra o Império: Antônio Borges da Fonseca*. João Pessoa: Editora União, 1994.
Amaral, Braz do. *História da independência na Bahia*. Salvador: Progresso, 1957.
Andrade, Maria José da Silva. *A mão-de-obra escrava em Salvador de 1811 a 1860*. São Paulo: Corrupio, 1988.
Asiegbu, Johnson U. J. *Slavery and the Politics of Liberation, 1787–1861: A Study of Liberated African Emigration and British Anti-slavery Policy*. New York: African Publishing Corporation, 1969.
Bakos, Margareth M. "A escravidão negra e os Farroupilhas." In Sandra Pesavento (ed.), *A Revolução Farroupilha*. Porto Alegre: Mercado Aberto, 1997: 79–97.
Barreto, Juliana, et al. *Cidades negras. Africanos, crioulos e espaços urbanos no Brasil escravista do século xix*. São Paulo: Alameda, 2006.

Barry, Jack. *A Dictionary of Sierra Leone Krio* (1966). Access 4 January 2007: eric—Education Resources Information Center, n° ed012454.
Basile, Marcelo. "Projetos de Brasil e a construção nacional na imprensa fluminense (1831–1835)." In Marco Morel, Lucia Maria Bastos P., Neves and Tania Maria Bessone da C. Ferreira (eds.), *História e imprensa: representações culturais e práticas de poder.* Rio de Janeiro: dp&a/faperj, 2006: 60–93.
Bassir, Olumbe. "Marriage Rites among the Aku (Yoruba) of Freetown." *Africa*, 24, no. 3 (1954): 251–256.
Basto, Artur de Magalhães. "O Pôrto contra Junot." *Revista de Estudos Históricos* (Porto), 1, no. 4 (1924): 121–147.
Behrendt, Stephen D. "Crew Mortality in the Transatlantic Slave Trade in the Eighteenth Century." *Slavery & Abolition*, 18, no. 1 (1997): 49–71.
Bethell, Leslie. "Britain, Portugal and the Supression of the Brazilian Slave Trade: The Origins of Lord Palmerston's Act of 1839." *English Historical Review*, 80 (1965): 761–784.
Bethell, Leslie. "The Mixed Commissions for the Suppression of the Transatlantic Slave Trade in the Nineteenth Century." *Journal of African History*, 7, no. 1 (1966): 79–93.
Bethell, Leslie. *The abolition of the Brazilian Slave Trade: Britain, Brazil and the Slave Trade Question.* Cambridge: Cambridge University Press, 1970.
Bolster, W. Jeffrey. *Black Jacks: African American Seamen in the Age of Sail.* Cambridge, MA: Harvard University Press, 1997.
Botelho, Tarcísio Rodrigues. "População e nação no Brasil do século xix." PhD dissertation, Universidade de São Paulo, 1998.
Braidwood, Stephen J. *Black Poor and White Philanthropists: London's Black and the Foundation of the Sierra Leone Settlement.* Liverpool: Liverpool University Press, 1994.
Brown, Vincent. *The Reaper's Garden: Death and Power in the World of Atlantic Slavery.* Cambridge, MA: Harvard University Press, 2008.
Campbell, Mavis. *The Maroons of Jamaica, 1655–1796: A History of Resistance, Colaboration and Betrayal.* Trenton, NJ: Africa World Press, 1990
Candido, Mariana P. *An African Slaving Port and the Atlantic World: Benguela and its Hinterland.* Cambridge: Cambridge University Press, 2013.
Candido, Mariana P. "Enslaving Frontiers: Slavery, Trade and Identity in Benguela, 1780–1850." PhD dissertation, York University, 2006.
Capela, José. *As burguesias portuguesas e a abolição do tráfico da escravatura, 1810–1842.* Oporto: Afrontamento, 1979.
Carretta, Vincent. *Equiano the African: Biography of a Self-Made Man.* Athens: The University of Georgia Press, 2005.
Carvalho, Daniela Vallandro de. "Experiências negras de recrutamento, guerra e escravidão: Rio Grande de São Pedro, c. 1835–1850." PhD dissertation, Universidade Federal do Rio de Janeiro, 2013.
Carvalho, Marcus J. M. de. *Liberdade: rotinas e rupturas do escravismo, Recife, 1822–1850.* Recife: Editora da Ufpe, 1998.
Carvalho, Marcus J. M. de. "Que crime é ser cismático? As transgressões de um pastor negro no Recife patriarcal, 1846." *Estudos Afro-Asiáticos*, 36 (2000): 97–122.
Carvalho, Marcus J. M. de. "De portas adentro e de portas afora: trabalho doméstico e escravidão no Recife, 1822–1850." *Afro-Ásia*, 29/39 (2003): 41–78.
Carvalho, Marcus J. M. de. "'É fácil serem sujeitos de quem já foram senhores': o abc do Divino Mestre." *Afro-Ásia*, 31 (2004): 327–334.
Carvalho, Marcus J. M. de. "O 'galego atrevido' e 'malcriado', a 'mulher honesta' e o seu marido, ou política provincial, violência doméstica e Justiça no Brasil escravista." In Rachel Sohiet, Maria Fernanda Bicalho, and Maria de Fátima Gouveia (eds.), *Ensaios de história cultural, história política e ensino de história.* Rio de Janeiro: Faperj/Mauad, 2005: 201–234.
Castillo, Lisa Earl. "Entre memória, mito e história: viajantes transatlânticos da Casa Branca." In João José Reis and Elciene Azevedo (eds.), *Escravidão e suas sombras.* Salvador: EDUFBA, 2012: 65–110.

Castillo, Lisa Earl, and Parés, Luis Nicolau. "Marcelina da Silva e seu mundo: novos dados para uma historiografia do candomblé ketu." *Afro-Ásia*, 36 (2007): 111–150.

Castro, Yeda Pessoa de. *Falares africanos na Bahia*. 2ª ed. Rio de Janeiro: Topbooks/ABL, 2005.

Chacon, Vamireh. "Introdução." In *Autos do inquérito da Insurreição Praieira*. Brasília: Senado Federal, 1979: i–cxii.

Chalhoub, Sidney. *Visões da liberdade: os últimos anos da escravidão na corte*. São Paulo: Companhia das Letras, 1989.

Chalhoub, Sidney. "The politics of silence: race and citizenship in Nineteenth-Century Brazil." *Slavery and Abolition*, 27, no. 1 (2006): 73–87.

Chalhoub, Sidney. *A força da escravidão: ilegalidade e costume no Brasil oitocentista*. São Paulo: Companhia das Letras, 2012.

Chebel, Malek. *Dictionaire des symboles musulmans*. Paris: Albin Michel, 1995.

Christopher, Emma. *Slave Ship Sailors and their Captive Cargoes, 1730–1807*. Cambridge: Cambridge University Press, 2006.

Cole, Gibril R. *The Krio of West Africa: Islam, Culture, Creolization and Colonialism in Nineteenth-Century*. Athens: Ohio University Press, 2013.

Cole, Gibril R. "Liberated Slaves and Islam in Nineteenth-Century West Africa." In T. Falola and M. Childs (eds.), *The Yoruba Diaspora in the Atlantic World*. Bloomington: Indiana University Press, 2004: 383–403.

Comissoli, Adriano. "O juiz de dentro: magistratura e ascensão social no extremo sul do Brasil 1808–1831." *Redos: Revista do Corpo Discente do Programa de Pós Graduação em História da Ufrgs*, 2, no. 4 (2009): 24–34.

Conrad, Robert Edgar. *Children of God's Fire: A Documentary History of Black Slavery in Brazil*. Princeton: Princeton University Press, 1983.

Conrad, Robert Edgar. *Tumbeiros, o tráfico de escravos para o Brasil*. São Paulo: Brasiliense, 1985.

Corrado Jacopo. "The Rise of a New Consciousness: Early Euro-African Voices of Dissent in Colonial Angola". *e-Journal of Portuguese History*, 5, no. 2 (2007). http://www.ejph/v5n2/v5n2a03.

Costa, Francisco Augusto Pereira da. *Anais Pernambucanos*. 6 vols. Recife: Fundarpe, 1983–1985.

Crooks, J. J. *A History of the Colony of Sierra Leone, Western África*. London: Frank Cass, 1972 [orig. 1903].

Cunha, Manuela Carneiro da. *Negros, estrangeiros: os escravos libertos e sua volta à África*. São Paulo: Brasiliense, 1985.

Curto, José. *Álcool e escravos: o comércio luso-brasileiro do álcool em Mpinda, Luanda e Benguela durante o tráfico atlântico de escravos (c. 1480–1830) e o seu impacto nas sociedades da África Central Ocidental*. Lisbon: Vulgata, 2002.

Curto, José. "Resistência à escravidão na África: o caso dos escravos fugitivos recapturados em Angola, 1846–1876." *Afro-Ásia*, 33 (2005): 67–86.

Curto, José, and Raymond R. Gervais. "A história da população de Luanda no período final do tráfico transatlântico de escravos, 1781–1844." *Africana Studia*, 5 (2002): 75–130.

Danmole, Hakeem Olumide. "The Frontier Emirate: A History of Islam in Ilorin." Phd dissertation, University of Birmingham, 1980.

Davis, Natalie Zemon. *Slaves on Screen: Film and Historical Vision*. Cambridge, MA: Harvard University Press, 2000.

Dias, Jill. "Angola." In Joel Serrão and A. H. de Oliveira Marques (coord.). *Nova história da expansão portuguesa*. x: *O império africano, 1825–1890*. Part 2. Valentim Alexandre and Jill Dias (eds.) Lisbon: Estampa, 1998: 349–367.

Dobronravin, Nikolay. "Escritos multilingües em caracteres árabes: novas fontes de Trinidad e Brasil no século xix." *Afro-Ásia*, 31 (2004): 297–326.

Dobronravin, Nikolay. "Literacy Among Muslims in Nineteenth-Century Trindad and Brazil." In Behnaz A. Mirzai, Ismael M. Montana and Paul Lovejoy (eds.). *Slavery, Islam, and Diaspora*. Trenton: África World Press, 2009: 217–236.

Dobronravin, Nikolay. "Não só mandingas: *Qaṣīdat al-Burda*, poesia ascética (*zuhdiyyāt*) e as *Maqāmāt* de al-Ḥarīrī nos escritos dos negros muçulmanos no Brasil oitocentista." *Afro-Ásia*, 53 (2016): 185–226.
Domingues, Daniel Barros and, David Eltis. "The Slave Trade to Pernambuco, 1561–1851." In David Eltis and David Richardson (eds.), *Extending the Frontiers: Essays on the New Transatlantic Slave Trade Database*. New Haven and London: Yale University Press, 2008: 95–129.
"dossiê—'Para inglês ver'? Revisitando a Lei de 1831," edited by Beatriz Mamigonian and Keila Gringer. In *Estudos Afro-Asiáticos*, 29, no. 1, 2, and 3 (2007): 87–340.
Edmundo, Luís. *O Rio de Janeiro no tempo dos vice-reis, 1763–1808*. Brasília: Senado Federal, 2000.
Elbl, Ivana. "The Horse in Fifteenth-Century Senegambia." *International Journal of African Historical Studies*, 28, no. 1 (1991): 85–109.
El-kareh, Almir Chaiban El-Kareh. "A Companhia Brasileira de Paquetes a Vapor e a centralidade do poder monárquico." *História Econômica & História de Empresas*, 2 (2002): 7–27.
Eltis, David. *Economic Growth and the Ending of the Transatlantic Slave Trade*. New York and Oxford: Oxford University Press, 1987.
Eltis, David. *The Rise of African Slavery in the Americas*. Cambridge: Cambridge University Press, 2000.
Eltis, David. "The Diaspora of Yoruba Speakers, 1650–1865: dimensions and implications." In T. Falola and M. Childs (eds.), *The Yoruba Diaspora in the Atlantic World*. Bloomington: Indiana University Press, 2005: 17–39.
Eltis, David, and David Richardson. *Atlas of the Transatlantic Slave Trade*. New Haven: Yale University Press, 2010.
Escorel, Silvia. "Vestir poder e poder vestir: o tecido social e a trama cultural nas imagens do traje negro (Rio de Janeiro—século xviii)." MA thesis, Universidade Federal do Rio de Janeiro, 2000.
Falheiros, Elaine. "Luis e Antônio Xavier de Jesus: mobilidade social de africanos na Bahia oitocentista." MA thesis, Universidade Federal da Bahia, 2013.
Falola, Toyin. *A Mouth Sweeter than Salt: An African Memoir*. Ann Arbor: University of Michigan Press, 2004.
Farias, Juliana Barreto. "Mercados minas: africanos ocidentais na Praça do Mercado do Rio de Janeiro, 1830-1890." PhD dissertation, Universidade Federal do Rio de Janeiro, 2013.
Farias, Juliana Barreto. "Ardis da liberdade: trabalho urbano, alforrias e identidades." In Mariza de Carvalho Soares (ed.), *Rotas atlânticas da diáspora africana: da baía do Benim ao Rio de Janeiro*. Niterói: EDUFF, 2007: 225–256.
Farias, Juliana Barreto, Carlos Eugênio L. Soares, and Flávio dos Santos Gomes. *No labirinto das nações: africanos e identidades no Rio de Janeiro, século xix*. Rio de Janeiro: Arquivo Nacional, 2005.
Ferreira, Roquinaldo Amaral. *Cross-Cultural Exchange in the Atlantic World: Angola and Brazil during the Era of the Slave Trade*. Cambridge: Cambridge University Press, 2012.
Ferreira, Roquinaldo Amaral. "Dos Sertões ao Atlântico: tráfico ilegal de escravos e comércio lícito em Angola, 1830-1860." MA thesis, Universidade Federal do Rio de Janeiro, 1996.
Ferreira, Roquinaldo Amaral "Fazendas em troca de escravos: circuitos de créditos nos Sertões de Angola, 1830–1860." *Revista Estudos Afro-Asiáticos*, 32 (1997): 76–96.
Ferreira, Roquinaldo Amaral. "Escravidão e revoltas de escravos em Angola (1830–1860)." *Afro-Ásia*, 21/22 (1998-99): 9–44.
Ferreira, Roquinaldo Amaral."Transforming Atlantic Slaving: Trade, Warfare and Territorial Control in Angola, 1650-1800." PhD dissertation, University of California/Los Angeles, 2003.
Ferreira, Roquinaldo Amaral. "Abolicionismo e fim do tráfico de escravos em Angola, séc. XIX." *Cadernos do CHDD*, Special Number (2005): 159–176.
Ferreira, Roquinaldo Amaral. "Biografia, mobilidade e cultura atlântica: a micro-escala do tráfico de escravos em Benguela, séculos XVIII–XIX." *Tempo*, 20 (2006): 33–59.

Ferreira, Roquinaldo Amaral. "'Ilhas crioulas': o significado plural da mestiçagem cultural na África atlântica." *Revista de História*, 155 (2006): 17–41.
Ferreira, Roquinaldo Amaral."The Suppression of the Slave Trade and Slave Departures from Angola, 1830s–1860s." In David Eltis and David Richardson (eds.), *Extending the Frontiers: Essays on the New Transatlantic Slave Trade Database*. New Haven and London: Yale University Press, 2008: 313–334.
Ferretti, Sergio. *Querebentan de Zomadonu: etnografia da Casa das Minas*. São Luis, Edufma, 1985.
Figueiredo, Betânia Gonçalves. "Barbeiros e cirurgiões: atuação dos práticos ao longo do século XIX." *História, Ciências e Saúde—Manguinhos*, 6, no. 2 (1999): 277–291.
Figueiredo, Betânia Gonçalves. *A arte de curar: cirurgiões, médicos, boticários e curandeiros no século XIX em Minas Gerais*. Belo Horizonte: Argumentum, 2008.
Florentino, Manolo. *Em costas negras: uma história do tráfico de escravos entre a África e o Rio de Janeiro*. São Paulo: Companhia das Letras, 1997.
Florentino, Manolo. "Alforria e etnicidade no Rio de Janeiro oitocentista: notas de pesquisa." *Topoi*, 5 (2002): 25–40.
Florentino, Manolo. "Slave Trading and Slave Traders in Rio de Janeiro, 1790–1830." In José C. Curto and Paul Lovejoy (eds.), *Enslaving Connections: Changing Cultures of Africa and Brazil During the Era of Slavery*. Amherst: Humanity Books, 2004: 59–79.
Franco, José Luciano. *Comercio clandestino de esclavos*. Havana: Editorial de Ciencias Sociales, 1980.
Frank, Zephyr. *Dutra's World: Wealth and Family in Nineteenth-Century Rio de Janeiro*. Albuquerque: University of New Mexico Press, 2004.
Freyre, Gilberto. *Os escravos nos anúncios de jornais brasileiros do século xix*. 2ª ed. São Paulo: Editora Nacional; Recife: Instituto Joaquim Nabuco de Pesquisas Sociais, 1979.
Fyfe, Christopher. *A History of Sierra Leone*. London: Oxford University Press, 1962.
Gallagher, J. "Fowell Buxton and the New African Policy, 1838–1842." *Cambridge Historical Journal*, 10, no. 1 (1950): 36–58.
García Martinez, Orlando, and Michael Zeuske. *La sublevación esclava en la goleta Amistad: Ramón Ferrer y las redes de contrabando en el mundo atlántico*. Havana: Ediciones Unión, 2012.
Gayibor, N. L. "Les Villes négrières de l'ancienne Côte des Esclave d'Ada à Grand-Popo." In Robin Law and Silke Strickrodt (eds.), *Ports of the Slave Trade (Bights of Benin and Biafra)*, Occasional Paper Number 6 Center for Commonwealth Studies. Stirling: University of Stirling, 1999: 35–47.
Gomes, Flávio dos Santos. *Experiências atlânticas: ensaios e pesquisas sobre a escravidão e o pós-emancipação no Brasil*. Passo Fundo: Editora da Universidade de Passo Fundo, 2003.
Gomes, Flávio dos Santos, Carlos Eugênio Líbano Soares, and Juliana Barreto Farias. "Primeiras reflexões sobre travessias e retornos: cabindas, redes do tráfico e diásporas num Rio de Janeiro atlântico." *Textos de História*, 12, no. 1/2 (2004): 65–105.
Gomes, Telmo. *Navios Portugueses século XIV a XIX. A memória do passado, uma referência para o futuro*. Lisbon: INAPA, 1995.
Goulart, Mauricio. *A escravidão africana no Brasil (das origens a extinção do tráfico)*. São Paulo: Ômega, 1975.
Graden, Dale. *Disease, Resistance, and Lies: The Demise of the Transatlantic Slave Trade to Brazil and Cuba*. Baton Rouge: Louisiana State University Press, 2014.
Graden, Dale. *From Slavery to Freedom in Brazil, Bahia, 1835–1900*. Albuquerque: University of New Mexico Press, 2006.
Grant, Douglas. *The Fortunate Slave: An Illustration of African Slavery in the Early Eighteenth Century*. London: Oxford University Press, 1968.
Gudeman, Stephen, and Stuart Schwartz. "Purgando o pecado original: compadrio e batismo de escravos na Bahia no século xviii." In João José Reis (ed.), *Escravidão e invenção da liberdade: estudos sobre o negro no Brasil*. São Paulo: Brasiliense, 1988: 33–59.
Handler, Jerome. "Survivors of the Middle Passage: Life Histories of Enslaved Africans in British America." *Slavery & Abolition*, 23, no. 1 (2002): 25–56.

Harrell-Bond, Barbara E., Allen M. Howard, and David E. Skinner. *Community Leadership and the Transformation of Freetown (1801–1976)*. The Hague: Mouton, 1978.

Hartman, Saidiya. *Lose your Mother: A Journey Along the Atlantic Slave Route*. New York: Farrar, Straus and Giroux, 2007.

Hébrard, Jean. "Esclavage et dénomination: imposition et appropriation d'un nom chez les esclaves de la Bahia au xixe siècle." *Cahiers du Brésil Contemporain*, no. 53–54 (2003): 31–92.

Hiskett, Mervyn. *The Sword of the Truth: the Life and Times of the Shehu Usuman dan Fodio*. New York: Oxford University Press, 1973.

Holloway, Thomas H. *Polícia no Rio de Janeiro: repressão e resistência numa cidade do século xix*. Rio de Janeiro: Fundação Getúlio Vargas, 1997.

Hutter, Lucy Maffei. *Navegação nos séculos XVII e XVIII. Rumo: Brasil*. São Paulo: EDUSP, 2005.

Karasch, Mary. *Vida dos escravos no Rio de Janeiro, 1808–1850*. São Paulo: Companhia das Letras, 2000.

Kiddy, Elizabeth W. *Blacks of the Rosary: Memory and History in Minas Gerais, Brazil*. University Park: The Pennsylvania State University Press, 2005.

Kiddy, Elizabeth W. "Who Is the King of Congo? A New Look at African and Afro-Brazilian Kings in Brazil." In Linda M. Heywood (ed.), *Central Africans and Cultural Transformations in the American Diaspora*. Cambridge: Cambridge University Press, 2002: 153–182.

Kipple, Kenneth F., and Brian T. Higgins. "Mortality Caused by Dehydration During the Middle Passage." In Joseph E. Inikori and Stanley L. Engerman (eds.), *The Atlantic Slave Trade: Effects on Economies, Societies and Peoples in Africa, the Americas, and Europe*. Durham: Duke University Press, 1992: 321–337.

Klein, Herbert. *The Middle Passage: Comparative Studies in the Atlantic Slave Trade*. Princeton: Princeton University Press, 1978.

Klein, Herbert, and Stanley L. Enferman. "Long-Term Trends in African Mortality in the Transatlantic Slave Trade." *Slavery & Abolition*, 18, no. 1 (1997): 36–48.

Klein, Herbert, Stanley L. Engerman, Robin Haines, and Ralph Shilomowitz. "Transoceanic Mortality: The Slave Trade in Comparative Perspective." *William and Mary Quarterly*, Third Series, 58, no. 1 (2001): 93–118.

Kraay, Hendrik. "'Em outra coisa não falavam os pardos, cabras, e crioulos': o 'recrutamento' de escravos na guerra da independência na Bahia." *Revista Brasileira de História*, 22, no. 43 (2002): 109–128.

Kraay, Hendrik. *Race, State, and Armed Forces in Independence Era Brazil: Bahia, 1790's–1840's*. Stanford: Stanford University Press, 2001.

Kraay, Hendrik. "'As Terrifying as Unexpected': the Bahian Sabinada, 1837–1838". *The Hispanic American Historical Review*, 72, no. 4 (1992): 501–527

Lara, Silvia Hunold. "Biografia de Mahommah G. Baquaqua." *Revista Brasileira de História*, 8, no. 16 (1988): 269–284.

Lara, Silvia Hunold. "The Signs of Color: Women's Dress and Racial Relations in Salvador and Rio de Janeiro, c. 1750–1815." *Colonial Latin American Review*, 6, no. 2 (1997): 205–224.

Last, Murray. *The Sokoto Caliphate*. New York: Humanities Press, 1967.

Last, Murray. "Some Economic Aspects of Conversion in Hausaland." In N. Levtzion (ed.), *Conversion to Islam*. New York: Holmes & Meier, 1979: 236–246.

Law, Robin. "Abolition and Imperialism: International Law and the Suppression of the Slave Trade." In Derek R. Peterson (ed.). *Abolitionism and Imperialism in Britain, Africa, and the Atlantic* (Athens: Ohio University Press, 2010), 150–174.

Law, Robin. *Ouidah: The Social History of a West African 'Port', 1727–1892*. Athens: Ohio University Press; Oxford: James Currey, 2004.

Law, Robin. "A comunidade brasileira de Uidá e os últimos anos do tráfico atlântico de escravos, 1850–66." *Afro-Ásia*, 27 (2002): 41–77.

Law, Robin. *The Slave Coast of West Africa, 1550–1750: The Impact of the Atlantic Slave Trade on an African Society*. Oxford: Clarendon Press, 1991.

Law, Robin. *The Ọ̀yọ́ Empire, c. 1600–c. 1836: A West African Imperialism in the Era of the Atlantic Slave Trade*. Oxford: Clarendon Press, 1977.

Law, Robin. "The Chronology of the Yoruba Wars of the Early Nineteenth Century: A Reconsideration." *Journal of the Historical Society of Nigéria*, 5, no. 2 (1970): 211–222.

Law, Robin. "Ethnicities of Enslaved Africans in the Diaspora: On the Meanings of 'Mina' (Again)." *History in Africa*, 32 (2005): 247–267.

Leitão, Humberto, and José Vicente Lopes. *Dicionário da linguagem de marinha antiga e actual*. 2d ed. Lisbon: Centro de Estudos Históricos Ultramarinos, 1974.

Leitman, Spencer. "The Black Ragamuffins: Racial Hypocrisy in Nineteenth-Century Southern Brazil." *The Americas*, 33, no. 3 (1977): 504–514.

Lima, Solimar Oliveira. *Triste Pampa: resistência e punição de escravos em fontes judiciárias no RS— 1818–1833*. Porto Alegre, IEL/EDIPUCS, 1997.

Lima, Valéria. *J.-B. Debret, historiador e pintor: a viagem pitoresca e histórica ao Brasil (1816–1839)*. Campinas: Editora UNICAMP/CECULT, 2007.

Lindoso, Dirceu. *A utopia armada: rebeliões de pobres nas matas do tombo real*. Rio de Janeiro: Paz e Terra, 1983.

Lindsay, Lisa. "'To Return to the Bosom of their Fatherland': Brazilian Immigrants in Nineteenth-Century Lagos". *Slavery & Abolition*, 15, no. 1 (1994): 22–50.

Lindsay, Lisa, and John Wood Sweet (eds). *Biography and the Black Atlantic*. Philapdelphia: University of Pennsylvania Press, 2014.

Lockett, James. "The Deportation of the Maroons of Trelawny Town to Nova Scotia, then Back to Africa." *Journal of Black Studies*, 30, no. 1 (1999): 5–14.

Lovejoy, Paul. "Autobiography and Memory: Gustavus Vassa, alias Olaudah Equiano, the African." *Slavery and Abolition*, 27, no. 3 (2006): 317–347.

Lovejoy, Paul. "Identidade e a miragem da etnicidade: a jornada de Mohammah Gardo Baquaqua para as Américas." *Afro-Ásia*, 27 (2002): 9–39.

Mac Cord, Marcelo. *O Rosário de Dom Antonio: irmandades negras, alianças e conflitos na história social do Recife, 1848–1872*. Recife: Editora da UFPE/FAPESP, 2005.

Maestri Filho, Mário José. *O escravo no Rio Grande do Sul: a charqueada e a gênese do escravismo gaúcho*. Porto Alegre: EST/EPUCRS, 1984.

Maestri Filho, Mário José. *O escravo no Rio Grande do Sul: trabalho, resistência, sociedade*. Porto Alegre: Editora ufrgs, 2006.

Maestri Filho, Mário José. *O sobrado e o cativo. A arquitetura urbana erudita no Brasil escravista: o caso gaúcho*. Passo Fundo: UPF Editora, 2001.

Maestri Filho, Mário José. *Deus é grande, o mato é maior! Trabalho e resistência escrava no Rio Grande do Sul*. Passo Fundo: UPF Editora, 2002.

Mamigonian, Beatriz Galotti. *Africanos livres: a abolição do tráfico de escravos no Brasil*. São Paulo: Companhia das Letras, 2017.

Mamigonian, Beatriz Galotti. "Do que o preto 'mina' é capaz: etnia e resistência entre africanos livres." *Afro-Ásia*, 24 (2000): 71–95.

Mamigonian, Beatriz Galotti. "In the Name of Freedom: Slave Trade Abolition, the Law, and the Brazilian Branch of the African Emigration Scheme (Brazil-British West Indies, 1830s–1850s)." *Slavery Abolition*, 30, no. 1 (2009): 41–66.

Mann, Kristin. *Slavery and the Birth of an African City: Lagos, 1760–1900*. Bloomington and Indianapolis: Indiana University Press, 2007.

Marques, João Pedro. *Os sons do silêncio: o Portugal de Oitocentos e a abolição do tráfico de escravos*. Lisbon: Imprensa de Ciências Sociais, 1999.

Marques, João Pedro. "Arsénio Pompílio Pompeu de Carpo, um percurso negreiro no século xix." *Análise Social*, 36, no. 160 (2001): 609–638.

Marques, João Pedro. "Tráfico e supressão no século XIX: o caso do brigue Veloz." *Africana Studia*, 5 (2002): 155–179.

Martin, Bradford Gary. *Muslim Brotherhoods in Nineteenth-Century Africa*. Cambridge: Cambridge University Press, 1976.

Mattos, Hebe Maria. "Identidade camponesa, racialização e cidadania no Brasil monárquico: o caso da Guerra dos Maribondos em Pernambuco a partir da leitura de Guillermo Palácios." *Almanak Braziliense*, no. 3 (2006). Available at: <http://www.almanak.usp.br>.
Mattoso, Kátia M. de Queirós. *Da revolução dos alfaiates à riqueza dos baianos no século xix*. Salvador: Corrupio, 2004.
Mattoso, Kátia M. de Queirós, Herbert S. Klein, and Stanley L Engerman. "Notas sobre as tendências e padrões dos preços de alforrias na Bahia, 1819–1888." In João José Reis (ed.), *Escravidão e invenção da liberdade: estudos sobre o negro no Brasil*. São Paulo: Brasiliense, 1988: 60–72.
Mattoso, Kátia M. de Queirós. *Testamentos de escravos libertos na Bahia no século xix: uma fonte para o estudo de mentalidades*. Salvador: Centro de Estudos Baianos, 1979.
Mattoso, Kátia M. de Queirós. *Être esclave au Brésil, xvie-xixe siècle*. Paris: Hachette, 1979.
Maupoil, Bernard. *Contributiom à l'étude de l'origine musulmane de La géomancie dans Le Bas-Dahomey*. Paris: Imprimerie Protat Frères, 1945.
Mello, José Antônio Gonsalves de. *Gente de Nação*. Recife: Massangana, 1989.
Mendes, Fábio Faria. "A economia moral do recrutamento militar no Império brasileiro." *Revista Brasileira de Ciências Sociais*, 13, no. 38 (1998): 81–96.
Menezes, José Luiz Mota. *Atlas Histórico Cartográfico do Recife*. Recife: Prefeitura da Cidade do Recife/Fundaj, 1988.
Miller, Joseph. *Way of Death: Merchant Capitalism and the Angolan Slave Trade, 1730–1830*. Madison: Wisconsin University Press, 1988.
Miller, Joseph. "The Significance of Drought, Disease, and Famine in Agriculturally Marginal Zones of West-Central Africa." *The Journal of African History*, 23, no. 1 (1982): 17–61.
Morais, Francisco de. "Estudantes brasileiros na Universidade de Coimbra." *Anais da Biblioteca Nacional do Rio de Janeiro*, 62 (1940): 141–335.
Monteiro, Hamilton. *Crise agrária e luta de classes*. Brasília: Horizonte, 1980.
Moreira, José Mendonça de Mattos. "As matas das Alagoas: providências acerca delas e sua descrição, Porto Calvo, 1797." In Luís Sávio de Almeida (ed.), *Mata e Palmares nas Alagoas*. Arapiraca: Edufal, 2004: 21–39.
Moreira, Paulo Roberto Staudt. *Faces da liberdade, máscaras do cativeiro: experiências de liberdade e escravidão, percebidas através das cartas de alforria—Porto Alegre (1858-1888)*. Porto Alegre: EDIPUCS, 1996.
Moreira, Paulo Roberto Staudt. *Os cativos e os homens de bem: experiências negras no espaço urbano*. Porto Alegre: EST, 2003.
Moreira, Paulo Roberto Staudt, and Tatiani de Souza Tassoni. *Que com seu trabalho nos sustenta: as cartas de alforria de Porto Alegre (1748–1888)*. Porto Alegre: EST, 2007.
Morel, Marco. *O período das regências (1831-1840)*. Rio de Janeiro: Jorge Zahar Editor, 2003.
Morel, Marco, and Mariana Monteiro Barros. *Palavra, imagem e poder: o surgimento da imprensa no Brasil do século xix*. Rio de Janeiro: DP&A, 2003.
Morton-Williams, Peter. "The Ọ̀yọ́ Yoruba and the Atlantic Trade, 1670–1830." *Journal of the Historical Society of Nigeria*, 3, no. 1 (1964): 25–45.
Mosher, Jeffrey C. *Political Struggle, Ideology, and State Building: Pernambuco and the Construction of Brazil, 1817–1850*. Lincoln: University of Nebraska Press, 2008.
Moura Filho, Heitor Pinto de. "Taxas cambiais do mil-réis (1795–1913)." *Cadernos de História*, 11, no. 15 (2010): 9–34.
Nishida, Mieko. *Ethnicity, Gender, and Race in Salvador, Brazil, 1808–1888*. Bloomington: Indiana University Press, 2003.
Northrup, David. "African Mortality in the Suppression of the Slave Trade: The Case of the Bight of Biafra." *Journal of Interdisciplinary History*, 1 (1978): 47–64.
"Olaudah Equiano, the South Carolinian? A Forum." *Historically Speaking: The Bulletin of the Historical Society*, 7, no. 3 (2006). Available at: <http://www.bu.edu/historic/hs/janfeb06.html#forum1>.
Oliveira, Maria Inês Côrtes de. *O liberto: seu mundo e os outros*. Salvador: Corrupio, 1988.

Oliveira, Maria Luiza Ferreira de. "Sobreviver à pressão escapando ao controle: embates em torno da 'lei do cativeiro' (a Guerra dos Marimbondos em Pernambuco, 1851–1852)." *Almanak Braziliense*, no. 3 (2006). <Available at: http://www.almanak.usp.br>.

Oliveira, Maria Luiza Ferreira de. "As guerras nas matas de Jacuípe." *Clio*, 33, no. 2 (2015): 100–138.

Oroge, E. Adeniyi. "The Institution of Slavery in Yorubaland with Particular Reference to the Nineteenth Century." PhD dissertation, Center of West African Studies, University of Birmingham, 1971.

Palacios, Guillermo. "Revolta camponesa no Brasil escravista: a 'Guerra dos Maribondos' (Pernambuco 1851–1852)." *Almanak Braziliense*, no. 3 (2006). Available at: <http://www.almanak.usp.br>.

Palmié, Stephen. *Wizards & Scientists: Explorations in Afro-Cuban Modernity & Tradition*. Durham: Duke University Press, 2002.

Parés, Luís Nicolau. "Milicianos, barbeiros e traficantes numa irmandade católica de africanos minas e jejes (Bahia, 1770–1830)." *Tempo*, 20 (2014). Available at: http://www.historia.uff.br/tempo/site/wp-content/uploads/2014/11/TEMPO_0000365_06-11_PT.pdf.

Parrón, Tâmis Peixoto. *A política da escravidão no Império do Brasil, 1826–1865*. Rio de Janeiro: Civilização Brasileira, 2011.

Parrón, Tâmis Peixoto. "Política do tráfico negreiro: o Parlamento imperial e a reabertura do comércio de escravos na década de 1830." *Estudos Afro-Asiáticos*, 29, no. 1–3 (2007): 91–121.

Peel, J. D. Y. "The Cultural Work of Yoruba Ethnogenesis." In E. Tonkin, E. M. McDonald, and M. Chapman (eds.), *History and Ethnicity*. London and New York: Routledge & Kegan Paul, 1989: 198–215.

Phillips, Richard. "Dystopian Space in Colonial Representation: Sierra Leone as 'The White Man's Grave'." *Geografiska Annaler*, 86, no. 3/4 (2002): 189–200.

Piersen William D. *Black Yankees: The Development of an Afro-American Subculture in Eighteenth-Century New England*. Amherst: University of Massachusetts Press, 1988.

Pires, Ana Flávia Cicchelli. "O caso da escuna *Destemida*: repressão ao tráfico na rota da Costa da Mina—1830–1831." In Mariza de Carvalho Soares (ed.), *Rotas atlânticas da diáspora africana: da baía do Benim ao Rio de Janeiro*. Niterói: EDUFF, 2007: 157–189.

Putnam, Lara. "To Study the Fragments/Whole: Microhistory and the Atlantic World." *Journal of Social History*, 39, no. 3 (2006): 615–630.

Pybus, Cassandra. *Epic Journeys of Freedom: Runaway Slaves of the American Revolution and their Global Quest for Liberty*. Boston: Beacon Press, 2006.

Quintas, Amaro. *O sentido social da Revolução Praieira*. Recife: Editora da ufpe, 1977.

Quiring-Zoche, Rosemarie. "Luta religiosa ou luta política? O levante dos malês na Bahia segundo uma fonte islâmica." *Afro-Ásia*, 19–20 (2000): 229–238.

Quiring-Zoche, Rosemarie. "Bei den Male in Brasilien. Das Reisebuch des 'Abdarrahman al-Bagdadi." *Die Welt des Islams*, 40, no. 2 (2000): 196–334.

Rebouças, Diógenes, and Filho, Godofredo. *Salvador da Bahia de Todos os Santos no Século XIX*. Salvador: Odebrecht, 1985.

Rediker, Marcus. *The Amistad Rebellion: An Atlantic Odyssey of Slavery and Freedom*. New York: Viking, 2012.

Rediker, Marcus. *The Slave Ship: A Human History*. New York: Viking, 2007.

Rediker, Marcus. *Between the Devil and the Deep Blue Sea: Merchant Seamen, Pirates, and the Anglo-American Maritime World, 1700–1750*. Cambridge: Cambridge University Press, 1987.

Reichert, Rolf. *Os documentos árabes do Arquivo Público do Estado da Bahia*. Salvador: Centro de Estudos Afro-Orientais da UFBA, 1970.

Reis, João José. "De escravo a rico liberto: a trajetória do africano Manoel Joaquim Ricardo na Bahia oitocentista". *Revista de História*, 174 (2016): 15–68.

Reis, João José. *Domingos Sodré, um sacerdote africano: escravidão, liberdade e candomblé na Bahia do século xix*. São Paulo: Companhia das Letras, 2008.

Reis, João José. *Rebelião escrava no Brasil: a história do levante dos malês em 1835*. 2d ed. São Paulo: Companhia das Letras, 2003.

Reis, João José. "Candomblé in Nineteenth-Century Bahia: Priests, Followers, Clients." *Slavery & Abolition*, 22, no. 1 (2001): 116–134.
Reis, João José, and Eduardo Silva. *Negociação e conflito: a resistência negra no Brasil escravista*. São Paulo: Companhia das Letras, 1989.
Reis, João José, and Hendrik Kraay. "'The Tyrant Is Dead!' ": The Revolt of the Periquitos, Bahia, 1824." *Hispanic American Historical Review*, 89, no. 3 (2009): 399–434.
Ribeiro, Gladys Sabina. *A liberdade em construção: identidade nacional e conflitos antilusitanos no Primeiro Reinado*. Rio de Janeiro: Relume Dumará, 2002.
Ricci, Maria Lúcia de Souza. *A atuação política de um publicista: Antonio Borges da Fonseca*. Campinas: Pontifícia Universidade Católica, 1995.
Richardson, David. "Shipboard Revolts, African Authority, and the Slave Trade." In Sylviane A. Diouf (ed.), *Fighting the Slave Trade: West African Strategies*. Athens: Ohio University Press, 2003: 199–218.
Rodrigues, Jaime. *Em mar e em terra: história e cultura de trabalhadores escravos e livres*. São Paulo: Alameda, 2016.
Rodrigues, Jaime. "Um sepulcro grande, amplo e fundo: saúde alimentar no Atlântico, séculos XVI ao XVIII." *Revista de História*, 168 (2013): 325–350.
Rodrigues, Jaime. *De costa a costa: escravos, marinheiros e intermediários do tráfico negreiro de Angola ao Rio de Janeiro (1780–1860)*. São Paulo: Companhia das Letras, 2005.
Rodrigues, Jaime. *O infame comércio: propostas e experiências no final do tráfico africano de escravos para o Brasil (1800–1850)*. Campinas: Editora da UNICAMP/CECULT, 2000.
Ryan, Patrick J. *Imale: Yoruba Participation in the Muslim Tradition*. Missoula: Scholars Press; Cambridge: Harvard College, 1978.
Russell-Wood, A. J. R. *Fidalgos and Philanthropists: the Santa Casa da Misericordia of Bahia, 1550–1755*. London: Macmillan, 1968.
Saavedra, Renata Franco. "População, recenseamento e conflito no Brasil imperial: o caso da Guerra dos Marimbondos." MA thesis, UNIRIO, 2011.
Sampaio, Gabriela dos Reis. *Juca Rosa, um pai-de-santo na Corte imperial*. Rio de Janeiro: Arquivo Nacional, 2009.
Santos, Ynaê Lopes dos. "Além da senzala: arranjos escravos de moradia no Rio de Janeiro (1808–1850)." MA thesis, Universidade de São Paulo, 2006.
Santos Filho, Lycurgo de Castro. *História geral da medicina brasileira*. 2 vols. São Paulo, Hucitec/EDUSP, 1991.
Schama, Simon. *Rough Crossings: Britain, the Slaves and the American Revolution*. New York: Harper Collins, 2006.
Scherer, Jovani de Souza. "Experiências de busca de liberdade: alforrias e comunidade africana em Rio Grande, século xix." MA thesis, Universidade do Vale dos Sinos, 2008.
Sherwood, Marika. *After Abolition: Britain and the Slave Trade since 1807*. London and New York: I. B. Tauris, 2007.
Silva, Alberto da Costa e. *Francisco Félix de Souza, mercador de escravos*. Rio de Janeiro: Nova Fronteira, 2004.
Silva, Alberto da Costa e. *Um rio chamado Atlântico: a África no Brasil e o Brasil na África*. Rio de Janeiro: Nova Fronteira, 2003.
Silva, Alberto da Costa e. *A manilha e o libambo: a África e a escravidão de 1500 a 1700*. Rio de Janeiro: Nova Fronteira, 2002.
Silva, Alberto da Costa e. "Buying and Selling Korans in Nineteenth-Century Rio de Janeiro." *Slavery & Abolition*, 22, no. 1 (2001): 83–90.
Silva, Eduardo. *Dom Obá II d'África, o príncipe do povo: vida, tempo e pensamento de um homem livre de cor*. São Paulo: Companhia das Letras, 1997.
Silva, Ricardo Tadeu Caires. "Memórias do tráfico ilegal de escravos nas ações de liberdade: Bahia, 1885–1888." *Afro-Ásia*, 35 (2007): 37–82.
Silva, Ricardo Tadeu Caires. "Caminhos e descaminhos da abolição: escravos, senhores e direito nas últimas décadas da escravidão (1850–1888)." PhD dissertation, Universidade Federal do Paraná, 2007.

Skinner, David E. "Islam and Education in the Colony and Hinterland of Sierra Leone (1750–1914)." *Canadian Journal of African Studies/Revue Canadienne des Études Africaines*, 10, no. 3 (1976): 499–520.

Skinner, David E. "Mande Settlement and the Development of Islamic Institutions in Sierra Leone." *The International Journal of African Historical Studies*, 11, no. 1 (1978): 32–62.

Smallwood, Stephanie E. *Saltwater Slavery: A Middle Passage from Africa to American Diaspora*. Cambridge, MA: Harvard University Press, 2007.

Soares, Carlos Eugênio Líbano. *Zungu: rumor de muitas vozes*. Rio de Janeiro: APERJ, 1998.

Soares, Carlos Eugênio Líbano, and Flávio dos Santos Gomes. "Negras minas no Rio de Janeiro: gênero, nação e trabalho urbano no século xix." In Mariza de Carvalho Soares (ed.), *Rotas atlânticas da diáspora africana: da baía do Benim ao Rio de Janeiro*. Niterói: EDUFF, 2007: 191–224.

Soares, Carlos Eugênio Líbano. "'Dizem as quitandeiras': ocupações étnicas em uma cidade escravista, Rio de Janeiro, século xix." *Acervo*, 15, no. 2 (2002): 3–16.

Soares, Carlos Eugênio Líbano, and Flávio dos Santos Gomes. "Com o pé sobre um vulcão": africanos minas, identidades e a repressão antiafricana no Rio de Janeiro (1830–1840)." *Estudos Afro-Asiáticos*, 23, no. 2 (2001): 335–377.

Soares, Luiz Carlos. *O 'Povo de Cam' na capital do Brasil: a escravidão urbana no Rio de Janeiro do século xix*. Rio de Janeiro: FAPERJ/7Letras, 2007.

Soares, Mariza (ed.). *Rotas atlânticas da diáspora africana: da baía do Benim ao Rio de Janeiro*. Niterói: EDUFF, 2007.

Soares, Mariza. *Devotos da cor: identidade étnica, religiosidade e escravidão no Rio de Janeiro, século XVIII*. Rio de Janeiro: Civilização Brasileira, 2000.

Sparks, Randy J. *The Princes of Calabar: An Eighteenth-Century Atlantic Odyssey*. Cambridge, MA: Harvard University Press, 2004.

Souza, Marina de Mello e. *Reis negros no Brasil escravista: história da festa de coroação de Rei Congo*. Belo Horizonte: Editora UFMG, 2002.

Souza, Mônica Lima e. "Entre margens: o retorno a África de libertos no Brasil, 1830–1870." PhD dissertation, Universidade Federal Fluminense, 2008.

Stamm, Anne. "La société créole à Saint-Paul de Loanda dans les années 1838–1848." *Revue française d'histoire d'Outre-mer*, 59, no. 217 (1972): 578–610.

Sweet, James H. *Domingos Álvares, African Healing, and the Intellectual History of the Atlantic World*. Chapel Hill: University of North Carolina Press, 2011.

Tavares, Luís Henrique Dias. *A independência do Brasil na Bahia*. Rio de Janeiro: Civilização Brasileira, 1977.

Tavares, Luís Henrique Dias. *Comércio proibido de escravos*. São Paulo: Ática, 1988.

Tavares, Luís Henrique Dias. *Da sedição de 1798 à revolta de 1824 na Bahia*. Salvador: EDUFBA; São Paulo: UNESP, 2003.

Thomas, Hugh. *The Slave Trade: The Story of the Atlantic Slave Trade, 1440–1870*. New York: Simon & Shuster, 1997.

Thompson, Estevam Costa. "Negreiros nos mares do Sul: famílias traficantes nas rotas entre Angola e Brasil em fins do século xviii." MA thesis, Universidade de Brasília, 2006.

Tibbles, Anthony (ed.). *Transatlantic Slavery: Against Human Dignity*. London: HMSO, 1994.

Tishke, Joel, Tóyìn Fálọlá, , and Akíntudé Akínyẹmí (eds.). *Ṣàngó in Africa and the African Diaspora*. Bloomington and Indianapolis: Indiana University Press, 2009.

Turner, Michael J. "*Les Brésiliens*: The Impact of Former Brazilian Slaves upon Dahomey." PhD dissertation, Boston University, 1975.

Verger, Pierre. *Flux et reflux de la traite des nègres entre le golfe de Benin et Bahia de Todos os Santos*. Paris: Mouton, 1968.

Verger, Pierre. *Os libertos: sete caminhos na liberdade de escravos da Bahia no século xix*. São Paulo: Corrupio, 1992.

Versiani, Flávio Rabelo, and José Raimundo Oliveira Vergolino. "Preços de escravos em Pernambuco no Século xix." *Textos para Discussão*, Departamento de Economia da UNB, 252 (October 2002).

Vieira, Alexandre Ribeiro. "The Transatlantic Slave Trade to Bahia,1582–1851." In David Eltis and David Davidson (eds.), *Extending the Frontiers*. New Have, CT: Yale Univeristy Press, 2007: 130–154.

Westermarck, Edward. *Pagan Survivals in Mohammedan Civilizations*. London: Macmillan, 1933.

Wissenbach, Maria Cristina Cortez. "As feitorias de urzela e o tráfico de escravos: Georg Tams, José Ribeiro dos Santos e os negócios da África Centro-Ocidental na década de 1840." *Afro-Ásia*, 43 (2011): 43–90.

Wissenbach, Maria Cristina Cortez."Cirurgiões e mercadores nas dinâmicas do comércio atlântico de escravos (séculos xviii e xix)." In Laura de Mello e Souza, Júnia Furtado, and Maria Fernanda Bicalho (eds.), *O governo dos povos: relações de poder no mundo ibérico na época Moderna*. São Paulo: USP/Alameda, 2009: 281–300.

Yon, Danoel A. "Making Place, Making Pace: St. Helena and the South Atlantic World". In Boubacar Barry, Elisée Soumoni, and Livio Sansone (eds.), *Africa, Brazil and the Construction of Trans-Atlantic Black Identities*. Trenton: Africa World Press, 2008: 114–126.

Zanetti, Valéria. *Calabouço urbano: escravos e libertos em Porto Alegre (1840–1860)*. Passo Fundo: UPF Editora, 2002.

Zuquete, Afonso Eduardo Martins (ed.). *Nobreza de Portugal*. Lisbon: Editorial Enciclopedia, 1960.

NAME INDEX

For the benefit of digital users, indexed terms that span two pages (e.g., 52–53) may, on occasion, appear on only one of those pages.
Listed here are individuals contemporary to Rufino. Other names are listed in the Subject Index.

Aberdeen, Lord (British minister), 73, 96, 122–23, 164, 170, 189–90, 272–73n17
Adams, Cap. John (Royal Navy officer), 181–82
Afonjá (chief of Ilorin), 3–4, 5, 6–8
Al-Bagdádi, Iman 'Abd al-Raman (Turkish traveler in Brazil), 138, 229–32, 239–40
Alimi (Fulani Muslim cleric in Ọ̀yọ́), 5, 6–7
Almeida, Domingos José (Farroupilha war minister), 38–39
Almeida, José Joaquim de (slave trader), 135
Altavilla, João (Brazilian representative on Mixed Commission), 147–48
Amaral, Joaquim Thomas do (Brazilian representative on Mixed Commission), 169–71, 182, 190, 191–92,
Antonio, Gabriel (slave trader), 93–95,
Antonio, Cap. Quirino (slave trader), 134
Aquino, Joaquim Tomás de (African leader in Recife), 232–33
Araujo, Cap. José Pinto de (slave trader), 133
Augusto, Luis (slave trader), 99–100
Azevedinho see Lisboa, José Francisco de Azevedo

Bandeira, Viscount de Sá da (Portuguese Foreign Affairs minister), 126–27, 127f
Baquaqua, Mohammah Gardo (enslaved Muslim in Pernambuco), 205
Barbosa, Manoel José (steward on the *Ermelinda*), 166, 184–85
Beaupaire-Rohan, Henrique de (Brazilian lexicographer and politician), 31
Benedito (African cook), 97
Bidwell, C. B. (clerk at Mixed Commission), 170

Bixoumi/Bishoumi (Rufino"s mother), 5–6
Blanco, Pedro (slave trader), 180–81
Bonaparte, Napoleon, 127, 139
Bowen, Thomas (Christian missionary in Africa), 154
Boyle, Samuel (dockworker in Freetown), 177
Braga, Antonio Rodrigues (president of Rio Grande do Sul), 36–39
Brito, Joaquim Ribeiro de (slave trader), 70–71, 83, 105–6, 112, 113–14, 258n22
Brito, Cap. Silvério de (slave trader), 135
Brízida (freedwoman), 26
Bronaio, Cap. A. J. (slave trader), 94
Burstal, Richard Acheson (British boatswain), 138, 166–69, 171
Burton, Richard (British writer, traveler), 160, 270n6

Campos, Joaquim Pinto Menezes (Portuguese resident of Freetown), 190, 191
Cardoso, Cap. José Antonio de Souza (slave trader), 68,
Carneiro, Angelo Francisco (owner of the *Ermelinda*), 83, 113–17, 124, 164–65, 166, 189–91, 192–93, 196, 199–200, 259n32, 266n14, 266n15,
Carpo, Arsénio Pompilio Pompeo de (slave trader), 78–79, 106–7, 115–16, 122–23, 139, 166
Carvalho, Antonio João de (black Angolan detained in Rio), 55
Carvalho, Cap. Matias José de (slave trader), 134–35
Cézar, João Baptista (slave trader), 97, 99, 100–4, 105
Chachá, *see* Souza, Francisco Félix de

Cintra, Elias Coelho (slave trader), 94
Clarke, Dr. Robert (visitor in Sierra Leone), 144–46, 148, 149–50, 151–52, 153–55, 155f, 182, 208–9,
Clarkson, Thomas (British abolitionist), 182
Coelho, Antonio Fernandes (slave trader), 133
Coelho, Cap. Daniel (slave trader), 134
Coimbra, Joaquim Gomes (slave trader), 98–99, 101–2,
Constantino, Manoel José (slave trader), 95, 105–7
Cordeiro, Cap. Joaquim Maria (slave trader), 185–86,
Costa, Duarte José Martins da (Rufino's shipmate on the *Ermelinda*), 89–90, 93, 110–12, 111f, 200, 265n8
Costa, Sabino Antônio da, 232, 237
Coutinho, Cap. Joaquim Antonio de Carvalho (captain of the *Ermelinda*), 87–88, 93, 118–19, 138, 139, 165–66, 168, 171–72, 176, 179, 181, 183–84, 190–91,
Cowper, Henry Augustus (British consul in Recife), 71, 73, 96, 114, 189–90
Crowther, Samuel Ajayi (Anglican missionary), 155–56, 157–58, 163

Delgado, Manuel (slave trader), 98–99
Dias, Cap. José Rodrigues (transported Rufino to Sierra Leone), 193
Divino Mestre (Christian pastor in Recife), *see* Pereira, Agostinho José
Doherty, Richard (governor of Sierra Leone), 158–59
Dreys, Nicolao (French merchant in Porto Alegre), 20, 23
Elizio, Felinto (a.k.a. Francisco Manoel do Nascimento, Portuguese poet), 82
Equiano, Olaudah (abolitionist author), 143f, 163

Feijó, Diogo Antonio (Brazilian politician), 47, 53
Ferguson, William (British representative on Mixed Commission), 164–65
Ferreira, Cap. Francisco Pedro (slave trader), 131–33
Ferreira, José Maria Henriques (slave trader), 135
Ferreira, Jovino Lopes (a Muslim in Recife), 235, 237
Ferreira, Marcelino (slave ship sailor), 140
Figueiredo, José Bento da Cunha (president of Pernambuco), 225–26
Findlay, Alexander (governor of Sierra Leone), 156–57, 159
Fodio, Uthman Dan, *see* Uthman dan Fodio
Fonseca, Borges da (liberal rebel in Recife), 219
Frederico (fugitive enslaved sailor), 48–49

Galvão, Cândido da Fonseca (a.k.a. Dom Obá II), 209–10
Gomes, Francisco (Rufino's young master), 20
Guerra, Manoel Alves (slave trader), 98–99, 104
Guimaraens, Joaquim Leocadio d'Oliveira (slave trader), 98–99,

Hamilton, Anthony (dockworker in Freetown), 179
Henrique, Roberto (Xangô devotee in Recife), 232, 238
Henriques, Manoel José (African protester in Rio de Janeiro), 52–53
Holman, James British visitor in Sierra Leone), 148

Isabelle, Arséne (French traveler in Porto Alegre), 23–24, 26–27, 63
Ivo, Cap. Pedro (Praieira leader), 217

Jardim, José Pereira (Rufino's first master in Porto Alegre),
Jeremie, Sir John (governor of Sierra Leone), 159–60
João, José (Brazilian sailor in London), 49
Jones, C. B. (court clerk in Sierra Leone), 176, 177

Koelle, Sigismund (German linguist in Sierra Leone), 154

Lawrence, Cap. John C. (U.S. Navy officer), 76, 77–78, 182
Lawrence, Richard (representative of the *Ermelinda*'s owners in court appeal), 176, 179, 183–84, 190–91, 193, 194, 196
Lima, Joaquim do Couto (slave trader in Luanda), 106–7
Limamo, Abdalá (Muslim cleric in Recife), 236–37
Lisboa, Antonio Carneiro (slave trader), 83–84, 190, 191, 194
Lisboa Junior, Antonio Carneiro (slave trader), 83–84, 185
Lisboa, Francisco (slave trader, official owner of the *Ermelinda*), 83, 87, 113, 164–65, 190, 193, 194
Lisboa, José Francisco de Azevedo (slave trader a.k.a. Azevedinho), 71, 83–84, 88–89, 95, 96, 98–108, 114, 164–65, 189–90, 263n12, 263n18, 263n23

Machado, Antonio Felix (passenger of the *Ermelinda*), 166
Machado, Francisco Alvares (president of Rio Grande do Sul province), 29
Manuel (black healer in Pernambuco), 233

NAME INDEX

Maranhão, José Pacheco de Albuquerque (planter in Pernambuco), 220
March, William "Billy" (dockworker in Freetown), 176, 177
Martius, Karl Friedrich Philipp von (German traveler in Brazil), 12–15, 279n9
Mason, Anthony (*Ermelinda's* keeper in Freetown), 177, 179
Matson, Lt. Henry James (captor of the *Ermelinda*), 68–70, 122–24, 128, 134–35, 136, 138, 172–73, 267n15
McFoy, Thomas (merchant and clerk in Freetown), 177, 179,
Medeiros, Manoel Joaquim de Souza, (police chief in Rio Grande), 29, 40
Meireles, Joaquim (African slave trader), 90–91
Mello, Antonio Lopes Pereira de (passenger on the *Ermelinda*), 112
Mello, Ignácio Luís Madeira de (commander of Potuguese forces in Bahia), 9
Melville, Elizabeth Helen (British resident in Freetown), 149, 150–52, 153, 154
Melville, Michael (governor of Sierra Leone and member of the Mixed Commission), 130, 131, 134, 149, 162, 164–65, 169–70, 171–72, 175–76, 272n15,
Mendonça, Joaquim Pereira de (slave trader), 106–7
Menezes, Joaquim José de Carvalho e (Luanda resident), 77, 81
Mercês, Cândido Fernandes das (African sailor), 90–91
Mesquita, Bento Botelho Pinto de (petty shipper on the *Ermelinda*), 112, 116t
"Millar", Mr., 97–98, 101–2, 106
Monteiro, Cap. Antonio da Silva (slave trader), 136
Moreira, Alexandre (African merchant), 140
Moreira, Joaquim Baptista (Portuguese consul in Recife), 83–84, 261n9
Muhammad (a.k.a. José, a Hausa freedman in Rio Grande), 29–31
Musewo, see Petro, Toki

Nagô, Antônio (undocumented African freedman), 55–56
Nicolau José (Rufino's son), 197–99
Niterói, Hermenegildo Frederico (Brazilian representative on Mixed Commission), 162, 169–72, 174, 182, 184, 190, 191–92, 272n15, 272–73n17

Obertally, Anna Francisca Ferreira (slave trader), 91–92, 116, 124
Ocochê/Ocoxé/Okọṣe (Rufino's father), 5–6
Oliveira, Cap. Francisco Antonio de (slave trader), 113–14, 133
Oliveira, Frederico Inácio de (Xangô devotee), 234, 238
Oliveira, José Joaquim d' (Rufino's interrogator), 215,

Oliver, William Brown (Royal Navy officer), 97

Palmerston, Lord (Henry John Temple), 126, 127–28, 127f
Parkinson, John (British consul in Recife), 88–89
Peçanha, José Maria de Salles Gameiro de Mendonça (Rufino's master in Porto Alegre), 21–23, 24–26, 27, 34–39, 40–42, 198
Perdigão, João da Purificação Marques (bishop in Recife), 224–25
Pereira, Agostinho José (a.k.a. Divino Mestre), 222–25, 232, 233–34,
Pereira, Cap. Manoel José (slave trader), 136
Pereira, Manoel Nunes (slave trader), 136
Petro, Toki (a.k.a. Musewo, African resident in Freetown), 90–91
Pinto, Joaquim Rodrigues (slave trader), 134
Prior, James (Royal Navy officer and author), 138–39

Queiroz, Euzébio de (Rio's police chief), 40, 41–42, 49, 53, 55–56, 57–58, 70

Rankin, Harrison (British doctor in Sierra Leone), 130, 152f, 181–82, 183f
Reffell, Joseph (merchant canoeman in Freetown), 174–79
Rego, José da Silva (slave trader), 91–92
Resende, José Antonio (slave trader), 87–88, 93
Ribeiro, Marciano Pereira (interim president of Rio Grande do Sul), 37–39
Rocha, Cap. Francisco José da (slave trader), 135
Rocha, Joaquim José da (slave trader), 67–68

Sá, José Bernardino de (slave trader), 133, 268n18
Saint-Hilaire, Auguste de (French traveler in Brazil), 24
Salami, Abdul (Emir of Ilorin), 6–7
Santos, Cap. Antônio Teodoro dos (slave trader), 68
Savage, William Henry (lawyer and businessman in Freetown), 156–57
Senna, Cap. José Pedro da Silva (interim *Ermelinda's* captain), 181, 182–84, 194, 274n10
Sharp, Granville (British abolitionist), 141–42, 143f
Silva, Bento Gonçalves da (leader of Farroupilha revolt), 38–39
Silva, Elias Baptista da (slave trader), 83–84, 113–14,
Silva, Francisco José da (slave trader), 130–31, 268n11

Silva, João Gomes da (apothecary, Rufino's master in Bahia), 10–16, 119
Silva, Joaquim Vieira da (Xangô devotee), 234, 238, 239*b*
Silva, Manoel Antonio Ferreira da (slave trader), 23
Silveira, Manoel Matoso da (slave trader), 165
Silvestre (Brazilian sailor in London), 49
Solagberu (leader of Yoruba Muslims), 6–7
Souza, Domingos Martins de (crew and trader on the *Ermelinda*), 110–11, 199–200
Souza, Francisco Félix de (a.k.a. Chachá, slave trader), 134, 181
Spix, Johann Baptist von (German traveler in Brazil), 12, 13–15

Tams, George (German traveler in Angola), 75–81, 111, 115–16, 122–25, 265n6
Thorpe, John Dawes (proctor of Mixed Commision), 176, 179
Tollenare, Louis-François de (French merchant in Brazil), 13–14

Uthman dan Fodio (leader of jihad in Hausaland), 4, 230–31

Van Luyek, Jan (interpreter for Mixed Commission), 170, 171
Vianna, Antonio Fernanders (slave trader), 98–99
Vieira, Antonio Gonçalves de Carvalho (passenger on the *Ermelinda*), 109

Walsh, Robert (British traveler in Brazil), 66*b*, 172, 193, 194
Wilkinson, Thomas (captain of the *Ermelinda* on return voyage), 184
Williams, James (wharfinger in Freetown), 176, 179
Williams, Sam (wharf constable in Freetown), 177
Wise, Henry (US consul in Rio de Janeiro), 109–10

Yadalieu, Mohammed (Yoruba imam in Sierra Leone), 157

SUBJECT INDEX

For the benefit of digital users, indexed terms that span two pages (e.g., 52–53) may, on occasion, appear on only one of those pages.

Aberdeen Bill, 173, 194–95
Abolitionism/abolitionists, 27
Abreu, Martha, 23
Abrilada revolt, 84, 261n9
Alafin (or king of Ọ̀yọ́), 3, 5, 6, 7–8
Alagoas, province of, 82, 89–90, 217
Alfa, 157; *see* Alufá
Alufá, 5, 198, 206–7, 209, 227–28, 231, 247n2
Azores, 134
Agualusa, José Eduardo, 122
Aku, 149, 152, 153, 270n6
  ethnic marks of, 155*f*
  merchants, 154–55, 174, 175
  origins, 153, 154, 270n22
  religion (Islam and others), 155–59, 160–53, 162, 201, 231
Ambriz, 68, 104, 123, 124–25
Amistad revolt, 180
Amulets, 6, 35, 44–45, 56, 64–65, 80–81, 151–52, 158–59, 160, 208–9, 210, 229–30, 233–34, 272n13, 277n12
Angola (ethnicity), 12–14, 27–28; manumission of, 28; in Rio de Janeiro, 43, 55, 120; in Recife, 202, 204
Arabic language, vii, 5, 6, 29–31, 35, 40–41, 57–59, 207–8, 223–24, 230, 235, 241, 277n27
  Rufino and, 156, 157, 161, 196, 208, 210–12, 214, 226
Are-ona-kakanfo, 3; *see* Ọ̀yọ́; Ilorin
Argentina, 37, 144, 218
Astrology, 208–9

Baálè, 3
Badagry, 16–17, 140, 203
Benguela, 24–25, 27–28, 43, 68, 75, 113–14, 122, 126–27, 134–35, 136, 193, 194, 204, 266n13

Benin, Bight of, 3, 7–8, 27–28, 90–92, 181
  slave trade ports in, 16–17, 140
  slave trade to Bahia from, 16–17, 257n10, 269n6
  slave trade to Pernambuco from, 203–4
Benin, Kingdom of, 98–99, 103
Benin, Republic of, vii, 89–90, 205
Benin River, 96–97, 99, 103–4, 105–6
Biafra, Bight of, 3
Bible, 158–59
Bolster, W. Jeffrey, 63–64
Bonny, 149
Borgu, 3
Bulom, 148–49

Cabanada Rebellion, 260n2, 261n9
Cabinda
  as slave trade port, 68, 70–71, 91, 105, 133, 134–35, 136, 140, 186
  canoe rowers from, 80–81
  slaves in Brazil from, 25, 27–28, 35, 43, 204, 232–33
Cape Verde, 89–90, 104, 166, 204; slaves in Brazil from, 43
Cabundá (ethnicity), 43
Calabar, 43, 149
Canada, 142–43
Candomblé, 53, 207–8*b*, 239*b*, 242, 277n11
Cannibalism, Africans' fear of white, 163–64
Capela, José, 114, 126–27
Caribbean, 139, 142–43, 147–48, 163, 185, 260n7
Cassange/Kasanje (ethnicity), 43, 75
Catholicism, 81, 210, 214, 215, 235–36, 237; *see* Christians
Chile, 135, 144

Cholera epidemic in Pernambuco, 233
Christians
  black preacher in Brazil, 222–23
  Sierra Leone, 141, 155–56, 157–59
  and Muslims in Recife, 230, 243
  see Church Missionary Society; Catholicism; Christianity
Christopher, Emma, 63–64
Chronica Nacional, 227–28
Church Missionary Society (CMS), 157–59
Cole, Gibril, 208
Congo (ethnicity),
  slaves in Brazil from, 13–14
  in Recife, 202, 204, 232–33
  in Rio de Janeiro, 43
  in Rio Grande do Sul, 27–28
  in Sierra Leone, 149
Congo River, 136
Conservative Party (Brazil), 219
Constitution, Brazil's (1824), 1834 amendment, 36–37
  and religious tolerance, viii, 222, 234, 240
Cooks
  enslaved 13–15, 21–22, 48, 64–65
  aboard slave ships, 63–65, 86–87, 131–32, 139
'Coromantins' (ethnicity), 149
Correio Mercantil (newspaper), 5–6, 56–57, 187, 206–7, 214–15, 217, 221, 226, 227
Costa da Mina, 27–28; *see* Bight of Benin; Mina Coast; Slave Coast
Cuba
  and the slave trade, 126–27, 136–37, 144, 185, 244
  and the *Amistad* revolt, 180

Dahomey, 3, 89–90, 134
Diário de Pernambuco (newspaper), 187, 199, 207–8*b*, 210–11, 225, 226, 232, 233
  debate in Recife between African Muslims and non-Muslims, 229–40
Diário do Rio de Janeiro (newspaper), 47, 48
Dias, Jill, 77–78, 81, 115–16
Diseases
  aboard slave ships, 66, 66–67*b*, 87–88, 97–98, 123, 146
  on the African coast, 101, 107–8, 162, 169–70, 181–82
Divination, 80–81, 154, 158–59, 196, 209, 230–31, 233–34, 280*b*; Ifá, 154, 280n4
Duarte and Warren (firm), 100

Education
  Christian in Sierra Leone, 147–48, 149–50, 155–56, 157–58
  Islamic in Brazil, 238–39
  Islamic in Sierra Leone, 156–57, 196, 208
  see Fourah Bay; Muslims

Egba, Kingdom of, 154, 270n1
Egypt, 210–11, 222–23
Eltis, David, 16–17, 65, 127
Equipment Act (1839), 126–37
England, 109–10, 130, 156, 163, 260*f*;
  see United Kingdom
Èṣù, 5
Europe, 47–48, 49
  anti-slave trade campaign in, 69*f*, 142*f*
Europeans in Africa, 75, 76, 77–78, 79–81, 100, 104, 109–10, 125, 146, 147–48, 149–51, 154–55, 156–57

Farias, Paulo F. de Moraes, 277n27.
Faria, Sheila, 45
Farroupilha Revolt (1835-1845), 29, 31, 34
  slaves and, 36–38, 40
Ferreira, Roquinaldo, 75
Fetishism, 237, 238, 240; *see* witchcraft
Florentino, Manolo, 43, 45, 265n7, 266n15
Foreign Office, 48, 123–24
Foster & Brothers (firm), 190–91, 199–200
Fourah Bay, 156, 157, 158*f*, 159, 160–61, 168, 179, 196, 201, 208, 270–71n9
Fourah Bay College, 157–58
Freedpersons, vii, 16, 27–29, 31, 47–48, 49, 52, 55, 63, 91, 93, 196, 198–99, 217, 219–20, 223–24
Freetown
  ethnic melting pot, 148–49, 150–52, 158*f*, 160;
  see individual ethnicities
  seat of Mixed Commission, 144, 147*f*, 169*f*, 175–76, 191–92
Freyre, Gilberto, 204
Fulani
  jihad in Hausaland, 3–4, 5, 6–8, 230–31
  in Sierra Leone, 148–49, 151–52, 152*f*, 159
Futa Jalon, 148–49
Futa Toro, 208

Gabon, 43
Ghana, 104
Gold Coast, 104
Gotto, 104
Goulart, Mauricio, 42–43

Haitian Revolution, 144; in popular verses in Recife, 223
Harrell-Bond, Barbara E., 157
Hartman, Saidiya, 164
Hausa (ethnicity), 57–58, 230–31, 270n1, 270–71n9, 278n32
  as Mina slaves in Brazil, 27–28
  in Bahia, 12–13, 16, 207–8*b*
  in Rio de Janeiro, 43
  in Rio Grande do Sul, 28, 29–31, 40–41, 25124;
  in Sierra Leone, 157–58
  revolt in Ọ̀yọ́, 3–5, 6–8

Healing, Islamic, 209, 210, 231, 233, 238–39, 242–43
Hunger
   among refugees in Nova Scotia, 142–43
   among Sierra Leone settlers, 141–42
   aboard slave ships, 64–65
Howard, Allen M., 157
Huggins, Brian T., 66

Ijebu, 97, 154, 270n1
Ile Kewu, 208
Ilesha, 154, 270n1
Ilorin, 3–4, 5, 6–7, 16–17
Ìmàle, vii, 5, 6; *see* Malês
Independence, War of (Bahia), 9–10
Inhambane (ethnicity), 43

Jamaica, 139, 143–44, 154–55, 156
Jeje (ethnicity), 12–13, 16, 91, 119–20
Jihad, 3–4, 5, 212–14, 230–31
Jaboatão, 217, 221
Jornal do Commercio (newspaper), viii, 5, 40, 45–47, 53, 56, 111, 160, 206–7, 209–11, 215, 227–28, 247n2

Kaferi/Kafir, 235
Karasch, Mary, 42–43, 58–59
Ketu, 154, 270n1
Kipple, Kenneth E., 66
Kosso (ethnicity), 149, 158*f*,
Kru (ethnicity), 148–49, 151, 158*f*, 166–67, 168, 270n20

Lagos, city of, 7–8, 16–17, 56, 128, 140, 203, 239*b. see* Onim
Law, Robin, 6, 7–8
Libambo, 78–79
Liberalism, 10–11
Liberia, 130–31, 159, 182
Liberated Africans, 138, 153. *see* Aku; Freetown; Sierra Leone.
Limba, 148–49
Little Popo, 140,
Luanda
   ethnic melting pot in, 79–81; European life in, 75–77
   marriage and funeral rites in, 81
   population in 1837, 75, 259n2
   slave trade in, 75, 76, 78–79, 84–87, 90, 91–92, 95, 104, 105–8, 109, 110, 111–17, 118, 120–25, 134–35, 138, 141–65, 166, 185–86, 200
   slavery in, 77–78
Luanda disease, 64; *see* scurvy

Machila, 77; *see* tipoia
Macuas, 43
Madrassa, 208; *see* education

Malaria, 16, 77–78, 91, 101–2, 182; *see* disease
Malês (Yoruba Muslims in Brazil), vii, 29
   in Recife, 229
   revolt of the, 18–19, 34, 48, 52, 57–59, 224; see Ìmàle; see Muslims; slave revolts
Malomi/malam, 29
Mandingos, C 148–49, 151–52, 156–57, 160, 201
Manipanso, 80–81, 80*f*
Manumission 3–4, 15–16, 28, 31, 34–35, 90, 202
   and Maribondo revolt, 218–19
   and Farroupilha Revolt, 37
   in Rio de Janeiro, 43, 45, 244, 2657
   in Rio Grande do Sul, 28, 34–36, 37–38, 40, 196, 198, 221, 229, 2523
Maranhão, province of, 12
Marques, João Pedro, 96, 263n12, 263n23
Martin, Bradford G., 242
Matamba, 75
Mecca, 58, 214–15
Medina/Al Madinah, 214–15
Mesquita & Dutra, 86
Middle Passage, 66, 70–71, 84–86, 91, 95, 102–3, 113–14, 115, 131–32, 133, 163, 200, 204,
Miller, Joseph, 68–70
Mina (ethnicity), 15–16, 23–24, 27–28, 29, 31–33, 35, 43, 44–45, 48–50, 51, 52–53, 54, 55, 56, 57, 92–93, 140–41, 194, 196, 200
   see Costa da Mina; Mina Coast; Bight of Benin
Mina Coast, 27–28, 56, 112, 196; *see* Bight of Benin; Costa da Mina: Slave Coast
Minas Gerais, 21–22, 218
Mixed Commissions Against the Slave Trade
   countries involved 144; in Sierra Leone, 98, 130, 134, 137, 147–48, 149, 156, 160, 162, 166, 169–70, 169*f*, 181
   Ermelinda's owners sue for compensation, trial of the *Ermelinda* by, 170–73, 174–79, 182–84, 190–92, 193, 194–95, 272–73n17
Moange (ethnicity), 43
Mofumbe (ethnicity), 43
Mokoe (ethnicity), 149
Molembo, 68, 73, 140, 203, 204, 269n6
Monjolo (ethnicity), 43
Monogamy, 236
Montevideo, 21
Morel, Marco, 47
Morocco, 210–11
Mozambique (ethnicity), 24–25, 43
Mozambique (region), 27–28, 43, 88–89, 126–27, 163, 204, 263n8
Muhammad (The Prophet), 31, 215, 236–37
Muslims
   in Bahia, vii, 5–6, 18–19, 198, 229–30
   in Òyọ́, 3, 18–19
   in Recife, 229

Muslims (*cont.*)
  in Rio de Janeiro, 57–59, 229
  in Rio Grande do Sul, 28–33
  in Sierra Leone, 148–49, 151–52, 156–57, 158–59, 160
  see Aku; Malês
Nagô (ethnicity), 34, 91–92
  in Bahia 16–17
  in Recife, 202–3, 204, 223–24, 226
  in Rio e Janeiro, 43, 51, 57–58
  in Rio Grande do Sul, 27–29, 41–42
  slave revolts by, 17–19
  see Akus; Malês; Mina; Yoruba
National Guard (Brazil), 47
Navy, British (or Royal Navy), 49, 71, 73, 75, 96–99, 101, 120, 122–23, 126, 128, 130–31
  see Mixed Commission; England
Nazaré, town of, 217, 218–19, 220–21
Nigeria, vii, 3–4
Novo Redondo, 68, 75
Nupe, 3, 48–49

Oery, 103–4
Onim, 56, 140, 204, 239; *see* Lagos
Ouidah, 73, 134, 135–37, 140, 154–55, 203, 204, 205
Òrìṣà, 5, 6, 155–56
Ọ̀yọ́, 3–8, 9–10, 16–17, 18–19, 91–92, 153–56, 161, 209, 243, 270n1

Pão d'Assucar (newspaper), 47, 56–57
Pará, province of, 218
Pau d'Alho town, 217, 218, 219–21, 225; *see* slave revolt in Recife
Pedro I, Emperor, 9, 19, 20, 36–37, 47, 83–84, 261n9
Pelourinho Plaza (Bahia), 18, 119–20
Periquitos Revolt, 10–11
Peru (country), 114
Piauí, province of, 12
Pirates, 100, 105, 138,
Plantations, vii, 9–11, 42–43, 55–56, 73–74, 233
  and slave revolt, 217–21
Polygamy, 235–36, 238
Porto Novo, 16–17, 140
Portugal, 9–10, 13–14, 19, 21–22, 36–37, 77–78, 89–90, 93–94, 109, 113, 115
  and slave trade policy, 16–17, 73, 75, 78–79, 126–28, 144
Praieira Rebellion, 217

Qaṣīdat al-Burda, 31–32
Quilimane (ethnicity), 43
Quilombo, 18, 25
Qur'ān, 6, 151–52, 157–58; *see* Qur'ānic surahs
Qur'ānic surahs, 31–33, 87, 208, 210, 222
  Al'Imran and An-nissa, 212–16

Ramandan, 229–30, 236
Rebolo (ethnicity), 43
Recôncavo (plantation region in Bahia), 9–10, 17
Rediker, Marcus, 63–64
Rio Grandense, O (newspaper), 227–28,
Rodrigues, Jaime, 91–92
Ronco do Maribondo revolt, 218, 240
Royal African Corps, 151
Royal Navy, *see* Navy, British
Ryan, Patrick, 230–31

Sabinada Revolt, 223–24
Saint Helena island, 123–24, 138–39, 141, 186
Santa Casa de Misericórdia da Bahia charity hospital, 10–16
Santa Catarina province, 89–90, 171
Santos Filho, Lycurgo, 15
São Tomé and Príncipe islands, 43, 130–31, 133, 134, 181, 193, 204
Scurvy, 64–65, 106
Sherbro (ethnicity), 148–49
Ships, Royal Navy (by name), *Bonetta*, 120; *Brisk*, 120; *Buzzard*, 120; *Dolphin*, 135; *Fair Rosamond*, 96–97, 101–2, 104–5; *Fantôme*, 120, 123; *Persian*, 133, 136; *Rolla*, 130–31; *Signet*, 181; *Water Witch*, 120–25, 134–35
Ships, slave (by name, except *Ermelinda*), *Abismo*, 70; *Amizade*, 70; *Andorinha*, 105, 114; *Aracati*, 71, 105–7; *Belona*, 131–33; *Bom Jesus*, 204; *Bom Fim*, 133–34; *Bonsucesso*, 94–95; *Borboleta*, 204; *Cacique*, 83–84; *Camões*, 96–99, 101, 103–4; *Corisco*, 123–24; *Cospe Fogo*, 94–95, 105; *Dois Irmãos*, 88–89; *Dona Bárbara*, 88–89; *Dona Elliza*, 136; *Destemida*, 73; *Ermelinda Segunda*, 185–86; *Especulador*, 94–95; *Euro*, 123; *Feliz Ventura*, 130–31; *Feiticeira*, 70, 113–14; *Firme*, 135; *Flor da América*, 136; *Flor do Tejo*, 114; *Francelina*, 71, 94–95; *Furão*, 107–8; *Galiana*, 180–81, 182; *General Silveira*, 94; *Josefa*, 70, 105; *Juliana*, 120–35; *Leopoldina*, 71; *Livramento*, 94–95; *Maria Gertrudes*, 70, 113–14; *Maria Thereza*, 203; *Mariquinha*, 94–95; *Nossa Senhora da Boa Viagem Abismo*, 70; *Nossa Senhora da Guia*, 203; *Nova Fortuna*, 135–37; *Nova Inveja*, 133; *Nova Sorte*, 90–91; *Novo Abismo*, 70, 71; *Novo Destino*, 140–41; *Orozimbo*, 134–35; *Paula*, 65–70, 82; *Pelicano*, 204; *Pernambucano*, 71; *Picón*, 135–36; *Resolução*, 180; *Rosa*, 71; *Santo Antonio*, 180; *São Domingos*, 55–56; *São João Baptista*, 180; *São João II Rosália*, 140; *São José*, 70–72, 82, 105–6; *Temerário*, 71; *Tentadora*, 140; *Triunfo*, 55–56, 94; *Ulisses*, 91–92; *União*, 84–86; *Veloz*, 70, 96–99, 101–2; *Velha de Dio*, 113–14; *Veloz Feiticeira*, 70; *Vencedora*, 112; *Viajante Feliz*, 114; *Venus*, 70; *Vulcano*, 70

SUBJECT INDEX

Ship, steam, 199
Sierra Leone Company, 142–44
Silva, Alberto da Costa e, 96
Silva, Luiz Geraldo, 63–64
Silva, José Mariano da Costa e, 130–31
Skinner, David E., 157, 209
Slave Coast, 27–28, 91, 140, 257; *see* Bight of Benin; Costa da Mina
Slave revolts,
  in Bahia vii, 5–6, 17–19, 47–48, 207–8*b*, 222
  in Pernambuco, 217, 218–21, 222–24
  fear in Rio de Janeiro, 52–55, 56–58, 59
  fear in Rio Grande do Sul, 25–26, 29–33
  in Ọ̀yọ́, 3 5, 6
Slave population (numbers), 48, 63, 130
  in Bahia, 9, 16–17, 75
  in Recife, 201, 221
  in Rio de Janeiro, 42–44, 45, 46*f*, 48
  in Rio Grande do Sul, 23, 27–29
Slave punishment, 25–27, 78–79
Slave Trade Society, 189–90
Slavery
  in Bahia, 17, 18*f*, 118–19
  in Luanda, 77–78
  in Recife, 220
  in Rio de Janeiro, 44–45, 48
  in Rio Grande do Sul, 20, 23–24, 25–27, 35, 37–38
Smallpox, 22, 123; *see* diseases
Smallwood, Stephanie, 109–10
Soares, Luís Carlos, 43
Sokoto Caliphate, 3–4, 6–7
Songo (ethnicity), 43
Spain, and the slave trade, 73

Telegraph, 100–1, 263n17
Temne (ethnicity), 148–49, 159
Tessubá, 230–31, 280n4
Typhoid, 91; *see* diseases
Tipoia, 77; *see* Machila
Tuberculosis, 12–13, 16; *see* diseases

United Kingdom, 141, 142, 191–92; *see* England
United States, 109–10, 142–43, 180–81, 205

Weapons, 25–26, 78, 88–89, 218–19
Witchcraft, 159, 164, 182, 208–9, 210–11, 231, 240
Wolof (ethnicity), 148–49, 151–52

Xangô, 233–34, 236, 239*b*, 240, 242; *see* Candomblé

Yellow fever, African resistance to, 91; in Luanda, 77; *see* diseases
Yoruba/Yorubaland, vii, 3, 4, 16–17, 58, 97, 168, 175–76, 196, 206–7, 215, 241, 243, 270n1
  in Bahia, 9–10, 16–17, 19
  in Recife, 202, 203, 204
  in Sierra Leone, 153, 208–9
  Muslims, 5–8, 57–58, 198–99, 206–7, 230–31
  see Aku; Nagô; Ọ̀yọ́; Malê; Ilorin

Zanetti, Valéria, 35